Gramsci's Laboratory

Historical Materialism Book Series

The Historical Materialism Book Series is a major publishing initiative of the radical left. The capitalist crisis of the twenty-first century has been met by a resurgence of interest in critical Marxist theory. At the same time, the publishing institutions committed to Marxism have contracted markedly since the high point of the 1970s. The Historical Materialism Book Series is dedicated to addressing this situation by making available important works of Marxist theory. The aim of the series is to publish important theoretical contributions as the basis for vigorous intellectual debate and exchange on the left.

The peer-reviewed series publishes original monographs, translated texts, and reprints of classics across the bounds of academic disciplinary agendas and across the divisions of the left. The series is particularly concerned to encourage the internationalization of Marxist debate and aims to translate significant studies from beyond the English-speaking world.

For a full list of titles in the Historical Materialism Book Series available in paperback from Haymarket Books, visit:
https://www.haymarketbooks.org/series_collections/1-historical-materialism

Gramsci's Laboratory

Philosophy, History and Politics

Alvaro Bianchi

Translated by
Sean Purdy

Haymarket Books
Chicago, IL

First published in 2019 by Brill Academic Publishers, The Netherlands
© 2019 Koninklijke Brill NV, Leiden, The Netherlands

Published in paperback in 2021 by
Haymarket Books
P.O. Box 180165
Chicago, IL 60618
773-583-7884
www.haymarketbooks.org

ISBN: 978-1-64259-421-8

Distributed to the trade in the US through Consortium Book Sales and Distribution (www.cbsd.com) and internationally through Ingram Publisher Services International (www.ingramcontent.com).

This book was published with the generous support of Lannan Foundation and Wallace Action Fund.

Special discounts are available for bulk purchases by organizations and institutions. Please call 773-583-7884 or email info@haymarketbooks.org for more information.

Cover design and art by David Mabb. Cover art is a detail of *Construct no. 35, Morris & Co. Medway / Rodchenko, untitled textile design*, pen on wallpaper on canvas (2006).

Printed in the United States.

10 9 8 7 6 5 4 3 2 1

Library of Congress Cataloging-in-Publication data is available.

Finding the real identity underneath the apparent differentiation and contradiction and finding the substantial diversity underneath the apparent identity is the most essential quality of the critic of ideas and of the historian of social development.

GRAMSCI, PN1, Q1, § 43, pp. 128–9

Contents

Preface to the Second Edition IX
Notes on Text and Translation XIV

1 Introduction 1

2 Eternal/Provisional 7
   1   Spaces 21
   2   Times 32

3 Materialism/Idealism 39
   1   Anti-Bukharin 49
   2   Anti-Croce 77

4 Structure/Superstructure 103
   1   Politics 123
   2   Relations 137

5 State/Civil Society 152
   1   Bobbio 157
   2   Machiavelli 165

6 War of Movement/War of Position 176
   1   East 185
   2   Trotsky 192

7 Revolution/Restoration 225
   1   Gioberti 247
   2   Fascism 257

8 Conclusion 268

References 273
Name Index 286
Subject Index 288

Preface to the Second Edition

I had always suspected that there would be a second edition of this book. The first Brazilian edition of *Gramsci's Laboratory* sold out quickly and a few years ago the book was no longer available in bookstores. When I published it in 2008, after a few years of intense research, I aimed to reach two different audiences. The first one, formed by those interested in interpreting Antonio Gramsci's thinking, was composed of specialists, most of whom make the author's thinking an object of study or an analytical tool. The second group consisted of political and social activists who wanted to change the world.

When I finished writing the book, I was assaulted by a doubt that should haunt all researchers – or so I would imagine – and I asked myself insistently about the relevance of yet another book on the Sardinian, moreover one that sought to expose the most important aspects of his thinking. The reception it received from readers and the debates that took place following its publication are, to a certain extent, a response to these doubts. Gramsci was presented differently to readers. Although there were honorable exceptions, superficial and careless readings of the work of the Sardinian Marxist, the use of outdated editions, anachronistic approaches and a great lack of knowledge of the political and intellectual environment in which the *Prison Notebooks* were produced, predominated in Brazil.

The publication of the book coincided with a new conjuncture in Gramscian studies in Brazil to some extent created by the publication of a new, careful and better organised edition of the works of Gramsci. This book was thus, at the same time, the effect and one of the causes of the emergence of a reorientation in Gramscian studies in our country. The use of critical editions, the reconstruction of the sources of his thought and the contextualisation of his ideas in the political and intellectual environment of his time allowed us to expose the complexity and richness of his ideas. As a consequence, new interpretations came to light disregarding common sense. Young researchers explored these paths, substantially renewing studies in the field. Authors until then unknown in Brazil or little studied were then considered important sources of Gramscian thought. Francesco De Sanctis, Benedetto Croce, Georges Sorel, Vilfredo Pareto, Gaetano Mosca, Albert Mathiez and Robert Michels were some of the intellectuals reassessed in this research. Greater care was also consolidated in the appreciation of texts and documents hitherto considered irrelevant; there was more intense use of digital and physical archives; scholars aimed for an in-depth knowledge of the history of nineteenth-century Italy and the first half of the twentieth century; finally, research in Brazil has become more careful and attentive to method.

At the same time, new approaches and themes have been taken into account in the political debates held around the work of Antonio Gramsci. Those who accompanied these debates should have soon realised that *Gramsci's Laboratory* was a book that took sides, rejected the prevailing readings and sought to align the work of the Sardinian Marxist with a political tradition that was not ashamed to define itself as revolutionary. I thus followed this path, suggested by Edmundo Fernandes Dias, from the middle of the 1980s onwards. This new reading was far from consensual.

Soon after the launch of the book, I had the opportunity to present it and debate it publicly alongside Carlos Nelson Coutinho. With his usual generosity, he highlighted what united us in the discussion, particularly the critique of the liberal interpretation that Norberto Bobbio had made of the Sardinian Marxist. But he also did not fail to present his reservations, considered unjust my criticisms of the edition of the *Prison Notebooks* that he had organised (and which he called *critical-thematic*) and opposed what he considered to be an excessive emphasis on the concept of war of movement and the convergence that I made between the work of Gramsci and that of Leon Trotsky.

I think he had a point in complaining about the criticism of his edition. It has a pedagogical value and has served as a tool for a resumption of Gramscian studies in Brazil. The didactic experience brought me to the conclusion that it is practically impossible to form a new audience of attentive readers taking as a starting point the critical edition published in Italy. The fragmentary nature of Gramsci's notes in prison makes the work of deciphering his writings difficult and discouraging for young students, making a thematic edition unavoidable. But it is in the work of investigation that this edition reveals its limits. If I had exclusively relied on it, I could never have written this book. I still think that the new Brazilian edition is not a critical edition or 'critical-thematic' and I believe that from a certain point it makes it difficult to advance research and understand the complex problems presented by the Gramscian text.

The thorniest question of my dialogue with Carlos Nelson was, however, the one that concerned the complex relationship between Gramsci and Trotsky. On this point, I believe that some misunderstandings and confusions were involved. I never said that Gramsci was a Trotskyist. In a certain way, I consider this an anachronistic question. In 1927, when Gramsci was arrested, the left-wing opposition existed only in the Soviet Union. The identification of Amadeo Bordiga's ideas with the Trotskyist Opposition, very common in Italy, is strongly contested by the existing documentation. If any political relationship existed between Bordiga and Trotsky, it ended before the founding of the International Left Opposition in 1930, to which the Italian never belonged.

Only from January 1930 onwards, the first nucleus of the left opposition in Italy appeared around Alfonso Leonetti, Pietro Tresso and Paolo Ravazzoli. In prison, Gramsci inquired about the so-called 'opposition of the three'. But the conditions for an answer to this inquiry were extremely adverse and it is very likely that he was not successful in his attempts. Most of the Italian interpreters, linked to the historical tradition of the Communist Party, have so far been unable to recognise that Gramsci's criticisms of the direction of the Communist Party of Italy by Palmiro Togliatti, which became more acute from 1930, coincided in many respects with the opinions that the oppositionists raised. These same interpreters made a point of considering that Gramsci had already resolved the 'Trotsky question' in the *Prison Notebooks*, affirming his opposition; for some, the Sardinian Marxist took Stalin's side in the internal struggles of the communist movement. For others, he would have been on Bukharin's side. I do not think it is possible to sustain such theses based on the *Prison Notebooks*. Criticism of Stalin is evident in several passages and cannot be ignored. But it also cannot be ignored that Gramsci wrote more than a hundred pages against Bukharin, much more than he wrote against Trotsky, which makes the hypothesis of his adherence to the ideas of the latter very fragile. It is also extremely inconsistent to attempt to prove a rapprochement between Gramsci and Togliatti, although Piero Sraffa later intermediated an encrypted dialogue between the two.

I constructed my argument on the Trotsky question on the basis of much more consistent textual evidence than those presented by these interpreters. And through this I tried to demonstrate that the Sardinian Marxist had not resolved 'the Trotsky question' in the *Prison Notebooks* and that the last notes he wrote in prison suggest an important change of opinion. In any case, the important thing was to emphasise that Gramsci was never Stalinist, or even Bukharinian, which should be evident in any reading free from prejudices, and that he never abandoned a revolutionary strategy or the idea of insurrection, which is also clear when the texts are not selected as one pleases.

Throughout these discussions, my doubts gradually faded and I realised that this book had taken its place not only in the restricted circle of Gramsci scholars in Brazil, but also among those who wanted to understand reality and even change it. The time had thus arrived for a new edition of the book that meets the demands of the public and allows its ideas to continue to freely circulate. I think it is important to emphasise that time has also revealed to me the evident gaps in the argument, or even ideas and notions that could be more effectively explained. Two themes in particular appear to require further development: the role of intellectuals in contemporary society and the different forms of the passive revolution.

In the seminars of the Research Group on Marxism and Political Thought realised after the publication of the book, my attention was drawn to a distinction that is implicit in the work of the Sardinian among the new organic intellectuals born in the very environment of production and the *novissimi* intellectuals. While the former have in the modern entrepreneur their most typical figure, the latter arise and develop in that particular articulation of factory work and party activism that could be verified in the experience of the councils during the Red Biennium in Turin. If I were to rewrite the passages I devoted to the Gramscian notion of intellectuals, I would try to explore this articulation.

I would also treat the notion of passive revolution differently. Gramsci uses this concept to designate processes of innovation and political and economic conservation that takes place through state initiatives. In articles I wrote before and after the publication of this book, I explored this notion and its ability to explain contemporary political processes. Gradually I began to realise that it is used to describe processes that can be very different from each other. In the *Prison Notebooks* you can find three different models of passive revolution, which are not identical to each other. The *French* passive revolution, was a movement of reaction to a revolutionary process, in which the people had assumed strong political activism, and the order was restored through an agreement between the political forces of the bourgeoisie and the urban petty bourgeoisie with the remnants of the old regime. Gramsci synthesised this process with the formula *revolution-restoration*. The *Piedmontese* passive revolution anticipated the revolution itself, preventing it from taking place, making the moment of restoration unnecessary, which gave way to the expansion of a pre-existing state order. The synthesis formula is that of the *revolution without revolution*. The *American* passive revolution is distinguished by its fundamental forces of production and relations of production and not politics. It is a process of transformations within the productive apparatus that act as counter-tendencies to the fall in the rate of profit by establishing a new control over the labour force inside the factory. Its formula is that of *Americanism and Fordism*. I believe that this distinction between these different forms was not adequately explored in the book.

Even so, I decided to publish the book with the original argument intact. I changed the text only to correct misspellings, eliminate some excesses and reformulate certain phrases to make them more precise. I do not believe that a definitive book on the thought of Gramsci is possible and I never intended to write one. There is no reason therefore to not recognise gaps and inaccuracies.

Such recognition may stimulate further investigations and approaches. If there is a conclusion that arises from the reading of this book, it is that the Gramscian laboratory is open to political imagination and cannot be closed.

Notes on Text and Translation

The texts most cited throughout the book will be referred to according to the symbols below. To facilitate reading and the comparison between different editions, I cite the *Prison Notebooks* always based on the critical edition (below Q) adopting the following nomenclature: Qxx, §yy, p. zz, where Q indicates the critical edition, xx the number of the Notebook, yy the paragraph and zz the page.

CC	Gramsci, Antonio 1999ss, *Cadernos do cárcere*, 6 vols, Rio de Janeiro: Civilização Brasileira.
CF	Gramsci, Antonio 1982, *La città futura. 1917–1918*: a cura di Sergio Caprioglio, Turin: Einaudi.
CPC	Gramsci, Antonio 1978, *La costruzione del Partito Comunista 1923–1926*, Turin: Einaudi.
CT	Gramsci, Antonio 1980, *Cronache Torinesi. 1913–1917*: a cura di Sergio Caprioglio, Turin: Einaudi.
L	Gramsci, Antonio 1992, *Lettere 1908–1926*: a cura de Antonio A. Santucci, Turin: Einaudi.
LC	Gramsci, Antonio 1973, *Lettere dal carcere*: a cura di Segio Caprioglio e Elsa Fubini, Turin: Einaudi.
LCW	Lenin, V.I. 1960ss, *Collected Works*, 4 ed., Moscow: Progress.
MECW	Marx, Karl and Friedrich Engels 1976, *Collected Works*, New York: International Publisher.
NM	Gramsci, Antonio 1984, *Il nostro Marx. 1918–1919*: a cura di Sergio Caprioglio, Turin: Einaudi.
Q	Gramsci, Antonio 1977, *Quaderni del carcere*: edizione critica dell'Istituto Gramsci. A cura di Valentino Gerratana, Turin: Einaudi.
SF	Gramsci, Antonio 1966, *Socialismo e fascismo: L'Ordine Nuovo (1921–1922)*, Turin: Einaudi.

Translator's Caveat

Where possible, the translator used the most recently published scholarly translations in English of direct citations of Gramsci from the critical edition used by the author in the original text, which will be referred to in the symbols below and with the same nomenclature in the citations in footnotes as the original. Already existing translations in English were also used in other translations of direct citations in the original book and are cited in the symbols below in the footnotes. Where an English translation was unavailable for citations by either Gramsci or other authors, the translator made an original translation, retained the citation from the original in Portuguese or Italian, and indicated that it was an original translation with the symbol OT (Original Translation).

GR Gramsci, Antonio 2000, *Gramsci Reader: Selected Writings 1916–1935*, edited by David Forgacs, New York: New York University Press.
FSPN Gramsci, Antonio 1995, *Further Selections from the Prison Notebooks*, translated and edited by Derek Boothman, London: Lawrence and Wishart.
LP1 Gramsci, Antonio 1988, *Gramsci's Prison Letters: Lettere dal Carcere*, London: Zwan.
LP2 Gramsci, Antonio 1994, *Letters from Prison*, 2 vols, edited by Frank Rosengarten, translated by Raymond Rosenthal, New York: Columbia University Press.
MECW Marx, Karl and Freidrich Engels 1976ss, *Collected Works*, New York: International Publisher.
PN1 Gramsci, Antonio 1992, *Prison Notebooks*, Vol. I, edited with Introduction by Joseph A. Buttigieg, translated by Joseph A. Buttigieg and Antonio Callari, New York: Columbia University Press.
PN2 Gramsci, Antonio 1996, *Prison Notebooks*, Vol. II, edited and translated by Joseph A. Buttigieg, New York: Columbia University Press.
PN3 Gramsci, Antonio 2007, *Prison Notebooks*, Vol. III, edited and translated by Joseph A. Buttigieg, New York: Columbia University Press.
PPW Gramsci, Antonio 1994, *Pre-Prison Writings*, translated by Virginia Cox, edited by Richard Bellamy, Cambridge: Cambridge University Press.
SPW Gramsci, Antonio 1978, *Antonio Gramsci: Selections from the Political Writings, 1921–1926*, translated and edited by Quintin Hoare, London: Lawrence and Wishart.

CHAPTER 1

Introduction

It is difficult to understand the reasons that lead some authors to become part of a certain intellectual environment. There are, of course, those with media talent who compensate for their lack of original ideas and become bestsellers. These books are read and commented on. Their platitudes feed informal conversations and even some articles. But these are not the authors referred to here; rather, I am speaking of those who conform to a common intellectual or academic common sense.

For instance, why are Habermas and Bourdieu so widely cited? It is probably not on account of their literary style. They do not have the easy prose of texts that are apt for a public, accessible and large audience. Their arguments are not simple and the theories they present are dense and complex enough to drive away those 'unoccupied readers' to whom Miguel de Cervantes addressed the opening words of *Don Quijote de la Mancha*.

And yet, complex concepts such as 'public sphere' or 'habitus' emerged from the pages of their books and have become common currency in intellectual exchange, flooding first the specialised academic journals and then the pages of the cultural supplements of newspapers and magazines. In this downstream, much of the theory dwells on the accidents that border the stream and what flows into common sense is far from meeting the requirements of rigour and precision that the original authors had met. In this process, the concepts fail to express a complex and multifaceted reality, acquiring the status of theoretical slogans, distinguishing marks of fine thinking and conversation.

This route is surprising due to the difficulty inherent in these authors' works. There is little or nothing in them that would allow us to foresee this destiny. After reading their articles and books, a confession could be heard amidst a dismayed sigh: theory is very difficult. And yet, the fate of the work, its reception, seems to go against the intention of its authors and what their works had to say. Because if your ideas and concepts, your books and articles, are read and reread, anticipated and guarded, this is not due to a misunderstanding or a media operation; rather, it is because they always had something to tell us, although this something does not always reflect what one had expected to hear or read.

The work of Antonio Gramsci seems to have had a similar fate. Comprised in part of articles published in the press and intended, according to its own author, to 'perish at the end of the day', as well as study notes taken in precarious conditions and condemned to die with its author, this work survived the very circumstances of its composition and became a sign of the distinction of fine thinking and conversation. 'Hegemony', 'historical bloc', 'intellectual' and 'civil society', key notions of patient and meticulous, complex and intricate reflection, these became mainstays of the intellectual and political vocabulary from the beginning of the mid-1970s.

And they did so as part of a shared theoretical-political common sense. The context of the struggle against Latin American dictatorships, concomitant with the process of the crisis and decomposition of traditional organisations of the left, created on our continent an environment conducive to this reception. It was not just a fad. His work showed a surprising longevity below the Rio Bravo and in fact had a greater staying power than one might imagine. The recent completion of new and carefully edited editions of Gramsci's works in Mexico and Brazil illustrates the diffusion of his thought.

The surprising thing about this diffusion is that it represented a clear mismatch with the path that Gramsci's work has undergone in Italy: a retraction of Gramscian studies in the peninsula was accompanied by their wide diffusion in Latin America.[1] The political situation in which this unequal development occurred is important to this understanding. Marked by the collapse of 'real socialism' and the end of the Italian Communist Party, the evolution of these studies could be separated from the determinations of the political conjuncture and of the moment.[2] But the crisis of the 'Gramsci party' reverberated negatively in the Italian context through the diffusion of the work of the individual identified as its founder. The appeal of Gramsci's ideas was not the same, which would explain the decline in research dedicated to them.

It was this same context, however, that freed the Sardinian Marxist from his second imprisonment, allowing for the internationalisation of Gramscian studies and the opening up of new problems presented either by the transformations of the contemporary world or the recognition of new political and social realities.[3] The transformations in this field of study can be illustrated by the creative appropriation of Gramscian notions, particularly that of

---

[1] See Liguori and Meta 2005, p. 7 and Aricó 2005, p. 109.
[2] See Durante 1999, pp. 3–4.
[3] On the internationalisation of Gramscian studies, see the collection organised by Righi 1995. For the diffusion of Gramsci in Latin America, see the pioneering study of Aricó 2005. In Argentina, Raúl Burgos 2005 published a detailed study on the trajectory of the group *Past and Present*, directed by José Arico. Gramsci's diffusion in Brazil was the subject of controversy involving Coutinho 1999, pp. 279–313 and Dias 1996b. Two authors sought to address the issue more broadly: Simionatto 2004; and Secco 2002 and 2006, chapters VI and VII.

hegemony, in new areas of research, such as international relations, cultural studies, pedagogy and psychology.

Although it has generated extremely fertile research, the appropriation of Gramscian categories, whether in these new national contexts or in new areas of investigation, did not always have as a presupposition a rigorous reconstruction of the Sardinian Marxist's thought. The starting point for many of these new studies was thus a philologically weak reading of the work of Gramsci and, mainly, that of the *Prison Notebooks*.

Contradictorily, it was in the Italian context of the decline of Gramscian studies that a more rigorous methodological approach became possible in the treatment of the text and sources. Thus, at the end of his encouraging work reconstructing the trajectory of the debate around Gramsci's work, Guido Liguori could see the emergence of a research programme in which the actual contextualisation of the thought of the Sardinian Marxist would permit a 'conceptual excavation' capable of identifying the multiple sources of its reflection as well as its place in history.[4] Who knows if this programme of conceptual excavation may also be one that puts an end to the conceptual slavery and imprisonment of Gramsci's thinking in the theoretical and political structures of common sense?

The philological methodology that has characterised recent research does not make the text easier; on the contrary, it reveals its own difficulty. Such methodology also does not provide the 'true' interpretation or even an interpretation free of assumptions. But it has allowed a greater rigour in the reconstruction of Gramsci's laboratory, avoiding what Dante Germino[5] called expropriation, as opposed to interpretation, of the text.

Assuming the unfinished character of the *Notebooks* and the provisional nature of the formulations in them, this approach has been engaged in an 'effective contextualisation' of Gramscian thought capable of allowing a rigorous reconstruction of the course of conceptual formulation throughout the texts. A positive appropriation of Gramscian thought, that is, the 'use' of concepts that were patiently distilled in his laboratory, in contexts and situations other than those deployed in the original context, is possible and even desirable. It only makes sense then to go back once again to the *Notebooks* because in them it is possible to find a living thought capable of informing a renewed theoretical and political practice engaged in social emancipation projects. But this use must presuppose a consistent interpretation.

---

4 Liguori 1996, p. 254.
5 Germino 2002, pp. 130–1.

This book is aimed as much at those concerned with the interpretation of the thought of Antonio Gramsci as those who want to change the world. But it makes more sense for those who want to do both at the same time. Marx's oft-quoted eleventh thesis on Feuerbach – 'Philosophers have only interpreted the world, in various ways; the point is to change it'[6] – was for Gramsci the matrix of a political theoretical programme. The *Notebooks* could be read as the theoretical reflection of a practice that was denied by the prison. But they are more than that. The very theoretical reflection in them is part of a pedagogical project that aimed for the formation of new working-class intellectuals.[7]

The purpose of this book is to *interpret* a central point of this reflection: the relation between philosophy and politics in the *Notebooks*. The unity between theory and practice in them unfolded theoretically in the unity between philosophy, history and politics. This unity was developed in the research project that Gramsci carried out in prison under the 'determination in the final instance' of politics. Understand: it is the research project itself that is political, hence this determination. To recognise this unity means to affirm that history (and historiography), as well as philosophy, even that which affirms its axiological neutrality, are also constitutive of the political field from which they want to keep their distance.

The affirmation of this unity does not, however, cancel the particularity of historiographical and theoretical work. 'Scientific rigour', the methods and techniques mobilised in research and the relentless testing of the results obtained are essential requirements even for engaged research. Gramsci was aware of these requirements and his philosophical research contained a self-conscious theoretical practice, just as his historical research involved an historiographical practice. His thinking is not politicised, as many have hastily asserted, but political.

Politics is thus the central and most important theme developed in the *Notebooks*, but obviously it is not the only one. In the same way, in Gramsci's philosophical reflection the most important and developed part is his 'philosophy of politics', but this does not make sense of all his reflections.[8] The attempt to reduce the relationship between philosophy and politics in the *Notebooks* to the effort of a refoundation of Marxist philosophy like a gnosiology of politics, or gnosiology of superstructures,[9] is, therefore, exaggerated.

---

6   MECW, Vol. 5, p. 5.
7   Cf. Lisa 1981, p. 377.
8   Cf. Martelli 1996, p. 59.
9   Buci-Glucksmann 1980a.

In this way, the choice of the theme that traverses the reflections presented to the reader here is justified. One last explanation becomes necessary. Every work has a public. The most generic definition I can think of for it is defined by the fact that the author resides in America, and particularly in Brazil. An Italian reader might deem a synthetic exhibition of the thought of Vincenzo Gioberti or of Bendetto Croce unnecessary in a work dedicated to the *Notebooks*. But this is not the case on our continent. Gramsci already has his permanent resident visa in America, where he has been generously welcomed like many other immigrants. But he is still a foreigner and his culture is, to a large extent, strange.

With the exception of Machiavelli, figures like Guicciardini, Cuoco, Gioberti, Croce and Gentile do not attend our universities. In teaching courses related to Gramsci's political thought, I noticed that one of the difficulties faced by younger students was the result of the strangeness provoked by the relation of otherness with Gramscian culture. To shorten this oceanic distance, I always sought to reconstruct Gramsci's dialogue with his sources, which also afforded opportunities for these sources to speak for themselves.

∴

This book is the result of research carried out within the Research Group on Marxism and Political Thought, based at the Center for Marxist Studies (CEMARX) in the Institute of Philosophy and Human Sciences at the State University of Campinas (UNICAMP). The research project received, in its final phase, institutional support from the National Council for Scientific and Technological Development (CNPq). Preliminary results of this project were published in the journals *Outubro, Crítica Marxista, Novos Rumos, Revista de Sociologia e Política*, and *Universidade e Sociedade*. Two courses – one in the graduate programme in Political Science in the second semester of 2005 and another in the undergraduate programme in Social Sciences in the first half of 2006 – provided the opportunity for a more detailed reflection on the themes I had attended to in previous years.

The research work mobilised a group of young researchers, undergraduate and graduate students from UNICAMP, who participated actively in seminars and study groups. They were important interlocutors, as well as a source of encouragement for the conclusion of this work. It was also for them that I wrote this book, with the expectation that it would stimulate their own research. Others who participated in these seminars included Marco Vanzulli of the University of Milano-Bicocca; Rita Medici of the University of Bologna; and Ruy Braga of the University of São Paulo. Carlos Zacarias de Sena Junior from the State University of Bahia and Marcos Del Roio from the State University of

São Paulo-Marília Campus kindly read preliminary versions and contributed research. Dora Kanoussi from the Autonomous University of Puebla followed the research from a distance, facilitated books that were hard for me to access and kindly accepted to write the preface to the first edition. Tatiana Fonseca Oliveira perused the used bookshops of Napoli until she found the books I had requested. Colleagues from the Political Science Department of UNICAMP and particularly Sebastião Velasco e Cruz, Rachel Meneguello and Andrei Koerner provided me with the necessary institutional conditions to carry out the investigation. Colleagues at the Center for Marxist Studies at UNICAMP (CEMARX), among them Armando Boito and Andréia Galvão, welcomed me in a fraternal way.

Special mention should be made of my friend Edmundo Fernandes Dias, who died in 2013. It was he who presented the work of Gramsci to me, stimulating me to study the critical edition and introducing me to the text of Gianni Francioni. Many of the ideas presented here are a development of his reading of the work of the Sardinian Marxist. To Edmundo and all those already mentioned, I am grateful for the support and dialogue while, of course, relieving them of any responsibility for the contents of this text.

CHAPTER 2

Eternal/Provisional

On 2 June 1928, when the State Prosecutor took the floor against Antonio Gramsci and other leaders of the Communist Party of Italy (PCI) imprisoned with him, a violent statement of motives condemning him was handed down. The pronouncement expressed a complete irrationality: 'for twenty years we must prevent this brain to function'.[1] The process against the Communist leader by the fascist police had been ongoing since November 1926. But prison did not prevent his brain from functioning. Even before the sentence, in a letter written to his sister-in-law, Tatiana Schucht, in March 1927, Gramsci stated: 'I am obsessed (this is a phenomenon typical of people in jail, I think) by this idea: that I should do something *für ewig* ... I would like to concentrate intensely and systematically on some subject that would absorb and provide a centre to my inner life'.[2]

The main difficulty that the *Prison Notebooks* present to the reader lies in the paradox that this research project *für ewig* (for eternity) was materialised in the form of provisional and unfinished notes. Nothing indicates that Gramsci at any point during his work abandoned this initial approach. The variety of topics covered, the depth of treatment and the strategic aim of the reflection clearly indicates the pretension to write beyond the immediate conjuncture. On the contrary, there is strong evidence that as his work progressed, his objectives broadened. In the letter mentioned above, the first sketch of what became known as the *Prison Notebooks* was presented. There were four themes that Gramsci intended to address:

> (1) a research project on the formation of the public spirit in Italy during the last century; that is, research on Italian intellectuals, their origins, their groupings in relation to cultural currents, their various modes of thinking, etc.; (2) a study of comparative linguistics; (3) a study of Pirandello's plays and the transformation of theatrical taste in Italy which Pirandello represented and helped bring about; (4) an essay on serialised fiction and popular taste in literature.[3]

---

1 Apud Fiori 1979, p. 285.
2 LP2, 1, p. 83.
3 Ibid.

Connecting these different themes was the creative popular spirit in its various manifestations.[4] *Für ewig*, for eternity. It was not those questions of the analysis of conjuncture that attracted Gramsci in prison. His project sought to present a group of themes that rescued some of his youthful concerns: his linguistic studies and his activity as a literary critic. The reasons for this venture appeared to be of an intellectual and psychological order. The Italian Marxist sought to organise his life in prison so as to make it, if not tolerable, at least bearable. The letter to his sister-in-law failed to record those motivations that connected him to a life of full freedom. In the letter, the prisoner remembered in an autobiographical way his 'intellectual remorse' for having abandoned his linguistic studies. He also narrated his activity as a literary critic during the years 1915 and 1920: 'Did you know that I ... discovered and contributed to popularizing Pirandello's theatre?', he asked his sister-in-law.[5]

But the project also incorporated a strong political and social dimension, particularly present in the first area of concentration, in which the formation of the leading Italian intellectual groups was investigated. On this dimension Gramsci referred in the letter quoted above: 'You remember my text, very short and superficial, about Southern Italy and about the importance of B. Croce?' he asked Tatiana, mentioning his text 'Some Aspects of the Southern Question', a pre-prison writing in which Gramsci discussed the southern social formation, incorporating the place occupied by intellectuals in class analysis.[6] There are no doubts about the political character of this text, hence the importance of this revealing reference. But this political dimension still appeared diluted in this first project, as it is possible to verify in Gramsci's declaration of intention to broadly develop the thesis outlined in 'Some Aspects of the Southern Question' but 'from a "disinterested" point of view, für ewig'.[7]

The results of this activity planned by Gramsci were the 33 notebooks he filled during his years in prison. There are notes on the Italian theatre, linguistics and popular culture, but also ones on philosophy, history, economics and, above all, politics. The variety of themes is enormous, prompting Eric Hobsbawm to observe that in these notebooks it is possible to find important and original contributions in all fields of the so-called human sciences, with the exception, perhaps, of economics.

---

4 LP2, 1, pp. 83–4.
5 LP2, 1, p. 84.
6 LP2, 1, p. 83. The essay, written in 1926, was only published in 1930 in the magazine *Lo Stato operaio*, maintained by the PCI in Paris. PPW, pp. 313–37.
7 LP2, 1, p. 83.

The prison project, however, had to be postponed for 'technical reasons', as the author liked to say. His friend Piero Sraffa had opened an account at a Milan bookstore in which Gramsci could order books, but it was not until the beginning of 1929 that he received authorisation to make notes in a notebook and the necessary material for doing so. In Notebook 1, whose writing began on 8 February 1929, he began his work with the following annotation:

> Notes and jottings.
> Main arguments:
> 1) *Theory of history and historiography.*
> 2) *Development of the Italian bourgeoisie until 1870.*
> 3) *Formation of Italian intellectual groups*: development, attitudes.
> 4) *The popular literature of 'serial novels' and the reasons for its continued success.*
> 5) *Cavalcante Cavalcanti*: his position in the structure and art of the Divine Comedy.
> 6) *Origins and development of Catholic Action in Italy and in Europe.*
> 7) *The concept of folklore.*
> 8) *Experiences of prison life.*
> 9) *The 'southern question' and the question of the islands.*
> 10) *Observations on the Italian population*: its composition, function of emigration.
> 11) *Americanism and Fordism.*
> 12) *The question of language in Italy*: Manzoni and G.I. Ascoli.
> 13) *'Common sense'* (cf. 7).
> 14) *Types of periodicals*: theoretical, critical-historical, of general culture (dissemination).
> 15) *Neo-grammarians and neo-linguists* ('this round table is square').
> 16) Father Bresciani's progeny.[8]

These notes in Notebook 1 revealed the development that the original project had received. To the themes of culture listed in the letter of 1928, others were added such as theory and social and political analysis, including questions of the theory of history, the formation of the Italian bourgeoisie and the 'Southern Question'. Important, too, was the inclusion of an item on Americanism and Fordism, rescuing themes that motivated his reflections during the Red Biennium in Turin. Gramsci himself presented the matter to his sister-in-law,

---

8   PN1, p. 99.

in a letter of 25 March 1929 indicating a concentration of his interests around a number of reduced areas: 'I decided to occupy myself predominantly and take notes on these three subjects: 1) Italian history in the nineteenth century, with special reference to training and development of intellectual groups; 2) The theory of history and historiography; 3) Americanism and Fordism'.[9]

Gramsci began writing these notebooks with jottings on quite varied subjects and comments on books and articles he read in prison. The titles that the author placed before each paragraph repeated themselves several times, indicating that the project would focus on specific themes as intended. But gradually issues related to political and social analysis would appear more intensely.

From the early 1930s, there was a marked politicisation of the Gramscian research project. The turning point seems to be an enigmatic two-line note written between December 1929 and February 1930, according to the dating of Francioni.[10] In it, Gramsci records in French: 'Leon Blum's saying. *"Le pouvoir est tentant. Mais seule l'opposition est confortable"*'.[11] There begins here what Francioni calls an '"explosion" of the most directly political theoretical reflection'.[12] Important in this movement are § 43, under the heading 'Types of Periodicals' – a long note devoted to the question of intellectuals – and § 44 'Political class leadership before and after assuming government power' in which the concept of 'passive revolution appears, for the first time, according to expression of V[icenzo]. Cuoco'.[13]

What are the reasons for this turn? The explanation must be sought outside the Gramscian text. To motivate such an inflection were the dilemmas of the struggle against fascism; the sectarian turn of the Communist International, given by the 6th Congress (1928) and consolidated by the 10th Plenum of the Executive Committee (1929); and the increasing Stalinisation of the Soviet Union. The events of 1930 in the PCI and in the Communist International coincide with the beginning of a series of discussions that Gramsci maintained with his companions in misfortune.[14] The most important theme of Italian politics at the time for Gramsci was the question of the Constituent Assembly and its effectiveness in the struggle against fascism, but this was articulated, as nar-

---

9 LC, p. 264. OT. This letter is dated incorrectly 24 February 1929 in the new Brazilian edition of *Cadernos do cárcere (Prison Notebooks)*. CC, Vol. 1, p. 78. In the edition of the *Cartas do cárcere (Letters from Prison)* organised by the same team, the date is recorded correctly. Gramsci 2005, Vol. 1, p. 328.
10 Gramsci 1984, p. 140.
11 PN1, Q1, § 40, p. 124.
12 Francioni 1987, p. 30.
13 PN1, § 44, p. 136.
14 Fiori 1979, pp. 308–18 and Buci-Glucksmann 1980a, pp. 303–10.

rated by Athos Lisa, one of the participants, with the question of 'intellectuals and the party' and the theme of 'the military problem and the party'.[15] It was from this point on that the critique of politics took centre stage in the Gramscian research project.

Gramsci's new concerns in prison and his conversations with his colleagues pointed in that direction. In a note written in Notebook 8, probably between the months of November and December 1930,[16] Gramsci reinforced his concerns that he had indicated in a letter to Tatiana on 25 March 1929, by expanding them and giving them the form of a research programme. He wrote:

> Loose notes and jottings for a history of Italian intellectuals (...)
>
> *Principal essays: General introduction.* Development of Italian intellectuals up to 1870: different periods. – The popular literature of serial novels. – Folklore and common sense. – The question of literary language and dialects. – Father Bresciani's progeny. – Reformation and Renaissance. – School and national education. – B. Croce's position in Italian culture up to the World War. – The Risorgimento and the Action Party. – Ugo Foscolo and the formation of the national rhetoric. – Italian theater. – History of Catholic Action: Catholics, integralists, Jesuits, modernists. – The medieval commune: the economic-corporative phase of the state. – Cosmopolitan function of Italian intellectuals up to the 18th century. – Reactions to the absence in Italy of a culture that is national-popular in character: the futurists. – The unitary school and its significance for the entire organization of national culture. – 'Lorianism' as one of the characteristics of the Italian intellectuals. – The absence of 'Jacobinism' in the Italian Risorgimento. – Machiavelli as a technician of politics and as a complete politician or a politician in deed.
>
> Appendices: Americanism and Fordism[17]

This note was preceded by a set of reservations that Gramsci made to his own work that permitted him to more precisely define the meaning attached to them by their author. The purpose of these notes was not an 'encyclopedic compilation' on intellectuals. The 'Principal essays' (*Saggi principale*) were of a provisional character and from them it would be possible to construct some independent trials, but not an organic and systematic work. However, it is

---

15   Lisa 1981, p. 376.
16   See Francioni 1984, p. 142.
17   PN3, Q8, pp. 231–2.

important to highlight that this note did not circumscribe the scope of Gramscian research as a whole, which is indicated by the inscription 'Appendices' in the plural, followed by only a single indication – 'Americanism and Fordism' – denoting the intention to aggregate other items. The rest of the page is blank, but it is possible that Gramsci wanted to enumerate other subjects there that did not fit in this set of essays on intellectuals.

At the stage in which the already written notebooks were found, it is possible to perceive that not all the written material would find a place in this set of essays on intellectuals. In addition to the theme 'Americanism and Fordism', already anticipated in the letter to Tatiana as an appendix, which reveals its autonomous character, we could also include in this category those notes registered under the title 'Notes on Philosophy', present in Notebooks 4, 7 and 8. On the other hand, even themes indicated in these 'Principal essays' would later receive a very different development, such as the study on Benedetto Croce present in Notebook 10, which was not limited to his role in the postwar period.[18]

What is the place of this enumeration of the 'Principal essays' in the internal history of the *Prison Notebooks*, Francioni asks: 'Not properly a reformulation of the whole Gramscian research program, but an organic project for the systematization and the development of a vast and autonomous section'.[19] The place of the question of intellectuals in the whole of Gramsci's reflections and in the *Notebooks* should not be minimised. Indeed, not only is this question found in his pre-prison writings, but this subject was present in all the different plans that Gramsci made for the writing of the *Notebooks*. Yet the question of intellectuals, in spite of its importance, did not exhaust the research. He himself made this clear, in a letter dated 17 November 1930, close to the date of the Note, which summarises its content:

> I've focused on *three or four main topics*, one of them being the cosmopolitan role played by Italian intellectuals until the eighteenth century, which in turn is split into several sections: the Renaissance and Machiavelli, etc. If I had the possibility of consulting the necessary material, I believe that there is a really interesting book to be written that does not yet exist; I

---

18 Gerratana 1997, p. 16. According to the dating of Francioni, the Essays in Notebook 4 were already fully drafted at the time of the writing of Notebook 8, while the beginning of the Notes on Philosophy in Notebook 7 coincide with Notebook 4 and succeed it. Evidently, the Notes on Philosophy of Notebook 8 came after the note written on the first page. Francioni 1984, pp. 141–2.

19 Francioni 1984, p. 78.

say book, meaning only the introduction to a number of monographs, because the subject presents itself differently in different epochs and in my opinion one needs to go back to the times of the Roman Empire. Meanwhile, I write *notes*, also because reading the relatively little that I have brings back to mind my old readings of the past.[20]

The theme of this letter was taken up again in another on 3 August 1931, after, therefore, the writing of this note. In this missive, the Sardinian Marxist assessed the difficulties for the development of his research and, probably, for the plan of the 'Principal essays' itself. 'I had intended to reflect on a certain set of questions', he affirmed, to then observe that 'it was inevitable that at some point these reflections would lead to a phase of documentation, and thus to a phase of work and of elaboration for which great libraries are needed'. The absence of the technical means which would allow him to advance the study of these 'questions' did not, however, impede him from continuing the work: 'This does not mean that I'm completely wasting my time, but I no longer have the great curiosity to proceed in any given general direction, at least for the time being', he concluded in dismay.[21] He then affirmed, framing his research on intellectuals within a broader theme, something that he had hitherto not revealed in the different notebooks:

> One of my greatest interests during the past few years has been to pinpoint certain characteristic features in the history of Italian intellectuals. This interest arose from the desire, on the one hand, *to probe the concept of the state, and on the other, to understand certain aspects of the historical development of the Italian people.*[22]

A few hours after writing this letter, during the night of the same day, 3 August, the worsening health of its author manifested itself sharply. It is not possible to attribute the transformations through which his research and writing plan would pass exclusively to the precarious state of his health, but it certainly influenced its rhythm. After that night, he abandoned, as Gerratana notes, the translation exercises and concentrated his efforts on the deepening of the research and the restructuring of a new series of notebooks, which he called 'Special'.[23] In a letter to Tatiana on 22 February 1932 he anticipated this inten-

---

20 LP2, 1, p. 360. Emphasis Added.
21 LC, pp. 459–60 cited by Joseph Buttigieg, PNI, Introduction, p. 30.
22 Ibid. Emphasis Added.
23 Gerratana 1997, pp. 37–8.

tion, requesting her to send to him small notebooks, 'to reorder these notes, dividing them by argument and thus systematizing them'.[24] According to the dating of Francioni,[25] shortly after the letter, probably between March and April 1932, Gramsci wrote in Notebook 8, on the page following the design of the 'Main Essays', the latest version of his work plan, denominating it 'Regrouping of Subjects':[26]

> Regrouping of subjects:
> 1. Intellectuals. Scholarly issues.
> 2. Machiavelli.
> 3. Encyclopedic notions and cultural topics.
> 4. Introduction to the study of philosophy and critical notes on a Popular Manual of Sociology.
> 5. History of Catholic Action. Catholic integralists – Jesuits – modernists.
> 6. A miscellany of various scholarly notes (Past and present).
> 7. The Italian Risorgimento (in the sense of Omodeo's L'età del Risorgimento Italiano but emphasizing the more strictly Italian motifs).
> 8. Father Bresciani's progeny. Popular literature. (Notes on literature).
> 9. Lorianism.
> 10. Notes on journalism.[27]

This is not a complete plan, but it is the last of Gramsci's projects for the *Notebooks*. For Gerratana, although not definitive, the proposal of the 'Regrouping of the Subjects' contained a project of monographic notebooks that would be materialised in the so-called Special Notebooks.[28] Francioni, in turn, considers these 'Regrouping of the Subjects' 'an incomplete index' with a view to the construction of the monographic notebooks and, at the same time, an alternative design of the 'Principal essays' on the intellectuals listed on the previous page.[29]

The writing of the Special Notebooks began in 1932, thematically grouping together the previously written material, reformulating it and adding new and

---

24 LC, p. 576. OT.
25 Francioni 1984, pp. 85–93.
26 [Translator's Note: in PN3, Q8, §2, Buttigieg translates this not as 'Regrouping of Subjects' but simply 'Grouping of Subjects'. I have maintained the translation of the present author's translations from the original Italian.]
27 PN3, Q8, §2, p. 233.
28 Gerratana 1997, p. 38.
29 Francioni 1984, p. 86.

unpublished passages. As he transcribed the material for the new notebooks, he also corrected and revised the older ones, without, however, compromising the reading of the original passages. The Special Notebooks started were the following (the numbering was provided later by Gerratana in the critical edition):[30]

- Notebook 10 – *'The philosophy of Benedetto Croce'* (100 pages).
- Notebook 11 – Untitled, but whose content corresponds to item 4 of the 'Regrouping' (*Introduction to the Study of Philosophy and critical notes on a Popular Manual of Sociology* – 80 pages).
- Notebook 12 – 'Notes and Loose Jottings for a group of essays on the history of intellectuals and culture in Italy' (24 pages in large format).
- Notebook 13 – 'Brief Notes on Machiavelli's politics' (60 pages in large format).
- Notebook 16 – 'Cultural Topics. I' (74 pages).
- Notebook 18 – 'Niccolo Machiavelli II' (3 pages in large format).
- Notebook 19 – Untitled, but whose content corresponds to item 7 of the 'Regrouping' (Italian Risorgimento – 132 pages).
- Notebook 20 – 'Catholic Action – Catholic Integralists – Jesuits – Modernists' (23 pages).
- Notebook 21 – 'Problems of Italian National Culture 1. Popular Literature' (32 pages).
- Notebook 22 – 'Americanism and Fordism' (46 pages).
- Notebook 23 – 'Literary Criticism' (75 pages).
- Notebook 24 – 'Journalism' (18 pages).
- Notebook 25 – 'On the Margins of History. History of Subaltern Groups' (17 pages).
- Notebook 26 – 'Cultural Topics. II' (11 pages).
- Notebook 27 – 'Observations on "Folklore"' (7 pages).
- Notebook 28 – 'Lorianism' (18 pages).
- Notebook 29 – 'Notes for an Introduction to the Study of Grammar' (10 pages).

As one can see, the notebooks 11, 12, 13, 16, 18, 19, 20, 21, 23, 24, 26 and 28 coincide with the themes of the 'Regrouping'. On the other hand, the contents of Notebook 10 – 'The Philosophy of Benedetto Croce' – only partly comprises the plan of the 'Principal essays' but not the 'Regrouping'; the theme of Notebook 22 – 'Americanism and Fordism' – coincides with the plan of Notebook 1 and the appendix of the 'Principal essays'; there is no mention in the plans

---

[30] For questions of the method of the critical edition, see Gerratana 1997.

previous to the contents of Notebook 25 – 'On the Margins of History. History of Subaltern Groups'; the 'Observations on Folklore' of Notebook 27 were foreseen in Notebook 1 and the 'Main Essays'; and the 'Notes for an Introduction to the Study of Grammar' of Notebook 29 were written in the letter of 19 March 1927 and in the plan of Notebook 1.

The writing of the Special Notebooks was quite uneven, as a result of either the conditions of life in prison or the debilitated health of its author. The Special Notebooks from number 16, in particular, written from the middle of 1933 onwards, were greatly affected by these conditions. Gramsci, however, maintained this intellectual activity until the middle of 1935, when the deterioration of his physical state prevented him from continuing. Soon after, he was transferred to a medical clinic with restricted freedom, where he could no longer perform his work on the *Notebooks*. At the beginning of April 1937 he was freed, but died a few days later, on 27 April.

The discrepancies between the projects designed by Gramsci and the Special Notebooks is a problem to be clarified and about which it is only possible to construct hypotheses. Fabio Frosini in the Seminar on the *Notebooks*, held in Rome in 2000, sought to address this issue.[31] With this purpose, he suggested the explanation that the thematic regrouping had been abandoned (but not repudiated) by Gramsci at first. According to Frosini, between the spring and summer of 1932, Gramsci would have oscillated between two hypotheses of work: the one present in the 'Regrouping of Subjects' which would be the finished research and which would seek to organise the collected material and another present in the list of the 'Main Essays' with a view to inaugurating a second phase of the research work on intellectuals and which, according to the letter to Tatiana on 7 September 1931, should be completed by a set of essays on the theory of history and historiography and another on Americanism and Fordism.[32]

Investigating the structure and history of this material,[33] Frosini drew attention to the fact that the title that organises the cast of the 'Principal essays – Notes and Loose Jottings for a group of essays on the history of intellectuals' – is almost identical to Gramsci's title for Notebook 12 – 'Notes and Loose Jottings for a group of essays on the history of intellectuals and culture in Italy'. The similarity would indicate that Notebook 12 would be the materialisation of the project of exhibition designed in the 'Principal essays'.

---

31 See Frosini 2003, pp. 62–5.
32 Frosini 2003, p. 63.
33 Frosini 2003, p. 65.

The question identified by Frosini himself remains: the result of Notebook 12 presents a clear contradiction between the title and its content and a congruence between that content and the thematic proposal contained in the 'Regrouping of Subjects' under the heading 'I. Intellectuals. Scholarly issues'.[34] Why was there this contradiction and congruence? Frosini suggests that this could indicate that the initial project was not actually carried out and that the project of the 'Regrouping of Subjects' was resumed as a minimal work programme after the very serious health crisis of 7 March 1933.[35]

But it is questionable whether, in fact, Notebook 12 began to be written as part of the programme announced by the set of 'Principal essays'. As late as August 1931, about six months, therefore, after the writing of the plan for the 'Principal essays', Gramsci expressed doubts about his research programme: 'It is safe to say that now I no longer have a real program of study and work'.[36] There are several reasons for the comings and goings of the projects. Noteworthy, for example, is the pressure that his friend Piero Sraffa exerted through Tatiana, encouraging him to take on more circumscribed projects so as to avoid the wasting of his physical and intellectual energy. After suggesting that Gramsci do some translations, Sraffa encouraged him to dedicate himself to the question of the intellectuals.[37]

Responding to Sraffa's pressure, Gramsci stated in a letter dated 7 September 1931 that 'If you will and the higher authorities allow me, I will make a sketch of the matter that should not have less than fifty pages'.[38] But he remained somewhat doubtful in this regard, as can be seen in a letter dated 2 May 1932:

> I do not know if I will ever send you the scheme I promised on the 'Italian intellectuals'. The point of view from which I look at the question some-

---

34 Frosini 2003, p. 66. In fact, § 1 of Notebook 12 has no title, but it is dedicated to the question of intellectuals, as well as § 3. § 2, in turn, is entitled '*Observations on the School*: In Search of the Educational Principle'. Notebook 12 is composed only of those three paragraphs quoted and gathers previously written essays present in Notebook 4.
35 Frosini 2003, p. 66.
36 LC, p. 459 cited in Buttigieg, PN1, Introduction, p. 30.
37 Gramsci clearly perceived this interlocution with his friend through his sister-in-law and it was him with whom he dialogued at various moments. In his letter of 7 September 1931, for example, he wrote his sister-in-law: 'I understand that you spoke with Piero [Sraffa], because certain things only he may have told you'. And in the same letter he sent a message clearly intended for his friend but carefully constructed, in order to avoid censorship: 'I read, in an article by Senator Einaudi, that Piero is preparing a critical edition of the English economist David Ricardo; Einaudi praises the initiative very much and I am also very happy'. LC, pp. 480–1. OT. For the reconstruction of this interlocution, see Sraffa 1991.
38 LP1, p. 162.

times changes: it may be too early to summarise and synthesise. It is a matter still in a fluid state, which must be further elaborated later.[39]

It has not been sufficiently emphasised that this letter coincides with the beginning of the writing of Notebook 12. Doubts over the research programme and the mode of exhibition of the results of his research would affect, therefore, the proposal contained in the 'Principal essays'. Gramsci's doubts with respect to his work on intellectuals allows us to understand the provisional and incomplete character not only of the exposition of his research, but also of the research itself. The author of the *Notebooks* was very careful in this regard and on three occasions referred to their provisional nature.[40]

The first of these occasions is found in Notebook 4, inside the 'Notes on Philosophy I'. At the end of a note, probably written between May and August 1930, regarding teleology in the manual of historical materialism of Nicolai Bukharin, Gramsci puts in parentheses, without any connection to the theme addressed in this text, a warning:

> In general, remember that all these notes are provisional and written as they flow from the pen: they must be reviewed and checked in detail because they undoubtedly contain imprecisions, anachronisms, wrong approaches, etc., that do not imply wrongdoing because the notes have solely the function of quick memoranda.[41]

The second warning signal was written, probably, between November and December 1930, in Notebook 8. This is the text which, after the title 'Loose notes and jottings for a history of Italian intellectuals', precedes the cast of the 'Principal essays'. These lines have a clear methodological meaning, guiding the research procedures and the recording of results:

> (1) Provisional character – like memoranda – of these kinds of notes and jottings. (2) They may result in independent essays but not in a comprehensive organic work. (3) There can be no distinction yet between the main part of the exposition and the secondary elements, between what would end up being the 'text' and what should be the 'notes.' (4) These notes often consist of assertions that have not been verified, that may be

---

39   LP1, p. 213.
40   See the discussion of these texts in Frosini 2003, pp. 73–4 and Baratta 2004, p. 95n.
41   PN2, Q4, §16, p. 158.

called 'rough first drafts'; after further study, some of them may be discarded, and it might even be the case that the opposite of what they assert will be shown to be true. (5) That said, one should not be put off by the enormity of the topic and its unclear boundaries; there is no intention to assemble a jumbled miscellany on intellectuals, an encyclopedic compilation aimed at filling all possible and imaginable 'lacunae'.[42]

The tone of this second note is, as can be easily seen, one of extreme caution. The affirmation that the provisional nature of the notes would not entail any damage to their content contained in the first text was abandoned. Instead, the note in Notebook 8 clearly stated that perhaps serious errors were possible and that they would need to be abandoned or corrected. A third and final warning signal, written in 1932, appeared in the 'Warning' which opens Notebook 11. It is a second version of the text present in Notebook 4 quoted above:

> The notes contained in this book, as in the others, were written as they flow from the pen, from a quick memory. They should be thoroughly reviewed and closely monitored because they certainly contain inaccuracies, false approximations, anachronisms. Written without having in mind the books to which they refer, it is possible that after the control they should be radically corrected because exactly the opposite of what is claimed could be true.[43]

Here the author recognised not only that there could be errors but also that notes could be 'radically corrected'. The presence of this 'Warning' at the beginning of Notebook 11, the most finished of all, is significant. But significant for whom? For the author of the notes, a warning should be obvious and, therefore, dispensable. If the *Prison Notebooks* were just the beginning of an ongoing investigation, a 'field book' in which the researcher recorded their reflections and the result of their scientific activity, if these notes were intended solely for their original author, then, what sense would this warning have?

With these warning signs, Gramsci appears to foresee the fate that his *Notebooks* would have. It is known that he always offered resistance to the publication of works that he did not consider ready. In the already cited letter to Tatiana on 7 September 1931, he illustrated his attitude:

---

42 PN2, Q8, p. 231.
43 Q11, p. 1365. OT.

> During ten years of journalism, I wrote enough pages to fill some 15 or 20 volumes of 400 pp. each; however, they were written for the day and, in my view, they should have died once the day was over. I have always refused to compile even small anthologies.[44]

It was for this reason that he avoided, in 1918, authorising the publication of a selection of his articles. It also explains why, in 1921, he preferred to collect the manuscript that was already in the process of being published by Giuseppe Prezzolini, paying the costs of a part that was already in composition.[45]

But the warnings in the *Notebooks* seem to be based not only on the well-known prudence of their author, but also on the conviction of the incompleteness and provisional nature of the collected material and the perception that this condition might not be recognised by eventual readers. Writing about the work of Marx, Gramsci addressed the question head-on:

> Among the works of the given thinker, moreover, it is necessary to distinguish those which he completed and published from those that remained unpublished, because they were not completed, and were published by friends and disciples, with revisions, modifications, cuts, that is, with the active intervention of the editor. It is evident that the content of this work should be taken with great discernment and caution, because it cannot be considered definitive, but *only material still in elaboration, still provisional*; it cannot be ruled out that such works, especially if they were elaborated a long time ago without the author deciding to complete them (in whole or in part), would be repudiated by the author or considered unsatisfactory.[46]

While the above remarks were made in respect of Marx's work, they were also apt for his own writings. The whole content of this note seems to have a double meaning, referring simultaneously to Marx and to Gramsci himself. Thus, alongside the warnings about the notes' provisional character, it invites future readers to exercise prudence and patient dialogue with the text.[47] The invitation by the Sardinian Marxist, however, was only heard belatedly.

---

44 LC, p. 480 cited in Buttigieg, PN1, Introduction, p. 5.
45 Ibid.
46 Q16, §2, p. 1842. Emphasis Added. OT.
47 Cf. Baratta 2004, p. 89.

1   Spaces

After Gramsci's death, his sister-in-law Tatiana and the communist leader Palmiro Togliatti took on the task of recovering the *Notebooks* and taking them safely to Moscow. The first news of their publication was given by Togliatti himself in an unsigned article published on 30 April 1944 in the PCI newspaper *L'Unita*:

> The main theme [of the *Notebooks*] is a 'history of Italian intellectuals' in which the function assumed by the intellectuals is critically examined as an instrument of the ruling castes to maintain their dominion over the popular classes, the rebellion of some great thinkers in relation to this function and the relative events of Italian history and thought. The greatest attention is devoted to the 1800s and to our times and a whole notebook deals with the philosophy of B[enedetto]. Croce, the lay Pope ... whose dictatorship over the last century's intelligentsia covers and ensures the dictatorship of the reactionary bourgeois caste in the economic and political order.[48]

Togliatti's article already established a modality for the dissemination of Gramsci's work that would assume its material form with the thematic reorganisation of the text. In 1947, the publisher Einaudi launched the first volume of the works of Antonio Gramsci in Italian, *Letters from Prison*, and from 1948 onwards the *Notebooks*, thematically organised and published with the following titles: *Il materialismo storico e la filosofia di Benedetto Croce* (*Historical Materialism and the Philosophy of Benedetto Croce*, 1949); *Gli intelletualli e l'organizazione della cultura* (*Intellectuals and the Organization of Culture*, 1949); *Il Risorgimento* (*The Risorgimento*, 1949); *Note sul Macchiavelli, sulla politica e sullo Stato moderno* (*Notes on Machiavelli, on Politics and on the Modern State*, 1949); *Letteratura e vita nazionale* (*Literature and National Life*, 1950); and *Passato e presente* (*Past and Present*, 1951). The reorganisation is not completely arbitrary, insofar as it could be justified by the 'Regrouping of Subjects' in Notebook 8. Yet it is still problematic. The edition mixed material written in the Miscellaneous Notebooks with material from the Special Notebooks, fused notes written at different times, and changed their order.

In some cases, the material inserted by Gramsci in a notebook was simply discarded. In *Historical Materialism and the Philosophy of Benedetto Croce* eight

---

48   Togliatti 2001, pp. 94–5. OT.

paragraphs from Notebook 10 were missing and four were transcribed only partially. From Notebook 11, the warning and two notes remained unpublished.⁴⁹ As editor of the *Notebooks*, communist leader Palmiro Togliatti also eliminated passages that he considered compromising. He also added introductory texts that were intended to guide the reader in certain directions. Thus, in the editors' Preface to the first of the volumes, one can read: 'These writings of Gramsci could not be understood and valued properly if the progress achieved by the Marxist conception during the first three decades of this century, due to the theoretical and practical activity of Lenin and Stalin, had not been acquired'.⁵⁰

The statement repeats the crude portrait constructed by Togliatti in the article 'Antonio Gramsci capo della operaia italiana' (Antonio Gramsci leader of the Italian working class) published for the first time in 1937 in which Gramsci appears (and perishes) carrying 'the invincible flag of Marx-Engels-Lenin-Stalin'.⁵¹ For the secretary-general of the Italian Communist Party, Gramsci would be not only a bearer of this standard, but also a theoretical disciple of Stalin:

> Gramsci developed, from 1924 to 1926, an exceptional activity ... From this period the writings of Gramsci were devoted mainly to elucidating the theoretical questions of the nature of the party, its strategy, its theory and its organization, in which one feels the profound influence exercised over him by Stalin's work.⁵²

Togliatti's processing of Gramsci into a Stalinist was interpreted as an attempt to 'safeguard the name of Gramsci' before the Communist International,⁵³ but it resembles an attempt to safeguard himself and Stalinism, appropriating the prestige of the prisoner of Mussolini.

The problems of the first edition of the *Notebooks* are cumulative. First of all, they induce the reader to consider the Gramscian text as fully completed and coherent. Not only does the fragmentary nature of the work become opaque to the reader, but also the grouping of the notes followed the criterion of an 'encyclopedia in compendium of all sciences',⁵⁴ of a humanist and even aca-

---

49   See Francioni 1987, pp. 20–1.
50   Gramsci 1949, p. XVI. OT.
51   Togliatti 2001, p. 89. OT.
52   Togliatti 2001, p. 82.
53   Liguori 1996, p. 17.
54   Garin 1996, p. 291.

demic character, 'a disciplinary hierarchy of the medieval and idealistic type: first, philosophy, then culture in general, history, politics, and finally literature and art'[55] in which 'philosophers, historians, politicians, learned men could thus find texts of interest to them'.[56]

Second, the particular research modality of the author of the *Notebooks*, 'the rhythm of thought', as he liked to say, was erased and the real determinations of the concepts elaborated by him were lost. The very order in which the writings were published tended to dilute the emergence of political criticism in his prison work, and as a result of such reconstruction, the author came to resemble the image of a cultural critic and theoretician of superstructures, which has been so widely spread. The Preface to *Historical Materialism and the Philosophy of Benedetto Croce* reinforced the meaning of this reconstruction, defining the writings gathered there as 'the crowning of all research conducted by Gramsci in the prison years, the theoretical, philosophical justification of the imposition given to the problem of intellectuals and culture'.[57]

Third, the insertion of the publishers' prefaces and notes imposed a Stalinised reading guide strongly marked by the new policy of the PCI. Thus, in the Preface to *Historical Materialism and the Philosophy of Benedetto Croce*, its authors made the traditional warnings about the censorship carried out by the prison administration and the need to codify the text by avoiding mention 'of the proletariat, communism, Bolshevism, Marx, Engels, Lenin, Stalin, the Party'.[58] The same authors then exemplified the Gramscian procedure, citing a passage that would become famous and inserting in brackets the editors' explanations:

> That this is not futile is demonstrated by the fact that ... the greatest modern theorist [Lenin] of the philosophy of praxis [Marxism] has – on the terrain of political struggle and organization, and with political terminology – and in opposition to the various tendencies of 'economism', revalued the front of cultural struggle and constructed the doctrine of

---

55 Monasta 1985, p. 32.
56 Baratta 2004, p. 65.
57 Gramsci 1949, p. xvi. OT. On the first edition of the *Notebooks*, see Gerratana 1997, pp. 57–72. Chiara Daniele 2005 brought together extensive documentation regarding the publication of this first edition by Palmiro Togliatti. For the debate that preceded and followed this edition, and particularly its nexus with the political turn of the Italian Communist Party after the Second World War (the so-called 'Salerno Turn'), see Liguori 1996, pp. 28–52. On the political meaning of the editing operation of the Notebooks 10 and 11, see the hypothesis of Francioni 1987, p. 45.
58 Gramsci 1949.

hegemony [of the hegemony of the proletariat – that is, of the working-class alliances] as a complement to the theory of the state-as-force [that is, the doctrine of Marx and not the falsification made by Trotsky] and as a contemporary form of the 1848 doctrine of 'permanent revolution'.[59]

The overlapping of these problems had a profound impact on the reception of Gramsci. The arbitrary ordering of the notes written in prison tended to produce the impression of a finished text, as already noted. In these circumstances the concepts appear most often in their more mature formulations and it is possible from there to reduce the context of discovery to enlightenment. The hypothesis of Gramscian 'enlightenment' is reinforced by the impossibility of separating the research from the exposure. What is registered in the *Notebooks* is always part of the investigation. Now, the publication of the notes almost exclusively taken from the Special Notebooks tends to give the research a more coherent and finalised character than it actually had; moreover, it reinforces the impression that Gramsci arrived at these conclusions first. In prison, like Paul on the road to Damascus and Rousseau in Vincennes, Gramsci would have, in an instantaneous mode, mentally constructed his philosophy of praxis.

To get an idea of the degree of confusion caused by the rearrangement of Gramscian texts by the thematic edition of the *Prison Notebooks*, one can take as an example the interpretation that Nicos Poulantzas makes of the question of historicism that is presented in these notes. Contesting Gramsci in the same schematic way as the Althusserian thesis of the epistemological rupture between the young and the mature Marx, the author of *Political Power and Social Classes* affirmed:

> we can locate a clear break between on the one hand the works of Gramsci's youth (e.g. the articles in *L'Ordine Nuovo*) and even *Il materialismo storico e la filosofia di Benedetto Croce* (*Historical Materialism and the Philosophy of Benedetto Croce*), with their typically historicist approach, and on the other, the works of his maturity concerning political theory (e.g. *Notes on Machiavelli*, etc.), i.e. precisely those works in which the concept of hegemony is elaborated.[60]

Now, it is not just *Historical Materialism and the Philosophy of Benedetto Croce* that is part of the *Prison Notebooks*; indeed, several of the paragraphs that make

---

59   GR, Q10 / I, § 12, p. 195.
60   Poulantzas 1978, p. 138.

up that 'work' were written after Gramsci started the writing of Notebook 13, which contains most of the texts that form part of *Notes on Machiavelli, on Politics and on the Modern State* (1949). Certainly Poulantzas had no way of knowing about the dating of the paragraphs in the *Notebooks*, which was only established in the indispensable study of Gianni Francioni.[61] But as early as 1967, Gerratana had commented on the process of preparing a critical edition, highlighting its fragmentation, at the congress of Gramsci Studies in Cagliari. Such a congress was not foreign to the French, since Jacques Texier had played an important role by commenting on the presentation of Norberto Bobbio.[62] Although a careful reading of the editors' preface to *Historical Materialism and the Philosophy of Benedetto Croce* was sufficient not to make such a gross misunderstanding, it must be acknowledged that the thematic edition induced the error.[63]

Soon after they were published, the texts began to travel around the world. Only three years after the publication of the *Letters from Prison* in Italy, they were translated into Spanish and published in Argentina by Lautaro Publishers.[64] The edition of this text would be followed by the publication by the same publisher of *El materialismo histórico y la filosofía de Bendetto Croce* (*Historical Materialism and the Philosophy of Benedetto Croce*, 1958); *Los intelectuales y la organización de la cultura* (*Intellectuals and the Organization of Culture*, 1960); *Literatura y vida nacional* (*Literature and National Life*, 1961); and *Notas sobre Maquiavelo, sobre la política y sobre el Estado moderno* (*Notes on Machiavelli, on Politics and on the Modern State*, 1962). However, the volumes *The Risorgimento*

---

61 Francioni 1984.
62 See Texier 1975.
63 Louis Althusser and his disciples had the merit of having projected Gramsci's work into French philosophical debates. But his studies published in the 1960s reveal only superficial knowledge, incompatible with the extent of the criticism they intended to promote. Thus, for example, in the midst of his pretentious criticism of historicism, Althusser comes to interpolate between brackets within a Gramsci note dedicated to the critique of the *Popular Manual* an erroneous observation, indicating to the reader that this work was from Benedetto Croce, instead of Nicolai Bukharin, as anyone knew who had attentively read the text that the French philosopher criticised (Althusser 1980, p. 70). The misunderstandings and ignorance are not unique to Althusser and his disciples. Critically commenting on the reading that Althusser made of Gramsci, Aricó wrote (in 1987!) that *Para leer el Capital* (*Reading Capital*) was the 'title of the Spanish translation of his celebrated *Pour Marx*, written in collaboration with some of his disciples' (Aricó 2005, p. 132).
64 The publishing house Lautaro, directed by Sara Maglione de Jorge and Gregorio Levin, was controlled by the Argentine Communist Party (PCA). It was left to a leader of this party, Héctor Pedro Agosti, to coordinate the edition of Gramsci in Argentina.

and *Past and Present* would have to wait until the end of the 1970s to see the light of day when they were published by the Mexican publishing house Juan Pablos.[65]

It may not be a coincidence, as Jaime Massardo[66] has pointed out, that the first edition of the *Notebooks* outside Italy occurred in the only country in Latin America that, according to Gramsci, would not have to go through a phase of Kulturkampf and the advent of a modern state.[67] However, for Aricó, translator and presenter of several of these books, everything may have simply been a misunderstanding, insofar as the publication and acceptance of Gramsci occurred due to a 'virtual ignorance of the specificity of his work' by the Argentine Communist Party (PCA). For this reason, the Sardinian would have remained marginal in the culture of the Argentine communists.[68]

Even so, at the margin this culture revived an important intellectual political current nucleated in the magazine *Pasado y Presente*, published in Córdoba beginning in April of 1963, by José Aricó, Oscar del Barco and others, expelled from the PCA a few months later.[69] It was through this cultural movement coming from Argentina that the thought and work of Gramsci began to circulate more intensely in Brazil. Gramsci's name, however, was already known in Brazil. Young intellectuals linked to the Communist Party of Brazil (PCB) quoted him and his ideas found space in magazines edited by party militants, such as *Revista Brasiliense*, directed by Caio Prado Jr. In the late 1950s, Elias Chaves Neto used his ideas in political analyses in addition to mentioning Héctor Agosti.[70] And in the beginning of the 1960s, Antonio Cândido, Carlos Nelson Coutinho and Leandro Konder made references to the philosophical thought and the literary criticism of Antonio Gramsci.[71] It was, however, Michael Löwy[72] that first consistently used Gramscian thought for the analysis of political problems for the first time in an article published, again, in *Revista Brasiliense*.

---

65   Burgos 2004, pp. 32 and 42–3 and Aricó 2005, pp. 49–50.
66   Massardo 1999.
67   PN2, Q3, §5, pp. 11–13.
68   See Aricó 2005, p. 49.
69   In this regard, Arico's essay-testimony is essential (2005, pp. 89–108). In detail, the work of Raúl Burgos 2004 reconstructs this trajectory. Kohan 2005 in a brief review censored Burgos for remaining attached to Aricó's own version, emphasising that Gramscian studies in Argentina was not limited to the *Pasado y Presente* group and would also have included the magazine *La Rosa Blindada*, directed by José Luis Mangieri. While the first criticism may be pertinent, the second is not. Gramsci was never a central author for the *La Rosa Blindada* collective.
70   Secco 2002, p. 24.
71   See Coutinho 1999, p. 283.
72   Löwy 1962.

It was in this context of the diffusion of Gramscian thought in Latin America, beginning in the mid-1960s, that the preparation of the Brazilian edition of the *Prison Notebooks* was initiated by the publishing house Civilização Brasileira. Since at least October 1962, as Coutinho clarified[73] from an analysis of the correspondence between the editor-owner of the Brazilian publishing house, Ênio Silveira, with the then director of the Istituto Gramsci, Franco Ferri, there were contacts for the publication of Gramsci's work in Brazil. The project was always under the direction of Silveira, who chose the translators and the presenters of the volumes and defined which books would be published.

This first Brazilian edition was, of course, based on the thematic edition of Togliatti. To avoid an anachronistic judgement, it is worth mentioning that this was the only issue available in the late 1960s and that the Argentine edition followed the same criteria. With translation and preparation of the originals by Luiz Mário Gazzaneo, Carlos Nelson Coutinho and Leandro Konder, the Brazilian edition reproduced the problems of the original edition and added some of its own. The prefaces of the Italian edition were summarily suppressed, leaving the Brazilian reader unaware that it was a reconstruction of the original text, but the notes 'clarifying' passages of the original were retained.

The translation also had its own problems. The problems were much greater in the volume *Notes on Machiavelli, on Politics and on the Modern State*, translated by Luiz Mário Gazzaneo, with the most striking being the passage in which the '*quarantottesca*' revolution[74] – referring to the revolutions of 1848 – was magically transformed into 'Revolutionary Jacobin'.[75] Also serious is the translation of *liberismo*, of frequent use in the Italian language referring roughly to *liberalismo*, also existing in Italian, but which refers to the political movement for the defence of individual freedoms.[76]

Both the editor-owner and the translators of this edition had links to the PCB. But, repeating the phenomenon that had already occurred in Argentina, it was only on the margin of this party and among intellectuals that the work of Gramsci had repercussions. As Coutinho[77] recognised, this first diffusion of Gramsci's work in Brazil was still very marked by the Togliattian reading and emphasised the philosophical and cultural aspects of the work. The initial impetus given to the diffusion of the *Notebooks* in Italy was, therefore, repeated.

---

73 Coutinho 1999a, pp. 32–8.
74 Q13, §7, p. 1566.
75 Gramsci 1991, p. 92.
76 Gramsci 1991, p. 32.
77 Coutinho 1999, p. 286.

Coutinho[78] has clarified that contrary to what even he imagined, the editor Ênio Silveira, already in the beginning of the negotiations with the Istituto Gramsci, had opted to suppress the volumes *The Risorgimento* and *Past and Present*, which did not fail to have a major impact on Gramsci's reception in Brazil.[79] Thus, the non-publication of these volumes was not a result of the Institutional Act of December 5, 1968 (AI-5)[80] as the same author wrote.[81] But surely AI-5 and a radical change in the cultural and political environment that had its beginning in this period conditioned the reception of Gramsci in Brazil and probably determined the commercial failure of these first editions.

Fortunately, from 1975 it was possible to count on a critical edition of the *Prison Notebooks*, published in Italy by the same publisher Einaudi, under the responsibility of Valentino Gerratana. The edition brought to light the entirety of the notebooks written by Gramsci in prison – with the exception of the four devoted to translation – organised sequentially. Following the occasional indications of Gramsci in his letters and in his own *Notebooks*, the critical edition numbered chronologically from 1 to 29 (the notebooks of translation were excluded from the enumeration), as well as the paragraphs inside them. The notebooks were divided in miscellanies, where the scattered notes predominate on various themes (volumes 1 to 9, 14, 15 and 17) and the Special Notebooks (10 to 13, 16, 18 to 29), but presenting them contiguously in accordance with their numbering.

The Gerratana edition also divided the paragraphs into 'A' texts, written in the miscellaneous and rewritten notebooks, with or without modifications, in the special notebooks as 'C' texts; and 'B' texts, of single writing, most present in the miscellaneous notebooks. Such presentation allows a reconstruction of the course of Gramsci's reflection throughout his years of imprisonment. There was no shortage of critics of the edition, such as those presented by Gianni Francioni, who suggested a new dating of the *Notebooks* and proposed a clearer separation between miscellaneous and special ones.[82] Such criticisms, however,

---

78 Coutinho 1999a, p. 35.
79 Critical evaluations of this edition and its impact on Brazilian Gramscian studies can be seen in Nosella 2004, pp. 27–35 and Dias 1996b.
80 [Translators Note: AI-5 was a broad executive decree enacted by the military regime in Brazil in December 1968 that abolished the Congress, did away with habeas corpus, instituted widespread censorship, and initiated the most repressive phase of the military dictatorship.]
81 Coutinho 1999, p. 285.
82 On the heated debate about the Gerratana edition and the publication of a new edition of the works of Gramsci, see Liguori 1996, pp. 247–53.

do not detract from the value of the Gerratana edition, which has become an indispensable tool for a deeper treatment of Gramsci's intellectual production.

Its great virtue is, as the editor points out, the possibility of capturing the unity of thought of Antonio Gramsci in the very process of its construction. It thus reveals the non-systematic, even anti-systematic, character, at the same time as it demonstrates the profoundly organic nature, of the intellectual enterprise carried out in the *Notebooks*. According to Gerratana, the 'study of the development of Gramscian thought in the *corpus* of the *Notebooks* ... makes us understand how this thought is alive and unitary through the very intermediary of its fragmentation'.[83]

The option of the Brazilian editors, and particularly of Carlos Nelson Coutinho, when they decided to launch a new edition of the *Prison Notebooks* by the publisher Civilização Brasileira in the late 1990s, was not, however, the Gerratana edition. They opted for a mixed mode, in which the thematic division is maintained, but the Special Notebooks are presented in these divisions, followed by the passages of the Miscellaneous Notebooks in which these matters were dealt with. The A texts of the Gerratana edition were, however, suppressed. The six volumes were organised as follows:

- Volume 1 – *Introdução ao estudo da filosofia. A filosofia de Benedetto Croce* (*Introduction to the study of philosophy. The philosophy of Benedetto Croce*).
- Volume 2 – *Os intelectuais, o princípio educativo. Jornalismo* (*Intellectuals, the educational principle. Journalism*).
- Volume 3 – *Maquiavel. Notas sobre o Estado e a política* (*Machiavelli. Notes on the State and Politics*).
- Volume 4 – *Temas de cultura. Ação católica. Americanismo e fordismo* (*Cultural Themes. Catholic action. Americanism and Fordism*).
- Volume 5 – *O Risorgimento. Notas sobre a história da Itália* (*The Risorgimento. Notes on the history of Italy*).
- Volume 6 – *Literatura. Folclore. Gramática. Apêndices. Variantes e índices* (*Literature. Folklore. Grammar. Appendices. Variants and indices*).

The merits of this edition are undeniable. The most obvious is the publication, for the first time in Portuguese, of a good part of the prison writings, notably of the texts that comprise Notebook 19 on the Italian Risorgimento. The discussion on the process of building the Italian national state by means of a passive revolution, which permits a more comprehensive understanding of the forms of the concept of hegemony in Gramscian thought and the limits of the leadership capacity of the ruling classes, was enriched by the publication of this book,

---

83 Gerratana 1997, p. 25.

the most extensive of them. However, the publication in Volume 1 of Gramsci's different projects for the *Notebooks* and the incorporation in volume 6 of two important tools for critical research should also be highlighted: the table of complete correspondences, that allows to locate all the paragraphs of the Gerratana edition in the Brazilian edition, and the dates elaborated by Gianni Francioni[84] for the writing of the *Notebooks*.

The translation corrects several faults and, among them, the expression 'quarantottesca', which is translated as 'from 1848 itself', which is still a good solution for a difficult problem.[85] *Liberismo*, on the other hand, returns to the Gramscian text.[86] As would be expected, the 'clarifications' of the editors of the Togliattian edition were also suppressed, as were the prefaces of the old thematic edition. The new edition, however, is not free of errors. Two of them are quite serious because they focus on the material that should allow critical research. In volume 1, the very important letter to Tatiana Schucht of 25 March 1929 appears with the date '24 February 1929'.[87] And in the reproduction of Francioni's chronology, the date of the writing of the 'Loose Notes' that begin in Notebook 8 appears mistakenly as 'between November and December of 1931' instead of 'between November and December 1930' and the 'Regrouping of Subjects' is also dated as being 'between November and December 1931' rather than 'between March and April 1932' according to Francioni.[88] Coincidentally, the dates mistakenly imputed to Francioni in the Brazilian edition are the same as those that Gerratana attributes to these passages in the critical edition.[89]

All those who are interested in the thought of Antonio Gramsci in Brazil now have in their hands a much more reliable and complete edition of the *Notebooks*. The credit is without doubt due to Carlos Nelson Coutinho, Luiz Sérgio Henriques and Marco Aurélio Nogueira. But the choice of those responsible for the new edition has not resolved all of the problems that have been observed over the years. Instead of adopting Gerratana's critical edition, they opted for

---

[84] Francioni 1984.
[85] CC, Vol. 3, p. 24.
[86] On the importance of the distinction between liberalism and liberism for Italian political thought, see Rego 2001, pp. 78–80. In a review of the Brazilian edition of the *Notebooks*, I mistakenly pointed out that although the use of the neologism liberism was acceptable, it would merit an explanatory note (Bianchi 2004). In fact, in Notebook 13, published in Volume 3 of the *Prison Notebooks*, the authors did not justify the use of the expression, but the justification was already found in the notes to the previously published Notebook 10. CC, Vol. 1, p. 483. I correct here my omission.
[87] CC, Vol. 1, p. 78.
[88] CC, Vol. 6, p. 460 and Francioni 1984, p. 142.
[89] Q, pp. 2395–6.

a mixed version, as already noted. The end result greatly hampers the reconstruction of the Gramscian lexicon. The philological work required for such reconstruction is often made unfeasible by the way in which the text is organised and the deletion of the A texts, the original versions. Unless the researcher makes use of the correspondence table and the Gerratana edition, this work may become impossible.[90]

The editorial decision can be justified in several ways and Coutinho argues in this manner in the beautiful introduction published in Volume 1. But it should be noted that at exactly the same time that the Mexican publisher Era completed its publication of the six volumes of the *Prison Notebooks*, based on the Gerratana edition, in Brazil a version came to light that synthesises a magnificent editorial effort, but one that is far from definitive. The new Brazilian edition is also far from being considered a 'thematic-critical' edition, as Carlos Nelson Coutinho and Andréa de Paula Teixeira refer to it.[91] And it is not the thematic organisation that prevents such treatment, but the deletion of paragraphs A, which makes the publication of the original texts incomplete, as well as the limits of its critical apparatus, far short of that elaborated by Gerratana.

If the goal was to please a wider audience that would fatally find difficulties with the aridity of the Gerratana edition, why not simply complete the old thematic collection, keeping it in the catalogue, and publish, in parallel, the critical edition, as was done in Mexico? The recent publication by Carlos Nelson Coutinho[92] of a collection of Gramsci's texts mostly extracted from the *Notebooks* has this evidently pedagogical character. The work of reading the *Prison Notebooks* is not made any easier by virtue of their themes having been grouped. Gramsci himself had already settled the question gathering the material in the so-called Special Notebooks. The reading of the *Notebooks*, unfortunately, will continue to be arduous.

---

90 On the importance of these texts it is worth mentioning the recent warning of Baratta: 'Here it is necessary to highlight another not insignificant problem related to the writer Gramsci. The reworking of his notes and points in the first edition of the *Special Notebooks* certainly represents a step forward in the direction of a long-sought "definitive" edition, but only in part: not always what is earned compensates for what is lost (in force, objectivity, effectiveness). Many misunderstandings and more than a little superficiality of reading originated in Italy from the scarce attention to the first writing of a good part of the Notebooks' (Baratta 2004, p. 98).
91 Coutinho and Teixeira 2003, p. 10.
92 Coutinho 2011.

2   Times

The pioneering studies of Valentino Gerratana and Gianni Francioni[93] established the tools that allowed for the development of new and original research, renewing Gramscian studies. From the critical edition of the *Notebooks* published by Gerratana in 1975, it became possible to overcome the systematic readings that artificially imposed an external order on the text and to carry out investigations that captured the unity of thought of Antonio Gramsci in the very process of its construction. Later, Francioni[94] undertook a meticulous dating of the paragraphs inside each notebook, allowing us to appreciate the internal history of the *Notebooks*.

Since 2000, based on these tools, the seminar on the *lessico gramsciano* (Gramscian Lexicon), held in Rome under the auspices of the International Gramsci Society-Italy, has explored a philological methodology renovating studies on the work of the Sardinian Marxist.[95] The research promoted by the *Fondazione Istituto Gramsci* and the progress of a new national edition of the Sardinian's writings have followed similar paths.[96] This method of restoration, as Gerratana[97] calls it, is strongly anchored in Gramsci himself. In a note written about Marx's work, the author stated:

> If one wishes to study the birth of a conception of the world which has never been systematically expounded by its founder, ... some preliminary detailed philological work has to be done. This has to be carried out with the most scrupulous accuracy, scientific honesty and intellectual loyalty and without any preconceptions, apriorism or *parti pris*. It is necessary, first of all, to reconstruct the process of intellectual development of the thinker in question in order to identify those elements which were to become stable and 'permanent' – in other words those which were taken up as the thinker's own thought, distinct from and superior to the 'material' which he had studied earlier and which served as a stimulus to him. It is only the former elements which are essential aspects of the process of development ... Search for the *Leitmotiv*, for the rhythm of the thought as

---

93   Gerratana 1997 and Francioni 1984.
94   Francioni 1984.
95   See, for example, Baratta 2004; Frosini 2003; Frosini and Liguori 2004; and Medici 2000.
96   On this subject, see the issue of the journal *Studi Sorici* dedicated to presenting the advances obtained in the context of the new national edition. Studi Storici 2011.
97   Gerratana 1997.

it develops, should be more important than that for single casual affirmations and isolated aphorisms.[98]

A thorough discussion of this paragraph and of those that follow it by Baratta[99] highlights the methodological value that Gramsci attributed to this passage. The care that the Sardinian demanded of the work of Marx becomes even more important for the reading of the *Notebooks* due to their fragmentary and inconclusive characteristics. The methodological requirements necessary for its study do not, however, nullify the value of the work, although they irrevocably compromise hasty interpretations. After the pioneering work of Gerratana and Francioni, it became possible to assume the fragmentary and inconclusive character of Gramscian thought, without ceasing to understand its unity or internal coherence.

The understanding of the living and unitary character of his thought imposes yet another methodological requirement: the reconstruction of the theoretical sources of the *Notebooks* and the *Letters from Prison*. The efficacious contextualisation of Gramscian thought and the reconstruction of its sources makes it possible to restore the critical dialogue that Gramsci established with authors who composed the literary environment of the period and to closely follow the process through which his new political lexicon was built. Such contextualisation allows us to rediscover the thought of the Italian Marxist in the historical confluence of the Italian revolution with the international communist movement.

The fundamental sources of the theoretical elaboration of the Sardinian Marxist should not, therefore, be sought exclusively within the Communist International[100] although the theoretical debates in this context are fundamental for our understanding. Nor should they be considered as belonging to a restricted geographical and intellectual context, although this may illuminate important theoretical aspects.[101] First of all, it is necessary to recognise the complexity of the sources of Gramscian thought and to verify how they fit into the Italian and European political-cultural context.

Such contexts are not, however, contemporaneous with each other. The notion of the 'discordance of temporalities', developed by Daniel Bensaïd,[102] is of great importance here. Rejecting the conception of linear and homogeneous

---

98 SPN, Q16, §2, pp. 713–15.
99 Barrata 2004, chapter IV.
100 For example, Gruppi 1987 and 2000.
101 Such as, for example, the studies of Bellamy 1987 and 1990.
102 Bensaïd 1995 and 1996.

time, Bensaïd rescues in Marx's work a notion of time marked by diversions and non-contemporaneity, capable of exploding and fragmenting the very evolutionary lines of positivist historiography revealing radical discontinuities and acrobatic jumps in space-time history. Instead of a teleological conception of history that would reduce it to mere waiting, a conception of history as tragedy. Instead of a historiographical narrative that placed order in the chaos of facts, a new writing of history. For it was a new writing of history that Gramsci began to produce in prison at the very moment he wrote his sister-in-law in March 1927, recounting his project of 'doing something *für ewig*' (for eternity).

His writing technique reveals the complexity of the project. The different notebooks were not written according to a chronological order. Several were written at the same time; some were temporarily set aside while others were initiated; blank pages were merged to be filled in later, all in one meticulous process of intellectual craftsmanship. The transcription of a note belonging to one 'Miscellaneous Notebook' and inserted into a 'Special Notebook', in turn, was not a mechanical fact. Inserting a note alongside others and within often different research themes, the transcription was part of the patient production of an intricate conceptual network that interconnected different themes through a multitude of fragments.[103]

In part, Buttigieg warned, the fragmentary character of the *Notebooks* is due to the 'philological' method that structures its composition and requires careful attention to the particular through which the universal comes to life.[104] In this dialectical relation between the universal and the particular the discordance of temporalities dictated by history was manifested objectively, but in a complex way, in the materiality of the Gramscian text. It was complex because the investigation and exposition shared the same base; in the *Notebooks* and the *Letters from Prison*, in this way, it is impossible to materially separate the moment of investigation from the moment of exposition.[105] Yet it is also because Gramsci's *Notebooks* were provisional expositions of an unfinished investigation.[106]

The structure of the work reveals the movement of Gramsci's reflection. In and through the complexity of the text, it becomes possible to rediscover the

---

103 Buttigieg 1990, p. 65.
104 Buttigieg 1990, p. 80.
105 Coutinho 1999, pp. 79–80.
106 According to Coutinho, 'the *Notebooks* contain a first systematic treatment of the material of *investigation*, although Gramsci did not have the time and conditions to work according to the *method of exposition*' (1999, p. 79). The same Coutinho seems to have distanced himself from this later on, writing that 'the "special notebooks" are attempts (although not always successful, it is true) of passing from the method of investigation, proper to the "miscellaneous notebooks", to that of exposition' (2003, p. 69).

historical temporality in which it was produced, the temporality of its epoch, and its biographical temporality, that of his own existence in prison. The temporality of the work is not the one that determines the other temporalities, but it is the one that reveals. It is through this that it becomes possible to reconstruct the thematic and conceptual lexicon that occurs in the *Notebooks*. It is here that the rhythms of the production of the work are crystallised under a sophisticated form of notation and that history – its own, that of its past and its present – permeates the text. The provisional character of the work, its fragmentary nature, that is, its non-contemporaneity, requires a new approach.

Gramsci warned that 'every research has its own determined method'.[107] The reading of the *Notebooks* demands that this maxim be taken seriously. To reveal the rhythm of the thought recorded in them demands attention to the plurality of his temporalities. Take a key notion, that of hegemony, and compare two versions. The first of these is present in Notebook 1 and was probably written between February and March of 1929; the second was inserted in Notebook 19, in the context of research on the *Risorgimento* and was likely written between February 1934 and February 1935. Gramsci said in them,

The politico-historical criterion on which our own inquiries must be grounded is this: that a class is dominant in two ways, namely it is 'leading' and 'dominant.' It leads the allied classes, it dominates the opposing classes. Therefore, a class can (and must) 'lead' even before assuming power; when it is in power it becomes dominant, but it also continues to 'lead.' The Moderates continued to lead the Action Party even after 1870, and 'transformism' is the political expression of this leadership action; all Italian politics from 1870 to the present is characterised by 'transformism,' that is, by the formation of a ruling class within the framework determined by the Moderates after 1848, with the absorption of the active elements that arose from the allied as well	The methodological criterion on which our own study must be based is the following: that the supremacy of a social group manifests itself in two ways, as 'domination' and as 'intellectual and moral leadership'. A social group dominates antagonistic groups, which it tends to 'liquidate', or to subjugate perhaps even by armed force; it leads kindred and allied groups. A social group can, and indeed must, already exercise 'leadership' before winning governmental power (this indeed is one of the principal conditions for the winning of such power); it subsequently becomes dominant when it exercises power, but even if it holds it firmly in its grasp, it must continue to 'lead' as well. The Moderates continued to lead the Action Party even after 1870 and 1876, and so-called

---

107 Q11, § 15, p. 122. OT.

as from the enemy classes. Political leadership becomes an aspect of domination, in that the absorption of the elites of the enemy classes results in their decapitation and renders them impotent. There can and there must be a 'political hegemony' even before assuming government power, and in order to exercise political leadership or hegemony one must not count solely on the power and material force that is given by government. This truth is clearly demonstrated by the politics of the Moderates, and it is the solution of this problem that made the Risorgimento possible in the forms and within the limits in which it was accomplished as a revolution without revolution [or, in V. Cuoco's words, as a passive revolution].[108]

'transformism' was only the parliamentary expression of this action of intellectual, moral and political hegemony. Indeed one might say that the entire State life of Italy from 1848 onwards has been characterised by transformism – in other words by the formation of an ever more extensive ruling class, within the framework established by the Moderates after 1848 and the collapse of the neo-Guelph and federalist utopias. The formation of this class involved the gradual but continuous absorption, achieved by methods which varied in their effectiveness, of the active elements produced by allied groups – and even of those which came from antagonistic groups and seemed irreconcilably hostile. In this sense political leadership became merely an aspect of the function of domination – in as much as the absorption of the enemies' elite means their decapitation, and annihilation often for a very long time. It seems clear from the policies of the Moderates that there can, and indeed must, be hegemonic activity even before the rise to power, and that one should not count only on the material force which power gives in order to exercise an effective leadership. It was precisely the brilliant solution of these problems which made the Risorgimento possible, in the form in which it was achieved (and with its limitations) – as 'revolution' without a 'revolution', or as 'passive revolution' to use an expression of Cuoco's in a slightly different sense from that which Cuoco intended.[109]

---

108   PN1, Q1, § 44, pp. 136–7.
109   SPN, Q19, § 24, pp. 212–15.

The note from Notebook 1 is of great relevance. Some expressions that have become widely used in Gramscian research appear here for the first time: leadership, domination, political hegemony and transformism. But the differences between the first and second citations are nevertheless important. The most subtle ones are the most revealing. Why does Gramsci put various expressions in the first version in quotation marks – 'leadership', 'domination' and 'political hegemony' – and remove those marks in the second? And why does he also do the contrary, using quotation marks in the second version for certain expressions – 'passive revolution' – and not in the first?

Analysing these discrepancies, Ragazzini[110] resorted to an unexpected 'philology of quotation marks' to explain the process of construction of the thematic and conceptual Gramscian lexicon. It was by means of a particular use of these marks that the author of the *Notebooks* underscored a stage of elaboration of the concepts, registering words and expressions of current use or those which did not belong to the ambit of the philosophy of praxis. In the second version of the text, the absence of quotation marks would indicate an incorporation of the terms into the Gramscian lexicon, assuming, however, a meaning that was no longer identical with that of the original. The reverse is also commonplace in the *Notebooks*, as can be seen from the use of the expression 'passive revolution'. In Notebook 1, it was completely assimilated by the Gramscian text, which incorporated it as part of its lexicon. But in Notebook 19 it appeared in quotation marks, and was followed by a warning that it was used 'in a slightly different sense' from the original.

This resource seems to be an imposition of the very process of Gramsci's theoretical production. The intense critical dialogue with the culture of his time caused him to appropriate concepts that, once rebuilt, became part of his own conception, assuming renewed meanings. His reading of Marx's philosophical work and its interpretations had already made him realise how many problems arise from the use of an outdated vocabulary. Hence the importance he attributed to the supposed affirmation of Napoleon Bonaparte before the Academy of Bologna: 'when you find something truly new, it is necessary to adapt a completely new word to it in order to keep the idea precise and distinct'.[111]

But what happens when it is not possible to construct this new vocabulary? In this case, the new meanings attributed to words must be made explicit, which Gramsci seeks to do in his writing, demarcating the new from the old. To make explicit these new senses, which old concepts assume, it is necessary to

---

110   Ragazzini 2002.
111   Q11, § 27, p. 1433. OT.

understand the older ones. It is necessary to reconstruct the critical dialogue that Gramsci established with Niccolo Machiavelli and Francesco Guicciardini, with Antonio Labriola and Georges Sorel, with Benedetto Croce and Giovanni Gentile, with Vladimir Lenin and Leon Trotsky. It was through them that Gramsci, in prison, communicated with the world and entered into dialogue with his time, rediscovering through the text the history that had been confiscated by the prison.

CHAPTER 3

Materialism/Idealism

From May 1930, Gramsci began to develop an extensive programme of philosophical research in prison. For this purpose, a new section had been opened in Notebook 4, with the purpose of collecting the notes of his investigation. This section, entitled *Philosophical Notes*, was developed in Notebooks 7 and 8 and most of the material presented therein was later reorganised in the Special Notebooks 10 and 11.

The writing of the *Philosophical Notes* in Notebooks 4 and 7[1] was carried out under the aegis of the research programme contained in the letter to Tatiana of 25 March 1929 and the same can be said of the paragraphs of the third series of the *Philosophical Notes*, contained in Notebook 8 and written up to February 1932. Built around the broader theme of 'theory of history and historiography' these first notes were organised around a set of recurrent items and their variants: 'Fundamental Problems of Marxism', 'Structure and Superstructure', 'Critical Notes and Observations on the Popular Manual', 'Croce and Marx', etc.

With the writing of these notes, the author intended to contribute to a renovation of historical materialism, theoretically working through its fundamental concepts. In this way, Marxist theory could put itself in a position to compete alongside the most advanced contemporary philosophy of his time identified in the figure of Benedetto Croce, responding to his neo-idealist criticism. It could, at the same time, subtract Marxism from the vulgar materialist current of which Bukharin's text was only one example.[2]

The 1929 letter, in which the author enumerated the main themes of this research, already prefigured his intention to treat Croce and Bukharin within the same problematic. After enumerating his new research priorities – nineteenth-century Italian history and the question of intellectuals; theory of history and historiography; and Americanism and Fordism – Gramsci listed the books he already had and asked for others:

---

1 The *Philosophical Notes I* present in Notebook 4 were written, according to Francioni, between May 1930 and November of the same year; the *Philosophical Notes II* from Notebook 7 were written between November 1930 and November 1931. Francioni 1984, pp. 141–2.
2 See Frosini 2003, p. 67.

> On the theory of history, I would like to have a French volume released recently: Bukharin, *Théorie du matérialisme historique*, Social Editions – Rue Valette 3, Paris (Ve.), and Marx's *Oeuvres philosophiques*, published by ed. Alfred Costes Paris: Tome I, *Contribution à la critique de la Philosophie du droit de Hegel* – Tome II, *Critique de la critique critique, contra Bruno Bauer and consorts*. – I already have the most important books of Benedetto Croce with respect [to these questions].[3]

The extent of the treatment given to Bukharin and Croce in the *Notebooks* was a demand derived from his purposes: the struggle against 'double revisionism' that had resulted in a 'Marxism "in combination"'. In the development of this struggle, the philosophical project of Gramsci became more comprehensive, gaining new contours. In the spring of 1932, an important turn in the philosophical research was registered by the sudden appearance in the *Philosophical Notes* of Notebook 8 of two new rubrics: 'Introduction to the study of philosophy' (§ 204, written between February and March 1932) and 'Points for an Essay on Croce' (§ 225, written in April of the same year). This turn, pointed out by Frosini[4] in his meticulous reconstruction of the philosophical question in the *Notebooks*, coincides with the wording of the 'Regrouping of Subjects' and with the beginning of the writing of the Special Notebooks, particularly Notebooks 10 and 11.

In these paragraphs, the philosophical question assumed a new orientation. It stopped being guided by research on historical materialism and its development and began to assume, on the one hand, an in-depth and critical study of Croce's thinking, and not just his relation to Marxism, and, on the other hand, a critique of the *Popular Manual* of Bukharin, with a view to constructing an alternative in the form of an *Introduction to Philosophy*.

According to Frosini,[5] this new Gramscian research orientation was dictated by an erroneous evaluation of the recent trends of the philosophical debate in the Soviet Union inspired by the reading of an article by D.S. Mirsky.[6] Mirsky's text was a version, frankly favourable to Stalin, of the philosophical debate that took place in the Soviet Union between the 'dialecticians' of Deborin and the 'mechanists', with which Bukharin was identified. In a political environment in which real theoretical debate was valued little, the intervention of the party

---

3 LC, pp. 264–5. OT. In the same letter, Gramsci asked for other books of Croce which remained in Rome: *Elementi di política, Breviario di Estetica* e *Hegel*. See LC, p. 263.
4 Frosini 2003.
5 Frosini 2003, pp. 70–2 and 113–22.
6 Mirsky 1931.

apparatus in the discussion was conceived as part of the 'progressive Bolshevization of all aspects of life in the Soviet Union'.[7] The 'bolshevisation' of philosophy was presented as part of the struggle against Trotskyism, the Bukharin right, Menshevism and even the 'petit bourgeois liberalism' that would be represented both in the conceptions of the 'dialecticians' led by A.M. Deborin as well as the 'mechanists' aligned with A.K. Timiriazev.

In jail, handling scarce information, Gramsci interpreted, bizarrely, the 'Bolshevisation' of philosophy as a new moment in the construction of socialism and the rebirth of historical materialism.[8] Particularly important in this interpretation was the emphasis given by Mirsky in his article on the need to establish a new nexus between theory and practice that implies 'in equal measure the subordination of theoretical thought to the demands of revolutionary practice and the firm foundation of all practical work in theoretical consciousness'.[9] Also worth mentioning is the important news given in this article of the publication of Lenin's philosophical notebooks, although Gramsci does not seem to quote them throughout the *Notebooks*.

From this emphasis, Gramsci deduced that in the Soviet Union 'a change has taken place from a mechanistic and purely external conception to one which is activist and, as has been pointed out, closer to a correct understanding of the unity of theory and practice, although it has not yet attained the full synthetic meaning of the concept'.[10] Far from being part of a revival of historical materialism, the 'theoretical and practical unity' was the effect of the shallow pragmatism and the instrumentalisation of philosophy operated by the Soviet bureaucracy. The cancellation of the debate between the 'dialecticians' and the 'mechanists' by means of government decree, the 'reform' of the Academy of Science, the purges in the editorial board of the magazine *Under the Banner of Marxism*, were not episodes of an intellectual and moral reform. If an analogy is possible, then it is with the counter-reform and its inquisitorial tribunals that these processes should be equated.

Gramsci's interpretation of this text by Mirsky should serve as a warning of the material limits of his investigation. But for the purposes of this work it is important to highlight the paradoxical result of this bizarre interpretation: the research that is the result of this turnaround represents the peak of creative development of *philosophical investigation* by its author in lines that are evidently not compatible with the mediocre 'Diamat' that was transformed

---

7   Mirsky 1931, p. 649.
8   See Frosini 2003, p. 119.
9   Mirsky 1931, p. 653.
10 SPN, Q11, § 12, p. 336.

into state ideology by Stalin in *Historical Materialism and Dialectical Materialism*. These results, principally included in Notebook 11, also synthesise a greater *approximation* to a definitive *form of exposition*, although they cannot be considered as the finished presentation of the results of the philosophical research, as did, for example, the Toglitatti edition, bringing them together in the volume entitled *Historical Materialism and the Philosophy of Benedetto Croce*.

It was from the revaluation of Labriola that Gramsci intended to carry this enterprise forward, as revealed in § 3 of the *Philosophical Notes I*, a note which must be read together with § 31 in Notebook 3. Labriola was for the Sardinian Marxist the starting point that would allow him to criticise the 'double revision' and the 'double combination' to which Marxism had been submitted. On the one hand, some of the elements of historical materialism had been absorbed by some idealistic currents, such as Croce, Sorel, and Bergson. On the other, the search for a 'philosophy' that contained Marxism had led the 'official' Marxists to find it either in vulgar materialism, such as Plekhanov, or in idealism, such as the example of Max Adler who attributed this position to Kantianism.

Antonio Labriola, however, distinguished himself from both, affirming the philosophical self-sufficiency of Marxism.[11] This affirmation constituted the framework for his critical dialogue with Georges Sorel in the series of letters in *Discorrendo di socialismo e di filosofia* (*Talking about socialism and philosophy*). Facing the revisionist movements that sought to make Marx compatible with the preceding philosophical culture, Labriola protested that: 'this doctrine [Marxism] contains in itself the conditions and modes of its own philosophy and is thus in its origin as in its substance, intimately international'.[12] Marxism would not, however, be closed to other forms of knowledge. Labriola saw the importance of the nexus that Marxism should establish with the empirical social sciences and the possibility of the latter 'incorporating the results of the empirical research conducted by the various disciplines'.[13] And it is from this perspective that one can understand the enthusiasm provoked in Labriola by Engels's *Anti-Dühring*:

> The effect of this work on the socialists of other countries should be, in my opinion, to supply them with those critical aptitudes which are required for writing all other Anti-Somethings needed for the rebuttal of those who try to thwart or infest the socialist movement in the name of so many confused notions in sociology.[14]

---

11   See the development given to this question by Leonardo Paggi (1973).
12   Labriola 2000, p. 216.
13   Vacca 1983, p. 79.
14   Labriola 1912, p. 54.

To the reservations that Sorel expressed regarding the development of a philosophy intrinsic and immanent to the assumptions and premises of historical materialism, Labriola responded by affirming the

> philosophy of practice [praxis], which is the core of historical materialism. It is the immanent philosophy of things about which people philosophise. The realistic process leads first from life to thought, not from thought to life. It leads from work, from the labor of cognition, to understanding as an abstract theory, not from theory to cognition.[15]

This revaluation of Labriola, in which praxis was promoted as a central category of historical materialism, was supported by a precise reading of Marx's *Theses on Feuerbach*. It thus created the conditions for a theoretical break with the dualist conceptions that marked the practical and epistemological separation between spirit and matter, intellectual work and manual labour, theory and practice.[16] At the same time, in affirming praxis as the foundation of human sociability and the philosophy of praxis as 'the theory of man at work',[17] one could affirm the overcoming of:

> all forms of idealism which regard actually existing things as mere reflexes, reproductions, imitations, illustrations, results, of so called a priori thought, thought before the fact. It marks also the end of naturalistic materialism, using this term in the sense which it had up to a few years ago.[18]

It was therefore in opposition to both idealism and vulgar materialism that the author of *Socialism and Philosophy* outlined his reading of the work of Marx and Engels. Conceiving of praxis in a historical and realistic way identified it with labour and productive activity, with scientific knowledge and experimentation, and with social mediation between man and nature.[19] The revaluation of praxis in philosophical discourse thus had a distinguishing function in that it marked the frontiers of Marxism from competing philosophies, but it was mainly a function of the transgression of these own frontiers, placing Marxism in open confrontation with competing philosophies with a view not to simply cancel them, but to dialectically overcome them.

---

15   Labriola 1912, p. 60.
16   See Paggi 1973, pp. 1323–4.
17   Labriola 1912, p. 85.
18   Labriola 1912, p. 60.
19   Cf. Martelli 2001, p. 88.

It was this programme of the affirmation of Marxism that mobilised Gramsci in prison. Commenting on the need to combat the philosophical subordination of Marxism to variants of idealism or naturalistic materialism, the Sardinian Marxist stated: 'Labriola is differentiated from both of these currents by his affirmation that Marxism is itself an independent and original philosophy. This is the direction in which one must work, resuming and developing Labriola's position'.[20]

In the transcription of the notes of the Miscellaneous Notebooks to the Special Notebooks, Gramsci proceeded through a cryptographic revision, aiming to evade censorship. In this revision, he replaced in most cases the expressions 'historical materialism' and 'Marxism' with 'philosophy of praxis'. Such a change may have been motivated by censorship, but the choice of 'philosophy of praxis' also had a theoretical-political meaning whereby Gramsci indicated what characterised Marx's philosophy and, at the same time, the direction in which it should develop.[21]

The development of this direction implied a confrontation with 'Marxism in combination' and 'double revisionism'. But it was not only a criticism of revisionism, as it could also reveal an original philosophical project. In the Special Notebooks, this criticism sought to assist the development of the philosophy of praxis. Yet, the forms of facing this problem and developing the philosophy through confrontation with these approaches were diverse. The approach made explicit by Gramsci revealed a contradiction. The absorption of Marxism by idealism was the result of the theoretical and political force demonstrated by the intellectual heritage of the author of *Capital*. The transformation of Marxism during the context of the culture of his time had made him part of the 'common sense' for a certain strata of the intelligentsia. This absorption could not, of course, preserve the revolutionary character of the theory; it was necessary to dismember and purify it, and thereby sterilise it. It is from this perspective that one may understand the intellectual enterprise of the young men Benedetto Croce[22] and Giovanni Gentile[23] and the critical dialogue they established with Marx's thinking.

Contradictorily, the development of Marxism after the death of Marx and Engels, instead of asserting its internal force, sought to combine it with non-Marxist philosophies, with deleterious effects for its own development as a conception of the world, weakening it before its philosophical adversaries. The

---

20 PN2, Q4, §3, p. 140.
21 See Medici 2000 and Frosini 2004a.
22 Croce 1927.
23 Gentile 2003.

moment that Marxism was absorbed as part of the culture of the time thus coincided with the weakening of its capacity of intervention in the 'struggle' of 'political hegemonies'. How did this come about?, Gramsci wondered.

The Sardinian Marxist understood this development through the analogy Renaissance-Reformation. Relying on a flexible reading of Croce's book, *Storia dell'età barocca in Itália* (*History of the Baroque Era in Italy*), he identified an aristocratic movement of high elaboration in the Renaissance, but one that was incapable of creating a socially inclusive cultural movement. The Reformation, in turn, despite its popular penetration, did not represent, at first, a new elaboration of a superior culture.[24] It was within this historical analogy that the historical development of Marxism could be explained:

> Renaissance-Reformation – German philosophy – French Revolution – secularism [liberalism] – historicism – modern philosophy – historical materialism. Historical materialism, in its dialectic of popular culture-high culture, is the crowning point of this entire movement of intellectual and moral reform. It corresponds to Reformation + French Revolution, universality + politics, it is still going through its popular phase, it has also become 'prejudice' and 'superstition'.[25]

In its phase of popular expansion, Marxism assumed the form of the Reformation. But in this manner it was confused with materialism. For reasons of 'didactic' order, Marxism in its phase of expansion had to confront the popular mentality by resorting to somewhat superior forms of culture, which were, however, insufficient to combat the cultured classes. This was one of the dominant tendencies of 'official' Marxism, as Gramsci liked to call it. Plekhanov was an outstanding exponent of this trend who, in his reconstruction of the 'sources' of Marx's philosophy, confused Marx's personal philosophical culture, that is, the philosophers he had studied, with the philosophical foundations of historical materialism itself:

---

24 For more details, see Frosini 2004b. According to Croce, the 'Renaissance movement remained aristocratic, of elected circles and in Italy herself, who was her mother and nourisher, did not leave the circles of the courts, did not penetrate to the people, did not become custom or "prejudice", that is, collective persuasion and faith. The Reformation, instead, had this efficacy of popular penetration, but it paid for it with a delay in its intrinsic development, with the slow and sometimes interrupted maturation of its vital germ' (Croce 1946b, pp. 11–12. OT).

25 PN2, Q4, § 3, p. 142.

> The study of the philosophical culture of a man like Marx is not only interesting but necessary, provided you do not forget that such a study is only a part of the reconstruction of his intellectual biography and that the elements of Spinozism, of Feurbachism, of Hegelianism, of French materialism, etc. are in no way essential parts of the philosophy of praxis, nor is it reduced to them, but what, above all, matters is precisely the overcoming of old philosophies, the new synthesis or the elements of the new synthesis, the new way of conceiving philosophy.[26]

The reduction of Marxism to its sources implied a subordination of the philosophy of praxis to them. Contradictorily, this process led Marxism to fall short of Marx and Hegel. In the identification of the philosophy of Marxism with the philosophy of materialism there was a regression to a 'metaphysics of matter', which was reunited through the eternal and absolute.[27] Achille Loria was one of the most grotesque cases in this respect and for this reason he caught the attention of Labriola, who referred to him when he wrote: 'Some vulgarisers of Marxism have stripped this doctrine of philosophy that is immanent to it by reducing it to a simple introduction of the variation of historical conditions by the variation of economic conditions'.[28] It was necessary, therefore, to mark a distance from this natural-scientific materialism by affirming historical materialism as its overcoming.

Italian neo-idealism with its 'metaphysics of the spirit' also led to this point of the history of philosophy that preceded Hegel. In fact, Benedetto Croce inserted himself in the Italian debate on the crisis of Marxism, which led him first to enter into a critical dialogue with it and with the author who introduced historical materialism to Italy, Antonio Labriola; and, afterwards, to a project that sought to annihilate theoretical Marxism itself. This project of annihilation occurred within the successive construction of a 'philosophy of the spirit', with its pretension to be the foundation of an operation of cultural hegemony that would complete the work of refuting historical materialism. Affirming that Marxism was also metaphysics of matter, Italian neo-idealism converged on this point with vulgar materialism.[29]

Both the metaphysics of matter and the metaphysics of the spirit suppressed the horizon that was, for Gramsci, Hegel's main contribution, the 'conscience of

---

26   Q11, § 27, p. 1436. OT.
27   Q11, § 62, p. 1489. OT.
28   Labriola 2000, p. 250. OT. See also the critique of Croce 1927, pp. 21–54 and Gramsci's comments in the *Notebooks* under the rubric Lorianism.
29   Martelli 2001, p. 71.

contradictions'.[30] This was precisely the contribution that Marx appropriated in a more intense way, overcoming the idealism present in Hegelian thought, understanding this consciousness as the expression of the contradictions of the historical epoch and affirming a new place for the philosopher, who came to be seen as 'an element of the contradiction', capable of converting it into a principle of knowledge and, therefore, of action.[31] For Gramsci, the superiority of the philosophy of praxis would be, precisely, in its ability to be a theory of contradictions 'existing in history and in society'.[32] According to the Sardinian Marxist,

> Hegel, straddling the French Revolution and the Restoration, joined the two moments of philosophical life, materialism and spiritualism, dialectically. Hegel's successors destroyed this unity, returning to the old materialism with Feuerbach and to the spiritualism of the Hegelian right. In his youth, Marx relived this whole experience: Hegelian, Feuerbachian materialist, Marxist; in other words, he reforged the destroyed unity into a new philosophical construction: this new construction of his, this new philosophy is already clearly evident in the theses on Feuerbach. Many historical materialists have done to Marx what had already been done to Hegel; in other words, they have gone from dialectical unity back to crude materialism, while, as has already been said, modern vulgar idealist high culture has tried to incorporate those elements of Marxism that it needed – also because this modern philosophy has itself sought, in its own way, to join materialism and spiritualism dialectically, just as Hegel had tried to do and as Marx really did.[33]

Combining the programme of the cultural elaboration of the Renaissance with the popular expansion of the Reformation was a key challenge for the affirmation of Marxism as a hegemonic force. From a practical point of view, this challenge should be solved by the formation of a new type of intellectuality, selected not in the traditional classes, but in the popular classes. From the theoretical point of view, this programme required a new concept of orthodoxy, forged on the basis of the indications already present in Labriola's reflection on the self-sufficiency of the philosophy of praxis.

---

30 Q11, § 62, p. 1487. OT.
31 Ibid.
32 Q10 / II, § 41, p. 1320. See also Losurdo 1997, pp. 105–9.
33 PN2, Q4, § 3, p. 143.

This question had already been addressed by Georgy Lukács in *History and Class Consciousness*, a book that Gramsci knew. The Hungarian stated that Marxist orthodoxy referred exclusively to method and to the concrete totality as the fundamental category of reality. In this perspective, orthodox Marxism would not be a dogmatism that implied an uncritical adherence to the results of Marx's research. It would also not be an affirmation of this or that thesis, nor the cult of a 'holy book'. For Lukács, 'orthodoxy refers exclusively to *method*'.[34]

As a method of investigation, dialectical materialism constituted for the Hungarian Marxist a theoretical horizon that could only be overcome by overcoming capitalism. In this way, the affirmation of Marxism as such implied the refusal of all attempts to overcome, complete or improve this method, attempts that only led to its vulgarisation and made it eclectic.[35]

In prison, Gramsci also faced the problem of constructing a non-dogmatic and critical concept of orthodoxy. In a political-cultural environment in which heterodoxy was commonly associated with heresy, the problem was highly complex. Gramsci would formulate, however, a definition of orthodoxy different from that presented by Lukács. For Gramsci, what defined orthodox Marxism was not its degree of methodological purity. Orthodoxy should be based on a fundamentally practical criterion:

> Orthodoxy should not be sought in this or that follower of the philosophy of praxis, in this or that tendency linked to currents estranged from the original doctrine, but in the fundamental concept that the philosophy of praxis 'suffices for itself', contains all the fundamental elements to construct a total and integral conception of the world, a philosophy and theory of the natural sciences, and not only that, but rather, also to vivify an integral practical organization of society, that is, to become a total, integral civilization.[36]

The differences between the two authors are subtle, but important. Lukács stated that orthodoxy did not reside in the faith in a 'thesis, nor in the exegesis of a "sacred" book'. Gramsci, in turn, referred to currents and individuals. The Hungarian abominated a Marxism transformed into 'eclecticism', whereas the Sardinian feared that Marxism would lose its power to 'vivify an integral practical organization of society, that is, to become a total, integral civilization'.

---

34   Lukács 1999, p. xxvi.
35   Ibid.
36   Q11, § 27, p. 1434. OT.

The two authors dealt with different problems. One emphasised the methodological complications derived from the incorporation of theories extrinsic to Marxism, while the other was worried about the practical implications of this merger. 'Currents', 'followers of the philosophy of praxis' and 'practical organisation' are strong words. The result of their use was a definition of orthodoxy forged for ideological combat.

The role that this definition of orthodoxy played in the thought of Gramsci becomes clearer when one understands its place within the material structure of the *Notebooks*. Such a definition first appeared in the *Philosophical Notes 1* present in Notebook 4, with the title 'The Concept of "Orthodoxy"',[37] between the first note devoted exclusively to the Popular Manual of Bukharin, entitled *'Notes and critical observations on the Popular Manual'*[38] and a note dedicated to Croce.[39] But it was from the criticism of the first that this definition of orthodoxy was coined, which is evident in the reference made to the 'disciples of Marx', something Gramsci knew could not be said of Croce.

1   Anti-Bukharin

Gramsci's relationship with Bukharin's philosophical and political thinking is extremely complex and even contradictory. A treatment of the issue, focused exclusively on Notebook 11, which criticised the theoretical positions of the Soviet Communist, may risk simplifying this relationship. The issue has not been satisfactorily clarified until now, although some synthetic studies have engaged with the theme[40] and a range of works have discussed the problem.[41]

Gramsci's shift of position regarding the theoretical positions of the Soviet leader is remarkable. It is well known that in the first half of 1925 he organised a 'Party School', with the aim of 'filling the gulf between what there should be and what there is not'.[42] The project was politically oriented with the purpose of ensuring that, after a period of illegality, the PCI would not succumb to an 'unstoppable impulse to action after action' without 'any consideration of

---

37   PN2, Q4, §14, pp. 155–6.
38   PN2, Q4, §13, pp. 154–5.
39   PN2, Q4, §15, pp. 156–8.
40   For example, Zanardo 1974.
41   Cf. Buci-Glucksmann 1980a, pp. 257–301 and 321–47 and Paggi 1973, pp. 1334–7.
42   PPW, p. 267.

the actual relations of social forces'.[43] In order to contain this impulse and to organise effective action, an adequate theoretical and political formation of all party members was necessary and not only for those who occupied positions of leadership.

Gramsci was concerned about the possibility of the Communist Party repeating the mistakes made by the socialists in the immediate postwar period, when the young adherents to the party, without political preparation or even notions of Marxist theory, were easily susceptible to petty-bourgeois opportunism.[44] The scant tradition of the Italian labour movement in struggle on the ideological front made the danger even greater. Hence, the importance of the school. Gramsci conceived the first course of this school in three series of lessons: 'one on the theory of historical materialism; one on the fundamental elements of general polities; one on the Communist Party and its principles of organization'.[45]

It is striking that for this first series of lessons, which dealt with historical materialism, the Italian Communist organised the course around 'a translation of the book by comrade Bukharin, on the theory of historical materialism', which contained 'a complete treatment of the argument'.[46] As confirmed by Buci-Glucksmann from the copy of the material of this course that was in the files of the CPI in the 1970s, the lessons replicated the introduction and the second chapter of Bukharin's book and complemented this with two texts by Engels on Hegelian dialectics and the materialist conception of history, and with excerpts from Marx's 'Preface of 1859' to his *Contribution to the Critique of Political Economy*.[47]

The text translated from Bukharin's manual contained a series of deletions and interpolations probably made by Gramsci himself. For example, of note was the cancellation of the passage in which Bukharin reduced historical materialism to sociology and criticised those who saw in it 'a living "method" of historical knowledge' demonstrable only in the works referring to 'concrete facts'.[48] In place of this passage, Gramsci added another of his works, in which he criticised the Crocean conception that identified a 'canon of historical science' in Marxism and extended historical materialism to the living movement

---

43 CPC, p. 51. OT.
44 PPW, pp. 265–6.
45 SPW, p. 291.
46 Ibid.
47 See Buci-Glucksmann 1980a, p. 261.
48 Bukharin 1925, Introduction.

of history.⁴⁹ Comparing the original version of the text with that produced by Gramsci, Paggi argues that it is possible to find evidence of the rejection of historical materialism as a sociology that would be later developed in the *Notebooks*.⁵⁰

In the *Notebooks*, Gramsci criticised Bukharin's treaty from the beginning to the end, starting with the title (Theory of Historical Materialism) and the subtitle (Popular Manual on Marxist Sociology). He claimed that the title of the book did not correspond to its content since if the objective was a systematic presentation of the theory of historical materialism, it should begin with a general introduction that defines what philosophy is, its relation to a conception of the world and how historical materialism would renew that conception. Only starting from these definitions would it be possible to reconstruct the assumptions of the theory of historical materialism.

But instead of following this path, Bukharin left the issue open and this lack of definition allowed him to ignore without justification the presupposition implicit in all his work: that 'the philosophy of historical materialism would be philosophical materialism'.⁵¹ Gramsci's criticism of Bukharin, nonetheless, was not always fair. In fact, the intellectual sophistication of the Soviet Communist catches the attention of the contemporary reader, accustomed to the crude ideas of the leaders of the current left. Moving with familiarity through the cultural and philosophical environment of his time, Bukharin achieved a true theoretical *tour de force* in his manual. The result, however, was not always satisfactory.

Gramsci's references to the text of the Soviet leader throughout the *Notebooks* were particularly imprecise where he denotes the absence of this book in his library. Martelli argues that Bukahrin's identification with eighteenth-century materialism was exaggerated and that his enterprise was very similar to that of Gramsci and could be summarised as an attempt to 'renew, update, the theoretical status of Marxism in the face of new instances of contemporary science and philosophy'.⁵² What is surprising in Gramsci's criticism of Bukharin are not some inaccuracies and exaggerations, but rather the choice to criticise him, after having used his book in 1925 at the CPI school. If the target was vulgar materialism, would it not have made sense to refute Plekhanov, whose work, *The Fundamental Principles of Marxism*, Gramsci possessed in prison? By pre-

---

49 See Paggi 1973, p. 1335.
50 Ibid.
51 PN2, Q4, § 13, p. 154.
52 Martelli 2001, p. 64.

ferring to criticise Bukharin, was Gramsci opting for a theoretical critique of the Soviet ruling group?

The critique of Bukharin and the lines of development of the philosophy of praxis began in a definition of the object and practice of philosophical reflection. The notion that articulated the *exposition* of this development was made explicit by Gramsci in Notebook 11 § 12, taking up that important programmatic note from the third series of the *Philosophical Notes* in which the title 'An Introduction to the Study of Philosophy' appeared for the first time.[53] In its last version, this note constitutes the first paragraph of a section entitled 'Notes for an Introduction and a Beginning of the Study of Philosophy and the History of Culture' and a subsection called 'Some preliminary points of reference':

One must destroy the prejudice that philosophy is a difficult thing just because it is the specific activity of a particular category of learned people, of professional or systematic philosophers. It is therefore necessary to show that all men are philosophers, by defining the characteristics of this ('Spontaneous') philosophy that is 'everyone's', namely common sense and religion.[54]	It is necessary to destroy the very widespread prejudice that philosophy is a very difficult thing because it is an intellectual activity with its own category of specialist scientists or professional and systematic philosophers. Therefore, it is necessary to demonstrate preliminarily that all men are 'philosophers', defining the limits and the characteristics of this 'spontaneous philosophy', typical of 'all the world', that is of the philosophy which is contained: 1) in language itself, which is a set of notions and concepts and not just words grammatically empty of content; 2) in common sense and in good sense; 3) in popular religion and therefore in the whole system of beliefs, superstitions, opinions, ways of seeing and acting that are revealed in what is generally called 'folklore'.[55]

This extremely broad definition of philosophical activity and those who exercised this activity was already noticeable in Gramsci even before his arrest. In an article published in the newspaper *L'Unità* on 1 April 1926, the Sardinian

---

53 PN3, Q8, § 204, p. 351.
54 PN2, Q8, § 204, pp. 351–2.
55 Q11, § 12, p. 1375. OT.

Marxist asked: 'What is a philosopher? It is necessary to distinguish *philosopher* from professor of *philosophy*. Just as every man is an artist in the same way, every man is a philosopher insofar as he is able to think and express an intellectual activity'.[56]

The bottom line was, of course, the concept of philosophy. In its first version in Notebook 8, Gramsci, by means of a note added later, referred to §17 of the second part of Notebook 10, written under the title *'Introduction to the Study of Philosophy. Principles and Preliminaries'*. The theme of this last paragraph was precisely the concept of philosophy. 'What should we understand by philosophy, by the philosophy of an historical epoch, and what is the importance and significance of philosophers' philosophies in each of these historical epochs?', asked the Sardinian.[57] The starting point for the elucidation of the question was Benedetto Croce's definition of religion – 'a conception of the world which became a norm of life'.[58] Focusing on the relationship between conception of the world and practical life, Gramsci stated that, in this case, 'most men are philosophers, insofar as they act practically and in their action (in the directive lines of their own conduct) a conception of the world is implicitly contained, a philosophy'.[59]

Taking Croce's definition as a starting point did not signify an uncritical adherence to its conception. In Notebook 11, Gramsci's free and critical appropriation of the Crocean definition becomes clear:

> Note the problem of religion taken not in the confessional sense but in the secular sense of a unity of faith between a conception of the world and a corresponding norm of conduct. But why call this unity of faith 'religion' and not 'ideology', or even 'politics'?[60]

The question, then, was that of the relationship between philosophy and politics. §204 of Notebook 8 occupied a position between Notebook 11 and Note-

---

56 Cited in Paggi 1973, p. 1337. OT.
57 Q10 / II, §16, 1255. OT.
58 Speaking of the 'religion of freedom', Croce wrote in his *History of Europe in the Nineteenth Century*: 'Now he who gathers together and considers all these characteristics of the liberal ideal does not hesitate to call it what it was: a "religion". He calls it so, of course, because he looks for what is essential and intrinsic in every religion, which always lies in the concept of reality and an ethics that conforms to this concept. It excludes the mythological element, which constitutes only a secondary differentiation between religion and philosophy' (Croce 1933, p. 18).
59 Q10 / II, §16, 1255. OT.
60 GR, Q11, §12, pp. 327–8.

book 10, guiding the polemic against Bukharin and against Croce. This preliminary reference already defined the ideological struggle and the importance of a struggle against Bukharin's naturalism-scientism and Croce's idealism. This struggle should not be reduced to an activity of intellectuals, but should encompass 'all men', inasmuch as they would also be carriers of a 'spontaneous philosophy', that is, they would all be part of a particular conception of world, and by that conception, all would belong to a particular social group.

Participation in a certain conception of the world would not always be of the same type. It could be passive, Gramsci declared, and so it is when one participates in 'a conception of the world mechanically imposed by the external environment …'.[61] Or it could be active, which would happen when the individual elaborated his own conception of the world in a critical and conscious way, and through it was linked to a social group that allowed them to 'take an active part in the creation of the history of the world, be one's own guide, refusing to accept passively and supinely from outside the moulding of one's personality?'[62]

But the active man, the Italian Marxist said, would not necessarily have a clear theoretical consciousness of his action, and it would even be possible for his conscience to be in contrast and opposition to his action. It would be possible, in a way, to say that he possesses two consciences, 'one which is implicit in his activity and which in reality unites him with all his fellow-workers in the practical transformation of the real world …'. But beyond this there would be another one, 'superficially explicit or verbal, which he has inherited from the past and uncritically absorbed'.[63] This 'verbal' consciousness would be, therefore, affirmed with words and would assert itself in '"normal times" – that is when its conduct is not independent and autonomous, but submissive and subordinate'.[64]

It should not be thought, however, that this verbal and superficial conception does not influence human behavior. It

> attaches one to a specific social group, it influences moral conduct and the direction of will, with varying efficacy but often powerfully enough to produce a situation in which the contradictory state of consciousness does not permit of any action, any decision or any choice, and produces a condition of moral and political passivity.[65]

---

61 GR, Q11, §12, p. 325.
62 Ibid.
63 GR, Q11, §12, p. 333.
64 GR, Q11, §12, p. 328.
65 GR, Q11, §12, p. 333.

There would thus be a permanent tension between the act and the conscience, and the resolution of this situation could only occur by overcoming the conscience linked to the past and the emergence of a new consciousness, for the unity between theory and practice. That all may be carriers of a 'spontaneous philosophy' did not mean that everyone was a philosopher 'without quotes', that is, philosophers in the full sense of the word:

> In the most immediate and relevant sense, one cannot be a philosopher, by which I mean have a critical and coherent conception of the world, without having a consciousness of its historicity, of the phase of development which it represents and of the fact that it contradicts other conceptions or elements of other conceptions.[66]

Gramsci was not willing to dilute the differences between philosophy and common sense. 'Philosophy is an intellectual order'[67] and as such is 'critical and coherent'.[68] In this sense, it is a thought methodically elaborated in contrast with a 'disjointed and episodic' conception[69] and makes up 'the diffuse, uncoordinated features of a generic form of thought common to a particular period and a particular popular environment'.[70] This difference makes it necessary that every philosophy that wants to become a substrate of a new and integral civilisation should present itself as an overcoming of the previous way of thinking and of existing concrete thinking:

> A philosophy of praxis cannot but present itself at the outset in a polemical and critical guise, as superseding the existing mode of thinking and existing concrete thought (the existing cultural world). First of all, therefore, it must be a criticism of 'common sense', basing itself initially, however, on common sense in order to demonstrate that 'everyone' is a philosopher and that it is not a question of introducing from scratch a scientific form of thought into everyone's individual life, but of renovating and making 'critical' an already existing activity. It must then be a criticism of the philosophy of the intellectuals out of which the history of philosophy developed and which, in so far as it is a phenomenon of individuals (in fact it develops essentially in the activity of single partic-

---

66 GR, Q11, §12, p. 326.
67 GR, Q11, §12, p. 327.
68 GR, Q11, §12, p. 325.
69 Ibid.
70 GR, Q11, §12, pp. 331–2.

ularly gifted individuals) can be considered as marking the 'high points' of the progress made by common sense, or at least the common sense of the more educated strata of society but through them also of the people.[71]

This critical and controversial statement presented the philosophy of praxis as a philosophy of combat. As such, it should challenge the philosophy of its time and the appropriation of this by common sense by presenting itself, through criticism, as the philosophical overcoming of this philosophy and of common sense and the practical overcoming of the existing separation between the professional philosopher (the intellectual) and the spontaneous 'philosopher'. The forms of this combat were also defined therein. Criticism of common sense must also be a critique of the philosophy of intellectuals because they assimilate the philosophy of the time as their intellectual horizon, as common sense, because of their participation in what Labriola denominated a 'literary environment'.[72] This diffusion of philosophy in the form of common sense also conforms to that conception of the popular world that lays its roots in the 'external environment'.

The relation between this 'higher philosophy' of the intellectuals and common sense was, according to Gramsci, assured by politics. For Catholicism, this nexus implied the maintenance of the distance between intellectuals from the 'simple' and discipline over the intellectuals so that this distance did not exceed certain limits. For Gramsci, the objectives of the philosophy of praxis were different. It does not seek to keep the 'simple' in 'their primitive philosophy of common sense, but rather to lead them to a higher conception of life'.[73] The stimulating contact between intellectuals and the people would, for this reason, have the objective of forging *'an intellectual-moral bloc which can make politically possible the intellectual progress of the mass* and not only of small intellectual groups'.[74] The *Notebook*'s research programme can thus be read as the theoretical basis for the formation of one's 'own group of intellectuals'.[75]

The place of the intellectuals in Gramsci's thought is extremely important. It began to be defined in the pre-prison period, reaching a high degree of elaboration in *Some Aspects of the Southern Question*, written in 1926, just before

---

71 GR, Q11, §12, p. 332.
72 Labriola 1912, p. 16.
73 GR, Q11, §12, p. 333.
74 Ibid. Emphasis Added.
75 See Kanoussi and Mena 1985, p. 40.

his arrest. In these rich notes, intellectuals, especially the southern ones, are considered one of the most important social strata of Italian national life.[76]

In prison, the theme of the intellectuals was resumed and, associated with the theory of hegemony and concept of the state in an organic sense, occupied a strategic position in Gramscian politics.[77] The relevance given by Gramsci to the theme was retained in the memory of his companions in misfortune. Athos Lisa says that in the discussions Gramsci had in jail, the subject of intellectuals was of fundamental importance and was associated with the central problem of the Constituent Assembly, that is, the forms of political struggle of the revolutionary movement in Italy.[78] In other testimonies, former prison comrades, such as Giovanni Lai[79] and Angelo Scucchia,[80] corroborated Lisa's declaration.

In the Gramscian approach, the question of intellectuals concerned the forms of exercising the functions of leadership and domination of the antagonistic social groups and, in this way, the training of specialised staff and managers. This problem is associated with the exercise of these functions by the bourgeoisie, but also with questions posed by the construction of a new society in the Soviet Union. In Notebook 11, the theme was raised in a synthetic manner and related to the criticism of the *Popular Manual* of Bukahrin. Intellectuals, Gramsci affirmed, conceive of themselves as 'independent of the struggle of the groups and not as an expression of a dialectical process by means of which every dominant social group elaborates a category of intellectuals of their own'.[81]

The question of the intellectuals was not, therefore, for Gramsci, sociological but political.[82] The thematic of intellectuals outlined in Notebook 11 and developed in Notebook 12 is, for Kanoussi and Mena, 'identical to that of the party as an organizational form of the masses and "collective thinker" that provokes an intellectual and moral reform and conforms to a national-popular collective will'.[83] The form of the groups of intellectuals was, therefore, a strategic issue, which explains the importance given to the subject by Gramsci in prison. With his conversations he was also educating these new intellectuals-militants. For Gramsci,

---

76 PPW, pp. 313–37.
77 LC, pp. 549–60.
78 Lisa 1981, p. 376.
79 Quercioli 1977, p. 208.
80 Quercioli 1977, p. 220.
81 Q11, §16, pp. 1406–7. OT.
82 Sassoon 1987, p. 255.
83 Kanoussi and Mena 1985, p. 69.

> Every new historical organism, or type of society creates a new superstructure, whose specialised and flag-carrying representatives – the intellectuals – can only be conceived as 'new' intellectuals, emerged from the new situation and not a continuation of the preceding intellectuality.[84]

The theme of intellectuals thus appeared in Notebook 12 as a history of intellectuals, describing the process of the constitution of these 'new' organic intellectuals and their nexus with the previous intelligentsia. The place occupied by the intellectuals in modern society was defined by the historical development of the state and by its 'expansion'. The expansion of the state should be understood not as a given, but as an historical process in which the incorporation of management functions and their own devices of hegemony occurs.[85] This process is characteristic of the West, in the well-known Gramscian metaphor, that is, of the central capitalist countries. But it is proper to a historical, concrete West, a set of countries that from the end of the previous century underwent a complex process of economic, social and political transformations known as the imperialist phase of capitalism.

It was precisely the perception of this incorporation of the functions of the management of the state that puts the subject of the intellectuals in the foreground in Gramscian thought. The discussion of intellectuals can be translated into an analysis of the relationship between leaders and followers, dominant and dominated, or in other words, a study of the construction and exercise of the supremacy of a class or a fraction of a class over the whole of society.

The beginning of Notebook 12, dedicated to the history of intellectuals ('Jottings and Scattered Notes for a Group of Essays on the History of Intellectuals') begins with an interrogation that defines the scope of research: 'Are intellectuals an autonomous and independent social group, or does every social group have its own particular specialised category of intellectuals?'[86] The question is directed against the meanings of an occupational definition of the status of the intellectual that restricts their scope to the liberal professions or academic activities. This first interrogation was accompanied by another, which follows:

> What are the 'maximum' limits of acceptance of the term 'intellectual'? Can one find a unitary criterion to characterise equally all the diverse and disparate activities of intellectuals and to distinguish these at the same time and in an essential way from the activities of other social groupings?

---

84 Q11, § 16, p. 1407. OT.
85 Sassoon 1987, p. 255.
86 GR, Q12, § 1, p. 301.

The most widespread error of method seems to me that of having looked for this criterion of distinction in the intrinsic nature of intellectual activities, rather than in the ensemble of the system of relations in which these activities (and therefore the intellectual groups who personify them) have their place within the general complex of social relations.[87]

For Gramsci, there were two main ways through which the real historical process of the formation of the various categories of intellectuals occurred. The first of these forms he denominated the so-called 'organic intellectuals', specialisations of partial aspects of the primitive activity of the new social type that the new class revealed. The issue was formulated for the first time in Notebook 4 and resumed, with a small but important variation, in Notebook 12, dedicated to the question of intellectuals:

Every social group coming into existence on the primal basis of an essential function in the world of economic production creates together with itself, organically, a rank or several ranks of intellectuals who give it homogeneity and a consciousness of its own function in the economic sphere ...[88]	Every social group, coming into existence on the original terrain of an essential function in the world of economic production, creates together with itself, organically, one or more strata of intellectuals which give it homogeneity and an awareness of its own function not only in the economic but also in the social and political fields.[89]

The alteration in the text recorded in Notebook 12 highlights, precisely, that the exercise of leadership is not restricted to the economic environment, but extends to other spheres of collective life. Therefore, if it is true that 'hegemony is born in the factory', as Gramsci asserts in Notebook 22,[90] it is also important to emphasise that hegemony is not restricted to the factory.[91]

---

87   GR, Q12, §1, p. 304.
88   PN2, Q4, §49, p. 199.
89   GR, Q12, §1, p. 301.
90   GR, Q22, §2, pp. 278–9.
91   The passage quoted in Notebook 22 is dated by Francioni between February and March 1934. Its first version is from February or March 1930. The passage from Notebook 4 on the intellectuals is from October or November 1930 and its version in Notebook 12 was written in mid-1932. The caveat regarding the social and political dimension of the function of the intellectuals was made, therefore, after the writing of the note on Americanism in Notebook 1 and before the second version of this one in Notebook 22. See Francioni 1984, pp. 140–5.

The second form is that which the Italian Marxist called the 'traditional intellectuals'. Every emerging social group found pre-existing social categories, representative intellectuals often from an historical continuity that was interrupted. Among these categories the most typical were ecclesiastics, who for a long time monopolised education, morality, justice and, of course, religious ideology, that is, the form that philosophy and science assumed in the medieval world. The ecclesiastics were organically linked to the aristocracy and possessed, in addition to the monopoly of ideology and its reproduction, land rights and the privileges attached to these properties. But it is possible to enumerate, also, the non-ecclesiastic administrators, scientists and philosophers supported by absolutism. If there are various types of intellectuals, what distinguishes them, then? The distinctive character lies in the whole system of relations in which intellectual activities are located.

Once this caveat was made, Gramsci introduced a definition of extreme importance: 'All men are intellectuals, one could therefore say; but not all men have in society the function of intellectuals ...'.[92] Strictly speaking, the non-intellectual does not exist to the extent that there is no human activity from which one can exclude any intellectual intervention, such that it is not possible to separate the *homo faber* from the *homo sapiens*. It was taken up again, in other words, from the already known definition presented in Notebook 11: 'all men are "philosophers"', provided that the limits of spontaneous philosophy present in language, religion, common sense, and good sense are defined. Thus, all men are intellectuals because outside their professions they are 'philosophers', artists, participating in a conception of the world or having a consciously defined line of conduct linked to this concept.

All are intellectuals, but only a few exercise this function in society. Intellectual activity is differentiated in degrees that can acquire a qualitative dimension, encompassing at one extreme the creators of various sciences and at the other the most humble administrators and disseminators of a previously accumulated cultural heritage. From an historical point of view, what is important to highlight is the formation of specialised categories in intellectual functions, in connection with the most important social groups. These groups struggle for the assimilation and ideological conquest of traditional intellectuals, a struggle that is more effective if the given group has its own organic intellectuals.

The relationship between these intellectuals and the world of production is mediated by the ensemble of superstructures of which the intellectuals are functionaries. The degree of organicity of intellectuals can be measured by a

---

92 GR, Q12, §1, p. 304.

gradation of the superstructures to which they are linked. The passage from the first writing of Notebook 4 to the second, in Notebook 12, shows that the concept of hegemony acquired sharper contours for Gramsci in 1932. It is therefore worth quoting the texts at length:

... it is possible to conclude, for now, that: the relationship between the intellectuals and production is not direct, as in the case of the fundamental social groups, but mediated, and it is mediated by two types of social organization: (a) by civil society, that is, by the ensemble of private organizations in society; (b) by the state. The intellectuals have a function in the 'hegemony' that is exercised throughout society by the dominant group and in the 'domination' over society that is embodied by the state, and this function is precisely 'organizational' or connective. The intellectuals have the function of organizing the social hegemony of a group and that group's domination of the state; in other words, they have the function of organizing the consent that comes from the prestige attached to the function in the world of production and the apparatus of coercion for those groups who do not 'consent' either actively or passively or for those moments of crisis of command and leadership when spontaneous consent undergoes a crisis.[93]

The relationship between the intellectuals and the world of production is not as direct as it is with the fundamental social groups but is, in varying degrees 'mediated' by the whole fabric of society and by the complex of superstructures, of which the intellectuals are, precisely, the 'functionaries'. It should be possible both to measure the degree of 'organicism' of the various intellectual strata and their degree of connection with a fundamental social group, and to establish a gradation of their functions and of the superstructures from the bottom to the top (from the structural base upwards). What we can do, for the moment, is to fix two major superstructural 'levels': the one that can be called 'civil society', that is the ensemble of organisms commonly called 'private', and that of 'political society' or 'the state'. These two levels correspond on the one hand to the function of 'hegemony' which the dominant group exercises throughout society and on the other hand to that of 'direct domination' or command exercised through the state and 'juridical' government. The functions in question are precisely organizational and connective. The intellectuals are the dominant group's 'deputies' exercising the subaltern functions of social hegemony and political government. These comprise:

---

93   PN2, Q4, § 49, pp. 200–1.

> 1. The 'spontaneous' consent given by the great masses of the population to the general direction imposed on social life by the dominant fundamental group; this consent is 'historically' caused by the prestige (and consequent confidence) which the dominant group enjoys because of its position and function in the world of production.
>
> 2. The apparatus of state coercive power which 'legally' enforces discipline on those groups who do not 'consent' either actively or passively. This apparatus is, however, constituted for the whole of society in anticipation of moments of crisis of command and direction when spontaneous consent has failed.[94]

This focus greatly extended the concept of the intellectual and inserted it into the elaboration of the concept of hegemony. If the relation between the function of the intellectuals and hegemony was already in the note of Notebook 4, written in 1930, it was Notebook 12, from 1932, in which it was expanded by articulating two conceptual pairs: a) civil society and political society or the state; b) direction and domination. The argument set out in the second text has been meticulously rebuilt, giving rise to a conception in which the relations between the concepts within a pair and the pairs between them are multidimensional. Instead of emphasising the antagonism between civil society and political society or that between the functions of direction and domination, the unity-differentiation within these concepts was noted. The place occupied by intellectuals is key to understanding this unity-differentiation, since they are the agents of both functions.

It is clear that this perspective presupposes a differentiation and hierarchisation between intellectuals to which reference has already been made. Gramsci even spoke of a certain division of labour. This differentiation is not only functional. The Italian Marxist distinguished between, for example, urban and rural intellectuals. Urban intellectuals grew together with industry, did not have

---

94   GR, Q11, 12, §1, pp. 306–7.

autonomy, and were limited to implementing the plan of production established by industrial chiefs.[95]

Rural intellectuals were, in turn, largely 'traditional'. These were linked to the peasant social mass and to the petty bourgeoisie of the city not yet absorbed and assimilated by the capitalist system. Rural intellectuals exercised on the peasant masses the function of political mediation, putting this mass in contact through its professional activity with the state administration. Such was the force of this mediation policy that the organic development of the peasant masses was linked in large part to the movement of intellectuals and depended on them. This is not the case with technicians of the factory. Their professional mediation did not translate into political mediation and did not exercise a political function over the intellectual masses.

The contact between the intellectuals and the people was a political condition of the cultural elevation of the masses. The 'intellectual progress of the masses' was also, in turn, political, insofar as it was accomplished through politics and resulted in a new relationship between the social groups in which theory and practice were finally unified. The process through which this progress was achieved was not, however, peaceful. Gramsci emphasised the conflictual character of the affirmation of a new personality and of a new hegemonic force:

> Critical understanding of self takes place therefore through a *struggle of political 'hegemonies'*, from opposing directions, first in the ethical field and then in that of politics, in order to arrive at the working out at a higher level of one's own conception of reality. Consciousness of being part of a particular hegemonic force (that is to say, political consciousness) is the first stage towards a further progressive self-consciousness in which theory and practice will finally be one.[96]

The unity between theory and practice, so much vaunted and so little understood, was thus, for Gramsci, a historical process and not a mechanical fact deduced from the action of the masses. The politics and the struggle between social groups would not be reduced to a practical activity. They also involve the conformation and affirmation of a philosophical identity that guarantees the unity of the social group and gives meaning to the transformative practice and constitution of the intellectual group. It was in this theory-practice nexus that Gramsci implanted the concept of hegemony.

---

[95] GR, Q11, 12, §1, p. 306.
[96] GR, Q11, §12, pp. 333–4. Emphasis Added.

The affirmation of a new conception of political struggle made this concept an important step forward in the political-practical process. But it also possessed a philosophical dimension, '[f]or it necessarily involves and supposes an intellectual unity and an ethic in conformity with a conception of reality that has gone beyond common sense and has become, if only within as yet narrow limits, a critical conception'.[97] This was, however, a philosophical-political programme and not a description of the prevailing philosophical elaboration in Marxism at the time. There would remain, within the philosophy of praxis, residues of mechanistic conceptions that would maintain theory as the 'handmaid of praxis'.[98] Such subordination of theory to practice was a sign of a still insufficient development of the philosophy of praxis. For Gramsci:

> Insistence on the practical element of the theory-practice nexus, after having not only distinguished but separated and split the two elements (an operation which in itself is merely mechanical and conventional) means that one is going through a relatively primitive historical phase, one which is still economic-corporate, in which the general framework of the 'base' is being quantitatively transformed and the appropriate quality-superstructure is in the process of emerging, but is not yet organically formed. One should stress the importance and significance which, in the modem world, political parties have in the elaboration and diffusion of conceptions of the world, because essentially what they do is to work out the ethics and the politics corresponding to these conceptions and act as it were as their historical 'laboratory'.[99]

The practicalism of this subordination expressed the incapacity of the workers' movement to overcome the level of immediate claims synthesised in a programme and in an economic-corporate type of practice. The alternative would certainly not be the constitution of theoreticism and the insulation of intellectual activity, which would remove the possibility of asserting itself as a material force and subjecting it to present reality. To overcome this economic-corporate level and move to the level of effective struggle for the constitution of a new hegemony would require merging the intellectual constitution of a new conception of the world to the practical constitution of this conception. The importance attributed by Gramsci to political parties is due to their ability to bring about this merger:

---

97 GR, Q11, §12, p. 334.
98 Ibid.
99 GR, Q11, §12, p. 335.

> ... the parties are the elaborators of new integral and totalitarian intelligentsias and the crucibles where the unification of theory and practice, understood as a real historical process, takes place. It is clear from this that the parties should be formed by individual memberships and not on the pattern of the British Labour Party, because, if it is a question of providing an organic leadership for the entire economically active mass, this leadership should not follow old schemas but should innovate. But innovation cannot come from the mass, at least at the beginning, except through the mediation of an elite for whom the conception implicit in human activity has already become to a certain degree a coherent and systematic ever-present awareness and a precise and decisive will.[100]

The ability to merge intellectual constitution and practical constitution of a conception of the world would be all the greater the more innovative and antagonistic radicalism of the conceptions one wishes to diffuse, that is, the greater the degree of conflict with the old ways of thinking. Although Bukharin's manual was part of a project of affirming a new 'intellectual progress of the masses', the theoretical approach he adopted would condemn these popular masses to a situation of ideological subalternity.[101] It is for this reason that Gramsci was so severe with Bukharin's philosophical attitude. Diluting Marxism in the philosophy of materialism, the Soviet leader was creating an obstacle to the affirmation of a new hegemony.

Conceived as a mass philosophy, that is, as an effective part of a project of 'intellectual reform', the philosophy of praxis should assume, according to Gramsci, a 'polemical form and in the form of a perpetual struggle'.[102] If the objective was to constitute a new philosophy of the masses, that is, a conception of the world capable of organising the intellectual life of the subaltern classes in which these same classes were actively involved, then it was in the first place 'common sense' that this philosophy should confront.

The subordination of the philosophy of praxis to the philosophical materialism promoted by Bukharin, rather than criticising this common sense, accepted it as a point of departure. For in the common sense, Gramsci asserted, the 'realistic' and 'materialist' elements that arise directly from the sensory experience of individuals predominated, constituting spontaneously a Ptolemaic, anthropomorphic and anthropocentric conception.[103] The Sardinian Marxist

---

100 GR, Q11, §12, pp. 335–6.
101 Cf. Frosini 2003, p. 106.
102 GR, Q11, §13, p. 345.
103 GR, Q13, §13, p. 344.

drew attention to the fact that contrary to what a 'philosophical' common sense could imagine, this common-sense materialism 'is by no means in contradiction with the religious element' and is even 'superstitious'.[104]

On the basis of this common-sense materialism was the belief that nature had been created by God even before the creation of man and that he would have found this nature in a finished form and received it as a gift. It was not just about common-sense materialism, since even in the Italian philosophical tradition it was possible to find not a few thinkers who espoused this view. In the thought of the philosopher of the Risorgimento, Vincenzo Gioberti, for example, human knowledge was nothing if not an intuition of the external world, but the very idea of an external world would not be conceivable without recourse to a supernatural sphere.[105]

Omitting criticism of the superstitious origin of common sense, the *Popular Manual* was not even capable of effectively combating the theological foundations of subjectivist idealism. This ineffectiveness also became apparent in Bukharin's criticism of Berkeley in the paper he presented at the International Congress on the History of Science and Technology, in London.[106] In this paper, the Soviet Marxist sought to face the subjectivist conception which reduced reality to a creation of the spirit and its influence on contemporary philosophy and science. To this end, he denounced the position that Berkeley's radical subjectivism had assumed from the seventeenth century, becoming a *communis doctorum opinio* with the 'tenacity of a popular prejudice'.[107]

Bukharin declared that only Adam, opening his eyes and seeing the world for the first time, could fall into the illusion that this world would exist only because he thought it and saw it.[108] To be faithful to the metaphor, it is not possible to think of the psychology of Adam, as the Soviet Marxist does, since he is the object of creation and not its subject. In the entire biblical narrative of Genesis, which is an extension of the creation of the world, only God is subject, and for this reason there is no description of the moment when Adam awakens in his first breath of life.

---

104   Ibid.
105   Haddock 1998, p. 709.
106   The paper is in the book *Science at the Cross Roads: Papers presented to the International Congress of the History of Science and Technology held in London from June 29th to July 3rd 1931 by the delegates of the USSR*. Gramsci noted in a letter of 31 August 1931 that he had just received the book, which calls attention to the speed with which it was edited and came to him. Probably the sending was an initiative of Piero Sraffa.
107   Bukharin 1971, p. 12.
108   Ibid.

But supposing it were possible within this biblical metaphor to think of this awakening, it would still be more likely that Adam would fall into the illusion that the world which he saw had a material existence external to him because he had been created by God. By relying on the reading of the Bible, religious common sense would thus be much closer to vulgar materialism than philosophical subjectivism, which would weaken and even invalidate the argument of the author of the *Popular Manual*.

Despite the harsh criticism, Gramsci shared Bukharin's opposition to solipsism. Discussing the musings of Giuseppe A. Borgese on subatomic particles, he asserted it was 'mere word-play, with science fiction, not with a new scientific or philosophical thought'. And he asked: 'Perhaps matter seen under the microscope is no longer really objective matter, but is, rather, a creation of the human mind having no objective or empirical existence?'[109] The answer to the question itself is a thorough rejection of the idea that thought could create matter:

> If it were true that the infinitely small phenomena in question cannot be considered as existing independently of the subject who observes them, they would in fact not even be 'observed', but 'created' and would fall into the same domain as the pure imaginative intuition of the individual ... One would not even be dealing with 'solipsism' but with witchcraft, with demiurgic powers.[110]

The insufficiency of Bukharin's critique of subjectivist philosophies would lie elsewhere in the confusion between the *communis doctorum opinio* and 'traditional prejudice'. It is necessary to distinguish, however, Gramsci affirmed, 'the great systems of traditional philosophy and the religion of the upper clergy – i.e. the conception of the world of the intellectuals and high culture ...'[111] from the philosophy of common sense '"the philosophy of non-philosophers", or in other words, the conception of the world which is uncritically absorbed by the various social and cultural environments in which the moral individuality of the average man is developed'.[112] Once this distinction was made, it would be evident how innocuous the Bukharinian approach was in combating the mysticism of speculative philosophy in that it would only reinforce the superstitions of those who should be emancipated from them.

---

109   FSPN, Q11, §36, p. 427.
110   FSPN, Q11, §36, pp. 430, 431.
111   GR, Q11, §13, p. 343.
112   Ibid.

However, Gramsci's critique of vulgar materialism was not always unequivocal and his conclusions sometimes appear contradictory. As a result, there were some who accused him of slipping or simply falling into idealism. One of them in Italy, Onorato Damen, did not hesitate, for example, to accuse Gramsci of being within the ambit of 'historicist neo-idealism' if not a 'philosophic pre-Marxism'.[113] A similar opinion appears, too, in Luciano Gruppi's reading, which claimed that the author of the *Notebooks* had fallen 'effectively into idealism'.[114] In the same sense, Carlos Nelson Coutinho considered that Gramsci '[n]ever completely surpassed the neo-Hegelian conception of Gentile and Croce, for which "All reality is spirit", nature itself being a "category of the spirit"'.[115]

Such readings tend to confuse Gramsci's criticism of the claim to epistemological objectivity, that is, the possibility cherished by the positivism of an absolutely objective, ahistorical and therefore unhuman knowledge, with a critique of the ontological objectivity of matter, that is, to its objective reality.[116] Within the realm of his criticism of Bukharin, Gramsci's emphasis is on the pretension of epistemological objectivity.[117] But the confusion is exacerbated by the fact that Gramsci himself does not make a clear distinction between the epistemological meaning and the ontological meaning of objectivity; indeed, he frequently passes rapidly within a single Note from one to the other.

Take, for example, the often cited §17 of Notebook 11, entitled 'The so-called "Reality of the External World"'. Gramsci stated in this paragraph that Bukharin's argument was misplaced. The subjectivist conception criticised by the author of the *Popular Manual* was the most complete and advanced form of modern philosophy and historical materialism would have, according to Gramsci, translated into 'realistic and historicist language what traditional philosophy expressed in speculative language'.[118] It was not, however, with any and all subjectivist conceptions of reality that Marxism would establish a critical dialogue. Here, as on other occasions, it was with Hegel that this dialogue had to be confronted. This caveat was accompanied by the explicit rejection of 'bizarre forms' assumed by this subjectivist conception, such as that of Tolstoy, who believed he could capture the moment when his spirit would not have had time to create nothing and therefore would see nothing. But it is one thing to face

---

113   Damen 1988, chapter 1.
114   Gruppi 1978, p. 119.
115   Coutinho 1999, p. 107.
116   Martelli 1996, p. 27.
117   Martelli 1996, p. 28.
118   Q11, §17, p. 1413. OT.

these 'bizarre forms', and it is quite another to forge weapons using the exponents of subjective philosophy. According to Gramsci,

> The proviso that must be made with the *Popular Essay* [Manual] is that of presenting the subjectivist conception as it appears in the critique of common sense and of embracing the conception of the objective reality of the external world in its most trivial and uncritical form without even suspecting that one can move against it the objection of mysticism.[119]

This 'trivial and uncritical' form was the result of a mechanical understanding of the question. Trying to flee from a reductionist solution to the problem, Gramsci asked: 'Can there be extra-historical and extra-human objectivity? But who will judge this objectivity? Who can put himself in this kind of "cosmo-in-itself point of view", and what would such a point of view mean?'[120] Only a god could claim such a universal point of view. It became necessary to answer the question by appealing 'to history and to man to demonstrate objective reality. Objective always means "humanly objective", which may correspond exactly to "historically subjective", that is, objective would mean "universally subjective" '.[121]

The difficulty of interpreting this paragraph lies in the displacement carried out by Gramsci's analysis of the ontological objectivity of the outside world for a critical analysis of the objectivity of knowledge. The paragraph thus goes from a critique of 'bizarre forms' of subjectivism that would deny the existence of matter outside of thought to a criticism of that epistemological objectivity, which would claim objective knowledge and a science free of assumptions. The continuation of the paragraph makes this shift explicit:

> Man knows objectively to the extent that knowledge is real for the whole human race *historically* unified in a unitary cultural system; but this process of historical unification takes place with the disappearance of internal contradictions that rip apart human society, contradictions that are the condition of the formation of groups and of the birth of ideologies that are not concrete-universal, but that expire immediately, because of the practical origin of their substance.[122]

---

119 Q11, §17, p. 1415, OT.
120 Ibid.
121 Q11, §17, pp. 1415–6.
122 Q11, §17, p. 1466.

The reference to the man who 'knows objectively' makes clear that it is the possibility of knowledge outside of history which Gramsci is questioning and not the objective existence of matter. Carlos Nelson Coutinho criticises this passage of the text, stating that 'it becomes difficult not only to explain the objectivity of the law of gravity before all men became aware of it, before it became a "universal subjective", but it is difficult even to understand the objectivity of social facts'. And he concludes: 'does the law of the tendency for the rate of profit to fall (although it is a human objectification, not a natural objectivity) have to wait to be a "universal subjective" to become an objective reality ...?'[123]

Appropriately, Coutinho noted that Gramsci in this passage is dealing with an epistemological rather than an ontological question. But the interpreter's argument is flawed, since he establishes an identity between gravitation and the 'law of gravity' and between the tendency of the rate of profit to fall and the law of the tendency of the rate of profit to fall, that is, between the real and the thought of the real. Certainly gravitation did not have to become a 'universal subjective' to be a force, but it needed Isaac Newton to be thought of as under the form of law. Gravitational force existed objectively before Newton, but the law of gravitation is a mathematical formula and it could not have had an objective existence before it was deduced by the English physicist.

As an explanatory model, the Newtonian law of universal gravitation presented theoretical limits that were addressed in the twentieth century by Einstein's theory of general relativity in a different 'historically subjective' context. If the law existed before its limits, would they be limits of nature? And would the theory of general relativity also have existed before it was enunciated by Einstein? In this case, would there be two natures, one Newtonian and another Einsteinian? As such, one must take care not to fetishise science and confuse the thought of reality with reality itself.[124]

The reference to Coutinho's 'law of gravity' is not accidental. It refers to the Preface to *The German Ideology* and to the sarcastic criticism that Marx and Engels directed to those who believed that people sank in the water only because they had the 'idea of gravity [Gedanken der Schwere]'.[125] But Cou-

---

123 Coutinho 1999, p. 106.
124 Gruppi defends a thesis similar to that of Coutinho, but clearly distinguishes that which is independent of us and what we objectify by an action or act of thought, arguing that Gramsci would confuse both dimensions (Gruppi 2000, pp. 119–20). For criticism of Gruppi, see Martelli 1996, pp. 37–8.
125 MECW, Vol. 5, p. 24.

tinho's statement reverses the original meaning of the Marxian-Engelsian irony in attributing to the law of gravitation, that is, the 'idea of gravity', the condition of 'objective reality'.

In this respect, it should be remembered that Gramsci's criticism is similar to that which the Hungarian Marxist Georgy Lukács subjected Bukharin's *Popular Manual* in 1925. Lukács declared that the Soviet Marxist came dangerously close in this work to what Marx called 'bourgeois materialism', rejecting 'all the elements in Marxist method which derive from classical German philosophy'.[126] This closeness to natural-scientific materialism would obscure the specific character of Marxism, to which 'all economic or "sociological" phenomena derive from the social relations of men to one another. Emphasis on a false "objectivity" in theory leads to fetishism'.[127]

How could one escape the solipsism proper to subjectivist idealism and this fetishism which characterises vulgar materialism? Gramsci presented the question in a set of mostly first-copy texts grouped together at the end of the Special Notebook dedicated to Bukharin under the subtitle 'Miscellaneous Notes'. Such a position implies that they constitute the peak of Gramsci's philosophical reflection.[128] He specifies in these paragraphs that before classical German idealist philosophy had been conceived as a receptive activity, which incorporated in thought an absolutely immutable external world, or an ordering activity, it was capable of arranging the world through thought, without, however, transforming it. Classical German philosophy, in turn, introduced an idealistic and speculative meaning to the concept of *creation*.[129]

Gramsci identified in German idealism a true revolution in thought and he considered, as has already been seen, that it was in this that the philosophy of praxis found its impulse. But what does this concept of creation mean? And how could one use it without falling into solipsism, assuming that the outside world is created by thought? According to Gramsci,

> To escape simultaneously from solipsism and from mechanistic conceptions implicit in the concept of thought as receptive and ordering activity, it is necessary to put the question in a 'historicist' fashion, and at the same time, to put the 'will' (which in the last analysis equals practical or political activity), at the base of philosophy. But it must be a rational, not an

---

126 Lukács 1966, p. 29.
127 Ibid.
128 These paragraphs were probably written in the last months of 1932 or early 1933. See Francioni 1984, p. 145.
129 SPN, Q11, § 59, p. 346.

arbitrary, will, which is realised in so far as it corresponds to objective historical necessities, or in so far as it is universal history itself in the moment of its progressive actualization.[130]

The synthesis of Gramsci's history of philosophy was undoubtedly very simplifying. But the solution he offered to escape from idealism and vulgar materialism was extremely rich in meanings. The solution was strongly anchored in Labriola's reading of the *Theses on Feuerbach*. It was through a revalorisation of historical praxis that the author of the *Notebooks* sought to solve the aporias of 'double revisionism'. It was for this reason that in order to highlight his solution, from Notebooks 10 and 11 onwards he preferred to speak of the philosophy of praxis rather than historical materialism, seeking in this way to stress the character of the history of its conception. Thus, paraphrasing a passage from Lenin in *Materialism and Empirio-criticism*,[131] Gramsci wrote:

> It has been forgotten that in the case of a very common expression [historical materialism] one should put the accent on the first term – 'historical' – and not on the second, which is of metaphysical origin. The philosophy of praxis is 'historicism', absolute secularization and earthliness of thought, an absolute humanism of history.[132]

In its historical dimension, thinking is part of the reality that one wants to think and insofar as it '*modifies* the way of feeling of the greatest number', that is, of the masses, it is also a material force capable of modifying one's reality.[133] The choice of words was careful and seems to mark the distance that separated the Gramscian philosophy of praxis (of Labriolan inspiration) from that presented by Giovanni Gentile, who sought to subsume Marxian thought within *attualista* (*actualist*) philosophy.

Taking as a starting point a particular reading of the same *Theses on Feuerbach*, of which he was the first translator in Italy, Gentile elaborated an impressive extension of the concept of praxis, in which activity became the praxis of

---

130   SPN, Q11, §59, p. 345.
131   Lenin said: 'Marx and Engels, as they grew out of Feuerbach and matured in the fight against the scribblers, naturally paid most attention to crowning the structure of philosophical materialism, that is, not to the materialist epistemology but to the materialist conception of history. That is why Marx and Engels laid the emphasis in their works rather on *dialectical* materialism than on dialectical materialism, and insisted on *historical* materialism rather than on historical materialism' (LCW, Vol. 14, p. 329).
132   SPN, Q11, §27, p. 465.
133   Q11, §59, p. 1486. Emphasis Added. OT.

thought and objectivity became the objectivity that was thought. Rather than a dialectical relationship between subject and object, there was a 'unilateral construction of the object by the subject'.[134] The key to this theoretical procedure was found in a mistranslation of the *Theses* in the version published by Engels.[135]

In the first of these *Theses*, in the moment when Marx discussed the limits of Feuerbachian materialism, Gentile translated the key noun of the paragraph, 'der Gegenstand' (the object, the thing), as '*il termine del pensiero*' (the term or conclusion of the thought), and then clarified in a footnote that 'objective activity' (*gegenständliche Tätigkeit*) meant 'activity that does, puts, creates the sensible object'.[136] In the same note, Gentile empties the revolutionary character of critical practical activity. Thus, where Marx wrote 'Hence he does not grasp the significance of "revolutionary", of "practical-critical", activity' [*Er begreift daher nicht die Bedeutung der 'revolutionären', der 'praktisch-kritischen' Tätigkeit*][137] Gentile translated: 'therefore he does not understand the meaning that the "revolutionaries" give to practical-critical activity' [*Perciò egli non intende il significato che I 'Rivoluzionari' dànno all'attività practico-critica*].[138]

This emptying by Gentile was completed in the third of the theses, the one that stated the condition of self-transformation (the word *Selbstveränderung* was deleted in the Engels version). Gentile translated the final strategic phrase of this thesis as such: 'The coincidence of the change of environment and human activity can be conceived and understood rationally [*concepito e inteso razionalmente*] only as subverted praxis [*prassi rovesciata*]'.[139] Gentile's error thus completely reversed the meaning of praxis, since the original German did not deal with a 'subverted praxis' but rather a 'subversive praxis (*umwälzende Praxis*)'.[140]

The transformation of the meanings of the *Theses* allowed Gentile to affirm that when 'you know, you construct, you make the object and when you make or construct an object, it is known; therefore the object is a product of the subject'.[141] Such objects constituted by this practice could be theoretical or

---

134 Martelli 2001, p. 89.
135 For the original version of Marx and the one published by Engels, as well as the comparison between the two, see Labica 1990.
136 Gentile 2003, pp. 68–9. OT.
137 Cf. Labica 1990, pp. 26, 31.
138 Gentile 2003, p. 69. OT.
139 Gentile 2003, p. 69.
140 In the original version of Marx, there is '*revolutionäre Praxis*' ('revolutionary praxis') rather than '*Umwälzende Praxis*'.
141 Gentile 2003, p. 77. OT.

practical, could be knowledge and facts, the neo-idealist philosopher said. But the permanent construction of the object would modify the circumstances, the education and the environment of the subject, thus modifying the subject himself. The effect would then react on the cause and 'the relationship itself is subverted, the effect being that the cause of the cause becomes an effect, remaining, however, cause'. In this way, 'the praxis that had as principle the subject and as an end the object, was subverted, regressing from the object (principle) to the subject (term)'.[142]

The central theme of Gentile's *The Philosophy of Marx*, the concept of praxis, was thus a key to an idealistic solution of the object-subject relation, declaring the identity between the two terms.[143] For the neo-idealist philosopher,

> Praxis means the relation between subject and object. Therefore, neither the individual subject, nor the individual object as such *sic et simpliciter*; but one in necessary relation with the other and vice versa. Therefore, also, the *identity* of opposites. Not an educator on one side and educated on another, as has been said, but educators who are educated; and educated who educate.[144]

Such an identity afforded Gentile with a solution to the relation between theory and praxis under the form, once again, of an identity. On the one hand, praxis was conceived as original, free and identical to thought, and, on the other, thought was conceived as a theoretical conscience of the practice in act and, therefore, as identical to praxis.[145] The question of the relationship between theory and practice was also central for Gramsci, as well as the place attributed to the *Theses on Feuerbach*. But the solution to the question was radically different from that of Gentile.

In prison, Gramsci undertook some translation exercises in the *Notebooks*, among which stand out some texts of Marx, such as the *Theses on Feuerbach* itself and the '1859 Preface' to *A Contribution to the Critique of Political Economy*, key texts for the reconstruction of Marxism that he intended to undertake.[146] Although not exact, the solutions that the Sardinian Marxist found in the exercise of translating the *Theses* were closer to the text of Marx than those of

---

142   Gentile 2003, p. 85. See the comments by Martelli 1996, p. 25.
143   Badaloni and Muscetta 1990, p. 3.
144   Gentile 2003, p. 160. Emphasis Added.
145   Badaloni and Muscetta 1990, p. 37.
146   On the importance of the books of translation of Gramsci, see Borghese 1981 and Francioni 1992.

Gentile. In the first thesis, for example, he translated the noun 'der Gegenstand' as 'l'oggetto' (the object) and in the final paragraph of the same Thesis, he precisely changed Gentile's translation of 'activity' to 'revolutionary activity' (*pertanto egli non concepisce l'importanza della attività "rivoluzionaria", dell'attività pratico-critica*').[147] The solution to the third thesis that Gramsci devised was not precise, however; although it was different from that advanced by Gentile. Instead of translating '*umwälzende Praxis*' into 'subversive praxis' (in Italian, *prassi rovesciante or prassi sovvertitrice*), as would be more exact,[148] Gramsci translated it as 'subversion of praxis' ('*rovesciamento della praxis*').[149]

Although not satisfactory, this latest version of Marx's text differs from that of Gentile and expresses, *in nuce*, the inability to identify one with the other.[150] According to Martelli,[151] in the Gramscian formula, the complement 'praxis' is defined with an active meaning and therefore equivalent to 'subversive praxis' ('*prassi rovesciante*'), to the contrary, therefore, of Gentile.[152] Martelli's interpretation gains strength when compared to the translation of the first thesis, in which practical-critical activity would not have the 'meaning' of 'revolutionaries', as in the Gentile version, but would be, in the Gramscian version, 'revolutionary activity'.

Revolutionary praxis does not create the object, as Gentile intended, but it transforms the world, as Marx stated in the eleventh of his *Theses on Feuerbach*. This was the sense in which Gramsci employed the notion of 'subversion of praxis' in the *Notebooks*. The expression was not in current use, but appears in a B text located in Notebook 8, in a theoretically significant context for the present discussion. In this note, in which Gramsci investigated the relationship between structure and superstructure, he wrote with respect to the 'existence

---

147 Q, p. 2355.
148 Cf. Martelli 1996, p. 25 and Martelli 2001, pp. 90–2.
149 Q, p. 2356.
150 Augusto Del Noce insisted on the thesis that Gramscian thought would be a chapter in the history of Italian neo-idealism and, particularly, of Gentilian *attualismo*. Cf. Del Noce 1978. Supporting this thesis is the assertion that one and the other would uphold his philosophy as an activism of the will. Domenico Losurdo criticises this thesis in a precise and competent way, marking the entire distance, not only political but also theoretical, which exists between the ideologue of fascism Giovanni Gentile and the communist leader Antonio Gramsci. Losurdo 1997, chap. III.
151 Martelli 1996, p. 27.
152 In Italian, the particle *di* (*della = di + la*) can establish a relation of specification, which determines the broader concept expressed by the name on which it depends, but it may also express, on the dependence of a name derived from the verb (as is the case of '*il rovesciamento*') a subjective specification, designating the logical subject of action. In this case, the subject is 'praxis'.

of the objective conditions for revolutionizing praxis', that is, for the revolution itself.[153] The existence of objective conditions for such a revolution would allow the emergence of subjective conditions, that situation in which 'the "rational" is actively and effectively real'.[154] The meaning attributed to the notion of 'subversion of praxis' was in this context that of 'subversion by praxis', the radical transformation of the existing order through revolutionary activity.

The political question posed in Notebook 8 was placed on a philosophical plane in §14 of Notebook 11. It is a text of great complexity and scope, which brings together §§174 and 186 present in Notebook 8, expanding and developing the content of these notes. Gramsci began the paragraph stating that the absence of a dialectical conception of the historical movement prevented the author of the *Popular Manual* from carrying out an effective critique of metaphysics and speculative philosophy. Bukharin's criticism of the philosophical systems of idealism would be characterised by the use of dogmatic terms.[155]

To overcome such dogmatism, Gramsci affirmed, it would be necessary to think about the historical value of philosophies, that is, to conceive of them as the '(necessary and inseparable expression of a particular historical action, of a particular praxis), but as superseded and rendered in "vain" in a succeeding period'.[156] The historicisation of philosophy would allow us to conceive thought in this way without falling into 'skepticism and moral and ideological relativism'. Responding to the challenges posed by this philosophy that he was criticising, Bukharin could not elaborate the concept of the philosophy of praxis as 'historical methodology'. It thus fell far short of the philosophical development of idealism since 'he does not succeed in posing and resolving from the point of view of the real dialectic, the problem that Croce has posed and has attempted to resolve from the speculative point of view'.[157]

In this last statement, Gramsci's judgement of the different versions of revisionism was clear. Placing Marxism short of the philosophical threshold that idealism itself had achieved, the determinism of Bukharin's manual provoked an unreserved censure on Gramsci's part. Contemporary idealism, and principally Croce and Gentile, represented for the Sardinian Marxist the limit that European bourgeois thought had reached and a challenge that needed to be overcome dialectically.

---

153   PN3, Q8, §182, p. 340.
154   Ibid.
155   SPN, Q11, §14, pp. 436–7.
156   SPN, Q11, §14, p. 436.
157   Ibid.

The criticism of the Soviet Marxist by the author of the *Notebooks* resided in the fact of Bukharin having confronted idealism and, in this struggle, instead of overcoming it, having remained in the safe haven of a less elaborate thought. Eliding the philosophical problems posed by contemporary idealism and retreating to the philosophical positions of vulgar materialism, Bukharin rediscovered a 'naïve metaphysics'.[158] The philosophy of the author of the *Popular Manual* was thus, according to Gramsci, a 'positivistic Aristotelianism'. Starting from a naïve metaphysics, the Soviet Marxist transformed Marxism into a '"sociology" of metaphysical materialism' whose aim was to investigate a 'law of causality and the search for regularity, normality, uniformity' present in society.[159] But in this search, his investigation eventually fell short of what it could have been. For revolution is not regularity, normality, and uniformity. It is not the expression of a homogeneous time in which repetition takes place. Revolution is irregularity, abnormality, discontinuity. And it was in search of a theory of revolution that Gramsci questioned the Bukharinian theory: 'But how can one derive from this way of seeing things the overcoming, the "overthrow" of praxis?'[160] How, through vulgar materialism, would it be possible to conceive of revolution?

Conceiving of revolution as a possibility requires abandoning the positivist idea of a homogeneous time. For Gramsci, Marxism was not a science of historical regularities and, for this reason, he announced his philosophy of praxis as 'an expression of the historical contradictions'.[161] And as such the philosophy of praxis is finite. Its time, however, is still the present that must be overcome. Its hour, the hour of its finitude, has not yet arrived. The philosophy of praxis is still an expression of the contradictions of our time and as such should be developed as a thought that conspires against the conditions of its existence. As a thought that understands itself as politics.

2   Anti-Croce

Benedetto Croce's place in Italian culture in the first half of the twentieth century is unique. The critic, born in Pescasseroli in the Abruzzo region, constructed his career on the sidelines of the university system. Yet this did not prevent him from exercising a hegemonic influence on the Italian cultural environment

---

158   SPN, Q11, § 14, p. 436.
159   Ibid.
160   Ibid.
161   SPN, Q11, § 62, p. 405.

whose only parallel was the place that Goethe occupied in nineteenth-century Germany.[162] For this, Croce used the magazine *La Critica* and the publishing house Laterza to saturate the cultural life of the peninsula with a single point of view: the cultural renaissance of Italy and the consequent annihilation of the vestiges of the still-existing thought of the eighteenth century, particularly that of positivism.[163]

It is no exaggeration to speak of cultural saturation. Between 1882, the date of his first juvenile texts, and his death in 1952, Croce published around 30,000 pages and carefully followed the frequent reprints of the 72 volumes of his work. To this large quantity of writings we would need to add his travel notebooks and the enormous epistolary correspondence that he maintained with some of the main exponents of the literary environment of his epoch.[164] The result was a colossal enterprise with a view to the reconfiguration of this literary environment and the full exercise of his cultural hegemony within it. With full awareness of the scope of this enterprise, Croce considered himself to have contributed decisively to affirm in Italy:

> the renewed concept of philosophy in its speculative and dialectical but not at all positivistic and classificatory tradition, the broad historical view, and the unity of erudition and philosophizing, so that the path that is opened that can acknowledge all ideal categories in their positivity and autonomy.[165]

In general, the search for these results unifies the different phases of Crocean thinking.[166] The intellectual means mobilised to achieve this goal varied, however, in time. This enterprise began, or at least gained form, with Croce's approach to Marxism. It is not accurate to say that he was a Marxist or even socialist, although he maintained an intense dialogue with both throughout his life.[167] His relationship with Marxism did not develop in a linear fashion

---

162 See Hughes 1979, p. 201; Garin 1996, pp. 3–4; Bellamy 1987, p. 72.
163 Jacobitti 1980, pp. 69–70.
164 Badaloni and Muscetta 1990, pp. 15–33.
165 Croce 1947a, p. 86. OT.
166 For a discussion of the different phases of Crocean thought, see Badaloni and Muscetta 1990, pp. 62–75.
167 On the basis of what Croce himself wrote, it is possible to say that he would not recognise himself in Finocchiaro's assertion that his thinking would have been Marxist (2002, p. 10). A more nuanced opinion is supported by Hughes 1979, pp. 82–9. According to Badaloni: 'Although he was not socialist or Marxist, Croce, like Gentile, needed Marxism to give a rational basis to his activity as a critic and historian' (Badaloni and Muscetta 1990, p. 62).

and it is possible to identify at least two phases therein. In this first, to which reference is now made, Croce was inserted in the debates of the time, and in the revisionist movement that affirmed the 'crisis of Marxism'.

As part of this revisionist strand, Croce attributed, in his essays *Materialismo storico ed economia marxistica* (*Historical Materialism and the Economics of Karl Marx*), published in 1899,[168] a positive value to certain aspects of Marxist theory, while at the same time attempting to correct what he considered to be the major flaws of this theory. In the Preface to the first edition of this work, he stated that, as with Georges Sorel, his goal was 'to rid the sound and realistic core of Marx's thought from the metaphysical and literary adornments of its author and of the little exegeses and hardly cautious deductions of the school'.[169]

This intellectual enterprise was interpreted as a liberating and revivifying mission because it was about liberating Marxism from the hands of Marxists and giving it a new life, albeit with more modest pretensions. It was within the scope of this project that the author of *Historical Materialism and the Economics of Karl Marx* defined that historical materialism was 'neither a philosophy of history nor a new method of historical thought; it must be simply a canon of historical interpretation', which suggested 'directing attention to the so-called economic basis of society, in order that the forms and mutations of the latter may be better understood'.[170]

To be successful, this valorisation of Marxism as a 'canon of interpretation' had to settle accounts with the notion of class struggle. Understood as a thought that calls attention to the 'economic substrate', Marxism could lose its revolutionary character, which would not occur if, instead of economic conditions, the permanent character of social antagonism were emphasised. According to Croce, history would be a class struggle only when there were social classes (a fact to which Engels had already drawn attention), when there were antagonistic interests and when the classes were aware of this antagonism. But these antagonistic interests would not always exist and if they did exist, they would not necessarily be conscious. Thus, the statement that 'history is a class war' also, according to Croce, should be reduced to the 'limited value of a canon and of a point of view, which we have allowed in general to the materialist conception'.[171]

---

168   The essays had originally been published between 1895 and 1899 in Italian periodicals and in the French journal *Devenir sociale*, edited by Georges Sorel. They are the result of the critical dialogue of Croce with Antonio Labriola, to whom the work was dedicated.
169   Croce 1927, p. 9.
170   Croce 1915, p. 35.
171   Croce 1915, p. 37.

Marx was, for Croce, a tool for the critique of positivist philosophy predominant in Italy and a means for the elaboration of his philosophy of the spirit, conceived by distinguishing between the different forms that defined how the spirit operated universally. In his conference presented in 1900 at the Pontaniana Academy of Napoli, entitled *Tesi fondamental di um'estetica come scienza dell'espressione e linguistica generale* (*Fundamental theses of an aesthetics as a science of expression and general linguistics*), Croce produced a first version of this philosophical system. The text, revised and expanded, became, in 1907, the book *Estetica come scienza dell'espressione and linguistica generale* (*Aesthetics as a science of expression and general linguistics*),[172] the first of the four volumes that Croce dedicated to the Philosophy of the Spirit.[173]

Croce's standard philosophical procedure consisted of a method of 'distinction-classification-definition' as an essential point.[174] Thus, the starting point of the exposition – literally, as this was stated in the first paragraph of his *Aesthetics* – could be nothing but a schematic and classificatory statement. In it, Croce distinguished between the two forms that knowledge acquired: 'it is either *intuitive* knowledge or *logical* knowledge; knowledge obtained through the *imagination* or knowledge obtained through the *intellect*; knowledge of the *individual* or knowledge of the *universal*'.[175] Such forms of knowledge would correspond, respectively, to Aesthetics and to Logic, which were diverse but not separate. The aesthetic form was considered independent of the intellective form and in that sense was the first form. Intelligence would need to express itself and, for this reason, could not exist without an aesthetic.[176]

The intuitive (Aesthetic) and intellective (Logic) forms exhausted for Croce the whole theoretical domain of the spirit, but its full knowledge would require the establishment of relations between the theoretical spirit and the practical spirit. With the theoretical form man would comprehend things and would appropriate them by means of the intellect or intuition and with practice would transform and create them.[177] The form or practical activity would, therefore, be correspondent to the will. Croce's argument was tautological, since he defined the will as 'activity of the spirit' and as being 'productive, not of

---

172 In English, Croce 1909.
173 The other volumes are *Logic as the Science of the Pure Concept*, published originally in 1908 (Croce 1917); *Philosophy of the Practical: Economic and Ethic* from 1908 (Croce 1913); and *Theory and History of Historiography* from 1915 (Croce 1921).
174 Garin 1996, pp. 3–31.
175 Croce 1909, p. 8.
176 Croce 1909, pp. 22–3.
177 Croce 1909, p. 30.

knowledge, but of actions'.[178] It would be repeated in these two forms – theoretical and practical – the same relationship that had already been established between aesthetic and intellective activity. The theoretical form would be the first and independent form; the practical form could not exist without it. This did not mean that the practical man needed a philosophical system to operate. What he needed for this was intuitions and concepts that would allow him to guide his action.

The first degree of practical activity would be, for Croce, merely useful or economic and the second would be moral activity: 'Economy is, as it were, the Aesthetic of practical life; Morality its Logic'.[179] The concept of economic activity would receive detailed treatment. Croce sought to overcome the confusion between the concepts of usefulness and selfishness. Since selfishness is immoral, confusion would place the Economy in a distinct, but not antagonistic position, to Ethics. But even the most scrupulous man should conduct his life for a sense of usefulness if he did not wish to operate without meaning.

The author of *Aesthetics* sought to resolve the issue in the same way as the relationship between Aesthetics and Logic was established. The altruist who seeks a moral end could only profitably seek it usefully (economically) by mobilising the accessible means with a view to achieving the desired end. Since only the individual could be the actor of the action, a rational (moral) end could only be desired as a particular end. Economic activity would be implied in ethical activity, but the reverse would not be true. Economic activity would thus be primary and independent in relation to ethical activity.[180]

The complex activity of thought was thus decomposed into four degrees: theoretical individuality and universality, referring to intuition and the expression of the individual (Aesthetics) and to the conception of the universal (Logic), respectively; and practical individuality and universality, corresponding to the volitions of the particular (Economy) and the volitions of the universal (Ethics). The relationship between these different moments or degrees of the spirit would constitute a regressive implication. Croce thus summed up his theory of the forms of the spirit:

> In this summary sketch that we have given, of the entire philosophy of the spirit in its fundamental moments, the spirit is conceived as consisting of four moments or grades, disposed in such a way that the theoretical activity is to the practical as is the first theoretical grade to the second

---

178 Croce 1909, p. 29.
179 Croce 1909, p. 33.
180 Croce 1909, p. 34.

theoretical, and the first practical grade to the second practical. The four moments imply one another regressively by their concretion. The concept cannot be without expression, the useful without the one and the other, and morality without the three preceding grades.[181]

The innumerable problems of formulating a philosophy of the spirit were unresolved, but the successive revisions of the first three volumes that composed his research and the addition of a fourth dedicated to history would demonstrate his solution. The attempt to restrict all human activity to those four forms implied the exclusion from the scope of the 'spirit' any action that could not be framed within them or in the arbitrary reduction of such activities to one of the previously defined forms.

Having based the presuppositions of his philosophy in his *Aesthetics*, Croce did not avoid debating the limits of the system itself, without arriving at a resolution of the tension between the formal and aprioristic classification of the forms of the spirit and an effective analysis of the human experience.[182] The tension manifested itself within Croce's work between the classificatory schematism of the four volumes of his *Philosophy of the Spirit* and the richness of the analysis present in the volumes of his *Scritti di Storia Letteraria e Politica* (*Writings on Literary and Political History*).

The most serious problems appeared precisely in the spheres in which this experience took the form of practical activity, the scope of what the author called 'philosophy of the practical', the fields of economics and ethics.[183] In the same year that Croce wrote the first version of his philosophy of spirit, in the *Fundamental Thesis* of 1900, he also wrote two letters to Vilfredo Pareto discussing 'economic principle'; these letters are included in *Historical Materialism and the Economics of Karl Marx*.[184] These letters were not, obviously, part of the first edition of this work, published a year before, but were included in the next edition in 1906. In addition to the importance for the reconstruction of the method which led Croce to his philosophy of the spirit, these letters, in the position they occupy in *Historical Materialism and the Economics of Karl Marx* reveal that what he called 'Economics' was the nodal point of his initial disaffection with Marx's work.

In the letter to Pareto of 15 May 1900, the relationship between the domains of Economics and Ethics was addressed. In this missive, the economic fact was

---

181   Croce 1909, p. 36.
182   Garin 1996, p. 21.
183   Croce 1913. See Martelli 2001, p. 121.
184   Croce 1915, pp. 66–74.

defined as 'the practical activities of men in so far as they are considered as such, independent of any moral or immoral determination'.[185] Establishing the autonomy of the *useful*, and distinguishing the economic action of a morality conceived in its categorical purity, Croce enunciated in these letters the bases for his philosophy of practice.[186]

The price of this statement was, however, high. Such a lax concept of economic fact would result in the subsumption by the economic of all activity with a view to transforming the environment in some way and therefore implied a reduction of law and politics to mere expressions of economic activity. This conceptual expansion would constitute a surprising economism. After first criticising the operation by Achille Loria and later Marx's supposed transformation of the economy into a 'hidden god', Croce paradoxically subsumed part of the superstructure in the economy.

In *Aesthetics* this procedure of subsumption was manifested in the treatment dispensed to the law: 'Law is a rule, a formula (whether oral or written matters little here) in which is fixed an economic relation willed by an individual or by a community'.[187] In *Philosophy of Practice*, the theme was resumed and dealt with in detail, preserving the formulation in its most important points: the law belonging to the sphere of practical activity, the distinction between morality and law, and the reduction of law to the economy.[188]

By the same token, political action for Benedetto Croce was that guided by the sense of *utility*, that is, it was action directed by an end considered *useful* by the agent and thus was relegated to the scope of the Economy. The criterion that would allow the evaluation of a political action would thus be a criterion of effectiveness. Directed with a view to achieving a useful end, such an action could not be qualified as moral or immoral, but only as effective or ineffective.[189] Once politics was defined this way, it became possible to distinguish it from moral and ethical action, that action directed towards the realisation of the *good*. It did not, however, deal with the affirmation of the morality or immorality of politics, but only that of amorality.

The distinction between philosophy and politics also implied a specialisation or specification of subjects. The distinction of spiritual forms was found in singular individuals and the specificity of their vocations.[190] The demarcation

---

185 Croce 1915, p. 70.
186 Bonetti 2000, p. 13.
187 Croce 1909, p. 36.
188 Croce 1913, pp. 465–585.
189 Croce 1945, pp. 1–2.
190 Bobbio 1955, p. 102.

Croce carried out among these forms in this way thus constituted physically separated sites: 'the philosopher' and the 'man of politics', to whom he continually referred.

The physical separation between these forms did not fail to pose a problem that the philosopher from Abruzzo tried to solve within the spirit. Although he distinguished between morality and politics, Croce formally ensured the link between them. This distinction was, nevertheless, a concrete and living unity,[191] a unit that was verified insofar as both were 'necessary moments of spiritual life'.[192] But the nexus also indicated the sense in which unification took place. Ethical and moral conscience and economic and political consciousness would share the same practical form, but following the mode of implication of the different degrees of the spirit, the economic and the political, as actions generated by the sense of utility, would be resolved in ethics.

As in the regressive implications of the different degrees of the spirit, the 'ethical spirit has in politics the premise of its activity and also its tool, almost as though it were a body which politics fills with renewed soul and bends to its own will'.[193] Although he expressed this relation between distinct concepts through Hegelian language, the Crocean enterprise was anti-dialectical, since the nexus existent between the different levels of spirit did not constitute a relation of mutual interpenetration and reciprocity, but of unilateral implication of the higher level in the inferior.[194]

If the discursive form was clearly of Hegelian inspiration, the conclusions which the Italian philosopher arrived at distanced him from the German. Understanding the state and morality was, for Croce, a theoretical problem of the purview of philosophy. Questions referring to the orientations of political action would be different. These would be practical issues and concern the politician not the philosopher. Political problems, as well as any practical problem, should be considered as a creative, and therefore personal and individual, enterprise. Croce decisively broke with Hegel on this point, affirming in politics the primacy of the individual over the state.

The affirmation of the autonomy of politics implied not only the distinction between ethics and policy, as analysed above, but also the distinction between the 'philosophy of politics' and the 'empirical science of politics'. Returning to the idea of an identity between philosophy and history, affirmed in his *Logica*

---

191 Croce 1945, p. 2.
192 Croce 1993, p. 241. OT.
193 Croce 1945, pp. 23–4.
194 See Fontana 1993, p. 60.

come scienza del concetto puro (*Logic as the Science of the Pure Concept*),[195] Croce wrote that the purpose of the philosophy of politics was the explanation of the history of political activity 'in its two-fold form – as economic history and merely political history and as ethico-political or moral history'.[196] The science of politics, in turn, would have the objective of establishing the knowledge which could make it quickly accessible to the spirit with a view to action or new inquiries. The procedure that would allow the empirical science of politics to achieve its objectives should be the reduction of historical multiplicity to a small number of 'types and classes', that is, 'Facts are taken in the abstract content ... and deprived of their own life, given by their spiritual form or by individuality'.[197]

Croce's judgement of the empirical science of politics was not, of course, positive, as indeed it was not for any 'empirical science'. He argued that returning to the material critically elaborated by philosophy and historical criticism, the empirical science of politics would empty the living contents of this material and its meaning. This negative judgement was also of a methodological nature: it would serve to prevent philosophy from being contaminated by a common practical philosophy.[198] It would thus be possible to avoid identification between logical truth and political truth, an error that could have as a consequence the absolutisation of practical thinking. But this negative judgement would also serve to warn against the transformation of individual whims and passions into theorems 'of the mechanical science which has made the state and society its objects'.[199] This last error would consist of a blurring of the boundaries between philosophy and praxis, believing that political action is a universal conceptual determination, when in fact such an action can only find its truth in its full individuality.[200]

Taking into account the intellectual environment of his time, and particularly the Italian one, this refusal of a political science was a rejection of the project carried out by Gaetano Mosca and Vilfredo Pareto, among others. Unlike these authors, who are committed to demonstrating the possibility of a knowledge of politics, Croce doubted the potential of a science that proceeded by 'pseudo-concepts' and classifications.[201] The scope he attributed to the empir-

---

195   Croce 1917.
196   Croce 1945, p. 45.
197   Croce 1945, p. 46.
198   When practice is the object of philosophy, this is a 'philosophy of practice'. When practice is the goal of philosophy, this is a mere 'practical philosophy'.
199   Croce 1945, p. 51.
200   See Zarone 1990, p. 89.
201   Croce 1945, p. 52. For Croce, the pure concept is omni- and ultra-representative and does

ical science of politics was very far away, therefore, from the one that Mosca tried to determine. For Croce, the empirical science of politics would have only a value restricted to its 'usefulness as an instrument'.[202] Recognising this instrumental value, it would prevent the science of politics from degenerating into philosophical aphorisms and absolute principles contaminating both philosophy and historiography.

This restriction of the scope and validity of political science reinforced the distinction that Croce carried out between theory and practice, philosophy and politics. Such a distinction and the emphasis it received allowed him to recommend to philosophers to not disturb politics with an inopportune philosophy. For this reason, he even denounced 'philosophical cretinism' and 'philosophical fixation', as Marx had done with parliamentary cretinism.[203] But the distinction also allowed 'to save historical judgment from contamination with practical politics, a contamination which deprives historical judgment of tolerance and fairness'.[204]

Once this distinction between politics and morality was developed in the first section of his *Elementi di politica* (*Elements of Politics*), Croce reviewed in the following section the history of the philosophy of politics so as to make his philosophy of politics the culmination point of all preceding philosophy of politics.[205] The starting point for this could not be anybody, if not Machiavelli, considered as an exponent of 'pure politics' and symbol of a deep crisis in the development of science. According to Croce, Machiavelli was the pioneer of the 'autonomy of politics', announcing for the first time in a clear way the antinomies between ethics and politics.[206]

---

not refer to this or that particular representation or to this or that group of representations. Pseudo-concepts, on the other hand, would be general representations that would simulate a false universality. The empirical sciences would operate from such pseudo-concepts. See Croce 1917, pp. 19–40 and Bonetti 2000, pp. 18–22. The solution elaborated by Croce allowed him to cut the Gordian knot between the *Kulturwissenschaften* and the *Naturwissenschaften* with a stroke of the pen, expelling arbitrarily all the scientific notions of the field of pure knowledge (Garin 1996, p. 23).

202 Croce 1945, p. 51.
203 Croce 1993, p. 281. OT. Cf. Bobbio 1955, p. 105.
204 Croce 1945, p. 56.
205 The *Elementi di politica*, originally published in 1925, was integrated in 1930 into the book *Politics and Morals* along with the *Frammenti di ethtica* (*Fragments of Ethics*), written in 1922. The first section of the *Elementi di politica*, was entitled 'Politica "in nuce"' and the second reference is 'Storia della filosofia della politica' ('History of the Philosophy of Politics'). For the history of this work, see the detailed note of Giuseppe Galasso in Croce 1994, pp. 423–86.
206 Croce 1945, pp. 58–9.

Establishing, on the one hand, knowledge as 'pure' thought and, on the other, policy as 'pure' power and 'pure' utility, he stated at the same time the radical distinction between thought and action, universal and concrete. As a theoretical activity, philosophy would be a disinterested activity confined to pure thought without falling into practice unless it was corrupted and lost its purity. As a practical activity, politics was a place of passions and interests, without ever reaching the level of philosophical truth, unless it ceased to be political and became the object of philosophy.[207]

This intellectual enterprise of Benedetto Croce had a strong impact on the young Gramsci. His admiration for Croce is undeniable, to the point of considering him 'the greatest thinker in Europe at this time'.[208] The important role assigned to the editor of *La Critica* in the constitution of a new conception of the world can be evaluated by the position that he occupied in the discussions of the Club of Moral Life, organised by Gramsci in 1917 to promote the education of the young socialists of Turin. In the letter to the pedagogue Giuseppe Lombardo Radice on the activities of the Club, Gramsci reported the organisation of studies on 'a chapter from something like Croce's *Cultura and vita morale* ... or a short piece from *La Critica* – anything that reflects the influence of the current Idealist movement'.[209]

Placing himself alongside Bendetto Croce and also Giovanni Gentile, the young Gramsci closed ranks against the positivist culture that prevailed within the Italian socialist movement. Gramsci identified himself during the first years of his political life more with the appreciation of human action present in Italian neo-idealism than with the gross economic determinism that had its maximum theoretical expression in the works of Achille Loria and his political representative in the socialist leaders Filippo Turati and Claudio Treves.

Gramsci's characterisation of Treves and his journal *Critica sociale* is clarifying in this regard. Commenting on Croce's dialogue entitled *The Death of Socialism*[210] the Sardinian affirmed that the dissolution of the 'myth' of socialism was necessary. Such a myth was actually a 'superstition'; it was the belief that socialism was a postulate of 'philosophical positivism'. This conception, which was not scientific, but simply mechanical, could be found in the 'theoretical reformism' of Claudio Treves, '[w]hich is nothing more than a pastime of positivist fatalism, whose determinants are energies social relations abstracted from man and will, incomprehensible and absurd: a form of arid mysticism,

---

207   Fontana 1993, p. 9.
208   CF, p. 22. OT.
209   PPW, p. 52.
210   Croce 1993, pp. 147–56.

without the jolts of a passion suffered'.²¹¹ But if Gramsci used Croce's argument it was not to agree with him about 'the death of socialism' but to affirm that it would not be dead as long as 'men of goodwill' continued to live.²¹²

On the political level, Italian neo-idealism also seemed to offer an attractive alternative whether it was against the conservatism of the Catholic Church or the question of the *Mezzogiorno* and Italian modernisation. Against reactionary clericalism, the call by Croce for a life without mythological religion, synthesised in an article from 1915 – *Religione e serenità* – republished by Gramsci himself in 1917, was considered a programme for modern man.²¹³ In prison, he did not spare his praise for this view: 'This point still seems to me today, the greatest contribution to world culture given by modern Italian intellectuals, it seems to me a civil achievement that should not be lost'.²¹⁴ It was as part of an anticlerical and lay movement that Gramsci felt close to neo-idealism.

With regard to the controversial issue of the *Mezzogiorno*, rather than the traditional North-South dichotomy, which found its supporters even among socialists of the time, Giovanni Gentile, and especially Bendetto Croce, they seemed to offer a more nuanced version of the historical constitution of the differences between the two regions. Concerning this question, Croce and Gentile were interpreted by Gramsci as a theoretical expression of the *Risorgimento* and of a bourgeois revolution that had to be taken to its last consequences to solve the southern issue. Gramsci's interpretation, however, went far beyond the point where Croce and Gentile would have liked to stop. It politically radicalised what for them were only timid ideas. At the point where he arrived, Gramsci no longer had the company of his masters.²¹⁵

The political-intellectual formation of the young Gramsci occurred within the self-styled Italian 'idealist renaissance'. But to assert, therefore, an identity of Gramsci with neo-idealism at this stage of his political-intellectual development would certainly be an exaggeration. Gramsci, however, shared some common themes with this neo-idealism and, in particular, the critique of positivism and naturalism.²¹⁶ It would not be an exaggeration to say, therefore, that it was through this current that the young Sardinian affirmed his own political and intellectual identity.

---

211   CF, p. 25. OT.
212   CF, p. 26.
213   Croce 1999, pp. 29–32.
214   LC, p. 466. OT.
215   See Losurdo 1997, p. 21.
216   Garin 1996, p. 354.

It was the impact provoked by the Russian Revolution of 1917 that made Gramsci begin to move away from Croce and Gentile. The withdrawal coincided with a second phase of Croce's relationship with Marxism, whose beginning can be dated to the aforementioned dialogue with respect to the 'death of socialism'. From the outset of World War I and, mainly, from the Russian Revolution onwards, this position was radicalised, developing into a frank antagonism.[217] In this new phase, Croce's goal was no longer the revision of Marxism, but its liquidation. Marx, affirmed the author of *Historical Materialism and the Economics of Karl Marx* in the 1917 Preface, was no longer a master deserving of homage. The war had shown the insufficiency of a conception based on class struggle. It was consequently necessary for Gramsci to increase the distance from his old mentor.

Croce's intellectual evolution was a demonstration of the trajectory of revisionism. Having begun his intellectual career influenced by Marxism, he had distanced himself sufficiently to be seen as an adversary. The anti-socialism of the Italian critic was already evident in *Cultura e vita morale* (*Culture and Moral Life*). After 1917, this anti-socialism had become a form of radical anti-communism. In his *Storia d'Europa nel secolo decimonono* (*History of Europe in the Nineteenth Century*), published in 1932 and conceived as an exaltation of the liberal bourgeoisie, communism was one of the 'opposing religions' to ethical principles and liberal politics, which had to be defeated so that these principles could be fully realised.[218]

In the shift from the anti-socialism of *Culture and Moral Life* to the anticommunism of *History of Europe*, it is possible to identify a clear radicalisation and a marked politicisation of the theoretical discourse. It was not just communism that threatened freedom. Historical materialism itself constituted a threat, since its 'materialist and determinist metaphysics' would lead the communists to wait for the crisis and 'cling rigidly and intransigently to the side of the democrats and liberals and help them, indeed, to seize power, but with the tacit understanding that immediately after that they would assault and overthrow and destroy them, as they had done with their common opponents'.[219]

A short text, written in 1928 for the American newspaper *St. Louis Post Dispatch* and published in Italy in 1934, sums up the belligerent attitude taken by Croce in relation to Marxism. The title of this text was already a veritable programme: 'Contro le sopravvivenze del materialism storico' ('Against

---

217 See Finocchiaro 2002, p. 9.
218 Croce 1933, pp. 35–44 and 425–38. See also Badaloni and Muscetta 1990, pp. 89–92.
219 Croce 1933, p. 208.

the Survival of Historical Materialism').[220] In the first paragraph, the author explained his purpose:

> If I were allowed to address a recommendation to historians, political theorists and the publicists of our day ... I would say that they should be careful to prevent their judgments and reasoning from being infiltrated by concepts derived from 'historical materialism' and to be diligent to expel them when they have entered and persisted.[221]

The reasons for this recommendation were theoretical and political. Croce already considered that historical materialism had been refuted and superseded by philosophical criticism. Implicitly, he assumed that he himself had carried out this mission to its end. But survivals and superstitions derived from historical materialism still persisted in public opinion. Particularly dangerous was Marx's supposed subversion of the Hegelian principle where he had converted the idea into matter and, specifically, in economic matters, which would assume 'the place of the ancient God and the character of the last and only reality'.[222]

For Croce, Hegelian panlogism had been converted into Marxian paneconomism. All thoughts, feelings, moral volitions, all science and art, all religions, traditions or customs would be for Marxism mere appearance or illusion, only the 'superstructure'.[223] In doing so, Marxism, according to the editor of *La Critica*, had manifested its radical opposition to the ethical and political conceptions of liberalism and even to the whole evolution of Western thought.

The political character of the accusation was reinforced by the concepts of historical materialism that Croce thought were most urgent to remove from common opinion: 'ruling class', 'bourgeoisie' and 'class struggle'. And he felt it necessary to depart from these concepts in order to be able to assert that 'freedom is not a function of the bourgeoisie or of another economy, but of the human soul and its deepest needs; and it has no quality or economic origin, but moral and religious one and is, to put it all in one word, the modern form of Christianity'.[224]

To the extent that Croce assumed this belligerent position, Gramsci distanced himself. But it was not a simple break. At the end of the 1910s, Gram-

---

220   Croce 1934. OT.
221   Croce 1934, p. 4.
222   Croce 1934, p. 5. Cf. Martelli 2001, pp. 58–62.
223   Croce 1934, p. 5.
224   Croce 1934, p. 10.

sci nourished the project of dialectically surpassing Italian neo-idealist philosophy, in the same way as Marx and Engels had done with German idealism.[225] Such a project was, at that time, a political project. What was involved was to overcome the political limits with which neo-idealist philosophy had condemned itself due to its opposition to the Russian Revolution.[226]

Gramsci's attitude toward neo-idealists, and especially toward Benedetto Croce, with whom he had identified more, evolved over the early years of the 1920s. Little by little, references to Croce practically disappeared from his writings, resurfacing however in 1926, in the important text *Alcuni temi della quistione meridionale* (*Some Aspects of the Southern Question*). But his judgement was now far from positive. In this text, the communist leader attributed to the Southern intellectuals, Benedetto Croce and Giustino Fortunato, a key role in agrarian bloc formed by the 'great amorphous disintegrated mass of the peasantry; the intellectuals of the petty and medium rural bourgeoisie; and the big landowners and great intellectuals'.[227] The functions of organisation, centralisation and domination within this bloc would fit the 'big landowners in the political field and the great intellectuals in the ideological field'. But it was in the ideological field that centralisation was more effective, hence the extremely negative judgement of the southern intellectuals: 'Naturally, it is in the ideological sphere that the centralization is most effective and precise. Giustino Fortunato Benedetto Croce thus represent the keystones of the Southern system and, in a certain sense, are the two major figures of Italian reaction'.[228]

The criticism developed in *Some Aspects of the Southern Question* was based on Croce's position as the intellectual organiser of a politically reactionary movement. This text was published in 1930 in the newspaper *Lo Stato operaio*, but it is very likely that Croce was not aware of it when in 1947 he reviewed the *Letters from Prison* published by the publisher Einaudi. It was in this review that he sought to appropriate the legacy of Gramsci who had strayed from Marxism and stated that 'as a man of thought he was one of ours, one of those who in the first decades of the century in Italy was to form a philosophical and historical mentality adequate to the problems of the present'.[229]

But he quickly changed his mind after reading the first volumes of the writings published since 1948. Already on the occasion of the publication of *His-*

---

[225] See Losurdo 1997, p. 31.
[226] On Croce's and Gentile's position in relation to the Russian Revolution, see Martelli 2001, pp. 175–81.
[227] SPW, p. 454.
[228] Ibid.
[229] Croce 1947a, p. 86. OT.

torical Materialism and the Philosophy of Benedetto Croce, the Abruzzian critic tried to reduce the impact of Gramsci's opposition to him. Croce said that the launch of the book had been preceded by 'daring ads' for which Gramsci, a 'serious man', could not be held responsible. Such ads, however, did not correspond to the content of the book: a set of provisory notes destined to be abandoned later on.[230]

The limits of these notes not only stemmed from the adverse conditions in which they were produced, but, according to Croce, were inherent in the Gramscian research programme itself: the reconstruction of a 'philosophy of praxis'. Such a programme subordinated thought to a 'practical desire', he wrote. In this way 'criticism of that particular philosophical work' – that of Croce himself, who avoided claiming that he was the target of criticism – became an 'empty discourse', leaving only the contrast of one practical desire to another practical desire, a contrast that was practical-political and not philosophical.[231]

Such a judgement about Gramsci's work would be repeated in a commentary written in 1950 in which Croce protested against what he believed to be the excessive and undeserved repercussion of the Gramscian *Notebooks*, stating that, contrary to what many said

> Gramsci could not have created a new thought and complete the portentous [intellectual] revolution attributed to him because ... his intention was solely to found in Italy a political party that has nothing to do with the dispassionate search for truth.[232]

Obviously, what troubled Croce, as he showed in the reviews that he published on some volumes of Gramsci's works, was the treatment that he himself received.[233] But the Gramscian criticism, and this he could not deny, was motivated by the very position of the organiser of contemporary culture that the director of *La Critica* attributed to himself. It was from an investigation into the question of intellectuals and of Croce's place in Italian political life that Gramsci intended to initiate his research in prison, as already demonstrated in the letter-programme addressed to Tatiana in March 1927 in which the project of a *für ewig* work was announced. The Croce question, therefore, was developed in prison as part of an investigation into the political history of Italian intellectuals.

---

230 Croce 1948, p. 78. OT.
231 Ibid.
232 Croce 1950, p. 231. OT.
233 Cf. Croce 1948, 1949a and 1949c.

The treatment given to Croce in the *Notebooks* was comprehensive. Croce was part of a study of intellectuals; he occupied an important place in the investigation of the theory of history and historiography; he became the central object of a comprehensive critique of revisionism of European Marxist currents and his place as leader of these currents; and he was the focus of research on the renewal of the philosophy of praxis as an exponent of a philosophy which had to be overcome. The hypotheses drawn by Gramsci before his arrest were, thus, resumed and expanded, receiving new orientations.

The perception of Croce's place in European culture was reinforced by a letter from Sorel to the editor of *La Critica*, in which the French philosopher revealed that Eduard Bernstein was inspired 'to some extent' by his works. The influence on Bernstein was exaggerated by Gramsci in a letter dated 18 April 1932, in which he stated that 'Bernstein himself wrote that he had been induced to rework all of his philosophical and economic thought after reading Croce's essays'.[234] The judgement about the influence of Croce on German Social Democracy was certainly exaggerated and revealed an overly Italian bias of this question on Gramsci's part. But it is important because it allows us to understand the real scope of the criticism of the philosopher. According to Gramsci, Croce was the 'leader of the revisionist tendencies: the early phase (at the end of the nineteenth century, he inspired Bernstein and Sorel) and now the second phase, which is no longer the moment of revisionism but of liquidation (ethico-political history in opposition to economic-juridical history)'.[235] To face him meant, therefore, to confront one of the main exponents of revisionism and one who had become one of his main opponents. Criticism of Croce was part of the 'struggle for hegemonies'.

The Italian Marxist was not unaware, however, of the specificity of this struggle and of the ideological combat. In political and military struggle, the tactic 'to break through at the points of least resistance in order to be able to assault the strongest point with maximum forces that have been precisely made available by the elimination of the weaker auxiliaries'. But on the ideological front 'the defeat of the auxiliaries and the minor hangers-on is of all but negligible importance. Here it is necessary to engage battle with the most eminent of one's adversaries'. A 'new science', and this is the case of Marxism, 'proves its efficacy and vitality when it demonstrates that it is capable of confronting the great champions of tendencies opposed to it and when it either resolves by

---

234 LC, p. 609. OT.
235 PNIII, Q8, § 225, p. 371.

its own means the vital questions which they have posed or demonstrates, in peremptory fashion, that these questions are false problems'.[236]

Marxism would not be given the right to choose its opponents on the ideological front. They would have to have been previously defined. And Croce was a principal opponent. It was inside Notebook 10, entitled *La filosofia di Benedetto Croce* (*The Philosophy of Benedetto Croce*), that Gramsci brought together and reorganised the Miscellaneous Notebooks concerning the Abruzzian critic, facing in this way his adversary. The Notebook is divided into two parts, the second of which includes the largest part of the notes. Three are three subtitles that organise this section: *'Introduzione allo studio della filosofia'* (Introduction to the study of Philosophy)) (Notebook 10/II, §§ 6, 9, 10, 12, 13, 17, 21, 24, 28, 35, 43, 44, 46, 48, 40, 52 and 54); *'Punti per lo studio dell'economia'* ('Points for the study of the economy') (Notebook 10/II, §§ 15, 23, 32, 37, 53 and 57); and *'Punti per um saggio su B. Croce'* ('Points for an essay on B. Croce') (Notebook 10/II, §§ 11, 14, 16, 18, 22, 26, 29, 31, 33, 34, 36, 38, 39, 41, 45, 47, 49, 51, 56, 58, 59, 60 and 61).

In the introductory notes to the study of philosophy, Gramsci developed the project of the reconstruction of the philosophy of praxis that had its parallel in that section of Notebook 11 entitled *'Appunti per uma introduione e avviamento allo studio della filosofia e della storia della cultura'* ('Notes for an introduction and beginning of the study of philosophy and history of culture'). The critical angle to Croce in these notes in Notebook 10 was philosophical, but the object of Gramsci's criticism was not the philosophy of the Crocean spirit *per se*, as Dora Kanoussi alerts us.[237] This is not, therefore, a study on the whole of neo-idealist thought: 'What he analyzes in detail and refutes with much attention and depth are the criticisms of the philosophy of praxis, criticisms that induce him to revise his own philosophy of praxis'.[238] Through this criticism, Gramsci sought to translate neo-idealism into the language of the philosophy of praxis, that is, to surpass its philosophy through the critical development of Marxism.[239]

In the Notebooks, overcoming Crocean philosophy became part of the philosophical programme of Marxism. Gramsci, in a note B present in *The Philosophy of B. Croce* in Notebook 10, recalled an article from his youth, published in 1917, in which he affirmed that 'Crocean philosophy could be the premise of a

---

236   SPN, Q11, § 22, p. 433.
237   Kanoussi 2000, p. 67.
238   Kanoussi 2000, pp. 67–8.
239   The notes on economy are, for the most part, directed to Croce's rejection in *Historical Materialism and Marxist Economy* of the law of value and the tendency for the rate of profit to fall. The theme is discussed in Bianchi 2002.

revival of the philosophy of praxis in our time'. The question, he argued, could not have been adequately developed due to the fact that he was still 'tendentially Crocean'.[240] In prison he considered this resumption of the philosophy of praxis as something that could no longer be postponed. The work of critiquing classical German philosophy by Marx and Engels should be continued through the criticism of Benedetto Croce's thinking. For Gramsci:

> This is the only historically fruitful way of determining a resumption of the philosophy of praxis, of elevating this conception that for the necessity of immediate political life has become 'vulgarised', to the extent that it should affect the solution of the most complex tasks that the current development of the struggle proposes, that is, the creation of a new culture that has the mass characteristics of the Protestant Reformation and the French Enlightenment and the characteristics of classicism of Greek culture and of the Italian Renaissance, a culture that, taking up the words of Carducci, synthesises Massimiliano [sic] Robespierre and Emanuele [sic] Kant, politics and philosophy, in a dialectical unity within a social group no longer merely French or German, but European and worldwide.[241]

In the Italian context, the critical appropriation of the German philosophical heritage meant a settling of accounts with Croce. The 'anti-x' advocated by Labriola,[242] received, in one of its possible translations – the struggle against the idealistic appropriation of Marxism – in the form of an 'anti-Croce':

> One must make this reckoning in the broadest and most profound way possible. Such a work of this type, an *anti-Croce* that in the modern cultural atmosphere could have the meaning and importance that the *Anti-Dühring* had for the generation preceding the world war, it would deserve a whole group of men devoting ten years of activity to it.[243]

Confronting Croce was thus to actively confront the idealist critique of Marxism, that is, to face the criticism with a philosophical programme of overcom-

---

240   As Gerratana explains in the critical edition of the *Notebooks*, one can easily see in the reading of the text published on 11 February 1917, that there is no mention of Crocean philosophy as the premise of a resumption of Marxism (Gerretana 1997, p. 21).
241   Q10 / I, § 11, p. 1233. OT.
242   Labriola 2000, p. 233.
243   Q10 / I, § 11, p. 1234. OT.

ing one's own idealism and of strengthening historical materialism. Gramsci thus rejected the defeatist position assumed by Max Adler and Otto Bauer in relation to idealism that implied an uncritical absorption of Kantianism. The defiant attitude towards Croce was an active response to the political consequences of his philosophy and his cultural militancy.

The notes gathered together under the heading 'Points for an essay on B. Croce' or the like had a different purpose. Gramsci discussed in them the relationship of Croce with his time from an eminently political perspective. The research here was based on the political history of intellectuals. In these paragraphs, Gramsci denounced the reactionary character of his intellectual enterprise. Establishing his political significance, the conservative historicism of this author was reduced to its ideological dimension.[244]

Certainly, Croce would not agree with this politicisation of his thinking, and even less so with the claim that his philosophy had a highly practical motivation. His radical distinction between ethics and politics, already present in his analysis of Machiavelli's work, developed through a clear division between thought and action, philosophy and ideology.[245] Such a split allowed the critic to assert the pure character of philosophy and thought that was presented as the place of the universal, as opposed to a politics that was affirmed as the place of particular interests and passions.

Gramsci denounced this split between thought and action and affirmed several times that Croce's attitude in his texts should not be considered 'as a philosophical judgment but as a political act of immediate practical significance'.[246] The conclusions that this philosopher intended to olympically attribute to a 'historical-philosophical judgment' were not but an 'act of will' with a 'practical end'.[247] It was this political characterisation of the historical-philosophical reflection of the neo-idealist critic that allowed Gramsci to write in Notebook 12 that 'Croce in particular feels himself closely linked to Aristotle and Plato, but he does not conceal, on the other hand, his links with senators Agnelli and Benni, and it is precisely here that one can discern the most significant character of Croce's philosophy'.[248]

The target of the criticism did not like this statement and complained about it in a small review of the book *Gli intellettuali e l'organizzazione della cul-*

---

244 Kanoussi 2000, p. 67.
245 Croce 1994, pp. 249–97. On Croce's analysis of Machiavelli and the Gramscian reading of Machiavelli, see Fontana 1993 and Medici 1990, pp. 161–207.
246 Q10 / II, § 41, p. 1291. OT.
247 LC, p. 384. OT.
248 GR, Q12, § 1, p. 303.

tura (*Intellectuals and the Organisation of Culture*).[249] He insinuated on this occasion that Gramsci's text might have been adulterated by the editors – 'I suspected an error committed in the transcription of Gramsci's text' – and said he knew that Senator Agnelli was the owner of Fiat, but that he did not know Benni and protested against the assertion that it was in the relation with these characters that the 'most relevant character' of his philosophy should be found.[250]

Gramsci's text should not be taken literally, as with many other texts he wrote. But it had a profound political significance, for it indicated the place of Croce's philosophy in the politics of the time as 'an extremely effective instrument of hegemony, although from time to time it was in contrast with this or that government'.[251] Crocean philosophy was a sophisticated philosophy of reaction. It was the philosophy of the modernisation of Italian capitalism through molecular transformations. The strongly political character of this thought was clearly evident in the aforementioned theoretical crusade against Marxism and in his review of Italian and European history. To position oneself against this philosophy was to combat the hegemony of Crocean thought.

The sense of Gramsci's criticism allows us to understand in greater depth that which is understood as the 'struggle of hegemonies' in the 'philosophical front'. It is not, as Badaloni has pointed out, a mere clash of ideas, but a confrontation of behaviours and conceptions which are characteristic of two different modes of production.[252] The 'struggle of hegemonies' comprises the conflict of rationalities that express different civilisational forms.[253]

In this confrontation, to settle accounts with the Crocean historiographic project was fundamental. For Gramsci, this enterprise of the editor of *La Critica* clearly stressed the change of attitude towards historical materialism. In a letter to Tatiana dated 9 May 1932, Gramsci summarised Crocean historiography as an attempt to complete the revision of Marxism that began at the end of the nineteenth century by the elaboration of a 'theory of history as ethico-political history as opposed to economic-juridical history that represented the theory derived from historical materialism after the revisionist process which it had suffered through the work of Croce himself'.[254] Gramsci's attitude to the notion

---

249 Croce 1949.
250 Croce 1949, p. 95.
251 LC, p. 481. OT.
252 Badaloni 1978, p. 11.
253 Dias 1996a, p. 10.
254 LC, p. 619. OT.

of 'ethico-political history', as in many other cases, expressed not a simple negation, but a complex critical appropriation of the Crocean concept by means of a translation operation that removed the notion from its original context and inserted it, in a subordinated way, into a new theoretical body. Originally circumscribed by the philosophy of the spirit, the history of moral or civil life was, for the philosopher, 'the only history, history par excellence'.[255] This history was conceived as an historiographical alternative to both deterministic naturalism, of which historical materialism would be a variant, and the ethical utilitarianism prevalent in the nineteenth century.

Croce's target was, above all, historical materialism, clearly indicating that his enterprise was no longer of a revisionist type, like that carried out in *Historical Materialism and Marxist Economy*, but an enterprise whose objective was the theoretical and political liquidation of Marxism. It was already beyond the time in which he stressed the validity of revaluing the 'economic substrate' of history which, according to him, was the main contribution of Marxism as a 'canon of historical interpretation'.[256] Now, according to the director of the journal *La Critica*, it was necessary to constitute a history that encoded 'in moral life, its principle and its object'.[257] Ethico-political history was thus presented as a reaction to economism and to the fatalistic mechanics identified with Marxism.

The moral history advocated by Croce would not, however, have the objective of opposing the history of the past to what it should have been. To avoid this confusion between the moral and a 'moralistic history', Croce adopted the expression 'ethico-political history'. He also distinguished the latter from the French *historie de la cvilisation* as well that of the German *Staatsgeschichte*. The first, born in the environment of the Enlightenment, would have been reduced to a 'history of intellectualism, positive science and the progressive collapse of religious beliefs or and their superstitions'.[258] The German history of the state, *Staatsgeschichte*, in turn, conceived this as the only ethical and true reality. For the author of *Politics and Morals*,

> Moral or ethico-political history must free itself from these defects of theory and of this contingent pressure, correcting itself and conceiving as an object not only the state and the state government and the expansion of the state, but as well as what is outside the State, cooperates with it, seeks

---

255 Croce 1994, p. 318. OT.
256 Croce 1915, p. 46.
257 Croce 1994, p. 320. OT.
258 Croce 1994, pp. 323–4.

to modify it, overthrow it and replace it: the formation of moral institutions in its broadest sense, including religious institutions and revolutionary sects, the feelings, customs, fantasies and myths of tendency and practical content.[259]

Conceived in this way, ethico-political history reached what was for Croce the 'very life of the state'. It was, therefore, within the scope of this ethico-political history that other historical dimensions (economy, culture, etc.) would find their resolution. It was this attempt to reduce the whole story to ethico-political history to which Gramsci's criticism turned. Such a procedure would result in no more than a '"speculative" history or philosophy'.[260]

This speculative character strongly marks the study *History of Europe in the Nineteenth Century*,[261] in which all history was reduced to the history of 'freedom'. But in this reduction, Gramsci said, Croce 'confuses "freedom" as a philosophical principle and speculative concept and freedom as ideology, that is, as a practical instrument of government, an element of a hegemonic morality'. But to rebuild its role as a 'practical instrument of government' it would be necessary to understand it from the practical nexus on which it was founded, that is, to recover in the ideology of freedom the very 'dialectic of history', the moments of 'strength and struggle'.[262]

At the same time that he was engaged in a critique of the political presuppositions of Crocean criticism, or precisely because of this, Gramsci was open to an appropriation of the very concept of 'ethico-political history' as an '"empirical tool" of historical research'.[263] Gramsci's statement has a distinctly provocative tone, in that it was Croce himself who stated that historical materialism would have value as an 'empirical canon of historical inquiry':

> Credit must therefore, at the very least, be given to Croce's thought as an instrumental value and in this respect it may be said that it has forcefully drawn attention to the importance of facts of culture and thought in the development of history, to the function of great intellectuals in the organic life of civil society and the state, to the moment of hegemony and consent as the necessary form of the concrete historical bloc.[264]

---

259 Croce 1994, p. 325.
260 LC, p. 619. OT.
261 Croce 1999.
262 LC, pp. 619–20. OT.
263 GR, Q10 / I, §12, p. 195.
264 GR, Q10 / I, §12, p. 195. See also LC, p. 661.

But it was not as a canon of historical inquiry that Gramsci appropriated this concept as part of his theory of hegemony. A notion that within the philosophy of the Crocean spirit presented itself as an historiographical key was translated by Gramsci into a notion of the 'science and art of politics', as he liked to say. Based on the assumption that history, politics and philosophy identify themselves, Gramsci interpreted the Crocean construction of an historiographical alternative to historical materialism as an intervention in the debate of the period. It was thus possible to retranslate that political intervention which Croce had raised in the form of a historiography into politics once again. Commenting on this political-historiographic enterprise carried out by the philosopher of Pescasseroli, Gramsci wrote:

> The approximation of the two terms 'ethics' and 'politics' to indicate the most recent Crocean historiography is the expression of the requirements around which Crocean historical thinking revolves: ethics refers to the activity of civil society, to hegemony; *politics* refers to the initiative and coercion of the governing state.[265]

Now, this judgement is of great importance not only for a theory of hegemony, which has often been emphasised, but also for a theory of the state in its expanded sense, as will be seen later. Within the framework of a Gramscian theory of revolution and of the state, the concept of ethico-political history gained a materialistic content and is clearly opposed to the moderate perspective that guided its original meaning.

The appropriation of the theory of ethico-political history was not done in an uncritical way. Gramsci was suspicious of the idea that the historiography of the southern philosopher was truly ethico-political. According to the Sardinian Marxist, Croce had failed both in his attempt to overcome both economism and mechanicism and in his attempt to rid modern thought of every trait of transcendence and theology. On the one hand, the Crocean reduction of the philosophy of praxis to an empirical canon of historical interpretation, calling historians' attention to the importance of economic facts did nothing more than reduce it to a form of 'economism', reducing the distance between Croce and Loria.[266] On the other hand, by reducing the whole of history to ethico-political history, Croce 'created a new form of rhetorical history; its present form is, in fact, speculative history'.[267]

---

265   Q10 / II, § 41, p. 1302. OT.
266   Q10 / I, § 13, p. 1236. OT.
267   LC, p. 620. OT.

It was not, therefore, in a schematic way that Gramsci accepted the theory of ethico-political history, nor was it inserted mechanically within the philosophy of praxis. The critical appropriation occurred as a transformation. For this, the theory of ethico-political history was withdrawn from the interior of Croce's speculative historiography and translated into a realistic language of the philosophy of praxis.[268] Gramsci thus appropriated not the whole Crocean conception of history but some of its elements, inserting them in an organic way into a different theory from the original and thus assigning it a different meaning.

The importance that Gramsci imputed to the thought of Croce and the necessity of realising this procedure of translation is shown in the comparison that he established between the political processes on which the concept of ethico-political history drew and the historical process of the transition to socialism in the Soviet Union under the leadership of Lenin:

> In the same period in which Croce made up his supposed club [to hit with], the philosophy of praxis in its greatest modern theoretician [i.e. Lenin] was elaborated in the same sense and the moment of 'hegemony' or of cultural direction was systematically revalued in opposition to some mechanistic and fatalistic conceptions of economism.[269]

This passage is key to the reconstruction of the concept of hegemony in Gramscian thought, but, in spite of being exhaustively quoted, it is seldom analysed with the necessary care. The construction of this statement by Gramsci was very careful and he was aware of its repercussions both for state theory and for the theory of revolution. With regard to state theory, he argued that the concept of hegemony did not contradict the theory of the coercive state, but complemented it. The functions of domination proper to political society would not be cancelled by the functions of political leadership that would have a privileged place in civil society. Hence the need for a theory that accounts for the state in its integral or organic meaning, that is, a theory that explains all state functions and not only domination/coercion or leadership/consensus.

Through the translation of the Crocean 'ethico-political history' into the language of the philosophy of praxis, Gramsci constructed a theory of hegemony that constituted a moment of a theory of revolution. Speculative historicism was thus superseded by a 'realistic historicism'[270] in which the automatic

---

268 On the translation of Crocean categories by Gramsci, see Frosini 2003, pp. 136–7.
269 LC, p. 616. Cf. Q10 / I, § 12, p. 1235.
270 Q10 / I, p. 1208. OT.

movement of the thesis ceded ground to the struggle of antagonistic social forces. Instead of quiet prediction, which constantly reaffirmed the thesis, the certainty that only struggle can be predicted scientifically.[271] The theory of hegemony was itself a moment of the theory of revolution and not a theory of reformism, as has often been read.

---

271 Q11, §15, P. 1403. OT.

CHAPTER 4

Structure/Superstructure

In the early 1950s, a learned historian conscientious of his profession protested against what he thought to be an underestimation of Marx's historical work. He referred to the profusion of studies developed at that time about his philosophy, politics and economics, while works of the calibre of *The Class Struggle in France* and *The Eighteenth Brumaire of Louis Bonaparte* passed almost unnoticed.[1] In his defence of a revaluation of these works, this historian did not cease to blame Engels for the subaltern place they occupied. In fact, in the 'Introduction to the German edition of 1895' of *The Class Struggle in France*, Engels led readers to believe that these historical works were nothing more than practical applications of theories formulated elsewhere.[2]

More than sixty years after this wise protest, many things have changed. Whether by historians, or by those interested in theorising a Marxist conception of the state, or politics, these previously underestimated works have been revalued.[3] But Krieger's criticism is still relevant. It is not uncommon for authors today to still promote a separation between the historical texts of Marx and the so-called methodological texts, or programmatic texts, converting him now into a philosopher, a historian, or a political activist.

A different, and even opposite, attitude is evident in the work of Gramsci. Throughout, it is possible to perceive a tenacious attempt to create a fusion between those materials of the work of Marx that resulted from methodological reflection (such as the 'Preface of 1859' and *The Poverty of Philosophy*) and those that came from concrete historical and political analysis (mainly *The Eighteenth Brumaire of Louis Bonaparte*). The operation carried out by Gramsci in order to affirm a non-economical reading of Marx's methodological texts was carried out through the mediation of his historical texts.

On more than one occasion, Engels, unjustly accused by Krieger, noted the importance of historical works for the understanding of Marx's theory and, in particular, the importance of *The Eighteenth Brumaire of Louis Bonaparte*.[4] And Benedetto Croce, echoing these comments of Marx's friend, used them in his

---

1 Krieger 1953, p. 381.
2 See MECW, Vol. 27, p. 506.
3 Cf. Codato and Perissinotto 2001 and Codato 2005.
4 See in this regard Engels's letters dated 21 September 1890 and 25 January 1894. See MECW, Vol. 49, p. 36 and Vol. 50, p. 267.

polemic against 'the alleged reduction of history to the economic factor'.[5] This observation was appropriated by Gramsci and in an ironic way was directed against Croce himself, stating the need to evaluate his thought 'not for what it professes to be but for what it really is and shows itself to be in concrete historical works'.[6]

Thus, a statement made earlier was repeated in a much clearer context for the problems dealt with here. Soon after criticising the pretension to reduce all political and ideological fluctuation to a mere manifestation of the structure, Gramsci recommended combating it with concrete political and historical works, stressing: 'Especially important, in this respect, are *The 18th Brumaire* and the writings on the Eastern Question but also others (*Revolution and Counter-Revolution in Germany*, *The Civil War in France*, and minor works)'.[7] Gramsci was categorical in stating that 'An analysis of these works allows one to get a better grasp of Marx's historical method, integrating, illuminating and interpreting the theoretical affirmations scattered throughout his works'.[8]

The merger promoted by Gramsci between methodology and concrete history was of such a form that the 'cautions' Marx introduced in his historical and political analysis penetrated the methodological formulation through the affirmation of the human will. That this will was not absent from the Marxian analysis there is no doubt. What about the first pages of *The Class Struggle in France*? Only after analysing the different class fractions and, especially that of the financial aristocracy, only after explaining the fiscal crisis of the state, only after exposing the 'sordid interests' that moved the different parliamentary cliques, only after that did the economic crisis appear.[9] The words were carefully chosen by Marx: the well-known world economic events that took place in the year 1848 – the agricultural crisis and the general crisis of commerce and industry in England – 'accelerated' the general discontent.[10] They did not create or produce, but precipitated a process that had its own temporality and existence, creating a new and potentially explosive singularity.

The richness of the interpretative tools existing in these works of concrete historical study is invaluable. There is nothing more just than promoting the revaluation of these texts. It is not only a matter of inserting them into histor-

---

5   Croce 1915, p. 17.
6   GR, Q10 / I, §12, p. 195.
7   PN2, Q7, §24, p. 173.
8   PN2, Q7, §24, pp. 173–4.
9   MECW, Vol. 10, p. 52.
10 Ibid.

ical studies referring to the themes addressed by them. That, strictly speaking, would not be even the most important. What is important is to find the true methodological value in them, verifying how those sharp formulations of theoretical and programmatic texts took flexible forms in historical and political analyses.

It was through the French Revolution that history entered into Marxian reflection. The marked influence that this revolution exerted on Marx's work is well known and those who have read his youthful writings will find a large number of references in them. For the circle of young German intellectuals that Marx frequented in the early 1840s, the French Revolution was a model and if they had seen Napoleon in the Rhineland they would not have hesitated to say that they had witnessed the 'spirit of the world' riding by them on horseback.

In the summer of 1843, Marx devoted himself to studying the history of this revolution. Mignet, Thiers, Condorcet, Madame Roland, and Madame de Staël were among his readings at the time and it is well known that in 1845 he planned to write a work on bourgeois society and communist revolution whose first chapter would be devoted 'to the history of the modern state, or to the French Revolution'.[11] Such a work never came to light. Nor did he write, or at least we have no knowledge of such, the history of the Convention, as he once intended to do.[12] The absence of a definitive work in this respect does not indicate, however, the absence of a reflection on the subject. This occurred, to a large extent, as part of an elaboration on social transformation. Why did Germany not follow the French example?, Marx inquired in one of his youthful texts. How are revolutions born and develop?, he asked himself in 1848 and in later years.

Thus, in his methodological or programmatic writings, when thinking about revolution, Marx fundamentally took the French Revolution as a reference. This model was applied to the field of historical interpretation, that is, in his study of the causes of revolution and also in his outline of a *mechanics* of the revolution, that is, of the various moments of the articulation of antagonistic social forces within the revolutionary process itself, moments that would be synthesised in the Marxian formula of the *permanent revolution*.[13]

The terrain that will be explored here is the first, the theoretical space defined by the attempt to create a mode of historical interpretation. The methodological and programmatic texts in which this mode was designed are

---

11   MECW, Vol. 4, p. 666.
12   McLellan 1990, p. 119.
13   Cf. Bianchi 2007b.

already quite familiar, beginning with *The Communist Manifesto*. This text, written in collaboration with Friedrich Engels between the end of 1847 and the first months of 1848 had a clear political objective. The *Manifesto* had been commissioned by the Congress of the Communist League and had to contain a 'detailed theoretical and practical programme of the Party', according to Marx and Engels in the preface to the German edition of 1872.[14] The links established in this programme between the upcoming revolution and the French Revolution of 1789 are evident and draw attention in the proposed interpretative scheme. The *Manifesto* says:

> ... the means of production and of exchange, on whose foundation the bourgeoisie built itself up, were generated in feudal society. At a certain stage in the development of these means of production and of exchange, the conditions under which feudal society produced and exchanged, the feudal organisation of agriculture and manufacturing industry, in one word, the feudal relations of property became no longer compatible with the already developed productive forces; they became so many fetters. They had to be burst asunder; they were burst asunder. Into their place stepped free competition, accompanied by a social and political constitution adapted to it, and by the economical and political sway of the bourgeois class.[15]

The formulation underwent further developments denoting the advance of Marx's research. In the *Manifesto* the central contradiction was still located in the relation between the development of the means of production and the relations of ownership, which nevertheless reveals a legal conception of social relations. But although it is not a completely mature statement, it is striking that it resembles the very famous passage written by Marx years later in the 'Preface of 1859' to the *Contribution to the Critique of Political Economy*. The juridical conception of social relations was, in this new text, left behind and the contradiction presented was that which occurred between the development of the productive forces and the relations of production. According to Marx:

> At a certain stage of development, the material productive forces of society come into conflict with the existing relations of production or this merely expresses the same thing in legal terms with the property rela-

---

14   MECW, Vol. 23, p. 174.
15   MECW, Vol. 6, p. 489.

tions within the framework of which they have operated hitherto, From forms of development of the productive forces these relations turn into their fetters. Then begins an era of social revolution.[16]

The crudeness of these formulas facilitated their dogmatic appropriation by a part of the nascent socialist movement and its consolidation in an economist and evolutionist version that had among its authors exponents of the Second International. This type of appropriation achieved paradigmatic status in the version developed by Karl Kautsky. In his well-known *Der Weg zur Macht* (*The Road to Power*), this conception appears in a crystalline way. In it, the ideological leader of German social democracy described how the development of capitalism had converted the working class into the foundation of social life and the bourgeoisie into something useless for the development of production. The proletariat had been transformed, according to Kautsky, into the largest class and the force on which state power was underpinned. It only lacked consciousness.

This consciousness was provided by the successes of social democracy in the struggle against its adversary and by the successful participation in electoral battles, which increased the power and sense of strength of the proletariat. In the tactics of German social democracy, parliamentary activity increasingly gained more weight. The bourgeois reaction would be based on

> the fear that the continual electoral victories of the Socialists will give the proletariat such a feeling of strength, and so overawe its opponents that it will be impossible to prevent the seizure of the powers of the state and the transformation of the relation of powers in the government.[17]

The possibility of defeat was not ruled out by Kautsky, but it did not prevent the final victory: 'The continuous and rapid advance of the whole proletariat, in spite of very heavy individual defeat, then becomes so notorious that nothing can destroy our confidence in ultimate victory'.[18]

Here the two theses that made the connection between the various forms that the ideology of progress assumed were present: the thesis of the irreversibility and linearity of time and the thesis of technical or moral improvement.[19] In Kautsky's statements, the ineluctable march of progress was expressed within

---

16   MECW, Vol. 29, p. 263.
17   Kautsky 1909, chap. 4.
18   Ibid.
19   Balibar 1995, p. 108.

a homogeneous time. History would be an automatic process, based on its process of self-transformation according to a movement that some call an arrow and others a spiral, which could be fast or slow, but it would undoubtedly reach its destination.

The gradual improvement of technique, of morals and – why not? – of conscience was another of the theses present in Kautsky. From one step to the next, humanity would walk forward and the same could be said for the number of votes for Social Democracy. Even occasional setbacks would be identified as necessary mishaps for the final victory. A victory that evidently never came.

There is no way to detach Kautsky's formulations from his antecedents in the *Manifesto* and in the 'Preface of 1859' cited above. For Marxists, it would be very easy to proceed in this form and qualify Kautsky's reading as a misrepresentation. It would also be easy to reject these passages as something foreign to the theoretical body of Marx's work and to summarise his theory through texts purged of all contamination. It is more difficult to carry out a reconstruction of Marx's theory, *through these passages*, elucidating the links between them and the whole of his thought, in order to reject the economism and determinism that appeared in formulations such as those of Kautsky.

The latter was the path followed by the Italian Marxist Antonio Gramsci. In a short and provocative article in polemic with François Furet, André Tosel pointed out that Gramsci interpreted the formulas present in the 'Preface of 1859' showing that they contain 'Principles, those of historical materialism, which ensure contact with the specificity of the revolutionary process'.[20] For a more accurate understanding of the issue it is necessary to depart from the material order of the *Notebooks* established by the Gerratana edition and analyse the elaboration of the question on the basis of a chronological criterion, looking for the manner in which such contact was established.[21]

Marx's text entered the *Notebooks* first in a set of notes A (Q7, §20) and C (Q11, §22) inscribed in the context of the criticism that the Sardinian Marxist carried out against Bukharin's popular manual. According to Francioni,[22] the first version (an A text) was written between November and December 1930 and in February 1931 and its second version (text C) between July and August of 1932. Gramsci wrote:

---

20   Tosel 1994, p. 42.
21   It should be made clear, however, that this chronological order is not accurate. It is a matter of constructing an interpretation and not of finding the truth of the text.
22   Francioni 1984, pp. 142 and 144.

The Popular Essay [Manual]. The fundamental issue is not dealt with: how does the historical movement arise out of the structures? Yet this is the crucial point of the whole question of historical materialism; it is the problem of the united between society and 'nature'. The two propositions – 1) society does not set itself tasks unless the necessary and sufficient conditions [premises] for their successful completion already exist; 2) no form of society disappears until it has exhausted all its possibilities of development – should have been analysed so as to bring forth their full significance and all their implications. Only on these grounds can all mechanistic views and every trace of superstitious belief in 'miracles' be eliminated. On these grounds also one must pose the problem of the formation of social groups and of political parties and, in the final analysis, of the function of great personalities in history.[23]

General inquiries. I. This fundamental issue is not dealt with: how does the historical movement arise on the basis of the structure. However, the problem is at least suggested in *Problemi fondamentali* by Plekhanov and could be developed. In addition, this is the crucial point of all the issues suggested about the philosophy of praxis and without having solved them one cannot solve the other, that of the relations between society and 'nature', which the *Essay* dedicated a special chapter to. Both propositions of the preface to the *Critique of Political Economy*: 1) Humanity always put itself to tasks that it can resolve; ... a task however only appears where the material conditions for its solution exist or, at least, are in the process of becoming; 2) A social formation does not perish before developing all the productive forces for which it is still sufficient and before new and higher production relations have occupied their place: before the material conditions of existence of the latter have incubated in the breast of the old society – should have been analysed in their full scope and consequence. Only on this ground can you delete all mechanicism and all traces of superstitious 'miracle'; only in this the problem of the formation of active political groups and, ultimately, also the problem of the function of the great personalities of history may be developed.[24]

---

23 PN3, Q7, §20, p. 171.
24 Q11, §22, p. 1422. OT.

Noteworthy in these texts is the statement that the author makes regarding the necessary elimination of all mechanicism and the importance he attributes to the 'Preface' in the abolition of all 'traces of "superstitious" miracle', of faith in the automatic transformation of society. The order of the Gramscian statement is of great importance for this and it is necessary to highlight that it is in the inverse position to that used by Marx.[25] According to André Tosel, these two principles that Gramsci reformulated would be 'the objective principle of the contradiction between relations of production and productive forces [and] the subjective principle of the maturation of the ideological-political conditions for the solution of the contradiction'.[26] The first of these rules produces optimism and confidence. It indicates the possibility of overcoming the current order. The second inspires fear and prudence. It warns that the previously mentioned overcoming does not occur in a mechanical form and without resistance 'and induces the politician not to take into account only the energy that its "part" can develop, but also the hegemonic impulses that the adversary can also emit'.[27]

In the passage from the first version to the second, the framework assumed a wider dimension by referring to Plekhanov. The critique of Bukharin took on a new dimension from the moment the name of the father of Russian Marxism was evoked. By establishing a Plekhanov-Bukharin nexus the target of criticism turned into the dominant Marxist tradition in Russia itself that found its place among expressive sections of the Soviet leadership.

Such themes were developed by Gramsci in a note in the same Notebook 11 (§ 29) devoted to the conception of the 'technical instrument' in Bukharin's manual, composed from texts previously present in Notebook 4 (§§ 12 and 19). The Soviet Marxist was not even mentioned in the notes of Notebook 4 and his appearance in a second draft indicates that Gramsci was willing to address the important issue of the relation between structure and superstructure within

---

25 The analysis of terminological differences is then left aside. It is worth comparing, however, the text of Gramsci with the original version of the 'Preface': 'No social formation is ever destroyed before all the productive forces for which it is sufficient have been developed, and new superior relations of production never replace older ones before the material conditions for their existence have matured within the framework of the old society. Mankind thus inevitably sets itself only such tasks as it is able to solve, since closer examination will always show that the problem itself arises only when the material conditions for its solution are already present or at least in the course of formation' (MECW, Vol. 29, p. 263). The complete translation of the 'Preface of 1859' may be found in the extracts from the translation books. Q, pp. 2358–60.
26 Tosel 1994, p. 42.
27 Badaloni 1978, p. 28.

the framework of his polemic against Bukharin's revisionism and its negative effects on the development of Soviet Marxism.

By equating the author of the *Popular Manual* with the infamous Achille Loria in this paragraph, Gramsci showed just how negative his judgement was: 'in this respect, the mode of thought presented in the *Essay* [Manual] is no different from that of Loria, if not even more censurable and superficial'.[28] The comparison between the two authors was intended as part of the criticism of positivism included in the *Notebooks* as well as its political dimension. Bukharin as much as Loria – the former in the international communist movement and the latter in Italian socialism – exerted a negative influence and constituted an obstacle to an intellectual and moral reform that would have to be overcome by criticism.[29]

The criticism of Loria and Lorianism, which had been present since Notebook 1, was strongly inspired by the devastating attack that Benedetto Croce had already carried out. Written in *Historical Materialism and the Economics of Karl Marx*, this attack revealed to the Italian public that Loria's theory was nothing more than a succession of plagiarisms and misrepresentations of the work of Marx. Plagiarism and misrepresentation was what the exponent of 'historical economism' had done with Marx's 'Preface of 1859'. In *La terra ed il sistema sociale*, for example, Loria completely transfigured the aforementioned passage from the 'Preface,' in which Marx commented on the contradiction between the development of the productive forces and relations of production. According to Loria,

> To a given stage of development of the *productive instrument* corresponds, and on it stands, a given system of production and, therefore, of economic relations, which constitute, later, the whole way of being of society. But the incessant evolution of productive methods generates, sooner or later, a radical metamorphosis of the *technical* instrument, to which that system of production and economy that was founded in an anterior stage of the technical becomes intolerable. Thus, the old economic form is destroyed by a social and economic revolution and substituted by a superior economic form corresponding to the new phase of the *productive instrument*.[30]

---

28   Q11, § 29, p. 1441. OT.
29   Buttigieg 1990, pp. 71 and 75.
30   Cited in Croce 1927, pp. 40–1. Emphasis added. OT.

In this distortion, the productive forces were reduced to technical means, which then subordinated the historical movement to the process of obsolescence of these means. The brutal automatism of this conception and the suppression of the human will in history that it implies motivated the harsh Crocean rebuttal that denounced the burlesque and feeble character of Loria's theory. According to Croce, Marx had indicated the importance of technical capacity in *Capital* and even invoked a 'history of technique' but had never dreamed of making the '"technical instrument" the ultimate and supreme cause of economic development'.[31]

Gramsci appropriated this refutation almost literally in some passages, extending it to the conception of 'technical instrument' present in Bukharin's manual. Thus, in Notebook 11 after quoting the 'Preface' of Marx and the text of Loria which had been transcribed by Croce, he then reproduced, almost word for word, the critique that the latter had made:

> The excerpt from the [Preface to] Zur Kritik contains the terms 'degree of development of the forces of material production', 'mode of production of material life', 'economic conditions of production' and the like, which affirm that economic development is determined by material conditions, but are not reduced only to the 'metamorphosis' of the technical instrument.[32]

And then, after thoroughly rejecting Lorian economism, Gramsci returned to the critique of Bukharin, stating that he had not even quoted the 'Preface' in his *Popular Manual* which was absurd, since this text was 'the most important authentic source for a reconstruction of the philosophy of praxis'.[33] The mechanistic conception developed by the author of the *Manual* hampered the proper understanding of the structure and superstructures. Defining the 'technical instrument' as any tool or utensil, even musical instruments could be considered as such. In his manual Bukharin had even bizarrely affirmed that 'the technique of music depends, first and foremost, on the technique of material production', which led him to consider

> the distribution of the members of an orchestra is determined precisely as in the factory, by the instruments and groups of instruments; in other

---

31 Croce 1927, p. 40.
32 Q11, § 29, p. 1440. OT. Cf. Croce 1927, p. 40.
33 Q11, § 29, p. 1441. OT. This time, Gramsci's statement is misleading, insofar as the Marxian text is quoted in the *Manual*. See Bukharin 1925, chap. 3.

words, the arrangement and organization of these members is here conditioned by musical technique.³⁴

This 'baroque way of thinking' confused rather than clarified the distinction between structure and superstructures and could give rise to a number of other 'baroque' issues. Would libraries and the laboratories of scientists be part of the structure or superstructure?, asked Gramsci. Are there instruments that form at the same time the structure and the superstructure? How can one explain the case of mathematics, which for centuries did not have instruments for its development? If it were possible to say, like Bukharin, that an art or a science had developed thanks to the improvements of 'technical instruments' why could one not also state that the development of art and science had promoted the improvement of the instruments?

The questions themselves are inadequate. But they allow us to understand 'how the causal element, removed from the natural sciences to explain human history is a pure arbitration'.³⁵ The key point discussed in the notes in Notebook 11 refers to the concept of structure. Gramsci emphasises that the philosophy of praxis does not study a machine (the 'technical tool') to understand the atomic structure of the material with which it is composed or the physical-chemical or mechanical properties of its components. The philosophy of praxis studies a machine only 'while it is a moment of the material forces of production, while it is the property of certain social forces, while it expresses a social relation and this corresponds to a certain historical period'.³⁶

Technique, as part of the material forces of production, is not outside of history. This technique, as well as the 'whole of the material forces of production is simultaneously a crystallisation of all past history and the basis of present and future history, is a document and simultaneously an active force of propulsion'.³⁷ In this way, the development of technique was not the cause of the historical movement, as stated by Loria and Bukharin. The development of the material forces of production, of which technique is only a part, is, dialectically, the effect of this movement and its cause.

This last statement must be treated cautiously to once again avoid mechanicism. The time of structure is slow. In historical development, the set of material forces of production is, according to Gramsci,

---

34 Bukharin 1925, chap. 6.
35 Q11, § 30, p. 1444. OT.
36 Q11, § 30, p. 1443.
37 Ibid.

> The least variable element in historical development, that which, in each concrete occasion, can be determined and measured with mathematical accuracy, which may give rise, therefore, to observations and criteria of an experimental character and, consequently, the reconstruction of a robust skeleton of the historical becoming.[38]

This account once again referred to the 'Preface of 1859', in which Marx warned that in the study of social transformations it was necessary to distinguish changes in the legal, political, religious, artistic or philosophical forms from those changes in the conditions 'which can be determined with the precision of the natural sciences'.[39] This observation was mobilised by Gramsci against Croce's accusation that historical materialism highlighted the structure instead of the superstructures, restoring a theological dualism in which the structure would occupy the place of a 'hidden god'. But by stating that the structure could be studied 'with the methods of the natural sciences' it was already clear that this was conceived in an 'ultra-realistic' mode and could not, therefore, occupy the place of a deity that created the real.[40]

Instead of conceiving the structure as immobile and absolute, it was conceived by the philosophy of praxis as 'reality itself in movement'. Croce's accusation was, therefore, according to Gramsci, 'empty and superficial'.[41] The philosophy of praxis, rather than highlighting the structure instead of the superstructures, recognised the historical development of them as closely related and necessarily reciprocal.

The question of superstructures also received extensive treatment in Gramsci. The attention dedicated to the subject does not, however, allow us to reduce his thinking to superstructures, as Norberto Bobbio tried to do in his speech at the congress of Gramscian studies in Cagliari in 1967.[42] Moreover, in the analysis of superstructures, Gramsci emphasised the nexus they maintained with the structures, based on the 'Preface of 1859'.

This analysis becomes clearer when it is located in the geography of Notebooks. The reference to this 'Preface' in Notebook 7 (§ 20) and in the passages cited above was preceded and succeeded by two important notes on the question of superstructure and ideology in Notebook 7, §§ 19 and 21. The issues were clearly articulated with the problem through the text of Marx and by its

---

38 Q11, § 30, p. 1433.
39 MECW, Vol. 29, p. 263.
40 GR, Q10 / II, § 41, p. 193.
41 Ibid.
42 See Bobbio 1975.

reinterpretation by Gramsci. In § 19, Gramsci protested against the vulgar and pejorative use of the term ideology when it designated the 'arbitrary elucubrations of particular individuals'.[43] Such use implied the affirmation that 'every ideology is "pure" appearance, useless, stupid, etc.'[44]

According to Gramsci, this reductionism prevented a fair theoretical analysis of the concept of ideology. It was necessary to distinguish, however, between

> historically organic ideologies – that is, ideologies that are necessary for a given structure – and arbitrary, rationalistic, 'willed' ideologies. Insofar as they are historically necessary, ideologies have a validity that is 'psychological'; they 'organize' the human masses, they establish the ground on which humans move, become conscious of their position, struggle, etc.[45]

Ideology is thus the mass aspect of every philosophical conception. With his protest against this terminological confusion, Gramsci sought to reserve the expression ideology in its strong sense to designate those that 'are necessary to a given structure'.[46] To that end, Gramsci remembered in § 21 of the same Notebook 7, Marx's statement in *Capital* regarding 'the solidity of popular beliefs',[47] as well as that passage from the 'Introduction' to a *Critique of Hegel's Philosophy of Right* in which reference was made to the material force of ideologies.[48]

Through such passages it would be possible to think of a materialist theory of ideologies in which the material forces are the content and the ideologies the form, with this distinction between form and content a methodological and non-organic distinction, 'because material forces would be historically inconceivable without form and ideologies would be individual fantasies without material forces'.[49] This theory was developed by Gramsci within the framework of the 'Preface of 1859'.

---

43 PN3, Q7, § 19, p. 170.
44 PN3, Q7, § 19, p. 171.
45 PN3, Q7, § 19, p. 171.
46 Ibid.
47 'The secret expression of value, namely, that all kinds of labour are equal and equivalent, because, and so far as they are human labour in general, cannot be deciphered, *until the notion of human quality has already acquired the fixity of a popular prejudice*' (MECW, Vol. 35, p. 70. Emphasis added).
48 'The weapon of criticism cannot, of course, replace criticism of the weapon, material force must be overthrown by material force; but theory also becomes a material force as soon as it has gripped the masses' (MECW, Vol. 3, p. 182. Emphasis added).
49 PN3, Q7, § 21, p. 172.

Repeatedly Gramsci paraphrased a statement made by Marx in this same text, writing that 'men become conscious of their social position and therefore of their tasks, on the terrain of ideologies, which is no small affirmation of reality'.[50] From this declaration, it is possible to understand the superstructure as an objective and operative reality which maintains an indissoluble nexus with the structure. Dora Kanoussi has insisted that such a declaration constitutes a third and indispensable canon of historical interpretation.[51]

The incorporation of this third 'canon' makes it possible to underline that superstructures – ideologies – are not arbitrary forms for the philosophy of praxis, they 'are real historical facts which must be combatted and their nature as instruments of domination revealed'.[52] The reasons for this necessary combat are of a political nature. It is through this that it becomes possible to 'make the governed intellectually independent of the governing, in order to destroy one hegemony and create another, as a necessary moment in the revolutionizing of praxis'.[53]

Contesting the accusation of Croce who stated that the superstructures were mere appearances to Marxism, Gramsci argued that as historical facts the superstructures were exactly that. But the conception of the superstructures as appearance did not mean for Marxism anything other than the affirmation of the historicity and the expiration of philosophy, alongside the affirmation of the historical validity of every system and its necessity.[54] The postulate that it is on ideological terrain that men become conscious of their social relations would only corroborate the necessity and validity of this 'appearance'.[55]

The fundamental difference between the philosophy of praxis and other philosophies is that the latter would be nothing other than inorganic, contradictory creations, since they try to reconcile oppositions and exclusions and, for this reason, they are extinguished as soon as the necessity to proceed with this

---

50 GR, Q10 / II, § 41, p. 196. According to Marx, 'change in the economic foundations lead sooner or later to the transformation of the whole immense superstructure. In studying such transformations it is always necessary to distinguish between the material transformation of the economic conditions of production, which can be determined with the precision of natural science and legal, political, religious, artistic or philosophic – in short, ideological forms in which men become conscious of this conflict and fight it out' (MECW, Vol. 29, p. 263).

51 Kanoussi and Mena 1985, p. 39 and Kanoussi 2000, p. 58.

52 GR, Q10 / II, § 41, p. 197.

53 Ibid.

54 Cf. Q13, § 10, p. 1570. OT.

55 Ibid.

conciliation ceases. The philosophy of praxis, on the contrary, clearly poses the contradictions of history and society. It is itself the 'theory of such contradictions' and, for this motive, does not intend to solve them intellectually, but to express them. Unlike speculative philosophies, Crocean neo-idealism among them, the philosophy of praxis is also a 'critique of ideologies'. As a 'theory of contradictions', the philosophy of praxis is therefore an instrument of the hegemony of the subaltern classes.[56]

This dialectical way of looking at the relationship between structure and superstructure was presented by Gramsci in a B text, entitled '*Il termine di "catarsi"*' (The term of 'catharsis') drafted probably at the end of May 1932, a few days before, therefore, the writing of the text referring to the two principles of the 'Preface of 1859' in Notebook 11. He notes that the term catharsis could be used to indicate the passage from the 'objective to the subjective and from necessity to freedom', from the merely economic moment to the ethico-political moment.[57]

In this cathartic moment, the structure would cease to be an external force capable of crushing individuals and condemning them to a situation of passivity and would become a condition of the freedom of these men, an instrument for the creation of new ethico-political forms by means of the superior elaboration of the structure in the superstructure. The determination of this cathartic moment was thus a crucial point of the philosophy of praxis, insofar as this would coincide with the historical movement itself. Gramsci concluded this note resorting to the 'Preface of 1859':

> Recalling the two points between which this process oscillates: – no society poses challenges for which there is no longer any solution or in which the necessary and sufficient conditions are in sight; – is that no society perishes before having expressed all its potential content.[58]

Gramsci sought to develop the concepts of structure and superstructure and establish the precise relation between the two approaches, approximating them to the concept of historical bloc[59] 'built by Sorel'.[60] This concept was reinterpreted in the light of 'Preface of 1859' and the statement that men become conscious of their own position and of their objectives on the terrain of super-

---

56   GR, Q10 / II, § 41, pp. 196–9.
57   See Q10 / II, § 6, p. 1244. OT.
58   Ibid.
59   GR, Q10 / II, § 41, pp. 196–9.
60   GR Q10 / II, § 41, p. 197.

structures. For Gramsci, 'this means that between structure and superstructure a necessary and vital connection exists'.[61]

The concept of the historical bloc in Gramsci had, however, the inverse meaning that it assumed in Sorel's work. In the latter, the concept described a system of images, a myth capable of maintaining access to the revolutionary flame, which must be taken 'in bloc as historical forces'.[62] But in Gramsci the concept of 'historical bloc' acquired 'a strong dialectical-material relationship with reality, assuming itself as the dialectic unity between productive forces, social relations of production and juridical-political superstructure at a given historical moment'.[63] It was in this sense that Gramsci defined the 'Concept of "historical bloc", i.e. unity between nature and spirit (structure and superstructure), unity of opposites and of distincts'.[64]

On this concept of 'historical bloc' it is important to register that it has often been misused as a synonym of class alliances. The origins of the misconception can be found in the use that the PCI made of the expression in the postwar period.[65] At the congress of Gramscian studies in January 1958, for example, Palmiro Togliatti spoke about the 'concept of alliance elaborated by Gramsci' characterised by the 'fundamental, organic nexus, which becomes the basis of a new historical bloc'.[66] Nevertheless, although the concepts were related, there was not established, at least in this intervention, a clear identity between historical bloc and social alliance.

This identity was stressed, however, in a crystalline way by Roger Garaudy in a series of interventions in the political debate of the late 1960s and early 1970s. The French philosopher argued that the concept of a historical bloc 'in Gramsci's conception' expressed 'at the same time the complex unity of the economic base of society and of the political superstructures and, on the other hand, a new organisation of class forces that take place'.[67] Thus, according to Garaudy, the concept of a historical bloc designated a strategic alliance, 'objectively founded on a new relationship between the base and the superstructure'.[68]

---

61   Ibid.
62   Sorel 1930, p. 32.
63   Galastri 2007, p. 141.
64   SPN, Q13, §10, p. 137.
65   On the use of the concept of historical bloc in the PCI, see the testimony of one of their leaders, Giorgio Napolitano 1970.
66   Togliatti 2001, pp. 251–2.
67   Garaudy 1971, p. 170. OT.
68   Ibid.

In a well-known but dated book, Hugues Portelli maintained, in an appropriate way, that the determination of an alliance of classes by transformations in the structure, as Garaudy had reasoned, consisted of a typically economistic procedure.[69] It was contrary not only to the spirit that animated the *Notebooks*, but also to the letter. Although he did not share some of Garaudy's assumptions, Portelli agreed with this assertion of the historical bloc as an alliance of classes.

It was not, however, in the sense of an alliance of classes and much less as a conciliatory slogan that Gramsci used this concept. In its original sense, the historical bloc was conceived as a critical tool aimed at interpreting historical relations, those that were, therefore, concrete and moving, existing between the structure and superstructure, objective conditions and subjective conditions, material forces of production and ideologies.

The concept of historical bloc thus allowed for the critical-historical analysis of the unification of the processes of the social reproduction of political relations and the political-ideological reproduction of the social relations that are most intense in contemporary capitalism. Semeraro favourably called the Gramscian conception 'reticular'.[70] In this conception, the historical bloc would designate the dialectical relationship between 'the "objective" depth of the material forces existing in society and the practice of a free and creative politics unleashed by socially organised groups'.[71]

Although enunciated in a precise way, the question was not completely resolved by Gramsci and he returned to the theme from an explicitly political perspective in an important note in the Philosophical Notes I denominated '*Rapporti struttura and superstructure*' (*Structure and Superstructure Relations*). This note, intended to discuss the methodological criteria of Marxist political analysis based on the 'Preface of 1859', would then be taken up again in the well-known Notebook 13, entitled '*Analysis* of *Situations. Relations of Force*'. The notes begins like this:

Relations between Structure and Superstructure. This is the crucial problem of historical materialism, in my view. Basics for finding one's bearings: 1) the principle that 'no society sets itself tasks for the accomplishment of which the necessary and sufficient conditions do not already	Analysis of Situations: Relations of Force. It is the problem of the relations between structure and superstructures which must be accurately posed and resolved if the forces which are active in the history of a particular period are to be correctly analysed and the relation between them

---

69 Portelli 1977, pp. 95–6.
70 Semeraro 2006, p. 53.
71 Semeraro 2006, p. 54.

exist' [or are not in the course of emerging and developing]; and 2) that 'no society perishes until it has first developed all the forms of life implicit in its internal relations' (check the exact wording of these principles).[72]

determined. Two principles must orient the discussion: 1. that no society sets itself tasks for whose accomplishment the necessary and sufficient conditions do not either already exist or are not at least beginning to emerge and develop; 2. that no society breaks down and can be replaced until it has developed all the forms of life which are implicit in its internal relations ...[73]

According to Francioni,[74] the passage in Notebook 4 was written in October 1930 and incorporated into Notebook 13 between May 1932 and the first months of 1934. Giuseppe Cospito believes that this note may have been written between October and December 1933, in any case after the severe health crisis of March of that year. Thus, although Gramsci had already completely revised his initial arguments on the structure-superstructure relationship and the 'Preface of 1859' in this period, he lacked the conditions for carrying out the necessary reformulation and thereby was content in introducing small but significant variants of the text.[75]

The passage kept its distance from Marx's original text, although Gramsci attached in the margin of the manuscript of Notebook 13 a literal translation made by himself. That the quotation was made initially through memory is evident by the observation itself, which recommended consulting the original text. But the modifications cannot be credited solely to gaps in memory and its interpretation is useful to clarify certain points of Gramscian thought.

The differences between the texts were pointed out by Nicola Badaloni[76] and are immediately apparent. Instead of 'productive forces', Gramsci used the expression 'forms of life' and what Marx called 'material conditions of existence' appeared in the Gramscian text as 'necessary and sufficient conditions'. To interpret this passage from the Gramscian text and its relation to Marx's preface, Badaloni[77] emphasised the link between the two 'principles' highlighted by Gramsci and his object: 'a critique of politics'.

---

72   PN2, Q4, § 38, p. 177.
73   SPN, Q13, § 17, p. 177.
74   Francioni 1984, p. 141.
75   Cospito 2000, p. 103. See also Cospito 2004.
76   Badaloni 1978, pp. 27–8.
77   Badaloni 1978, p. 28.

Gramsci's terminological options are of great importance. Deleting the word 'material' he removed the structure of this level of analysis, precisely the level that indicated the moment of transition to another social formation, the moment at which this 'problem' is placed historically. According to Badaloni, in the Gramscian summary, the problem 'becomes more general and is seen on the side of subjectivity', which can be appreciated by using term 'forms of life', which Gramsci uses quite frequently.[78]

The modification introduced by the Italian Marxist concerned the subjective principle. It was a question of *revaluing*, in the Marxian text, the place occupied by human intervention, introducing the theme of the will. Gramsci himself explained the problem by stating that

> The proposition that 'society does not set itself problems for whose solution the material preconditions do not already exist'. This proposition immediately raises the problem of the formation of a collective will. In analyzing critically what this proposition means, it is important to study how permanent collective wills are in fact formed and how these wills set themselves concrete goals that are both immediate and intermediate – in other words, how they set themselves a collective course of action.[79]

The result of this rearrangement of the Marxian text in order to highlight its 'rational core' is a powerful analytical tool capable of elucidating the connections existing between structure and superstructure. De Felice[80] pointed out that Gramsci's recurring appeal to the 'Preface of 1859', precisely the text that was taken as the point of departure from all the evolutionist and economistic readings on the part of the Marxist currents of the epoch, shows that its elaboration was part of an international debate on the theory-movement problematic and presented an interpretive alternative to historical issues represented by the Russian Revolution, by the defeat of workers' movement in the West and the capitalist solution to the crisis of capitalism.

Interpreted in this way, the 'Preface of 1859' had its content revalued. In the hegemonic thinking of German social democracy, it did nothing more than point out the destiny to which the gradual accumulation of the proletarian forces would lead, pushed by the very development of capitalism and strengthened by the electoral victories of the party. It was an ideological instrument of the morphism of the proletariat, to use an expression of Gramsci, who

---

78   Badaloni 1991, p. 47.
79   PN3, Q8, §195, p. 346.
80   De Felice 1978, p. 197.

would have nothing to do but wait for the inevitable outcome. This same text in the Gramscian formulation was transformed into a vigorous denunciation of all economism and automatism, as well as receiving a 'revolutionary' use, becoming 'an interpretative instrument of the proletarian revolution'.[81]

The maturity of the objective conditions, those explained in the first of the principles which constitutes the 'Preface of 1859', seems to Gramsci to be a fact which it is not necessary to insist on, a constant. The decisive question posed by Gramsci – 'how is the historical movement born on the basis of structure' – was therefore essential to the solution of the second principle, that related to the maturity of the political and ideological conditions. In so doing, Gramsci critically reworked a definition of the Marxism presented in his famous article *La rivoluzione contro il 'Capitale'* (*The Revolution Against Capital*) published in December 1917:

> ... Marxist thought has always identified as the most important factory in history not crude, economic facts, but rather men themselves, and the societies they create, as they learn to live with one another and understand one another; as, out of these contacts (civilization) they forge a social, collective will; as they come to understand economic facts, and to assess them, and to control them with their will, until this collective will becomes the driving force of the economy, the force which shaped reality itself, so that objective reality becomes a living, breathing force, like a current of molten lava, which can be channeled wherever and however the will directs.[82]

In this text, Gramsci was not intimidated by announcing the distance that could separate him of Marx.[83] Defending the capacity of political initiative demonstrated by the Bolsheviks in Russia in 1917, Gramsci, visibly marked by Italian neo-idealism, exaggeratedly claimed that they had denied the thought of Marx, 'contaminated by positivist and naturalistic incrustations'.[84] The article highlighted the affirmation of the 'primacy of the human will over the objective processes of economic relations', a principle that Gramsci claimed on the basis of an idealist conception closer to that of Fichte and Kant than to Hegel himself.[85]

---

81   Paggi 1973, p. 1321.
82   PPW, p. 40.
83   See Gerratana 1997, pp. 91–2 and Medici 2000, p. 65.
84   PPW, p. 40.
85   Gerratana 1997, p. 92. Edmundo Fernandes Dias 2000, p. 113 has a different opinion about

The young Gramsci wrote that 'the canons of Marxist historical criticism' captured reality *in the normal course of events*' in which the development of the experience of the classes occurred slowly. Repeating theses that could be found, for example, in Kautsky, Gramsci asserted that 'normally' the proletariat reacted against its miserable situation and in the conflict that opposed it to the bourgeoisie would become increasingly 'aware of their own potential, their own capacity to assume social responsibility for themselves, to become the arbiters of their own destiny'.[86] But the war that had accelerated historical time in Europe was not a normal situation: 'In Russia, the war has served to galvanize the people's will'.[87]

This radical voluntarism underwent considerable moderation insofar as Gramsci's relation with Marxism became more intense. Already in *L'Ordine Nuovo* period it was possible to note a new way of seeing the relationship between objective and subjective conditions in which the will continued to occupy a prominent position, but the decisive question was to identify the conditions under which it would become 'operative' and would appear as the 'decisive element'.[88] It was to this new direction that the research in the *Notebooks* would be oriented.

1 Politics

It is quite surprising that Antonio Gramsci was first introduced to the postwar Italian public first as a 'cultural theorist'. And more surprising is the persistence of this image. Certainly there is consistent approach to culture in the *Notebooks* and, in particular, to Italian culture. In the various outlines that preceded the beginning of the writing of the *Notebooks*, this question was persistently apparent. And even after the writing began, it remained. But at a determined moment, the Gramscian project began to be organised around another question: politics.

The moment in which the explosion of political reflection occurred has already been pointed out. It is the observation about power and opposition, credited to Leon Blum and inscribed in §40 of Notebook 1. If this is a key moment, it is because it inaugurates this reflection and not because it already

---

this text. For him, it is not about voluntarism, but the interpenetration of will and history.

86 PPW, p. 41.
87 Ibid.
88 Gerratana 1997, p. 102.

appears as finished or mature. Important themes of Gramscian thought will appear in the same *Notebook* in notes following this paragraph, in particular in § 43 'Riviste tipo' (Types of Periodicals) and in § 44 'Direzione política di classe prima and dopo l'andata al governo' (Political class leadership before and after assuming government power). But these paragraphs seem to define only one set of research problems and working hypotheses.

The imposition of these problems in these important notes was clearly historical and referred in a recurring way to Italian development and the difficulty of affirming national unity in the *Risorgimento*. The location of the second version of these, §§ 43 and 44 inside notebooks 20, 24 and especially 19, reinforced this emphasis. It was from these problems and after that first formulation that Gramsci seems to have identified the need for a more systematic reflection on political activity and what he called 'political science' or the 'science of politics'. In this reflection, the dialogue with Machiavelli occupied a strategic position.

The importance of research on the Florentine is already evident in Notebook 1 although this was not part of the index that Gramsci had outlined at the beginning. This was, however, one of the themes enumerated both in the collection of arguments in the 'Saggi principali' (Main Essays) as in the 'Raggruppamenti di materia' (Regrouping of Subjects) placed before in Notebook 8. Regarding the notes on Machiavelli, Leonardo Paggi has pointed out that it is possible to identify two major themes, which, although interconnected, appear formally distinct: 1) research on the Marxist interpretation of the work of the Florentine secretary; 2) the translation into Marxism of some concepts present in his work.[89]

The treatment given to the author of *Il Principe* (*The Prince*) in the *Notebooks* accompanied the gradual transformation of the Gramscian research programme and the new emphases it acquired. In the different plans for the texts, Machiavelli appeared first in that cast of the 'Main Essays', written at the end of 1930, and concentrated on the history of Italian intellectuals. The paragraphs referring to the Florentine secretary that can be found in Notebooks 1 and 2

---

89   Paggi 1984, p. 387. Cf. Finocchiaro 2002, pp. 125–6. To Paggi's observation it is necessary to add that Gramsci began his investigation in Notebook 1 in the framework of a reflection on the interpretation of Machiavelli's work, highlighting his own time and the need to treat it in a historical way. PN1, Q1, §10, p. 103. The research on 'autonomy of the political fact' in that second thematic block pointed out by Paggi would appear only later, in Notebook 4, §56. According to Francioni, this paragraph dates from November 1930 (Francioni 1984, p. 141). It was concomitant, therefore, of those discussions in prison narrated by Athos Lisa, discussions that marked a turning within the *Notebooks*.

appear clearly within this perspective. These are notes concerning the historical character of his work[90] and his position as a cosmopolitan intellectual.[91]

The notes in Notebook 2 are more or less contemporaneous with those inscribed in Notebook 4 and form part of the ensemble that received the subtitle Appunti di Filosofia I (Philosophical Notes I), probably written between May and October 1930.[92] But the approach in Notebook 4 was no longer just historical. Within it, the study of the work of Machiavelli and his commentators came to be part of a comprehensive investigation of the concept of politics and political activity within the ambit of the philosophy of praxis. The titles that Gramsci placed before his paragraphs already allow us to perceive this displacement: 'Machiavellism and Marxism';[93] 'Machiavelli and Marx';[94] and 'Marx and Machiavelli'.[95]

The privileged space of Machiavelli in this Gramscian project of reflection on theory and political activity is undeniable. Rita Medici[96] warned that this place seems to contradict the claim made by Gramsci himself, reviving a thesis of Labriola, regarding the independence of the philosophy of praxis and the refusal of any attempt to complete it with other doctrines.[97] If Gramsci was able to attribute this role to Machiavelli without this constituting an antinomy, it was because he saw in the Florentine secretary a 'first figure of the philosophy of praxis'.[98] This is why in the notes entitled 'Marx and Machiavelli' both authors did not appear opposite one another or as complementary, but rather as authors who shared the same place.[99]

Such a place seems to be justified at the beginning of Notebook 4 in a small note of eight lines entitled 'Machiavellism and Marxism'. Probably reflecting on the endless quarrel about the objectives of *The Prince* – who did Machiavelli teach? – Gramsci wrote:

> Two interpretations of Machiavelli: by tyrannical men of state who want to preserve and extend their dominion; and by those with liberal tenden-

---

90   PN1, Q1, §10, p. 103 and Q2, §31, pp. 280–1 and §41, pp. 287–8.
91   PN1, Q1, §150, pp. 229–30.
92   Francioni 1984, p. 141.
93   PN2, Q4, §4, p. 144.
94   PN2, Q4, §8, pp. 150–1.
95   PN2, Q4, §10, p. 152.
96   Medici 1990, p. 188.
97   See Labriola 2000, p. 216 and PN2, Q4, §3, p. 144.
98   Lefort 1986.
99   In the notes entitled 'Croce and Marx', on the contrary, both authors are placed in opposition.

cies who want to modify the forms of government ... Croce writes that this proves the *objective validity* of Machiavelli's views, and this is absolutely true.[100]

Yet, not all of Machiavelli's positions could be considered as carriers of an 'objective validity'. Those to which Gramsci attributes this status are those who could be integrated into the philosophy of praxis as canons of interpretation. On the other hand, the Machiavellian characterisation of human nature should be clearly rejected. According to the author of the *Notebooks*, the fundamental innovation introduced by Marx in political and historical science, when compared to Machiavelli, was the criticism of the idea of a fixed and unchanging 'human nature'.[101] The rejection of this idea would allow one to conceive of a political science that in its concrete content would identify itself with a historical science. Machiavelli considered politics as a practice that asserts itself in a circular time in which the regularity of human nature guarantees the constancy of historical cycles. The acuity of the Florentine for history was justified by its demonstrative effect on what might be. Hence his insistence on the need to articulate 'from a long experience in modern affairs and a continuous study of antiquity'.[102]

The refusal of a fixed human nature allowed Gramsci to free himself from the conception of a cycle of time without thereby giving up that important historical sensitivity. Also, the contemporary experience and study of history provided the key to the intelligibility of the present. Freeing Machiavelli's thought from the moorings that were imposed on him by this idea of human nature would reveal its rational nucleus. This nucleus, according to Gramsci, was:

> (1) the affirmation that politics is an independent and autonomous activity that has its own principles and laws, different from those of morality and religion in general (this position of Machiavelli's is of great philosophical significance, because it implicitly alters the conception of morality and religion; it alters the whole conception of the world); (2) the practical and immediate content of the art of politics, which is studied and articulated with realistic objectivity, in accordance with the first affirmation.[103]

---

100   PN2, Q4, § 4, p. 144.
101   PN2, Q4, § 8, pp. 150–1.
102   Machiavelli 2005, p. 5.
103   PN2, Q4, § 8, pp. 150–1.

In the first of the points enumerated in this quotation, Gramsci explicitly takes up the idea of 'autonomy of politics' from Croce's reading of the work of the Florentine. According to the philosopher,

> It is known that Machiavello discovers the necessity and autonomy of politics, of politics which is beyond or, rather, below moral good and evil, which has its own laws against which it is useless to rebel, politics that cannot be exorcized and driven from the world with holy water.[104]

In declaring that the Florentine secretary inaugurated the 'autonomy of politics', the author of *Politics and Morals* presented him as a forerunner of the distinction between the different spheres of the spirit. Contrary to those who read *The Prince* as a manual of practical politics, Croce emphasised that the concept of the 'autonomy of politics' present in him was a 'profoundly philosophical concept, and it represents the true foundation of a philosophy of politics'.[105]

The properly philosophical content of the discourse of the Florentine was revalued in detriment to that which Croce considered to be the casuistry and political preceptism that characterised Machiavellian thought. Machiavelli could thus not be considered the founder of an 'empirical science of politics', as many had thought. He was, in fact, the founder of the modern philosophy of politics.

This anti-Machiavellian reading of Machiavelli's work was possible because Croce separated the practical and political tendencies, that is, he removed politics as an act of reflection with respect to these practices and politics, removing the sphere of philosophy from the sphere of politics. A similar procedure was carried out in the separation between historiography and history as an act. The example given by Croce in this respect in *Theory and History of Historiography* was, precisely, the Florentine:

> Machiavelli is a historian in so far as he tried to understand the course of events; he is a politician or at least a publicist, when he posits and desires a prince, founder of a strong national state, as his ideal, reflecting this in his history ... Thus Machiavelli belongs partly to the history of thought in the Renaissance and partly to the history of the practice of the Renaissance.[106]

---

[104] Croce 1945, p. 59. The Crocean approach had already been anticipated, albeit very summarily, in his *Philosophy of Practice*. Croce 1923, pp. 266–8.
[105] Croce 1945, p. 60.
[106] Croce 1921, p. 169.

Machiavelli's claim to be the discoverer of the autonomy of politics underscored his role as a philosopher of the Renaissance and not as a politician of this historical epoch. Although he was in constant dialogue with the interpretation of Francesco De Sanctis, Croce distanced himself from the conclusions of this historian of the *Risorgimento*. In his monumental *Storia della letteratura italiana* (*History of Italian Literature*), De Sanctis attributed to the Florentine secretary the function of 'conscience and thought of the century' 'at the same time, the most profound negation of the Medieval and the clearest assertion of the new times'.[107] This dual function – negative and positive – that was accomplished by the Protestant Reformation in the rest of Europe assumed a different form in Italy. De Sanctis affirmed, then, that in the peninsula 'Luther was Niccolò Machiavelli'.[108] As man of the Renaissance, the Machiavelli of De Sanctis was also a reformer.

This dualism was also stressed by Croce. The Florentine secretary, he stated in *Politics and Morals*, was commonly identified with the Renaissance. But he also belonged to the movement of the Reformation and its desire, inside and outside Italy, to 'know man and to study the problem of the soul'.[109] The sense from which Machiavelli was identified with the spirit of the Reformation differed, however, from that affirmed by De Sanctis. For Croce, the Florentine was a reformer of philosophy and not of the society of his day. For this reason he could be embedded in a movement of research into the 'problem of the soul', of the human spirit. Machiavelli thus assumed the position of the precursor of the philosophy of the spirit.

The claim of the author of *The Prince* as the discoverer of the autonomy of politics that is still discussed to this day has become famous and has made Croce one of the exponents of the modern Machiavellist, although he had devoted to him only small articles and scattered pages, found mainly in *Politics and Morals* and in the *History of the Baroque in Italy*.[110] The influence of this Crocean reading on Gramsci's reflections in the *Prison Notebooks* is irrefutable. The references are too explicit to be ignored. Taking these references into account, Finocchiaro simply states that Gramsci 'accepts' Croce's fundamental thesis.[111] In fact, although he embraced the expression and makes regular use of it in the *Notebooks*, he did not do the same with its content. The

---

107 De Sanctis 1968, p. 454.
108 Ibid.
109 Croce 1945, p. 59.
110 See Cochrane 1961, pp. 115–16 and Medici 1990, p. 166.
111 Finocchiaro 2002, p. 133.

fundamentals and the results of this thesis were different for Croce and Gramsci[112] if not opposed.[113]

For Gramsci, the affirmation of an 'autonomy of politics' implied the recognition that politics could not be reduced to religion or ethics. As a field of knowledge and as an activity, that is, as a science and practice, theory and praxis, political science and politics had their own rules that distinguished them from other forms of knowledge and human activity. But, in Gramsci's work, such 'autonomy' does not seem to imply a radical separation between politics and morals. For this reason, Gramsci found in Machiavelli a precursor of the philosophy of praxis in a full sense, that is, the creator of a 'revolutionary science-action'.[114]

The question therefore concerned the 'dialectical relationship' that the 'autonomy of politics' could have with historical forms. The Crocean formula was entirely inadequate, if not mistaken. Would the relation of politics to art, morality, and philosophy be an indeterminate relation of mere implication, as the 'dialectic of the distinct' suggested? Gramsci clearly rejected this indeterminacy, and stated that art, morality, and philosophy 'serve' politics; they could be reduced to a moment of it, but to affirm the opposite would be a misconception. In this way, he posited the 'priority of the politico-economic fact – that is, the "structure" – as a dialectical point of reference and as a nonmechanical dialectical "causation" of the superstructures'.[115]

Establishing this structure-superstructure nexus was also to define the concept of politics within the philosophy of praxis. This was, for the author of the *Notebooks*, the first to be resolved in a treatment of Machiavelli's work. The definition did not concern only the place that a philosophy of politics should have within the philosophy of praxis. If politics is praxis, then this was an easily resolved issue: the philosophy of political praxis was the very philosophy of praxis.

The reflection on Machiavelli, which at first were found sparsely scattered in the *Notebooks*, gained pace and intensity inside the important Notebook 8, in a set of notes written between January and April 1932 and then rewritten, mostly in Notebook 13, between May 1932 and the first months of 1934.[116] The

---

112 Medici 1990, p. 167.
113 See Fontana 1993, pp. 7 and 52–73 and Frosini 2003, p. 164.
114 Martelli 1996, p. 170.
115 PN2, Q4, §56, p. 231.
116 See Francioni 1984, p. 144. Machiavelli was quoted in all the notebooks anterior to Notebook 8 with the exception of Notebook 7. But he never dedicated more than three paragraphs to the Florentine in them. In Notebook 8, instead, one can find references in Notebooks 21, 37, 43, 44, 48, 56, 58, 61, 78, 84, 86, 114, 132, 162 and 163.

correct approach to these notes tends to emphasise the metaphor of the 'modern prince', already present in §1 of Notebook 13 and the place of the political party in the process of constitution of a new state. Rita Medici drew attention to the lack of references to this thematic in the *Notebooks*.[117] Such a thematic is, without doubt, of great importance but it does not provide an internal criterion of the unity of the Gramscian approach to Machiavelli.

The question that could provide a criterion of unity was posed by Gramsci originally in Notebook 8: what is the place of political activity in the philosophy of praxis? The very imposition of the problem already marked a distance from that assumed by Croce to the extent in which Gramsci indicated, already in the question he asked about the unity between philosophy and politics.[118] Pointing out the differences between the two interpreters, Frosini argued that for Croce, the Machiavellian assertion of the autonomy was a discovery of philosophical value, while for Gramsci this philosophical dimension could be affirmed because it implied a revolution of the whole conception of the world and a reinterpretation of morality and philosophy as well. Thus, Gramsci 'subverts the Crocean perspective, insofar as he sees in politics itself the discovery in *nuce* of an entirely new philosophy'.[119]

Croce, as already seen, based his conception of politics on the distinction between different forms of the spirit, and defined it as a moment of autonomous practice independent of the other forms, although related to them through the circular nexus of the distinct. Gramsci sought to develop this concept in an opposite sense to that of this author in a rich passage of meanings:

> In a philosophy of praxis, wherein everything is practice, the distinction will not be between the moments of the absolute spirit but between structure and superstructure; it will be a question of establishing the dialectical position of political activity as a distinction within the superstructures. One might say that political activity is, precisely, the first moment or first level of the superstructures; it is the moment in which all the super-

---

117 Medici 2000, p. 162. In fact, in the Special Notebook dedicated to Machiavelli there are only two references to the 'modern prince'. Q13, §1, p. 1558 and §21, pp. 1601–2.

118 PN3, Q8, §61, p. 271. After subsuming the Gramscian interpretation of the 'autonomy of politics' in the Crocean philosophy of the spirit, Finocchiaro accuses Gramsci of confusing political activity with political science. See Finocchiaro 2002, p. 124. It would only make sense to assert such a confusion if Gramsci had accepted the separation of politics and philosophy, something which he always rejected.

119 Frosini 2003, p. 164.

structures are still in the unmediated phase of mere affirmation – willful, inchoate, and rudimentary.[120]

From this definition the identity between history and politics becomes comprehensible, as well as the statement that 'all life is politics'. All human praxis carries within itself a political dimension, even though this dimension does not fulfil all its content. If history is conflict, there is no denying that every conflict is also greater or lesser, explicitly or implicitly, politics. The concept of distinction, reworked within the ambit of the philosophy of praxis, allowed him to conceive the whole system of superstructures as a '(system of) political distinctions'.[121]

For Gramsci, it was, therefore, a question of developing this 'autonomy' of politics founded by Machiavelli, seeking from this definition the construction of a science of politics as the form of the philosophy of praxis, which had as its method a 'realistic objectivity'. The resumption of the principle of 'verità effettuale della cosa' (the effectual truth of the matter) was how Machiavelli aimed to approach politics as it is and not its imagination and, in this way, guide an effective political practice, assuming a strategic position in this venture.[122]

It was this cognitive principle, shared by both Marxism and Machiavelli, that allowed the author of the *Notebooks* to consider the latter as a prefiguration of Marxism.[123] In refusing the intellectual project of constructing in an idealised way a model of the state and assuming immediate political action as the object of investigation, the Florentine secretary was also refusing all traces of metaphysical idealism. His political thinking was thus materialistic and historical. According to Gramsci:

> In his treatment, in his critique of the present, he articulated some general concepts that are presented in an aphoristic and nonsystematic form. He also articulated a conception of the world that could also be called 'philosophy of praxis' or 'neohumanism,' in that it does not recognize transcendental or immanent (in the metaphysical sense) elements but is based entirely on the concrete action of man, who out of historical necessity works and transforms reality.[124]

---

120   PN3, Q8, §61, p. 271.
121   Ibid.
122   In a well-known passage of *The Prince*, the Florentine secretary warned: 'But since my intention is to write something useful for anyone who understands it, it seemed more suitable for me to search after the effectual truth of the matter [verità effettuale della cosa] rather than its imagined one'. Machiavelli 2005, p. 53.
123   See Lefort 1986, p. 245.
124   PN3, Q5, §127, p. 378.

The attribution of a strongly realistic streak to the Florentine secretary's thinking was common in Italian political science at the beginning of the twentieth century and essential in the phenomenon of 'Machiavellianism' or the 'return to Machiavelli' that characterised the reflection on politics in the context of the First World War.[125] The realism of Machiavelli was, however, problematised in the *Notebooks*. Gramsci went beyond a traditional analysis that saw in *The Prince* a reflection on politics as it is and perceived an articulated reflection on the *being* and *what should be* of politics. One can then comprehend the importance that Gramsci attributed to the epilogue of *The Prince*, in which he exhorted 'To seize Italy and free her from the barbarians':[126] it was a necessary part, a fundamental moment in which all the 'should be' was condensed into a call for concrete political action.

The assertion of Machiavelli's objective validity did not imply a neutrality to the means and ends. If realism has as its objective the definition of effective means to obtain a particular end, it is possible to consider that it is a political technique. Even from this definition, realism could not be identified with a vulgar cynicism, since the means would not be justified by ends, but by their effectiveness. The 'effective truth of things' would thus contain a criterion of efficient causality. The valid means would be those considered capable of producing the desired results.

As a political technique, realism would not exclude, *a priori*, any purpose. But the realism that is common to Machiavelli and to Marx is not about a technique, but a cognitive principle. As such, realism considers empirical reality to be the result of human activity and, therefore, accessible to knowledge. Such realism does not exclude all utopia, provided that it assumes a concrete character, this being the result of a patient and rigorous analysis of the real. The condition of historical legitimacy lies in the fact that the *should be* is previously inscribed in the *being*. The future takes root in the present and only in this condition does it makes a future 'predictable'.

It was to this point that Gramsci drew attention in a note first present in a paragraph in Notebook 8 (§ 84), and then transcribed to Notebook 13 (§ 16) emphasising the superficial and mechanical character of vulgar realism. The note disputed the preference that the reformist leader Paolo Treves had for the moderate realism of Francesco Guicciardini, in detriment to Machiavelli's engaged realism. This preference was very close to the moderation of the interpreter, thus justifying his own political position.

---

125 See Medici 1990, p. 14.
126 Machiavelli 2005, p. 87.

In his reply, Gramsci distinguished the 'diplomat' (Guicciardini) from the 'politician' and the 'political scientist' from 'politician in action'. The diplomat and the political scientist could have as a horizon an already constituted reality. But Machiavelli was not a mere scientist, but a party man, 'a politician in action' and as such had the objective 'to create new relations of forces and therefore could not fail to be concerned with the should be'.[127] Being and should be would thus maintain an intimate relation: 'The politician in action is a creator, a sustainer, but he does not create from nothing or move in the murky emptiness of his desires and dreams. He takes *effective reality* as his basis'.[128]

By adopting the expression 'realtà effettuale' (effective reality) instead of that which originally appeared in Machiavelli (verità effettuale), Gramsci further highlighted his objective and realistic content. The politician in action, like Machiavelli, should be able to read the effective reality, the relation of existing forces and in continuous movement. But the objectives of this reading are not the conservation and stabilisation of these forces, nor their accommodation, as in vulgar realism – that of Treves, for example. The position of the Florentine secretary, according to Gramsci, approached the philosophy of praxis insofar as he too sought to construct a 'popular realism'.[129]

For this popular realism, the reading of effective reality aims to find the possibilities of really effective transformation. It is not, therefore, intended to stabilise or to settle; it is about transforming the world. Popular realism is thus capable of revealing a reality that is equal to itself, but which contains, at the same time, what is different from itself. It is for this reason that, according to Gramsci:

> Applying the will to the creation of a new balance of really existing and operative forces, based on that determined force that is considered progressive, and empowering it to make it succeed is, always, to move on the ground of effective reality, but [also] to dominate and overcome it (or contribute to it). The 'should be' is therefore concrete, it is the only realistic and historicist interpretation of reality, it is the only history in action and philosophy in action, the only politics.[130]

Comparing the realism of Machiavelli and that of Marx, Claude Lefort argued that the well-known Thesis 11 *Ad Feuerbach* – 'Philosophers have hitherto only

---

127 Q13, §16, p. 1577. OT.
128 Q13, §16, p. 1578. Emphasis added.
129 Q14 §33, p. 1691. OT.
130 Q13, §16, p. 1578. OT.

interpreted the world in various ways; the point is to *change* it'[131] – would imply a call to action, but would add nothing to the knowledge of reality.[132] The interpretation of the French philosopher seems to separate theory and practice in an extraneous way to that of Marx, and especially strange to that of Gramsci's understanding. If 'reality is praxis', as Lefort himself points out,[133] then praxis gives meaning to the reality that one wants to know, as well as providing the point of view from which this cognitive practice is carried out.

The pretension of an absolute objectivity enclosed in the supposed autonomy of knowledge in any project of transformation of this reality eliminates the subject from the act of knowledge. However, the effective reality can only be known by a real subject. Hence Gramsci's emphasis on the position occupied by Machiavelli. For this, the Florentine secretary could not be considered just a 'scientist of politics'. As a 'politician in action' he should be understood as the theoretical and practical subject of a project of the transformation of reality.

Gramsci's interest in the work of Machiavelli in the *Prison Notebooks* must be interpreted as constituting a critical development and a new problematisation of the theme of the will.[134] For Gramsci, the fundamental character of Machiavelli's *The Prince* was in the fusion of political science and of political ideology in the dramatic form of the 'myth', as well as in the relation of unity that is established in this work between a universalised rationality and a particular 'collective will' personified in the figure of the *condottiero* (captain, leader). Thus, according to the Sardinian Marxist,

> In order to represent the process whereby a given collective will, directed towards a given political objective, is formed, Machiavellli did not have recourse to long-winded arguments or pedantic classifications of principles and criteria for a method of action. Instead he represented this process in terms of the qualities, characteristics, duties and requirements of a concrete individual. Such a procedure stimulates the artistic imagination of those who have to be convinced, and gives political passions a more concrete form.[135]

---

131   MECW, Vol. 5, p. 5.
132   Lefort 1990, p. 188.
133   Ibid.
134   See Medici 2000, p. 66.
135   GR, Q13, §1, p. 239.

Gramsci proposed a key interpretation of *The Prince* based on the Sorelian concept of myth, as a creation of the 'concrete fantasy' that would act on people to awaken and organise their collective will with a view to building a new state.[136] Hence, Gramsci affirmed, the character of the 'political manifesto' of the work of the Florentine secretary.[137]

It is interesting to compare the Machiavellian myth with that of the Sorelian version utilised by Gramsci. According to Sorel, a myth would allow one to represent immediate action 'in the form of images of battle in which their cause is certain to triumph'.[138] This set of images

> which, *taken together and through intuition alone*, before any considered analyses are made, are capable of evoking the mass of sentiments which correspond to the different manifestations of the war undertaken by socialism against modern society.[139]

As the 'framing of the future in some indeterminate time',[140] such myths would have the capacity, at the same time, to awaken the hope and mobilisation necessary for their fulfilment. Sorel considered that 'the general strike of the syndicalists and the Marx's catastrophic revolution are such myths'.[141] But he clearly stated his predilection for the trade union myth:

> Strikes have engendered in the proletariat the noblest, the deepest and the most moving sentiments that they possess; the general strike groups them all in a coordinated picture and, by bringing them together, gives to each one of them its maximum intensity; appealing to their painful memories of particular conflicts, it colours with an intense life all the details of the composition presented to consciousness. We thus obtain that intuition of socialism which language cannot give us with perfect clearness – and we obtain it as a whole, perceived instantaneously.[142]

---

136 Ibid.
137 The analogy with the *Communist Manifesto* is obvious and it is possible that Gramsci had in mind a passage in which Croce claimed to have been Marx's 'Machiavelli of the proletariat'. Croce 1915, p. 46.
138 Sorel 1999, p. 20.
139 Sorel 1999, p. 113. See also p. 118.
140 Sorel 1999, p. 115.
141 Sorel 1999, p. 20.
142 Sorel 1999, p. 118.

It was this status that Sorel attributed to the general strike that motivated Gramscis criticism. According to the Sardinian Marxist, the maximum realisation of political praxis in Sorel's conception was limited to an economic-corporate moment, a 'negative and preliminary' moment, embodied in the general strike in which the irrational and 'arbitrary' impulse predominated, pure spontaneity.[143] The Sorelian myth would have the capacity of dissolving the existing, of denying it. But this negation of the present would not be dialectical. It would not produce a new synthesis.

Sorel's conception lacked a 'constructive' moment. It abandoned the collective will in the 'primitive and elementary phase of its mere formation' and would soon disintegrate in a deformed multiplicity of particular wills. The element capable of welding these wills into a creative historical force was lacking. The Sorelian myth could thus stimulate the destruction of 'existing moral and juridical relations', but was incapable of being a 'producer of realities': 'destruction and negation cannot exist without an implicit construction and affirmation – this not in "metaphysical" sense, but in practice, i.e. politically, as a party programme'.[144]

Behind the spontaneity of revolutionary syndicalism, there would be nothing but a pure mechanism, 'a maximum of determinism, behind the idealism an absolute materialism',[145] that is, vulgar. Thus theoretical syndicalism and anarchism could be similar to liberalism. But liberalism is a theoretical program of classes 'designed to change – in so far as it is victorious – a state's ruling personnel, and to change the economic programme of the state itself ...'[146] and, therefore, it is a programme aimed at preserving a situation of class domination by imposing a new leadership and updating the state organisation. Revolutionary syndicalism, in turn, refers to the subaltern group (the working class) which, with this theory, 'is prevented by this theory to from ever becoming dominant, or by developing beyond the economic-corporate stage and rising to the phase of ethico-political hegemony in civil society, and of domination in the state'.[147]

In Machiavelli, on the contrary, political praxis assumed a *positive* and *constructive* character, embodied in a 'new state' and 'new national and social structures'.[148] The 'myth' would thus not be the moment of the irrational, but

---

143   GR, Q13, §1, p. 239.
144   GR, Q13, §1, pp. 239–40.
145   GR, Q13, §1, p. 240.
146   GR, Q13, §18, p. 210.
147   GR, Q13, §18, pp. 210–11.
148   GR, Q13, §1, p. 240.

the particular mediation of political praxis itself that would allow for the creation of a new order. The constitution of a new order and the difficulties of this process was a recurrent theme in Machiavelli.[149] In *The Prince*, the Florentine secretary stressed, there was 'nothing more difficult to execute, nor more dubious of success, nor more dangerous to administer, than to introduce new political orders'.[150] And in the same sense in the *Discorsi sulla prima deca di Tito Livio* (*Discourses on Livy*) he wrote that it was 'no less dangerous to find new modes and orders than to seek unknown waters and lands'.[151]

For Gramsci, the construction of a new order required this positive and constructive role of the prince-myth which allowed him to attribute to Machiavelli a 'precocious Jacobinism', identifying in this 'Jacobinism' the '(more or less fertile) germ of his conception of national revolution'.[152] If Machiavelli was an early Jacobin, the partisans of Robespierre were in turn the '"categorical embodiment" of Machiavelli's Prince'. It was, however, the aversion to Jacobinism that pushed Sorel away from politics and made his conception of 'myth' abstract.[153] In contrast, for the Sardinian Marxist, the Jacobins were an expression of a modern Machiavellism and an example of 'the concrete formation and operation of a collective will' and understanding this 'collective will, and of political will in general, in the modern sense: will as operative awareness of historical necessity, as protagonist of a real and effective historical drama'.[154] This was the content of the Jacobinism shared by Gramsci.

2   Relations

The question that Gramsci's research on the 'Preface of 1859' permitted him to engage with was, precisely, 'When can the conditions for awakening and developing a national popular collective will be said to exist?' To respond to this question, it would be necessary to analyse the group of social relations that allowed the development of the social will, 'Hence a historical (economic) ana-

---

149   See Medici 2000, pp. 141–2.
150   Machiavelli 2005, p. 22.
151   Machiavelli 1996, p. 5.
152   GR, Q13 §1, p. 242.
153   Gramsci shared this aversion in his youth. See Losurdo 1997, p. 26. Rita Medici stressed that Gramsci's youthful anti-Jacobinism was due not only to the influence of Croce and Gentile, emphasised by Losurdo, but also that of Sorel. Medici 2000, p. 70. In the same sense, see Del Roio 2005, pp. 37–9. For one treatment of the evolution of Gramsci's thinking on Jacobinism, see Medici 2004.
154   GR, Q13 §1, p. 241.

lysis of the social structure of the given country ...'.[155] Only from this analysis would it be possible to identify the 'field of possibilities that the relatively permanent and opposing forces use, to the extent of their political capacity, in the opposite direction'.[156]

The 'Preface of 1859' assumed a crucial position in the context of the research on relations of political forces between social classes. By means of a displacement of a note from the 'philosophical' plan of Notebook 4 §38 – 'Rapporti tra struttura e superestruttura' ('Relations between structure and superstructure') to the proper 'political' plan of Notebook 13 §17 – 'Analisi delle situazioni: raporti di forza' ('Analysis of the Situation: Relations of Force'), the seemingly insoluble theoretical question that Gramsci had been debating – the relations between structure and superstructure – assumed an effective meaning.[157]

The canons of historical methodology extracted by Gramsci from the principles presented in the 'Preface of 1859' gained, with the new framework, a strategic dimension. They connected with other themes and articulated themselves with new concepts, redesigning the conceptual fabric of *Notebooks*. In their new base, the canons of the 'Preface' allowed him to separate those that were occasional, the result of the action of political groups and personalities, from those that were permanent and a result of the action of social classes. While the analysis of the occasional fed a 'political criticism of a minor day-to-day character', the study of the permanent would stimulate 'socio-historical criticism'.[158]

The distinction that Gramsci made between big and small politics is of extreme importance for an accurate valuation of the scope of these canons. What made it possible to distinguish one from the other was, exactly, the strategic dimension that could, through these canons, be learned. This strategic dimension was highlighted by a minor change in the passage from the first to the second version of these paragraphs:

Big politics encompasses issues related to the founding of new states and to the struggle for the defense and *preservation of a given socio-political structure*.[159]	Big politics comprises issues related to the founding of new states, with the struggle for destruction, defense, conservation of given organic socio-economic structures.[160]

---

155 GR, Q13 §1, p. 241.
156 Paggi 1973, p. 1347.
157 Cospito 2000, p. 103.
158 GR, Q13, §17, p. 201.
159 PN3, Q.8, §48, p. 264. Emphasis added.
160 Q13 §5, pp. 1563–4. Emphasis added. OT.

Some of the changes made by Gramsci in this text had the evident goal of making it more accurate. Thus, he clarified that big politics does not only concern 'the struggle for defense and conservation' of a given structure, but also its destruction. It was also important to replace 'socio-political structure' with 'organic socio-economic structures'. Of course, big politics is still political and, for this reason, this last change appears strange. Why did he suppress the word 'politics'? And what does the addition of 'organic', as an adjective of structures, in the second version mean? This is one of the cases in which it is only possible to suppose why the changes were made, but one can imagine that they were intended to mark more clearly what distinguishes big politics that has as its objective the transformation or conservation of the relations of production, from small politics that aims at substitution of a fraction of the leading group by another.

In the same note, small politics was defined as 'everyday politics, parliamentary politics, of the hallway, of intrigue'.[161] In this dimension of activity, questions were only 'partial and everyday' and were placed face-to-face within a stable structure with 'the various fractions of the same political class'.[162] By stating how the struggle of big politics for the transformation and/or conservation of 'given organic socio-economic structures', emphasised the strategic nature of the antagonism. What is at stake in big politics is the conformation of a new hegemony, a new historical bloc whose possibility is inscribed in the social totality.[163]

The exclusion of social antagonism and of 'big politics' from the scope of state life and reduction of this to small games of intrigue between parliamentary cliques was, according to Gramsci, the 'high politics' of the ruling classes. It was this concealment of social conflicts that allowed them to reduce the agents to the condition of citizens, abstracting their social determinations and transforming them into isolated units.[164] In this concealment of liberalism, even when grouped in parties, these agents would not cease to be individuals. It was this illusion of reality that allowed Croce to affirm that in the state each one of its members was sometimes both a 'sovereign and subject'.[165]

The perception of the mechanism of illusion led Gramsci to recognise in Giolitti an exponent of 'big politics' even when he downgraded him to the level of 'small politics' or precisely for this reason. The exposition in the *Notebooks*

---

161   Q13, §5, p. 1573. OT.
162   Ibid.
163   Dias 1996a, p. 14.
164   Dias 1996a, p. 25.
165   Croce 1945, p. 16.

may be considered incomplete on this point. For beyond the illusion that turns big politics into small politics it would be possible to think of the one that develops in the opposite sense, transforming small politics into false big politics. If that first form was represented by the liberal Giolitti, this second found its representatives inside the Italian Socialist Party (PSI).

The removal of the word political did not, therefore, cancel the strategic dimension of the social conflict, but allowed Gramsci to emphasise that it was located beyond what was commonly called 'politics' – the small parliamentary skirmishes, the empty polemic in the newspapers, ministerial scandals. Big politics is present in everyday life, but in that dimension of the present in which it is possible to find antagonistic classes in open or concealed conflict.

Distinguishing *big politics* from *small politics* is tantamount to differentiating the *conjuncture* from the *situation*. Gramsci emphasised that in the study of a structure it was necessary to distinguish organic movements (permanent) from conjunctural movements (occasional, immediate, accidental). Unfolding the structure and its present is an operation that requires unravelling time in its varied manifestations: the time of the epoch, the situation and the conjuncture; of economy, society and politics; of strategy and tactics; of propaganda and agitation. This decomposition only makes sense when followed by the resolution of these multiple temporalities in the history of the present. The distinction should not serve as a basis for the radical separation of these temporalities. Its purpose should be the clarification of the relationship between these times.

It was with this distinction that Gramsci sought to establish a notion of the relationship between this concept and political activity. There are two moments where he attempted to define this concept, both of which appear within a section entitled 'Nozioni enciclopediche' ('Encyclopedic Notions').

Encyclopedic notions. Conjuncture. The origin of the word: it helps to understand the concept better. In Italian = Economic fluctuation. Linked to very rapidly changing postwar phenomena. [In Italian, the term 'conjuncture' still means 'favorable or unfavorable [economic] opportunity']. Difference between 'situation' and 'conjuncture': conjuncture is the ensemble of the immediate and transitory peculiarities of the economic situation, and one must therefore take this concept to

Encyclopedic notions. [...] Conjuncture. The conjuncture can be defined as the set of circumstances which determine the market in a given phase, if these circumstances are conceived as in movement, that is, as a set which gives rise to a process of always new combinations, a process that is the economic cycle. The conjuncture is studied to predict and consequently also determine, within certain limits, the economic cycle in a favourable sense to business. For this reason, it is also

refer to the most fundamental and enduring characteristics of the situation itself. The study of conjuncture, then, is more closely related to immediate politics, 'tactics' [and agitation], whereas 'situation' is related to 'strategy' and to propaganda, etc.[166]

defined as the oscillation of the economic situation, or the set of oscillations.[167]

The comparison between the two definitions shows that the author was concerned, in the first place, to define the so-called 'economic conjuncture'. The first definition, inscribed in Notebook 6, has a confusing wording, but it seems to indicate the difference between 'the ensemble of immediate and transitory peculiarities' (conjuncture) and 'the more fundamental and enduring characteristics' (situation). In the same sense, the note from Notebook 15 sought to define the concept in the context of research on the crisis and economic cycles. The properly political dimension of the concept was explored in the final passage of the first paragraph, in which the distinction was drawn between, on the one hand, the conceptual constellation of conjuncture-tactics-agitation and, on the other, situation-strategy-propaganda. Such constellations group together key concepts of criticism and political action.

The initial focus on the economic dimension of the conjuncture should be understood as part of Gramsci's criticism of economism. The denunciation of economism and automatism entailed the rejection of a fatalistic view of history, much in vogue at the time, which derived the revolutionary crisis directly from the economic crisis. Such derivation tended to approximate the different times of politics and economy and ended up diluting the superstructure in the structure. Gramsci's conception was antagonistic and tended to stress the discordance of these times. Mindful of the setbacks that could prevent the outbreak of political crisis or modulate it, he affirmed:

> It may be ruled out that immediate economic crises of themselves produce fundamental historical events; they can simply create a terrain more favourable to the dissemination of certain modes of thought, and certain ways of posing and resolving questions involving the entire subsequent development of national life.[168]

---

166 PN3, Q6, §130, p. 105.
167 Q15, §16, p. 1774. OT.
168 GR, Q13, §17, p. 208. A more in-depth discussion of the relationship between economic crisis and political crisis can be found in Bianchi 2002.

In this passage, Gramsci emphasised the asynchrony between the economic changes and political changes. Recognising this temporal diversity is an important antidote against all automatism. This recognition allows one to understand the discordance in the times of changes in the structure and the superstructure. This discordance leads one to perceive that the accelerated time of political and ideological forms, and of conflicts within these, makes the structure appear as fixed due to its slow movement. The action of the masses, as well their political and ideological movements, has its own temporality that is not necessarily the temporality of the economic crisis. On the contrary, for the most part, the movements of the masses lag behind conjunctural economic phenomena. According to Gramsci, in the economic analysis of reality,

> no account is taken of the 'time' factor, nor in the last analysis even of 'economics'. For there is no understanding of the fact that mass ideological factors always lag behind mass economic phenomena, and that therefore, at certain moments, the automatic thrust due to the economic factor is slowed down, obstructed or even momentarily broken by traditional ideological elements ...[169]

Identifying the discordance of the times of politics and economics is to recognise that a multiplicity of times can be contemporary in such a way. The interaction of these diverse temporalities presents as a final product not the result of a 'parallelogram of forces', but a historical singularity, a specific conjuncture. Conjuncture and situation were the terms with which the properly political analysis of the 'Preface to 1859' in §17 of Notebook 13 was conducted, in which such notions were related to big politics and small politics. The comparison between the first and second versions allows one to glimpse the process of the maturing of these notions in Gramsci's thinking. Concepts absent from the first version will occupy an important place in the second, serving as a point of articulation of the discourse and attributing depth and accuracy to it:

When studying a structure one must distinguish the permanent from the occasional. The occasional gives rise to political criticism, the permanent gives rise to sociohistorical criticism, the occasional	[I]n studying a structure, it is necessary to distinguish organic movements (relatively permanent) from movements which may be termed 'conjunctural' (and which appear as occasional, immediate, almost

---

169   GR, Q13, §23, p. 220.

helps one assess political groups and personalities, the permanent helps one assess large social groupings.[170]

accidental). Conjunctural phenomena too depend on organic movements to be sure, but they do not have any very far-reaching historical significance; they give rise to political criticism of a minor, day-to-day character, which has as its subject small ruling groups and personalities with direct governmental responsibilities. Organic phenomena on the other hand give rise to socio-historical criticism, whose subject is wider social groupings – beyond the people with immediate responsibilities and beyond the ruling personnel.[171]

Gramsci wanted to prevent the political crisis from being deduced directly from the economic crisis. For this reason, he clearly distinguished the conjuncture, in which the cyclical crisis of capitalism was revealed, from the situation, the time in which the organic crisis took place. The author of the *Notebooks* stated that during a crisis which lasted decades, insoluble contradictions revealed themselves, at the same time in which political forces that acted to defend this structure were struggling to overcome these contradictions. These efforts constituted the terrain of the occasional, a terrain on which the structure was updated.

The presence of such a crisis and the conflicts that are born within it revealed, according to Gramsci, 'that the necessary and sufficient conditions already exist to make possible, and hence imperative, the accomplishment of certain historical tasks'.[172] The strategic dimension that the Gramscian reading of the 'Preface of 1859' assumed appears here with force. Based on Marx's text it was possible to distinguish between organic movements and conjunctural facts applicable to 'all kinds of situations' and not only to the contexts of crisis and revolution. The absence of a fair relationship between these movements was by the Sardinian Marxist as a frequent mistake in historical-political analysis. But the consequences of this error were more serious in politics than in historiography, to the extent that while the latter aimed at reconstructing past history, politics aimed to build the present and the future.

---

170   GR, Q4 § 38, p. 177.
171   GR, Q13, § 17, p. 201.
172   Ibid.

Gramsci exemplified the use of these methodological criteria by means of a concrete case history, the same that motivated the original reflections of Marx: the French Revolution. Such a case was understood on an amplified historical scale. To extract all the necessary conclusions it must be borne in mind, Gramsci affirmed, that it was only in 1870–71, with the Paris Commune, that all the historical possibilities which came to light in 1789 had been historically exhausted. The internal contradictions of the French structure were manifested over the long term, in a historical period marked by transformations that took place in waves with an increasing length: 1789, 1794, 1799, 1804, 1815, 1830, 1848, 1870. The study of these successive waves would, according to Gramsci, allow one to 'reconstruct the relations on the one hand between structure and superstructure, and on the other between the development of the organic movement and that of the conjunctural movement in the structure'.[173]

The reconstruction of these complex relationships was one of the pillars of Gramscian theory building. To find in the apparent contingency of the conjuncture the structured and structuring forms that set the stage for the possible was an antidote to immediatism. To perceive the conjuncture as the moment in which the synthesis of the multiple contradictions in the structure assumed its current condition through the present conflict, constituting a historical particularity, was an antidote to fatalism. A fine sensitivity to the multiplicity of political and social times allowed Gramsci to dangerously navigate between Scylla and Charybdis. The contradictions often present in *Notebooks* attest to how dangerous this crossing was.

Gramsci sought to apprehend this multiplicity of times of politics and by means of a series of 'canons of research and interpretation' of the relations of forces. As an encounter of discordant times, the situations studied by Gramsci implied, according to Portantiero, 'the knowledge of the unequal development of the relations of force in each of the levels that, articulately, make up the social as a real object and as a concept'.[174]

Such canons would allow one to capture the existing trends in the real without considering them as 'historical causes'.[175] The application of these canons and the analysis of the real is not an end in itself. They only acquire meaning 'if they serve to justify a particularly practical activity, an initiative of will'. The analysis permits one to identify those points in which the concentration of the collective will can achieve the best results, 'suggest immediate tactical

---

173   GR, Q13, §17, p. 204.
174   Portantiero 1979, p. 60.
175   See GR, Q13, §17, p. 204.

operations; they indicate how a campaign of political agitation may best be launched, what language will best be understood by the masses, etc.'.[176]

The author of the *Notebooks* established as a starting point the analysis of the relation of forces linked to the objective structure. Such a relationship could be appreciated 'with the exact or physical sciences'.[177] The social groups rise on the basis of this structure, from the degree of development of the material forces of production, each occupying a given position in the social division of labour. At this level, classes exist objectively. They are a quantity, a place, a function. A 'rebel reality' is located here, but it is essential for verifying whether they exist in society, or if they can develop in society, the *necessary and sufficient conditions* for their transformation. That is, it allows one to verify the realism, the actuality and the degree of adequacy of the ideologies born on the soil of this rebellious reality and the contradictions generated in its development.

The positioning of this dimension as the first level of analysis reinforces the structured and structuring of the economic-social dimension in Gramsci's analysis. The assumption that the author of the *Notebooks* had reversed the positions occupied by the structure and the superstructure in his analysis of the real,[178] faces serious difficulties in sustaining itself when compared with §17. But Gramsci, as has already been said, did not intend to deduce the conjuncture from the structure. The result of the analysis of the objective relations of forces established a constant for the political situation, revealing the potential conflicts in reality and their possibilities of development, that is, of this adherence to the real. In this sense, Marx's analysis of the revolutions of 1848, investigating the social immaturity and politics of a proletariat still in the process of being constituted, is exemplary.

The fixity of the structure and the relation of the objective forces that takes place in it are the result of the slow maturation time of the productive forces. For Gramsci, these are 'the least variable in historical development, it is that once in a while can be identified and measured with mathematical accuracy, which can give rise, therefore, to observations and criteria'.[179] It is, therefore, in the *longue durée*, in what economists call 'secular tendencies' that this relationship finds its time.

The second level of analysis concerned the correlation of political-ideological forces, able to estimate the degree of homogeneity, self-consciousness and organisation of the various social groups. The various moments of col-

---

176 GR, Q13, §17, p. 209.
177 GR, Q13, §17, p. 204.
178 For example, Bobbio 1975.
179 Q11 §30, p. 1443. OT.

lective political consciousness may be captured here, the moments that horizontally and vertically combine, nationally and internationally, creating original and historically concrete arrangements. The definition of the different moments of this relationship of political-ideological forces also had a prescriptive character, in that it indicated where it should arrive: the formation of a renewed worldview in which the class recognises itself and recognises the *state form* proper to this conception.

The primitive moment of this relation was denominated by Gramsci as economic-corporate and expressed the situation in which one perceives 'the homogeneous unity and the duty of organise it, the unity of the professional group, but not yet that of the broader social group'.[180] The interests that weld this unity together are immediate, selfish and particular, unable to acquire a universal content and to create a 'an integral state civilization of their own'.[181] Economicism, whose criticism the author of the *Notebooks* devoted so much attention to, was for him considered as the theoretical effect of a consciousness and an organisation that has not yet succeeded in overcoming this economic-corporate phase.

The appropriation by the subaltern classes of the theoretical model of liberalism that sought to isolate politics from the other spheres of human activity – Croce, for example – had for Gramsci a perverse effect on these same classes. Such appropriation, by means of theoretical syndicalism, prevented the subaltern classes from becoming dominant and developing beyond the economic-corporate phase. In this way, the independence and autonomy of the subaltern group that the theoretical syndicalist movement said it represented were sacrificed to the intellectual hegemony of the dominant group.[182]

A less primitive form constitutes the next moment of this political-ideological relation. At that moment it would be possible to verify the solidarity of interests of all members of the social group, but still in the purely economic field, in which the question of the state, that is, of activity fully political, would not yet establish itself. As such, this new moment is an overcoming of narrow corporate marks, but expresses an identity that is still built in the economic sphere.

Although it has surpassed the strictly corporate dimension, the transformation of the subordinate group into a dominant one would not even be accomplished, as in the case of Fabianism; or inefficiently, as in social democracy; or through the immediate overcoming of the groups to a regime of perfect

---

180   Q11 §30, pp. 1583–4.
181   PN2, Q5, §123, p. 367.
182   GR, Q13, §18, pp. 210–11.

equality, as in anarchism. The economicism present in these moments of the construction of the ideological identity and organisation of the classes carried with it an important political consequence and formed a barrier to the constitution of a conception of the world by the subaltern classes themselves. For Gramsci, economicism was not merely a theoretical problem, it was an eminently political problem.

The third moment described was one in which there would be a strictly political phase of social groups and the transition from structure to the sphere of complex superstructures. This is the moment in which the 'hegemony of a fundamental social group over a series of subordinate groups' is formed.[183] According to Gramsci:

> it is the phase in which previously germinated ideologies become 'party', come into confrontation and conflict, until only one of them, or at least a single combination of them, tends to prevail, to gain the upper hand, to propagate itself over the whole social area – bringing about not only a unison of economic and political aims, but also intellectual and moral unity, posing all the questions around which the struggle rages not on a corporate but on a 'universal' plane, and thus creating the hegemony of a fundamental social group over a series of subordinate groups.[184]

It is at this moment that the process of development and self-organisation of social classes culminates, forming a new collective will, of which the political party, 'The modern Prince must be and cannot but be the proclaimer and organizer of an intellectual and moral reformation ...'.[185] The analysis of such a process summed up a patient reflection on the workers' movement in the first quarter of the twentieth century. The passage from one moment to another is not expressed theoretically by means of a cancellation, but by an overcoming. The construction of a hegemony implied, therefore, the re-elaboration of the economic or even corporate struggle of the subaltern classes as part of a totalising programme.

The way Gramsci understood this process and the reworking of the first moments in a new conception of the world and a political practice conforming to it can be understood from a note in which he discussed the 'Turin movement', the experience of the *Biennio Rosso*. Recalling the claims that this experience had been 'spontaneous' or 'voluntarist,' the former editor of the newspaper

---

183 GR, Q13, §17, p. 205.
184 Ibid.
185 GR, Q13, §1, p. 242.

L'Ordine Nuovo recognised the 'spontaneous' base of the real action to affirm that this could not have been nor was neglectful or unvalued. The spontaneous movement had been, according to Gramsci, '*educated* ... by means of modern theory but in a living, historically effective manner'.[186]

The process of building hegemony cannot fail to have an economic dimension.[187] The intellectual and moral reform in which this process was translated is the cultural elevation of 'the depressed strata of society'. This elevation begins in the very struggle of the party that represents and organises these strata, but which can only develop fully in a new state form and after 'a transformation in social positions and in the economic world'.[188] For this reason, intellectual and moral reform must be linked to a 'programme of economic reform', that is, 'the programme of economic reform is precisely the concrete form in which every intellectual and moral reformation presents itself'.[189]

The exact understanding of this relationship between 'intellectual and moral reform' and 'economic reform' is fundamental. Without the latter, the former would be pure voluntarism. 'Economic reform' also provided the limit to which concessions to allied groups was possible. According to Gramsci,

> Undoubtedly the fact of hegemony presupposes that account be taken of the interests and the tendencies of the groups over which hegemony is to be exercised, and that a certain compromise equilibrium should be formed – in other words, that the leading group should make sacrifices of an economic-corporate kind. But there is also no doubt that such sacrifices and such a compromise cannot touch the essential; for though hegemony is ethico-political, it must also be economic, must necessarily be based on the decisive function exercised by the leading group in the decisive nucleus of economic activity.[190]

The process of building hegemony, a process that develops parallel to the formation of self-consciousness and self-organisation of classes, corresponds to a certain extent to the passage from 'class in itself' to 'class for itself'. According to testimony from Angelo Scucchia to Mima Paulesu Quercioli, this was one of the first themes that Gramsci dealt with in his conversations with fellow detainees in Turi:

---

186 PN2, Q3, § 48, p. 50.
187 See Burgio 2003, p. 31.
188 GR, Q13, § 1, pp. 242–3.
189 GR, Q13, § 1, p. 243.
190 GR, Q13, § 18, pp. 211–12.

He considered, in fact, fundamental and primordial to deepen these concepts of the working class that 'class in itself' becomes the 'class for itself', that is, the class that acquires consciousness of its own historical function, political struggle and expresses the party.[191]

This passage in which the construction of the political subjects occurs was not conceived in a voluntarist way by Gramsci. The study of the different moments of this passage in the *Prison Notebooks* develops, rather than denies, Gramsci's reflection in the 'Introduzione al primo corso della scuola interna di partito' ('Introduction to the First Course of the Internal Party School'), written in 1925. It would not be correct, this text warns, to demand from a common worker a full awareness of the functions which his class was called to develop in the historical process. Before the conquest of the state, it would be impossible to completely change the consciousness of the entire working class. Gramsci took up again a problematic already developed by Trotsky in *Literature and Revolution*: consciousness would only change completely in the whole class when the proletariat becomes the dominant class, controlling the production apparatus and state power.[192]

So far, the relations of objective forces and political-ideological relations have been dealt with. Gramsci completed his analysis of the relations of forces with a third level, calling it the relation of military forces, considered by him to be '*directly decisive*'.[193] Here too, two moments were also distinguished: a first that could be called technical-military, representing a more strictly conflictual dimension; and another, politico-military.

The use of military terminology on this third level has no other meaning than to build an analogy with politics. Gramsci would not have developed all this exposition with respect to the relations of forces between the fundamental classes to, suddenly, shift his focus to interstate conflict in the international arena. The very discussion of this relation of military forces from the analysis of the *Risorgimento* allows us to understand the analogy.[194] The relationship of military forces is nothing if not a relation of strategic forces that occurs at the very moment of open confrontation or the preparation for it among the fundamental social classes.

Gramsci explained in Notebook 19 that the expression 'military direction' should not be understood only in the strict sense; 'one should rather under-

---

191 Quercioli 1977, p. 220.
192 CPC, p. 54. See Trotsky 2005 and Paggi 1973, p. 1349.
193 GR, Q13, §17, p. 206. Emphasis added.
194 See GR, Q13, §17, p. 207 and Q19, §28, pp. 2048–54.

stand it in a much more comprehensive sense and adherent to the proper political leadership'.[195] The military leadership comprises therefore not only the technical issues related to the mobilisation of an army, but also 'the political-insurrectional mobilization of popular forces'.[196] Faced with the affirmation of an 'directly decisive' moment identified with the 'political-insurrectional mobilization' it becomes difficult to sustain, as Coutinho proposes,[197] an antagonistic opposition between 'the idea of a frontal clash with the state' and 'the idea of a "long march" through the institutions of civil society'.

According to Athos Lisa's account, the 'military problem and the party' was one of the principal topics discussed by Gramsci in his conversations with other prisoners. Although his narrative is not always conceptually precise, it leaves no room for doubt about the importance of the theme and its relation to the problem of insurrection. According to Lisa, Gramsci stated that:

> The violent conquest of power demands from the party of the proletariat the creation of an organization of a military type, which, despite its molecular form, diffuses into all branches of bourgeois state organization and is able to violate it and to strike heavy blows to it at the decisive moment of struggle.[198]

One may notice here that Lisa was not aware of the Gramscian extension of the concept of the state, but this does not invalidate his general framing of the problem. The 'military question' was a question of insurrection. The suppression of the insurrectional horizon and the moment of revolutionary rupture, carried out by many interpreters of Gramscian political thought, requires that this third moment be neglected in the analysis of the relations of forces. It is symptomatic, therefore, that in his essay on Gramsci's analysis of conjuncture, Portantiero ignores, without further explanation, this third degree of the correlation of forces, interrupting the description in §17 of Notebook 13 before reaching the relations of military forces.[199] It was the revolution itself that was cancelled. The analytical suppression of the relations of military forces is equivalent to the annulation of that level considered by Gramsci 'directly decisive'.

The different levels of the analysis of the relation of forces express different levels of analytical abstraction. In addition to the logic of the exposition,

---

195 Q19, §13, p. 2048. OT.
196 Ibid.
197 Coutinho 1999, p. 135.
198 Lisa 1981, p. 378.
199 See Portantiero 1979, p. 69.

there is the logic of the historical movement itself. The scheme developed was symmetrical to that drawn by the two principles expressed by the 'Preface of 1859'. The three levels presented concerned different degrees of intervention of the human will. At the first level there would be the movement of the structure imposing itself, the 'rebel reality', independent of the immediate action of historical subjects. It is the objective principle of the contradiction between productive forces and relations of production; an *epochal* definition.

But it would be on the third level, in which the direct shock between the social subjects occurs, that this contradiction would be resolved. This is the level of the achievement of the will 'as operative awareness of historical necessity, as protagonist of a real and effective historical drama', the level of revolution.[200] The historical movement, Gramsci said, constantly oscillates between the first and third moments of the correlation of forces through the mediation of the second moment, that of the correlation of political forces. This was the level at which it would become possible to pass 'from the structure to the complex superstructures'.

It was here and nowhere else where Gramsci arrived at his reflection on the analysis of situations and relations of forces. The patiently constructed canons of investigation from the material of the 'Preface of 1859' were intended to identify the possibility of revolution and the conditions for its victory. The analysis of 'effective reality' was articulated in this way by meticulous research into the effectiveness of the forms of political struggle.

---

200   GR, Q13, §1, p. 241.

CHAPTER 5

State/Civil Society

There is no denying the existence of a hegemonic reading of Gramsci's work. In it, he would be proclaimed as a theoretician of superstructures, a prophet of 'organised' civil society and a defender of the 'conquest of spaces' in democracy. The epicentre of this reading can be found in a reductionist appropriation of the Gramscian concept of the state in its 'organic and broader' sense for which Norberto Bobbio's interpretation became paradigmatic. In this appropriation, the unity between structure and superstructure, political society and civil society, dictatorship and hegemony were split and a relation of antagonism was constituted between each of these terms. To overcome the false antagonisms instituted in these concepts and revalue the unitary and organic character of the Gramsci's thinking, a reading is needed that appreciates the fragmentary character of his work, the sources to which he resorts and the time of its production.

The starting point for the analysis of the concept of state may be a note, already present in Notebook 1, entitled 'La concezione dello Stato secondo la produttività [funzione] delle classi sociale' ('The conception of the state according to the productivity [function] of the social classes'). In this note, Gramsci stated: 'The productive classes (capitalist bourgeoisie and modem proletariat) can conceive the state only as the concrete form of a specific economic world, of a specific system of production'.[1] The state is the expression, in the field of superstructures, of a certain form of social organisation of production. Thus, the conquest of power and the affirmation of a new economic and productive world are inseparable and it is this unitary condition in which the very unity of the class occurs which is, at the same time, politically and economically dominant.

This definition, however, is only a starting point. Relevant questions and satisfactory answers are not found in this preliminary framework. Gramsci was aware of these difficulties. Even in this paragraph he shows that it is necessary to conceive of this articulation between economics and politics without neglecting the complex relations between economic and national political (local) and international development, as well as the rationalisation process

---

1 PN1, Q1, §150, p. 229.

through which the intellectuals make the historical function of the state appear as a determination of the absolute.

The second version of this note, inscribed inside Notebook 10, reveals that Gramsci considered it necessary to increase the precautions that would prevent the establishment of a reductionist conception of the state. This new version denotes an increasing effort by the author of the *Notebooks* with a view to purifying the historical materialism of every economistic residue. This commitment became more and more evident as the writing advanced in time and when previous notes were revised in the special notebooks.² In the second version of the text that is being analysed here, the Italian Marxist reproduced an important passage from the original version, but added some warnings:

> If it is true that for the fundamental productive classes (capitalist bourgeoisie and modern proletariat) the state is conceivable only as a concrete form of a particular economic world, of a certain production system, it is not said that the relationship between the means and the ends is easily determined and takes on the aspect of a simple and obvious scheme at first sight.³

The precautions taken here were fully justified. After all, how can one explain, for example, the case of his own country in the nineteenth century without taking care to avoid an instrumentalist conception? The need for the renovation of the state was not defined by a profound transformation in the social structure. Although this transformation was taking place, it had not yet generated social forces vigorous enough to drive social change. The emergent social forces represented, rather than the force of the present, the possibilities of the future and the changes that took place in the state did not reflect a previously existing economic organisation. The renewal of the Italian state thus preceded the modernisation of the economy.

Yet beyond this reality that was presented on Italian national soil, there was an international situation favourable to the expansion and victory of these forces. And it was the combination of the scarce and insufficient progressive forces and this international situation which allowed for the renewal of the Italian state, determining the limits through which it occurred.⁴ The Italian case shows that the relations between capitalist state and the economic world (relations between superstructure and structure) cannot be determined in an

---

2 See Cospito 2000, p. 101.
3 Q10 / II, § 61, p. 1360. OT.
4 Q10 / II, § 61, p. 1360.

easy way in the form of a simple scheme. To understand them, one has to keep in mind that these two groupings form a totality that has diverse temporalities within it. This mismatch between the times of superstructures and structures constitutes the chief difficulty faced by instrumentalist theories of the state, which define it as a mere reflection of the economic world and cannot explain the transitions to capitalism in which political transformations anticipate the full transformation of the economic world.[5]

The development of the economy and politics is closely linked and marked by reciprocal influences, actions and reactions, by the struggles that characterise the classes in presence and the superstructural forms of these in the national and international environment. Recognising these links does not mean that waiting for transformations in the economic world always provokes an immediate reaction that modifies the superstructural forms, or vice versa. A certain mismatch between the changes occurring in these ensembles is even foreseeable, although there is a tendency for one to adapt to the other. This tendency is nothing but the search for an optimisation of the conditions of production and reproduction of the capitalist social relations through the economic and political unity of the ruling class, a unit that is processed in the state.

In this way, the 'state is seen as the organ of one particular group, destined to create favourable conditions for the latter's maximum expansion'.[6] But for this expansion to be effectively carried out it could not appear as the accomplishment of the exclusive interests of the groups that are directly benefitted. It had to present itself as a universal expansion – an expression of the whole society – by way of the incorporation of the claims and interests of the subordinate groups in state life, subtracting them from their own logic and framing them within the prevailing order. This incorporation is the contradictory result of permanent struggles and the formation of unstable balances of power arrangements between the classes. It is a process limited by the necessities of the reproduction needs of the order itself, and is therefore restricted to the level of economic and corporate demands.

This is the point of the exposition in which it becomes necessary to define the contours of the state. The general elements have already been largely presented and the more attentive reader who is familiar with the theme will not have much difficulty in predicting where I want to go. The state is understood here in its 'organic and broader' sense as the ensemble formed by political society and civil society. In Notebook 6, written between November 1930 and

---

5   See Saes 1994, p. 20.
6   GR, Q13, §17, p. 205. In the original essay, Gramsci refers to the concept of 'state-government'. PN2, Q4, §38, p. 180.

January 1932[7] and composed mostly of B texts, this definition was presented explicitly by Gramsci, under the concept of the 'integral state'.

The formulation appeared for the first time within the analysis of the constitution of a social order after the French Revolution of 1789 in which the bourgeoisie could 'present itself as an integral "State", with all the intellectual and moral forces that were necessary and adequate to the task of organizing a complete and perfect society'.[8] The construction of the Gramscian text occurs within the nexus evident in the 'Preface of 1859'. By having necessary and sufficient conditions to overcome the old order, the bourgeoisie could complete the reorganisation of society. In the same sense, in reference to the political development of the French Revolution after 1793, Gramsci referred to the Jacobin initiative of unifying

> in a dictatorial manner the constitutive elements of the state organically and more broadly (the state, in the rigorous sense, and civil society) in a desperate effort to tighten their grip on the life of the people and the nation as a whole. Yet it also appears to have been the first root of the modern secular state, independent of the church, seeking and finding within itself, within its complex life, all the elements of its historical personality.[9]

It is clear that the definition of the state hitherto outlined sought to avoid a conception which would reduce it to the coercive apparatus. Consensus building also acquired a place in this state. In summary, though no less significant, Gramsci presented his conception in an already classic way, 'state = political society + civil society, that is, hegemony protected by the armor of coercion',[10] or as he expresses later in the same Notebook, 'state (in the full sense: dictatorship + hegemony)'.[11] The issue was framed in the Notebook's research plan in the following way in a letter dated 7 September 1931:

> I extend very much the notion of intellectual and I do not limit myself to the current notion that refers to the grand intellectuals. This study brings also certain determinations of the concept of state that is usually understood as political society (or dictatorship, or coercive apparatus to conform the popular mass according to the type of production and

---

7   See Francioni 1984, pp. 141–2.
8   PN3, Q6, §10, p. 9.
9   PN3, Q6, §87, pp. 74–5.
10 PN3, Q6, §88, p. 75.
11 PN3, Q6, §155, p. 117.

the economy of a given moment) and not as an equilibrium of political society with civil society (or hegemony of a social group over the entire national society exercised through the so-called private organisms, like the church, the labor unions, the schools, etc.) and precisely in civil society the intellectuals especially operate (Ben. Croce, for ex., is a sort of laic pope and is a very efficient instrument of hegemony even if from time to time he finds himself in contrast to this or that government, etc.).[12]

It is this definition that Christine Buci-Glucksmann synthesises with the formula 'expanded state'.[13] Although strong, this formula can generate, and has generated, excessive oversimplifications and some confusion. For this reason, the observations of Liguori with respect to this question are prudent: on the one hand, the concept of the expanded state harbours the distinction between the state and civil society without cancelling or suppressing either of the two terms and, on the other hand, the concept indicates 'that this unity comes, if the expression is allowed for me, *under the hegemony of the state*'.[14] In the same sense, Prestipino[15] stresses that the rudimentary formula

state = coercion and civil society = hegemony

is contrary to the complex Gramscian analysis, in which there is no rigid division of labour between the two spheres and which, to the contrary, aims to account for the new hegemonic tasks of the state.

Take these two key terms: political society and civil society. The concept of political society is clear in the Gramscian text. It is the state in the strict sense, that is, the governmental apparatus in charge of the direct administration and the legal exercise of coercion on those who do not consent either actively or passively, also called in Notebooks the 'political state' or 'state-government'. Gramsci does not ignore, at any moment, this dimension, that is, he does not lose sight of the coercive dimension of politics although he does not reduce politics to it.

More complex is the definition of the concept of civil society. Whether it is because in the Gramscian text, the concept has very imprecise contours, because there is not a single definition of the term or because in contempor-

---

12   LP2, Vol. 2, p. 67.
13   Buci-Gluksmann 1980, pp. 126–48.
14   Liguori 2006, p. 13.
15   Prestipino 2004, pp. 70–1.

ary political language, the term 'civil society' was incorporated, often making references to Gramsci himself, albeit with a different sense. For all this, the confusion is great.[16]

1   Bobbio

A considerable part of this confusion stems from the influential interpretation by Norberto Bobbio[17] (1975) of the concept of civil society in Gramsci. Identifying a dichotomy between civil society and the state, Bobbio stated that Gramsci distanced himself from the Marxist conception of the former term. While for Marx the moment of civil society coincided with the material basis of society, the structure, as opposed to the superstructure, for the Italian Marxist, civil society 'does not belong to the structural moment, but to the superstructural one'.[18] According to Bobbio, Gramsci shared with Marx the idea that civil society would determine the whole of historical development:

> both in Marx and in Gramsci, civil society, and not the state as in Hegel, represents the active and positive moment of historical development. Still, in Marx this active and positive moment is a structural moment, while in Gramsci it is a superstructural one.[19]

To sustain his thesis, Bobbio takes as a starting point a note of Gramsci on intellectuals:

> It should be possible both to measure the degree of 'organicism' of the various intellectual strata and their degree of connection with a fundamental social group, and to establish a gradation of their functions and of the superstructures from the bottom to the top (from the structural base upwards). What we can do, for the moment, is to fix two major superstructural 'levels': the one that can be called 'civil society', that is the ensemble of organisms commonly called 'private', and that of 'political society' or 'the state'. These two levels correspond on the one hand to the function of 'hegemony' which the dominant group exercises throughout society and

---

16   Several authors have identified the varied and often indiscriminate use of the concept of civil society. I highlight Costa 1997 and Foley and Edwards 1996.
17   Bobbio 1979.
18   Bobbio 1979, p. 30.
19   Bobbio 1979, p. 31.

on the other hand to that of 'direct domination' or command exercised through the state and 'juridical' government.[20]

This is undoubtedly the most frequent meaning of the term civil society in the *Prison Notebooks*. In this sense, *civil society* is understood as the 'ensemble of organisms commonly called "private"'. Regarding these 'organisms', it is important to emphasise their material character, as Gramsci does in the aforementioned Notebook 6, using the precise terms 'hegemonic apparatus of one social group'[21] and '"Private" apparatus of hegemony'.[22] The materiality of the processes of the conformation of hegemony was thus highlighted.[23] The struggle of hegemonies is not only a struggle between 'worldviews', as, for example, appears in Notebook 10; it is also a struggle of the apparatuses that function as material carriers of these ideologies by organising and disseminating them.

The list of such hegemonic devices is large, but well-known: churches, schools, private associations, unions, parties, and the press are some of them. The function of these organisms is to articulate the consensus of the great masses and their adherence to the social orientation formed by the dominant groups. This group of organisms, however, is not socially undifferentiated. The classist divisions and the struggles between different social groups traverse the hegemonic apparatuses and put various groups in opposition to each other. Using everyday political vocabulary, this alert is justified in that a Tocquevillian concept of 'civil society' becomes preponderant. In this concept, civil society signifies a set of associations located outside the state sphere, undifferentiated and potentially progressive, agents of social transformation and bearers of uncontradictory universal interests. Such a view is implicitly shared by Bobbio when he affirms an immanent positivity to this sphere.

But it is worth noting the existence of what Simone Chambers and Jeffrey Kopstein[24] appropriately referred to as 'bad civil society': the development of authoritarian or even totalitarian currents within civil society itself and not on its margins as was the case of Nazism in the Weimar Republic and fascism in the Italy of Gramsci. Perceived not as an undifferentiated whole, but as an ensemble marked by deep class antagonisms, civil society loses its illusory veil. It is not just about the unequal distribution of communicative resources that prevents free access to a public sphere, it is also about the defence of antagon-

---

20 GR, Q12, §1, p. 306 and Bobbio 1979, p. 85.
21 PN3, Q6, §136, p. 107.
22 PN3, Q6, §137, p. 108.
23 Liguori 2006, p. 24.
24 Chambers and Kopstein 2001.

istic societal designs. Instead of the place of the universalisation of particularist interests, it becomes seen as a space of the class struggle and the affirmation of antagonistic projects.[25] The political strategy for the occupation of spaces in civil society advocated by a reformist, if not a liberal thought, makes no sense to the author of the *Notebooks*. It is exactly about the creation of new autonomous spaces for the subaltern classes and the denial of political spaces for the ruling classes.

In addition to affirming the immanent positivity of civil society, Bobbio attributed to it the role of determining history. According to him, the concept of civil society expressed by Gramsci was derived directly from Hegel, and not from Marx, contrary to what many believe. For in Hegel, civil society would encompass not only the moment of economic relations, but also the spontaneous and voluntary forms of organisation that he identified in corporations, considered as 'the second ethical root of the state, the one planted in civil society'.[26] The Hegelian formula appears almost literally in an enlightening A text inserted by Gramsci in Notebook 6 that is also quoted by Bobbio:

> One must distinguish civil society as Hegel understands it and in the sense it is often used in these notes (that is, in the sense of the political and cultural hegemony of a social group over the whole of society; *as the ethical content of the state*) from the sense given to it by Catholics, for whom civil society is, instead, political society or the state, as opposed to the society of the family and of the church.[27]

The similarity between the Gramscian formula and that of Hegel is evident and made explicit. It should be noted, however, that the knowledge Gramsci possessed of Hegel's work was not always consistent.[28] Thus, it was probably via Croce that the Sardinian Marxist was approaching Hegel. It was a merit of Bobbio to highlight this Gramsci-Hegel nexus in an emphatic manner. But it is not possible to deduce from this nexus that Gramsci, freely appropriating the Hegelian concept, attributed to society (and therefore to the superstructure) the active place attributed to it by Marx.

---

25 Dias, 1996, pp. 66–8.
26 Hegel 2008, § 255, p. 226. It is worth emphasising that, for Hegel, the 'mediation of the need and the satisfaction of the individual through his work and the satisfaction of the needs of all others – the *system of needs*', was a constitutive moment of civil society. See Hegel 2008, § 188, p. 186.
27 PN3, Q6, § 24, pp. 20–1. Emphasis added.
28 See Semeraro 2001, p. 134 analysing Gramsci in PN1, Q1, § 152, pp. 231–2.

Gramsci's approach to Hegel, according to the Turin philosopher Bobbio, had the purpose of splitting the former from Marxist theory and his reconversion to idealism. As a 'theoretician of superstructures' Gramsci would thus see his theory reduced to the so-called 'ethical-political history' of Benedetto Croce.[29] The recurrent criticism that Gramsci makes of the hypothesis of the ethico-political moment by Croce, particularly in Notebook 10, however, disavows this reduction.

Coutinho[30] criticises Bobbio's interpretation, stating that if Gramsci's concept of civil society is not that of Marx himself, there would be no reason to assign to it the same function of determination in the last instance. And there is, in fact, nothing in the Gramscian text to affirm that he had reinvested in Hegel, putting it above his own formulations and affirming the superstructure as determinant of the historical process.

Bobbio's argument turns out to be unilateral when we analyse the other senses that the concept of civil society assumes in Gramscian thought. As Texier warned, the very passage quoted by Bobbio reveals that Gramsci defines civil society 'frequently' ('spesso', in the Italian text), but not exclusively, as a place of the 'political and cultural hegemony of a social group'.[31] In fact, this seems to be not the only meaning that Gramsci attributes to the term. See, for example, a passage from §18 in Notebook 13, entitled 'Some theoretical and practical aspects of "economism"' (*'Alcuni aspetti teorici e pratici dell "economismo"'*):

> The approach of the free trade movement is based on a theoretical error whose practical origin is not hard to identify: namely the distinction between political society and civil society, which is made into and presented as an organic one, whereas in fact it is merely methodological. Thus it is asserted that economic activity belongs to civil society, and that the state must not intervene to regulate it. But since in actual reality civil society and state are one and the same, it must be made clear that *laissez-faire* too is a form of state 'regulation', introduced and maintained by legislative and coercive means. It is a deliberate policy, conscious of its own ends, and not the spontaneous, automatic expression of economic facts.[32]

---

29   See Semeraro 2001, p. 185 and Liguori 2006, p. 31.
30   Coutinho 1999, p. 122.
31   Texier 1988, p. 8.
32   GR, Q13, §18, p. 210.

The idea that Gramsci would have excluded the capitalist economy from civil society, to the contrary of Marx, and even of Hegel, an idea supported not only by Bobbio, but also by Cohen and Arato,[33] does not withstand a detailed analysis of the above passage. In this text, civil society appears as the locus of economic activity itself, the terrain of immediate material interests, private property, bourgeois economic society, or what today would be called the business world.

These two meanings are used in different ways by Gramsci. In the first, civil society is associated with the forms of the exercise and affirmation of the supremacy of one class over society as a whole. It is part of a research programme aimed at clarifying not only the processes of bourgeois revolution and the founding of a new state, but also the longevity and strength of the capitalist West's political institutions and the possibility of the establishment of a new social and political order. In the second sense, often presented in quotation marks, the capacity of economic initiative that the state possesses in contemporary capitalism is stressed.

The link between these two forms of the manifestation of the concept is not always found in Gramsci, so that authors such as Badaloni[34] and Francioni[35] can affirm that Gramsci works with a triple distinction: economic society, civil society, and political society. From this perspective, the analysis of the three moments of the relationship of forces present in Notebook 13 would be an analysis of the relations that would be verified in economic society as relations of objective forces; in civil society, as relations of political-ideological forces; and in political society, as relations of political-military forces.[36]

However, what is important here is that civil society in one sense – the ensemble of private bodies responsible for the articulation of consensus – as in the other – the locus of economic activity – maintains a relation of unity-distinction with political society. The re-elaboration of the Crocean 'nexus of distincts' was an important contribution of Gramsci, fundamental for the understanding of these links between political society and civil society.

For Croce, as we have already seen, the Spirit differed in its theoretical and practical forms and these in their upper and lower degrees. The degrees of the beautiful and the true comprised the different degrees of the theoretical form, while the useful and the good conformed to the practical form. Croce emphasised that among these different degrees there was no relation

---

33   Cohen and Arato 2000, p. 174.
34   Badaloni 1978, pp. 37–47.
35   Francioni 1987, pp. 193.
36   See Medici's comments, 2000, pp. 166–7.

of opposition, but only one of unity and distinction, that is, beautiful, true, useful and good were not opposed to each other. The Crocean nexus of the distincts allowed its creator to undertake a conservative and speculative reform of the dialectic which denied internal negation in the concept. According to Croce:

> ... the distinctions of the concept are not the negation of the concept, nor something outside the concept, but only the concept itself, understood in its truth; the *one-distinct*; one, only because distinct, and distinct only because one. Unity and distinction are correlative and therefore inseparable.[37]

Gramsci's critique of this conception was explicit and aimed to overcome of the Crocean nexus of distincts. Gramsci was wrong, however, in assigning to Croce a 'dialectics of the distincts', since for this philosopher the dialectic would always be a relation between opposites.[38] Without abandoning the idea that within a unit it was possible to find not only opposites, but also distincts, Gramsci severely rejected the speculative character of the Crocean thought, which reduced the historical dialectic to an alternation of pure forms of the concept.[39] He also rejected the Crocean suppression of negation and the consequent endless reproduction of the thesis that would never be overcome by the antithesis.

Thus, for Gramsci the distinction was conceived as a form of non-antagonistic opposition, not antagonistic insofar as each distinct is in a relationship of '(dialectical) *tension* with the other'.[40] The possibility of this relationship of tense unity converting into an opposition was not discarded, however, by Gramsci. But this conversion was not an *a priori*. Martelli explains in this respect that 'even if the distincts are not opposed, in certain conditions they may become, that is, the opposition is nothing but the distinction, the diversity, the alterity that is subverted into antagonism'.[41]

By way of the categories of unity and distinction Gramsci thematised the 'elaboration of the structure in the superstructure',[42] that is, the process by means of which the particular that is based in economic society is universal-

---

37   Croce 1917, p. 77.
38   See, for example, Croce 1947b, pp. 92–3 and Martelli 2001, p. 116.
39   Prestipino 2004, p. 56.
40   Prestipino 2004, p. 68.
41   Martelli 2001, p. 116.
42   Q10 / II, § 6, p. 1244. OT.

ised in civil society. In this process, the economic society becomes the 'state', that is, in its becoming the structure is 'superstructuralised' as a civil society in the integral state.[43]

Keeping political society and civil society in a unity-distinction relationship serves to form two overlapping planes that can only be separated for purely analytical purposes. For this reason, Gramsci emphasised that unity ('identity') between the state and civil society is always 'organic' and that the 'distinction' is only 'methodical'.[44] This is not, however, the interpretation of Texier, for whom the organic unity pointed out by Gramsci between civil society and political society in the above citation applies only to the relationship between state (political society) and economy (civil society) and not to the relation hegemony-dictatorship.[45] The unity between political society and civil society as the locus of economic activity appeared explicitly in Gramsci in the aforementioned passage of 'Some theoretical and practical aspects of economism'. But unity between political society and civil society was also affirmed as the set of private bodies responsible for the articulation of consensus.

The incomprehension of this organic unity between civil society and political society has led some authors to claim that Gramsci characterised civil society as an autonomous sphere of the state.[46] Although Coutinho[47] rejected the radical dichotomy that these authors posited between civil society and the state, he shared to some extent the conception which attributes to civil society a 'material (and not only functional) autonomy in relation to state in the strict sense'.[48] Coutinho's statement was based on a questionable historical assumption – the exclusively contemporary character of civil society – and a theoretical conception that is difficult to sustain – of the establishment of an algebraic relation between domination and direction.

Historically, Coutinho stated, the material autonomy of civil society would be a 'specific trait of its manifestation in the most complex capitalist societies'.[49] This interpreter did not, however, acknowledge the ambiguity of the *Notebooks*, where Gramsci seems to oscillate between a position that affirmed the presence of civil society in pre-capitalist societies and another, in which

---

43 Prestipino 2004, p. 71.
44 Q10 / II, § 6, p. 1244. OT.
45 Texier 1988, p. 10.
46 See, for example, Baker 1998, p. 81 and Cohen and Arato 2000, p. 175. For a critique of the readings on civil society that have prevailed in the Anglo-Saxon academic universe, see Liguori 2006, pp. 37–8.
47 Coutinho 2006, pp. 41 and 46–7.
48 Coutinho 1999, p. 129 and 2006, p. 38.
49 Coutinho 1999, p. 131.

this would be a distinctive characteristic of societies in which there would be high levels of the socialisation of politics and the self-organisation of social groups.[50] As previously stated, the thesis is historically questionable and is based on a historiographically outdated conception of pre-capitalist societies, and particularly about the early medieval period.

It completely escapes the purpose of this text to discuss the historical impropriety of this thesis. Yet it should be emphasised that it is inconsistent with the text in the *Notebooks* in which State-Church relations in the medieval period provide an important analogical resource for the discussion of the contemporary state and its relations with civil society. But it is not just a historical analogy, as revealed by Gramsci's research on the '*formation of the group of Italian intellectuals*' and their place in civil society, already present in the index of Notebook 1, which dates from 1929. This research goes far beyond the scope of 'complex societies'.[51]

Certainly, it is not intended here to establish a transhistorical concept of civil society that identifies social and political forms that have developed in very different realities and in different ways. But here too history and politics are identified. The main question for Coutinho is not of a historiographical order, but of a political one.

His argument is rigorously constructed with the purpose of establishing an identity between the '*complex* societies of *recent* capitalism' and the affirmation of an algebraic conception of the relationship between consensus and coercion in which one variable presents behaviour inversely proportional to the other. According to Coutinho:

> The fact that a state is more hegemonic-consensual and less 'dictatorial', or vice versa, depends on the relative autonomy of the superstructural spheres, of the predominance of one over the other, predominance and autonomy which, in turn, depend not only on the degree of socialization of the politics reached by the society in question, but also of the correlation of forces between the social classes that dispute *supremacy* between themselves.[52]

No matter how Coutinho affirms the unity between coercion and consensus, the true sense of this unity is lost in his algebraic formula. For if an extension

---

50 Q10 / II, § 6, p. 1244. OT.
51 A historically well-informed analysis of the place of these intellectuals in the Middle Ages, close to Gramsci in many ways and far from Coutinho, can be found in Le Goff 1993.
52 Coutinho 1999, p. 131.

of civil society implies an emptying of the coercive functions of the state, this can only occur because one overrides the other. In this algebraic conception, the dialectic of the unity-distinction that characterises the Gramscian formulation is removed. The very exercise of hegemony was understood by Gramsci as a combination of coercion and consensus, even in political regimes in which liberal-democratic forms prevailed:

> The 'normal' exercise of hegemony in what became the classic terrain of the parliamentary regime is characterized by the combination of force and consent variously balancing one another, without force exceeding consent too much. Indeed one tries to make it appear that force is supported by the consent of the majority, expressed by the so-called organs of public opinion newspapers and associations – which are therefore, in certain situations, artificially increased in number.[53]

Thus, if, in the well-known formula of Notebook 6, hegemony was protected in the classic form of the 'armour of coercion', in the passage above, it is force that appears protected by hegemony.[54] The fact that some authors inspired by Gramscian thought give little importance to the coercive dimension of the state is, therefore, not defensible. Justifying the scant attention she dedicated to the subject in her work *Gramsci et l'Etat* (*Gramsci and the State*), Christine Buci-Glucksmann[55] stated that Marxist thought had emphasised coercion so much that she felt it appropriate to emphasise consensus to counterbalance the results. The result, however, is a one-dimensional analysis, in which the Gramscian 'double perspective' is lost, leaving only the articulation of consensus as a form of political affirmation. Gramsci thus becomes a Proto-Habermasian ...

2   Machiavelli

With respect to the dialectical relation of unity-distinction between force and consensus it is important to revisit the sources of Gramscian thought, and in first place, Machiavelli. The fundamental question appears in a note in which

---

53   GR, Q13, § 37, p. 261.
54   The note in Notebook 6 is dated by Francioni between March and August of 1931. The note in Notebook 13 appears as an A text already in Notebook 1 (§ 48, pp. 155–6) and is dated by Francioni between February and March 1929 and his second essay (that I quote) is dated between May 1932 and the first months of 1934 (Francioni 1984, pp. 140, 142 and 144).
55   Buci-Glucksmann 1987 and 1980b.

Gramsci intended to establish the distinction between 'small politics' and 'big politics': 'Machiavelli examines especially questions of big politics: the creation of new states, the conservation and protection of organic structures as a whole; *questions of dictatorship and hegemony on a large scale, that is, over the entire area of the state*'.[56]

The key theme, which unified the discussion of the historical interpretation of the Florentine's work and the translation of some concepts for the scope of Marxism was therefore the creation and preservation of new states.

It is in this theoretical-political context that the aforementioned passage becomes of great importance for an adequate appreciation of the relations between coercion and consent. Referring to the distinction that Luigi Russo analysed in Machiavelli, highlighting *The Prince* as a treaty on dictatorship and the *Discourses on the First Decade of Titus Livius* as a treaty on hegemony, Gramsci observed that in *The Prince* there was no shortage of references 'to the moment of hegemony or consensus alongside that of authority and force' and concluded that 'there is no opposition of principle [in Machiavelli] between the principality and republic, but above everything, it deals with the hypostases of the two moments of authority and of universality'.[57] In Gramsci's interpretation it becomes clear that the separation between authority and universality, force and consensus, dictatorship and hegemony were, for Machiavelli, arbitrary. It is in a note in which Gramsci made reference to a contemporary of Machiavelli, Francesco Guicciardini, where such arbitrariness is fully revealed:[58]

> Guicciardini's claim that two things are absolutely necessary for the life of a state: arms and religion. This formula of his can be translated into various other, less drastic, formulas: force and consent, coercion and persuasion, state and Church, political society and civil society, politics and morals (Croce's ethico-political history), law and freedom, order and discipline, or, with an implicit judgement of a libertarian flavour, violence and fraud.[59]

The reference was still to Machiavelli, since Guicciardini poses the question in a commentary on *Discourses on the First Decade of Titus Livius*. Machiavelli

---

56 Q13, § 5, p. 1564. OT. Emphasis added.
57 Ibid.
58 It is possible that the reference to Guicciardini is only indirect, resulting from a reading of an article by Paolo Treves. See the critical edition of Gerratana in Q, 2720.
59 FSPN, Q6, § 87, pp. 127–8.

stresses: '[I]t will be plain to anyone who carefully studies Roman History, how much religion helped in disciplining the army, in uniting the people, in keeping good men good, and putting bad men to shame' and that 'when religion is once established you may readily bring in arms; but where you have arms without religion it is not easy afterwards to bring in religion'.[60] In this respect Guicciardini wrote in his *Considerations on the Discourses of Machiavelli about the First Decade of Tito Lívio* (*Considerazioni Intorno ai Discorsi del Machiavelli sopra la prima deca di Tito Livio*): 'It is true that guns and religion are the main foundations of the republics and kingdoms and are so necessary that lacking any of them one can say that they can be said to lack vital and substantial parts'.[61]

The theme present in the *Discourses* was not out of place in *The Prince*. In this last work, Machiavelli wrote that 'the principal foundations of all states, the new as well as the old or the mixed, are good laws and good armies'.[62] The question of the foundations of power has a long tradition in political thought and his research was considered by many to be the object of political philosophy *par excellence*. In the Italian political tradition, marked by the presence of Machiavelli and Guicciardini, the insistence on the dual nature of political power was recurrent. The Piedmontese philosopher Vincenzo Gioberti, leader of the moderates in the first half of the nineteenth century, for example, in his 1843 book *On the Moral and Civil Primacy of the Italian Race* (*Del primate moral and civile degli italiani*) stated Machiavellianly that the sovereign power was founded:

> Partly in moral force, that is, on the law, partly in material force, that is, on the armies; and yet due to human malignity weapons are necessary to protect opinion, they cannot be developed like those ... if they are not consented to by many benevolent people.[63]

From Machiavelli and Guicciardini this tradition stood out for two reasons. First, because it unified the condition of the exercise of political power (coercion, 'the weapons') and the legitimacy of this power (the 'religion', 'the laws'), creating an inseparable nexus between the two. Second, because this dual source of political power was, in its inseparable character, affirmed as necessary in all forms of 'Republics' or 'kingdoms', 'new, old, or mixed'.

---

60 Machiavelli 1883, p. 26.
61 Guicciardini, 1933, p. 21.
62 Machiavelli 2005, p. 42.
63 Gioberti 1932, I, p. 95. OT.

The state is marked in this way by the presence of elements that maintain among themselves a tense relationship of distinction, without either of them even cancelling its pair in the historical process, but, on the contrary, each one shaping and even reinforcing the other. The organic separation of these elements is nothing more than a hypostasis and, as such, an arbitrary abstraction. It was this unitary conception of political power that Gramsci called the 'double perspective':

> Another point to be fixed and developed is the 'double perspective' in political action and state life. Several are the degrees through which one can present the double perspective, from the most elementary to the complex. But they can be reduced theoretically to two fundamentally corresponding degrees of the twofold nature of the Machiavellian Centaur, that of beast and human, of force and consensus, of authority and hegemony, of violence and civility, of the individual moment and that of the universal ('Church' and 'State'), of agitation and propaganda, of tactics and strategy.[64]

The image of the Centaur is strong and serves to highlight the organic unity between coercion and consent. Is it possible to split the half-beast from the half-man without the death of the Centaur? Is it possible to separate the condition of existence of political power from its condition of legitimacy? Is it possible to have coercion without consensus? But such issues can induce error. In this unitary conception, which was that of Machiavelli, but also of Gramsci, it is not just that coercion cannot exist without consensus. Consensus cannot exist without coercion.

There is, therefore, a 'dialectical relationship' between these two natures of political power.[65] Gramsci protested in the paragraph quoted above against those who made the 'double perspective' something petty or banal, reducing the two natures of political power to their immediate forms and placing them in a relation of succession – first one, then the other. This protest becomes full of meaning if it refers to that form of appropriation of the work of the Florentine secretary already cited that separated *The Prince* from the *Discourses*, reducing the first work to an analysis of the coercive moment of the foundation of a new political order and the second to an analysis of the moment of consensus and expansion of a state. The caveat that Gramsci makes

---

64   Q13, §14, p. 1576. OT.
65   Ibid.

with respect to *The Prince*, identifying in this work several references to the 'moment of hegemony' allowed him to refuse the separation between coercion and consensus. It was about recognising that the two natures of political power, although possessing distinct times, were coexistent.

It is worth asking, however, whether, in addition to being coexistent, coercion and consensus may also be coextensive, that is, if they can reach, with diverse intensities, the same spaces of political life. Gramsci, it is well known, emphasised that coercion was based in political society and consensus in civil society. But would this mean for him then that there would be different definitions of exclusive and excluding spheres for each function? The issue was not treated directly in Notebook 13, in which an important part of the reflection on Machiavelli was found, nor does it appear in the notebooks that precede it. But it does appear in several notes in Notebooks 14, 15 and 17.

This set of notebooks has very particular characteristics. The writing of Notebook 14 began in December 1932, after Notebook 13 began, therefore, with § 4. The three preceding paragraphs are from March 1935, as Francioni[66] observes from the study of the references cited therein. It was interrupted in February 1933, when Gramsci undertook the writing of Notebook 15, and resumed in March of 1935. In Notebook 15, for its part, Gramsci left an important warning on the first page of what would be the tone of these miscellanies: 'Notebook started in 1933 and written without taking into account those divisions of materials and regrouping of notes in the special notebooks'.[67] The last of these new notebooks is number 17. It starts after Notebook 15 was finished in August 1933, and was completed in June 1935, just before Gramsci interrupted his work.

The writing of these notebooks coincides with the moment in which Notebooks 10, 11, 12 and 13 were well under way or near completion and marks a phase of transition that lasted until the middle of 1933, constituting the last period of intense creative activity. After his transfer to Formia in December 1933 and with the worsening of his state of health, this creative work had almost reached its end. From there, the prisoner of fascism was limited, practically, to transcribing the special notebooks, in a more and more literal manner, from the texts already present in the miscellaneous ones.[68]

Why would Gramsci have started these new miscellaneous notebooks after having already begun the writing of the special notebooks? And why did the Machiavellian heading appear in these miscellaneous notebooks at a time

---

66 Francioni 1984, p. 116.
67 Q15, p. 1748. OT.
68 Frosini 2003, p. 26.

when the writing of Notebook 13 was advanced or in the process of conclusion? It is possible that he had found gaps in his research and that he revived the work on the miscellanies with a view to editing them, at the same time as he was writing the special notebooks. It is also possible that he intended to transcribe this material into new special notebooks, as Frosini suggests.[69] In fact, in the early months of 1934, after completing Notebook 13, the Sardinian Marxist began a new special notebook titled *Niccolò Machiavelli. II* in which he wrote only three pages, collecting three notes already present in Notebook 2. It is possible, therefore, that this would be the intended seat of the notes contained in Notebooks 14, 15 and 17.

In the themes present in these new miscellaneous notebooks, the notes in which Machiavellian concepts and themes are translated into the philosophy of praxis predominate. A comparison between some of the themes in Notebook 13 and in Notebook 14 is important for a more enriched understanding of the concepts of civil society and the state, as well as for a more precise identification of the links between consensus and coercion. Discussing the questions of 'collective man' and 'social conformity', Gramsci recorded in Notebook 13:

> Educative and formative role of the state, whose aim is always that of creating new and higher types of civilization; of adapting the 'civilization' and the morality of the broadest popular masses to the necessities of the continuous development of the economic apparatus of production; hence of evolving even physically new types of humanity.[70]

The conformation of the 'collective man' finds its crucial moment in the passage of the singular individual to the universalised sphere of classes, and more specifically, for that sphere in which classes present themselves as universal subjects, the sphere of politics. This passage was understood by Gramsci as an active 'pedagogical relation', distinct, therefore, from a mere school relation. It is in the link between governors and governed, leaders and led, intellectuals and non-intellectuals that it becomes possible to identify this relationship more precisely, and the process of the formation of a 'historical personality'. In this way, 'Every relationship of "hegemony" is necessarily an educational relationship of building new social and political subjects'.[71]

---

69   Frosini 2003, p. 27.
70   GR, Q13, §7, p. 232.
71   GR, Q10 / II, §44, p. 348.

It was this pedagogical relation, a relation of hegemony, that Gramsci had in mind when he emphasised the 'educative and formative role of the state'. It is the process of affirming civilisational forms that is stressed in this role. The incorporation of the singular individual in the collective man, the affirmation of a civilising form that finds its summary in the state, requires the active or passive acquiescence of these individuals. For this purpose, the law fulfils an important function. It is not, however, the law as a mere legal device that acts by means of legal sanctions. Gramsci presented in that paragraph of Notebook 13 an integral conception of the law, writing:

> this concept will have to be extended to include those activities which are at present classified as 'juridically indifferent', and which belong to the domain of civil society; the latter operates without 'sanctions' or compulsory 'obligations', but nevertheless exerts a collective pressure and obtains objective results in the form of an evolution of customs, ways of thinking and acting, morality, etc.[72]

We know since Durkheim that 'collective pressure' is still a form of coercion. Contemporary symbolic sociology, which followed the paths opened by the founder of *L'Année sociologique* greatly contributed to unveiling these forms of violence that manifest themselves outside the sphere regulated by the legal forms of law. There is nothing in the *Notebooks* to indicate that Gramsci knew the work of the French sociologist, although Benedetto Croce cites him in *Historical Materialism and the Economics of Karl Marx*.[73] Croce himself had already called attention in *Politics and Morals* to the need to have a concept of force that would go beyond physical violence and cover other forms of coercion: 'we must not limit the idea of force to the superficial meaning which the word usually suggests – almost the seizing of a man by the neck, bending him and forcing him to the ground, and similar meanings'.[74]

Gramsci did not share with Croce the origin of this statement in the context of a conception in which the base of this force, the state, 'is not a fact, but a spiritual category'.[75] But he could well subscribe to the statement that Croce had made about the relationship between strength and consensus:

> in the field of politics: force and consent are correlative terms, and one does not exist without the other. The objection will be raised that this

---

72   GR, Q13, §7, p. 232.
73   Croce 1915, p. 118.
74   Croce 1945, p. 12.
75   Ibid.

is a 'forced' consent. But every consent is more or less 'forced'; that is, every consent is based on the 'force' of certain facts and is therefore 'conditioned' ... There is no political body which escapes this vicissitude: in the most liberal State as in the most oppressive tyranny there is always a consent, and it is always forced, conditioned, changeable. Otherwise, neither the State nor the life of the State would exist.[76]

In Notebook 13, by putting the expressions 'sanctions' and 'obligations' in quotation marks when they are based in civil society, Gramsci departed from the connotation they assumed in common sense and approached the Crocean formula. But this was not a question, however, that was explicitly or even definitively settled by him, although there were signs that he considered it important. Gramsci's expanded conception of the law was a theoretical development of the idea of integral state. It was for this reason that he decided to inscribe it in the note in Notebook 13 even though it was completely absent from the first essay.[77]

The theme was taken up again in some notes of Notebook 14, precisely the one that opened a new cycle of research. Most of these notes were recorded under the heading *Machiavelli*, although the predominant themes did not concern the interpretation of the work of the Florentine secretary, who was rarely quoted directly in this Notebook. But the heading is important, as it pointed to the continuity of the topics covered in Notebook 13, the unity that exists between the various thematic blocks that are articulated in it and the insertion of these notes in a comprehensive research project.

Regarding an article by Mauro Fasiani, collaborator of the journal *Riforma Sociale*, the author of the *Notebooks* asked: 'Who is the legislator?'[78] The interrogation motivated a series of important reflections relevant to the development of an integral theory of the state. The first of these concerns the need to distinguish between 'voluntas legislatoris', that is, the intention of the legislator in the act of conception of the law, from 'voluntas legis' the set of unforeseen consequences arising from the application of a particular law. Research on 'voluntas legislatoris' does not exhaust the whole law, and research is necessary to really take account of 'voluntas legis'. The result of legislative activity is thus marked by the dialectical tension between the production of the law and its effective application.

---

76 Croce 1945, p. 13.
77 PN3, Q8, §52, pp. 266–7.
78 Q14, §9, p. 1662. OT.

This observation paved the way for another, more far-reaching theory of the integral state. If legislative will cannot be reduced to the will of the legislator, then, it is necessary to give a broader meaning to the word legislator, 'to the point of indicating it with the set of beliefs, feelings, interests and diffuse reasonings in a collectivity in a given historical period'.[79] The question reappeared a few pages later in a note inscribed under the same heading. Gramsci argued that the concept of 'legislator' should be identified with that of 'politician' and that since all are 'political', insofar as they are an active or passive part of political life, they are all also actively or passively 'legislators' as well.[80]

In its narrow sense, the word 'legislator' has a legal-state meaning, indicating those persons who have a mandate to carry out the legislative activity and have this activity recognised and regulated by the laws of a country. It happens that the activity of the 'legislator' is the same as with the activity of intellectual. Everyone is a legislator, but not all have a legislative function. Even adopting an expanded conception of law and the legislator, it is necessary to establish the sphere in which this right and this legislator fulfil a condition of legitimacy, that is, they are recognised as such by public opinion. It is also necessary to identify the actual effectiveness of this activity, that is, the extent to which those representatives practice, in fact, those rules that arise from the activity of the 'legislator' and that have a 'systematic normative expression'.[81]

The legislative act of the legislator cannot therefore be placed beyond history, assuming the position of the demiurge of the real. This act gains significance, insofar as it stimulates or represses trends already evident in social and political life. Such a meaning is thus the result of actions and reactions intrinsic to a given social sphere and to the legislative act itself. For this reason

> No legislator can be seen as an individual, save in the abstract and for convenience of language, because in reality, it expresses a determined collective will to make its 'will' effective, which it is only will because the community is willing to give it *effectiveness*.[82]

In this passage the dialogue with Machiavelli is revealed in the particular use that its author makes of the expression 'effectiveness' (*effetuale*). The dialogue became more intense when Gramsci affirmed in sequence that anyone who, in the legislative act, does not have a collective will, is no more than a 'flash in the

---

79   Fasiani apud Q14, § 9, p. 1663. OT.
80   Q14, § 13, p. 1668. OT.
81   Ibid.
82   Q14, § 9, p. 1663. OT. Emphasis added.

pan', an 'unarmed prophet'.[83] The prophet, the legislator, must have weapons at his disposal to legislate effectively. The reference to Machiavelli is less metaphorical than it seems at first sight, for Gramsci argued that the legislator is not only the one who 'elaborate[s] guidelines that should become a standard of conduct for others'. It is also the one that 'elaborates the instruments through which these directives will be "imposed" and their application verified'.[84]

This broader conception of the power to legislate comprised an organic or integral conception of the state in which the existence of 'legislative activity' was localised as much in the context of political society, which is quite evident, as in that of civil society. This double localisation meant that the effectiveness of this activity resided in the capacity to mobilise instruments of coercion both within the framework of the government as in the scope of the private apparatuses of hegemony:

> The highest legislative power resides in state personnel (elected and career officials), which have at their disposal the coercive legal forces of the State. But it cannot be said that the leaders of 'private' organizations and organisms also do not have at their disposal coercive sanctions, even up to the death penalty.[85]

This theme continues to be developed in §11 of the same Notebook, although under another heading 'Cultural Topics' (*'Argomenti di coltura'*). In this note the capacity of constitutions to adapt to different political circumstances was discussed, particularly those that would be unfavourable to the ruling class. The model of the author of the *Notebooks* was the analysis that Marx undertook of the Spanish Constitution of 1812.[86] In this perspective, Gramsci stated, revisiting the idea of the pedagogical function of the state: 'It can be said, in general, that constitutions are above all ideological "educational texts" and that the "real" constitution is in other legislative documents (but especially in the effective relationship of social forces in the political-military moment)'.[87]

The actual truth of the Constitution thus finds its mirror in the relation of forces between social classes and, particularly, the relation of social forces that is manifested in conflict, the 'political-military moment'. To conceive of law as

---

83   'From this comes the fact that all armed prophets were victorious and the unarmed came to ruin' (Machiavelli 2005, p. 22).
84   Q14, §13, p. 1668. OT.
85   Ibid.
86   See MECW, Vol. 13, pp. 424–33.
87   Q14, §11, p. 1666. OT.

an expression of these relations was, for Gramsci, a way of combating 'mechanistic abstraction and deterministic fatalism'. Such a conception needed to appreciate the historical and national particularities of each country to be truly effective, as well as the legislative capacity (in an expanded sense) and, therefore, coercive, which emanates from civil society. The relationship between religion and politics in the United States was, at this point, enlightening. In an observation of great timeliness, Gramsci recorded,

> In the United States, there is legally and in fact no shortage of religious freedom within certain limits, as recalls the case against Darwinism, and if legally (within certain limits) there is no lack of political freedom, this lacks in fact by economic pressure and by *open private violence*.[88]

The strength of the words leaves no doubt that Gramsci rediscovered coercion in the sphere of civil society. The sequence of this note also makes it possible to clarify that this private violence is coexistent and coextensive with state-legal violence. For the author of the *Notebooks*, the critical examination of the judicial and police organisation was of great importance for understanding of the political configuration of the United States, as it revealed how these organisations of political society 'leave unpunished and support *private violence* aimed at preventing the formation of parties other than the Republican and the Democratic'.[89]

It is worth asking the following question: does this mature elaboration of Gramsci that identified the presence of coercion in civil society and consent in political society not cancel his previous distinction of the functional specialisations of both spheres? That is, in this new theoretical apparatus would it still make sense to distinguish between civil society and political society? The theoretical development given to the question in Notebook 14 by Gramsci is not contradictory with the one found in Notebook 6, but it is certainly more subtle and sophisticated. Making a more literary use of concepts rather than literal, it is possible to sustain that in civil society, consensus is 'hegemonic', whereas in political society it is coercion. That is, the institutional spaces for exercising the functions of leadership and domination are not exclusive. Under the light of this theoretical development it becomes difficult to accept that Gramsci was a theorist of consensus, as many have claimed.

---

88   Ibid. Emphasis added.
89   Q14, § 11, pp. 1666–7. Emphasis added.

CHAPTER 6

War of Movement/War of Position

The understanding of the exact relationship between force and consensus is what strengthens the theory of the state in Gramsci. It allows us to think about the unity existing between civil and political society, the resistance of the state to the crises of capitalism, the forms of the crisis and the overcoming of these crucial moments. For Gramsci, the analysis of politics serves to justify a practical activity, indicating those points where the force of will must concentrate its energies, maximising its results. His theory of the state was, therefore, not only a theory to explain its longevity, but also a theory to explain its crisis and the conditions for overcoming the present state form. It was from this perspective that Gramsci engaged with a set of far-reaching conceptual pairs of great strategic reach: war of manoeuvre/war of position; East/West; permanent revolution/hegemony.

The analogy between political struggle and military strategy began to be developed in Notebook 1 as part of a discussion on political and military leadership in the Italian Risorgimento. In §§ 117 and 118 the author discussed the importance of political leadership, and even its predominance, in the organisation of armies. Gramsci pointed out that the larger the army, the greater the importance of subordinating the military-technical leadership to political leadership.[1] The deficiency in the leadership function implied a technical-military deficiency.[2]

It is clear that already in this first moment, Gramsci conceived the technical-military and political functions in a unitary way, a concept that is fundamental for his elaboration with respect to the relations of political-military forces. These relationships were dealt with in a more extensive manner in two other B texts present in the same Notebook, written probably between February and March 1930, a period of intense intellectual production on the part of the author.[3] In these texts, Gramsci discussed, among other subjects, the use of detachments similar to the *arditi*, assault troops deployed by the Italian army during the First World War.[4]

---

1 PN1, Q1, § 117, pp. 206–7.
2 PN1, Q1, § 118, p. 208.
3 See Francioni 1984, p. 140.
4 After the end of World War I, veteran movements adopted the title of *arditi* and a part of them maintained relations with fascism. Obviously inspired by previous movements, in the

In the first of these notes, § 133, the Sardinian Marxist disputed the tendency to generalise the tactic of '*arditism*'. He argued that this tactic corresponded not to an ideal form, but rather to a situation in which a) there was an inefficient regular army and b) the masses were in a state of passivity or demoralisation, and for this reason were replaced by special detachments. The general criterion for treating this phenomenon was 'that comparisons between military art and politics should always be made with a grain of salt, that is, only as stimuli for thought and as terms simplified *ad absurdum* ...'.[5]

In political struggle the element of discipline and hierarchy is not sustained by penal sanctions, but rather by conviction. Military detachments and political groups are, therefore, very different forms of organisation and correspond to distinct modes of action. Gramsci's view was clear with respect to this: political struggle is more complex than war. In 'political struggle, *there exist other forms* of warfare besides the war of movement and the war by siege or war of position'.[6] Different tactics might be appropriate for some classes but not for others; this was the fundamental question for the author of the *Notebooks*.[7] The critique was implacable: 'in political struggle one should not ape the methods of struggle of the ruling classes, and avoid falling into easy ambushes'.[8] But the criticism was directed at *arditism* and its generalisation rather than the 'war of movement', which was not identified with these forms:

> The tactics of the *arditi*, therefore, cannot be as important for certain classes as they are for others; for certain classes the war of movement and maneuver is necessary because it is appropriate for them, and in the case of political struggle the war of movement can be combined with a useful and perhaps indispensable employment of *arditi* tactics. But to fix one's mind on the military model is foolish: here too, politics must rank

---

spring of 1921 the *Arditi del popolo* emerged, an armed movement constituted with the aim of organising the defence against the fascist bands. Although many communists had readily adhered to the *Arditi*, the leadership of the PCI, then directed by the Bordigist fraction, denounced the movement for being monopolised by forces that were not 'strictly revolutionary' and announced in July of the same year the creation of detachments exclusively formed by communists. Gramsci's position in this respect, more pondered, can be seen in the articles 'Contro il terrore' and 'Gli Arditi del Popolo' published in *L'Ordine Nuovo*. SF, pp. 287–9 and 541–2. See also Hajek 1984, pp. 43–4.

5   PN1, Q1, § 133, p. 217.
6   Ibid. Emphasis added.
7   PN1, Q1, § 133, p. 218.
8   PN1, Q1, § 133, p. 217.

higher than the military element and only politics creates the possibility of maneuver and movement.⁹

The need to distinguish between forms of struggle was taken up again in §134, entitled 'Political struggle and military war' (*'Lotta politica e guerra militaire'*).¹⁰ In military warfare, the strategic goal is the destruction of the enemy army, occupation of its territory and peace as a result of this end. For the war to come to an end, it would not even be necessary for the strategic end to have actually happened if there was no doubt that it could be, so that peace could be established without the necessary destruction of the enemy and occupation of its territory.

The political struggle, Gramsci claimed, was much more complex, for it would not end with the destruction of the enemy. This would resemble the 'colonial war' in which the victorious army proposes to occupy the conquered territory in a stable way. In this paragraph, Gramsci pointed out that the different moments of the 'political struggle', as well as those of 'military warfare', demanded different forms of struggle, diverse tactics that should be employed with great consideration. These different moments could happen successively in time or coexist and, in this way, the various forms of struggle would be succeeded or coexist depending on the case. Gramsci analysed these combinations from the example of the anticolonial struggle in India:

> Thus India's political struggle against the English (and to some extent that of Germany against France, or of Hungary against the Little Entente) knows three forms of war: war of movement, war of position, and underground war. Gandhi's passive resistance is a war of position, which becomes a war of movement at certain moments and an underground war at others: the boycott is a war of position, strikes are a war of movement, the clandestine gathering of arms and of assault combat groups is underground war.¹¹

Gramsci did not rule out the use of detachments similar to the *arditi*. But the condition for the acceptance of 'arditism' was its use with much consideration to avoid a premature defeat. He still distinguished between modern arditism, represented by the Indian anticolonial movement, and the partisan guerril-

---

9   PN1, Q1, §133, p. 218.
10   PN1, Q1, §134, pp. 218–20.
11   PN1, Q1, §134, p. 219.

las (*partigiani*), forms of minority struggle against well-organised majorities.[12] This distinction aimed to highlight the positive role that modern arditism could play in the political struggle as part of a balanced set of diverse tactics. According to Gramsci:

> Therefore, in these mixed forms of struggle, which have a fundamentally military character but are above all political (every political struggle, however, always has a military substratum), the use of the arditi requires the development of an original tactical concept for which the experience of war can provide only a stimulus, not a model.[13]

The development of an 'original tactical development' was further elaborated in an A text in Notebook 7, probably written in November 1930 and transcribed as text C in the notes on Machiavelli in Notebook 13, probably between May 1932 and early 1934.[14] The context of the writing of the first note is important. It is included under the heading 'Structure and Superstructure' ('*Struttura and superstruttura*') within the 'Philosophical Notes II' ('*Appunti di Filosofia II*') and explicitly refers to the 'Philosophical Notes I' ('*Appunti di filosofia I*'), present in Notebook 4, particularly §§ 12, 38 and 45, presented under the same heading:

> Structure and Superstructure. (See the notes in the 'First Series'). On this subject, I believe, one could draw a comparison with the technique of warfare as it was transformed during the last war with the shift from war of maneuver to war of position. Take note of Rosa's little book that was translated by Alessandri in 1919–20; its theory is based on the historical experiences of 1905. (Besides, it appears that the events were not analyzed accurately. The 'voluntary' and organizational elements are ignored, even though they were much more widespread than Rosa was inclined to believe; because of her 'economistic' prejudice, she unconsciously ignored them.) This little book, in my view, constitutes the most significant theory of the war of maneuver applied to the study of history and the art of politics. The immediate economic factor (crises, etc.) is seen as the field artillery employed in war to open a breach in the enemy's

---

12   Gramsci cited as examples of these partisan guerrillas, the Macedonian committees and the Irish resistance. At least in this last case, it was far from being characterised as a minority.
13   PN1, Q1, § 134, p. 219.
14   Francioni 1984, pp. 142 and 144.

defences big enough to permit one's troops to break through and gain a definitive strategic victory – or, at least, to achieve what is needed for a definitive victory.[15]

The research programme in which the Note in Notebook 7 was inserted was engaged with the renewal of historical materialism and was already present in the note that opened Notebook 1 in the form of an investigation into the 'theory of history and historiography'. The military metaphor provided the opportunity to discuss, in the first place, the relation between economic crisis and political crisis, between a crisis that manifests itself within the framework of the economic development of society and another that appears in the sphere of political superstructures. A critique of economism was highlighted at this point in the text. The unfolding of Gramsci's methodological reflection became evident when criticism of economism was explicitly related to the critique of spontaneity of which Rosa Luxemburg would be an example.

The properly political content of Notebook 7 appears to the reader in the subtle shifting of the problematic within §10. Thus the structure-superstructure relation ceded place to a development of the military metaphor from the analysis of the Eastern and Western fronts of Russia during the First World War. In this displacement, the reflection on the theory of history and historiography ceased to be the vector which made sense to the research project. The properly political vector was stressed: investigation into the forms of proletarian struggle in the capitalist West. Here the differences between the first and second essays are important and deserve to be highlighted:

| In reality, the Russian army did attempt a war of maneuver and breakthroughs, especially in the Austrian sector (but also in Prussia, near the lakes of Mazovia) and had some partial successes that were extremely brilliant but ephemeral. A war of position in fact does not consist solely of a set of actual trenches; it comprises the entire organization and industrial structure of the territory that lies behind the arrayed forces, and it is especially dependent on the rapid-fire capacity and con- | In actual fact, the Russian Army did attempt a war of manoeuvre and sudden incursion, especially in the Austrian sector (but also in East Prussia), and won successes which were as brilliant as they were ephemeral. *The truth is that one cannot choose the form of war one wants, unless from the start one has a crushing superiority over the enemy. It is well known what losses were caused by the stubborn refusal of the General Staffs to recognise that a war of position was 'imposed' by the over-* |

---

15   PN3, Q7, §10, p. 161.

centration of cannons, machine guns, and rifles (and on an abundance of material that makes it possible to replace quickly any equipment lost after and enemy breakthrough).[16]

all relation of the forces in conflict. A war of position is not, in reality, constituted simply by the actual trenches, but by the whole organizational and industrial system of the territory which lies to the rear of the army in the field. It is imposed notably by the rapid fire-power of cannons, machine-guns and rifles, by the armed strength which can be concentrated at a particular spot, as well as by the abundance of supplies which make possible the swift replacement of material lost after an enemy breakthrough or a retreat.[17]

The analysis of the Western and Eastern fronts has only a metaphorical meaning and cannot be interpreted beyond this condition. In the passages in which Gramsci refers to military issues, he reveals an insufficient knowledge of the questions that, in any event, appear to have been contradicted by the development of military technique in World War II.[18] In any case, Gramsci seems to be careful in contradicting common assertions at the time that invalidated the war of manoeuvre.

Such care appears more clearly in the second edition of this note, present in the already mentioned Notebook 13, in which Gramsci introduced an important modification, emphasising that the modality of military conflict *was not an option of the forces in conflict* but rather an imposition arising from the existing relation of forces. This warning by Gramsci, read along with that present in the First Notebook in which he censured the habit of imitating ('aping') the methods of struggle of the ruling classes, constitutes an antidote against all reductionist readings of the notions of war of manoeuvre/position.

The war of position was not a positive programme of action but an objective requirement of the situation in which the social and political forces were found. If the war of position was imposed by the general relation of forces and would only be possible to impose a form of struggle when it had over-

---

16   PN3, Q7, §10, p. 162.
17   GR, Q13, §24, p. 226. Emphasis added.
18   Gramsci seems, however, to have keenly studied the military question, although his knowledge, unlike Trotsky, was only theoretical. A preliminary survey conducted by Leandro Galastri, based on the works quoted in the *Notebooks*, found references to about fifty titles, including books, booklets and articles.

whelming superiority over the enemy, then the war of position was the form of struggle convenient to the ruling classes. The political action of the subaltern classes should therefore have as its objective the disarticulation of the dominant classes.

The development of the analogy led Gramsci to a new shift where he revealed his principle intention. After presenting the consequences of the change in military paradigm for the 'art of war', Gramsci developed the analogy of the 'art and science of politics' in order to define the prevailing modes of political struggle, but not exclusively, of the 'most advanced states'. That the 'war of position' could be preponderant did not annul the 'war of manoeuvre' in the strictly military field nor in the political realm, as the author of the *Notebooks* made clear in the passage below:

This does not mean that the tactics of assault and incursion and the war of manuever should now be considered to be utterly erased from the study of military science; that would be a serious error. But in wars among the most industrially and socially advanced states, these methods of war must be seen to have a reduced tactical function rather than a strategic function; their place in military history is analogous to that of siege warfare in the previous period. The same revolution must take place in the art and science of politics, at least in those cases pertaining to the most advanced states, where 'civil society' has become a very complex structure that is very resistant to the catastrophic 'irruptions' of the immediate economic factor (crises, depressions, etc.): the superstructures of civil society resemble the trench system of modern warfare.[19]	Even those military experts whose minds are now fixed on the war of position, just as they were previously on that of manoeuvre, naturally do not maintain that the latter should be considered as expunged from military science. They merely maintain that, in wars among the more industrially and socially advanced states, the war of manoeuvre must be considered as reduced to more of a tactical than a strategic function; that it must be considered as occupying the same position as siege warfare used to occupy previously in relation to it. The same reduction must take place in the art and science of politics, at least in the case of the most advanced states, where 'civil society' has become a very complex structure and one which is resistant to the catastrophic 'incursions' of the immediate economic element (crises, depressions, etc.). The superstructures of civil society are like the trench-systems of modern warfare.[20]

---

19   PN3, Q7, §10, p. 163.
20   GR, Q13, §24, pp. 226–7.

The difference that can be noticed between the two versions concerns a greater emphasis on the need to avoid the cancellation of the war of manoeuvre from the strategic horizon. In the paragraph of Notebook 13 the protest against this cancellation was stronger, since it was related not only to the suppression of a 'manoeuvred war' from the 'the study of the military art' but rather to the cancellation *by* science of a form of struggle that still had a place.

Already in the first version of the text the notions of 'war of manoeuvre' and 'war of position' were strongly related to Gramsci's integral conception of the state. This relation would be resumed in Notebook 6, in a passage in which he discussed the possibility of a 'Garibaldine war', that is, the use of guerrilla tactics 'whether in politics or in military art'.[21] Gramsci denied the validity of this tactic, stating that it expressed an individualist and localist perspective that 'results in underestimating the adversary and his fighting organization'. According to Gramsci, this error arose in politics:

> from an inaccurate understanding of the nature of the state (in the full sense: dictatorship + hegemony). In war, a similar error occurs when the misconception is applied to the enemy camp (a failure to understand not only one's own state but also the nature of the state of one's enemy).[22]

The misconception denounced by Gramsci did not concern only the unfamiliarity of the hegemonic function played by the dominant classes, but also to the governing-dictatorial function of its political power. For this reason, he pointed out that the misunderstanding concerned the state in its 'integral meaning'. The appropriate tactic therefore consisted of an articulation in different degrees of the diverse modalities of confrontation. But this articulation would not be equal to a zero-sum game. An algebraic conception of the state that tends to consider civil society as more or less equal to political society, has as a corollary an algebraic conception of the forms of struggle of the subaltern classes, in which more 'war of position' equals less 'war of movement'. The algebraic solution is simplistic and verges from the constant care with which relationships between these different forms of struggle were treated by the author. In fact, Gramsci warned in §10 of the Notebook 7 against the cancellation of the 'war of movement'.

It should be noted, however, that Gramsci himself led the reader to understand that the passage from one form of struggle to another would imply a

---

21   According to Francioni 1984, pp. 142 and 144, the writing of §10 of Notebook 7 occurred in November 1930 and precedes that of §155 in Notebook 10, dated October 1931.
22   PN3, Q6, §155, p. 117.

cancellation. Thus, in §138 in Notebook 6, written, probably in August 1931 and entitled 'Past and Present. Transition from the war of maneuver (and frontal assault) to the war of position – in the political field as well' (*'Passato e presente. Passaggio dalla war manovrata (e dall'attacco frontale) alla guerra di posizione anche nel campo politico'*) this passage from one form of struggle to another was discussed in terms of which seem to indicate the annulment of one form by the other. After noting that the relationship between political science and the art of war was only indirect, emphasising its analogic character,[23] Gramsci wrote:

> The war of position calls on enormous masses of people to make huge sacrifices; that is why an unprecedented concentration of hegemony is required and hence a more 'interventionist' kind of government that will engage more openly in the offensive against the opponents and ensure, once and for all, the 'impossibility' of internal disintegration by putting in place controls of all kinds – political, administrative, etc. reinforcement of the hegemonic positions of the dominant group, etc. All of this indicates that the culminating phase of the politico-historical situation has begun, for, in politics, once the 'war of position' is won, it is definitively decisive. In politics, in other words, the war of manoeuvre drags on as long as the positions being won are not decisive and the resources of hegemony and the state are not fully mobilized. But when, for some reason or another, these positions have lost their value and only the decisive positions matter, then one shifts to siege warfare – compact, difficult, requiring exceptional abilities of patience and inventiveness.[24]

The argument presented in this paragraph is extremely complex, but it did not receive a second version in Notebook 13, as one might expect.[25] In this way, it remains without further posterior development that could better clarify its content. The analogy that was developed in it demonstrates a degree of abstraction that makes it ambivalent, hindering an unequivocal understanding.

---

23 To emphasise this indirect and metaphorical relationship is important, since the metaphor has an analytical relevance far superior in the sphere of politics than in the military field. If, instead of an analogy, equivalence between the two fields was constructed, the metaphor could not be sustained.
24 PN3, Q6, §138, p. 109.
25 The reasons for this are far from clear. Of the 211 paragraphs that comprise Notebook 6, only 25 were transcribed in C notes, with 186 paragraphs remaining, including §§138 and 155, dealing with the theme in questions, such as the B texts.

In this text, 'war of manoeuvre' and 'war of position' do not appear to be restricted to the conquest of power, but are related to what precedes this moment – the struggle for political power – as much as to what succeeds it – the construction of a new order. In view of the process of building socialism, the disarticulation of the capitalist state itself – conceived in its strict sense as the set of repressive apparatuses (political society) – by means of the 'frontal attack' could be conceived as a 'non-decisive' position although it is indispensable. The conquest of the state would thus be the beginning of the end, but not the end.

Still with respect to this paragraph it would be possible to interpret that once political power was conquered, it would become necessary to mobilise 'all the resources of the hegemony and of the state' with a view to building a new order. In this new phase, which not only denies the old order, but builds a new order and leads to a complete intellectual and moral reform, the 'war of position' in civil society would occupy a preponderant role. It is clear that this '"war of position", once won, is definitively decisive', as Gramsci claimed.

War of manoeuvre and war of position would thus find themselves in an inseparable nexus and would be related to different moments of the struggle for the affirmation of a new political and social order. Gramsci's development of the issue indicates that this link is analogous to that which is established within his concept of the integral state. Both conceptual planes are thus superimposed and it is possible to state that the war of manoeuvre prevails in the struggle *against* political society and the war of position affirms its supremacy in the struggle *in* civil society.

1   East

In order to clarify the previous theme, it is important to revisit a B note (§16) in Notebook 7. Although located within the Philosophical Notes II, this note was clearly out of place with the other themes covered in this section. Unlike §10 of that same Notebook, which formally framed the question within a research project on historical materialism, the imposition of §16 was directly political and began with the title: 'War of position and war of maneuver, or frontal war' (*'Guerra di posizione and guerra manovrata o frontale'*). It was in this new paragraph that the duality war of manoeuvre/war of position overlapped another conceptual duality: East/West (Orient/Occident).

The overlap was cautiously included, making reference to the theory of Leon Trotsky. The author of the *Notebooks* proposed to investigate whether this theory was not the political reflex of the theory of the war of manoeuvre and the reflex, in the final instance, of the particularities of a national social formation which are 'embryonic and unsettled and cannot become a "trench or fortress"'.²⁶ The distinction between East and West was presented at the end of the same paragraph:

> In the East, the state was everything, civil society was primordial and gelatinous; in the West, there was a proper relation between state and civil society, and when the state tottered, a sturdy structure of civil society was immediately revealed. The state was just a forward trench; behind it stood a succession of sturdy fortresses and emplacements. Needless to say, the configuration varied from state to state, which is precisely why an accurate reconnaissance on a national scale was needed.²⁷

The presence of Trotsky at the beginning of the paragraph is paradoxical for various reasons. First because Trotsky was a staunch opponent of the absolutisation of the war of manoeuvre in the field of military strategy, which he identified as the political theory of the offensive, defended by the extreme left in the 3rd Congress of the Communist International.²⁸ Secondly, because as Gramsci himself would acknowledge, in Notebook 13 Trotsky had raised the distinction between East and West for the first time in his speech on the New Economic Policy in Russia and the prospects of world revolution, during the 4th Congress of the Communist International in 1922.²⁹ On the occasion, the Bolshevik leader affirmed the difference between Russia and other countries. While in Russia it had been possible to gain power easily and quickly, this was unlikely to occur in Western Europe, where the proletariat would face 'not only the combat vanguards of the counter-revolution but also its heaviest

---

26   PN3, Q7, §16, p. 168.
27   PN3, Q7, §16, p. 169.
28   Anderson 1976a, p. 67.
29   'One attempt to begin a revision of the current tactical methods was perhaps that outlined by L. Dav. Br. [Trotsky] at the fourth meeting, when he made a comparison between the Eastern and Western fronts. The former had fallen at once, but unprecedented struggles had then ensued; in the case of the latter, the struggles would take place "beforehand". The question, therefore, was whether civil society resists before or after the attempt to seize power; where the latter takes place, etc. However, the question was outlined only in a brilliant, literary form, without directives of a practical character' (GR, Q13, §24, p. 228). This passage is not found in the first version of the note (Q7, §10) and its inclusion denotes the contradictory character of the relation that Gramsci maintained with the thought of Trotsky. Rosengarten 1984–85, pp. 78–80 considers Trotsky's Report 'an anticipation of ideas concerning proletarian hegemony in the West which Gramsci fully developed in the *Quaderni del carcere*'.

reserves'.[30] The distinction between East and West was under discussion within the Communist International and can be found in Lenin's book *Left-Wing Communism: An Infantile Disorder*. Debating abstentionists regarding participation in parliamentary activity, the Communist leader presented the reasons why the distinction between the political forms was important. According to Lenin, 'it was easy for Russia, in the specific and historically unique situation of 1917, to *start* the socialist revolution, but it will be more difficult for Russia than for the European countries to *continue* the revolution and bring it to its consummation'. On the other hand, 'it is more difficult for Western Europe to *start* a socialist revolution than it was for us [in Russia]'.[31]

The difficulties in Western Europe could be found, according to Lenin, in the existence of strong parliamentary institutions and in the 'bourgeois-democratic and parliamentary prejudices' that these institutions fed in the disorganised sectors of the workers' movement and, especially, among the small peasants.[32] Such prejudices constituted a political obstacle to be overcome. In this book, the fundamental problem was precisely the determination of the ways in which workers could overcome these obstacles.

The distinction between East and West was therefore not an original contribution of Gramsci and, indeed, seems to have been a current topic in the Communist International after 1922. Gramsci himself made this distinction in a text sent to the governing committee of the PCI in August 1926, drafted in terms similar to those used by Trotsky. He wrote:

> in the advanced capitalist countries, the ruling class possesses political and organizational resources that it did not possess, for example, in Russia. This means that even the most serious economic crises do not have immediate repercussions in the political sphere. Politics is always one step behind – or many steps behind – economics. The State apparatus is far more resistant than it is often possible to believe; and, at moments of crisis, it is far more capable of organizing forces loyal to the regime than the depth of the crisis might lead one to suppose. This is especially true of the most important capitalist States. In typical peripheral States such as the Italy, Poland, Spain or Portugal, the State forces are less efficient.[33]

---

30   Trotsky 1974, Vol. 2, p. 221.
31   LCW, Vol. 31, p. 64.
32   LCW, Vol. 31, p. 65.
33   PPW, pp. 297–8.

Three themes only briefly pointed out in this passage will constitute nodal points of the Gramscian elaboration in prison: a) the East/West distinction; b) a dialectical reading of the political/economic relations; and c) the formulation of a theory of revolution capable of accounting for the challenges raised by the two preceding issues. Gramsci did not work on these issues starting from an imaginary zero point. He did so from the political and theoretical tradition that emerged nationally in the Russian Revolution and became globalised in the early years of the Communist International, a background in which Gramsci sought to incorporate the rich Italian cultural tradition. As far as the East/West relationship is concerned, the contribution of the *Notebooks* is in a greater detailing and elaboration of notions that were only found in a rudimentary state beforehand.

This elaboration did not solve all the problems inherent in the metaphor and Gramsci was aware of the difficulties. The notions of East and West, he wrote, could be considered 'objectively real', although they are 'nothing more than a "historical" or "conventional construct"'.[34] North-South and East-West relations would be real relations, which could not be imagined without the development of civilisation. As spatial notions, any point could be simultaneously to the East and to the West of other points. But the assertion of an East or a West ceased to be a geographical issue and became a historical issue when it was stated that Japan is in the East and California in the West.

As historical notions, East and West are not constructions of man in general, according to Gramsci, but of the European educated classes, who through their cultural hegemony made everyone accept them.[35] In this sense, they ceased to be spatial notions and have come to mean 'relations between whole civilizations', alternately 'Arab', 'Muslim', 'Asian', etc.[36] Born in the Italian East, the *Mezzogiorno*, and very attentive to the Southern Question, Gramsci was on guard against an ethnocentric appropriation of these spatial notions. Although he used them, this does not mean that he accepted the historical content that they embodied.

Of course, with the notions that are being dealt with here it is difficult to completely ignore the spatial connotation, obscuring the temporal dimension of these historical-political situations. They can cover up the discordance of times, reducing it to geographical distance. In this respect, Perry Anderson is correct when he points out that 'the terms East and West assume that the social formations on each side of the divide exist in the same temporality, and can

---

34 PN3, Q7, §25, p. 175.
35 Ibid.
36 Ibid.

therefore be read off against each other as variations of a common category'.[37] After having conduced Gramsci to an alleged 'Western Marxism',[38] Anderson was not the most suitable person to question these concepts.[39] But his warning is pertinent because despite Gramsci, many of his readers regarded these terms as opposites.

The concepts of East and West, war of manoeuvre and war of position had for Gramsci a methodological value, inasmuch as he sought to distinguish between different national realities, as well as different stages of the class struggle. The utilisation of the concepts of war of position and war of manoeuvre to describe different moments of the relations of forces in the European context appeared in a pure state in Notebook 10. According to Gramsci:

> In Europe from 1789 to 1870 there was a (political) war of movement in the French Revolution and a long war of position from 1815 to 1870. In the present epoch, the war of movement took place politically from March 1917 to March 1921; this was followed by a war of position whose representative and – both practical (for Italy) and ideological (for Europe) – is fascism.[40]

In this paragraph, the war of manoeuvre coincided with a period of offensive of the workers' movement that began with the Russian Revolution and ended with the March Action of 1921 in Germany. From then on, according to the author of the note, a defensive period began, characterised by the war of position and represented in Italy by fascism. The use of the military analogy to designate the passing of one offensive moment in the struggle to another defensive moment was not completely compatible with the use of the geographic metaphor. A dense civil society, with its parties and unions, obviously would not have disappeared or arisen in the course of a month or even a year. Therefore, if the war of position was exclusively a requirement arising from the densification of civil society, there would be no sense in periodising in this way the passage from one to another.

The problem was already evident in the texts of Lenin and Trotsky, in which a strong rhetoric sometimes oversimplified complex issues. The inverse relationship between the socialist revolution and the construction of socialism that

---

37 Anderson 1976b, p. 50.
38 Anderson 1976a, pp. 24–48.
39 See the critique of Losurdo 1997, pp. 241–53.
40 GR, Q10 / I, § 9, p. 267. This passage, written between April and May 1932, was not found in the respective A text. PN3, Q8, § 236, pp. 378–9.

characterised East and West was, in the discourse of Lenin, and especially Trotsky, the consequence of an uneven (and combined) movement of the universalisation of the economy and politics of capitalism. But this inverse relationship could not be understood in an absolute way, precisely because of this unequal and combined development. Did the socialist revolution in Russia not accelerate the time of the revolution in Germany, dismantling some (but not all) of the existing obstacles? And would a revolution in Germany not advance the construction of socialism in Soviet Russia more quickly?

There are great difficulties in the shift from a synchronic reading, which values the distinctions between 'western' and 'eastern' societies, to a diachronic reading which values the different moments of the class struggle. Luciano Gruppi, for example, sought to separate these two dimensions in the definition of war of manoeuvre and war of position, arguing briefly that in the diachronic dimension these concepts 'want to indicate different phases of the historical course and the passage from rapid convulsions in the class and political structure of society to moments of relative stability'.[41]

Gruppi, states, however, that this would not be the most advantageous and insightful development that Gramsci would give to these notions. The richest meaning of these notions, according to the commentator, would occur when these notions did not indicate 'the shift from the offensive to the defensive and vice versa, but two substantially different strategies, two profoundly different historical situations'.[42] By the same token, Carlos Nelson Coutinho sought to articulate the synchronic and diachronic dimensions of the concept. For this, he affirmed that the diachronic difference occurs between 'periods marked by weakness of mass organization' and periods of 'more intense socialization of politics'. In the former, the 'war of manoeuvre' would prevail, the frontal clash with the state, while in the second, 'the gradual conquest of positions' would obtain.[43]

Developing the argument, Coutinho states that the 'war of manoeuvre' would be applicable 'not only to the absolutist and despotic "Eastern" states, but also to the elitist liberal states of the first two thirds of the nineteenth century, while the "war of position" would be valid for modern democratic states'.[44] Leaving aside that it would make no sense to confront the coercive state in a period marked by the 'weakness of mass organization', the question remains

---

41   Gruppi 2000, p. 138.
42   Gruppi 2000, p. 142.
43   Coutinho 1999, p. 149.
44   Ibid.

that the strength or weakness of this organisation is always the result of a relationship of forces and not a mechanical consequence of a state form.

Coutinho's interpretation reduced the diachronic dimension to the synchronic. But in this case, what was the meaning of Gramsci's periodisation? Why would the 'war of position' be the predominant form in Europe after 1921 and not before? And why would fascism be the ideological and practical expression of a war of position? Would the rise and consolidation of fascism in Italy and reactionary or fascist governments in other European countries coincide with a period of the 'more intense socialization of politics'? Had Gramsci and Togliatti not defined fascism as a 'movement of armed reaction that aims to disaggregate and disorganise the working class in order to immobilise it'?[45]

The solution proposed by Coutinho was constructed with a view to affirming the war of position as an exclusive strategy in the West, in the 'modern democratic states'. To conceive of a relation of identity between the densification of civil society and the increase in political participation is only possible when one loses sight of the conflicting character of one's own civil society. A more dense and complex civil society can be coexistent with the process of the 'socialization of political participation', but a denser and more complex bourgeois civil society can also mean (and frequently means) the expansion of the private apparatus of control and the pacification of the subaltern classes. There was not, therefore, any positivity inherent in the notion of the West as used by Gramsci.

In this sense, Del Roio argues that Gramsci wrote that he was confronting 'the entire West and with the duality West/East generated by its dominion'.[46] The notion of the West used in the *Notebooks* did not indicate a model, a programme or an ideal. It was only meant to express a historical-political situation: the existence of a denser civil society and, contradictorily, of greater obstacles to the socialist revolution. The notions of East and West gain richer meaning when they are articulated with the notions of war of manoeuvre and war of position. Only in this articulation it is possible for the researcher to recognise the necessary distinction between the time of state forms and the time of the class struggle.

---

45   CPC, p. 495.
46   Del Roio 1998, p. 117.

2 Trotsky

The reflection with respect to 'an original tactical development' became more important to Gramsci as he became aware of the turnarounds in the Communist International (CI) and the dilemmas of the construction of socialism in the Soviet Union, results of both the sectarian turn consolidated by the 10th Plenum of the CI's Executive Committee, held in 1929, and of the consolidation of the Stalinist bureaucracy in the Soviet power. Such processes had intense repercussions within the PCI and had stimulated a sectarian turn in the struggle against fascism and the refusal to defend the convocation of a Constituent Assembly.

The notes written from mid-1930 onward on the war of manoeuvre and war of position did not fail to express, albeit in highly coded language, Gramsci's concerns about these problems of strategy and tactics of the world communist movement. In this reflection, the imagined dialogue with the Bolshevik leaders Lenin and Trotsky assumed great importance. Gramsci's political elaboration on the 'war of position' ran contrary to the Stalinist strategy of the 'Third Period' and called for a Leninist formulation of the 'United Front'. According to Gramsci,

> In my view, Ilyich understood the need for a shift from the war of manoeuver that had been applied victoriously in the East in 1917, to a war of position, which was the only viable possibility in the West, where, as Krasnov observes, the armies could quickly amass huge quantities of munitions and where the structures of society were still capable of themselves becoming heavily fortified trenches. This, I believe, is the meaning of the term 'united front' ...[47]

Lenin was among the first to perceive this change. The PCI only belatedly understood the meaning of the political formula of the united front and Gramsci himself resisted it.[48] The first experiences of the building of a united front occurred in Germany, where the Communists launched, on the initiative of Paul Levi and Karl Radek, an open letter to the trade union organisations and workers' parties of that country, calling for a common struggle to defend the immediate interests of the working class.[49] The open letter did not find the

---

47   PN3, Q7, §16, pp. 168–9.
48   Regarding Gramsci's evolution in relation to the political formula of the united front, Marcos Del Roio's 2005 book is irreplaceable.
49   See Broué 1997, p. 206 and Hajek 1984, pp. 18–20.

expected response from the organisations to which it was addressed, and even faced opposition within the Communist Party of Germany (KPD). Divided, the party responded to police repression in Saxony in March of the same year with a precipitous insurrectionary general strike.

The failure of the insurrection ended with a severe defeat for the Communists and a dissolution of the party, which lost hundreds of thousands of members.[50] Internal conflicts swelled and Paul Levi publicly broke with the leadership of the party, being expelled soon after. The German question occupied a great deal of space in the discussions of the Congress of the CI held in July 1921, a few months after the defeat of the insurrection. The theses *On Tactics* adopted by Congress, however, reflected the compromise between the different currents. The text considered the March action as 'a step forward', while condemning 'a number of party members who contended that, under present conditions, the offensive represented the VKPD's main method of struggle'.[51]

The debates within the Third Congress already increasingly signalled the intense perception among the main communist leaderships, and especially among the Bolsheviks, that the most intense moments of the revolutionary ascension had already passed. But with respect to this, the resolutions passed still carried a heavy dose of ambivalence in relation to the conflict with the supporters of the offensive and the resulting agreements. The cautious tone in the analysis of the situation and the compromise with the supporters of the offensive did not conceal, however, that a new appreciation of the moment experienced by the class struggle had consolidated itself in the International.

The *Theses on the World Situation and the Tasks of the Communist International* demonstrated in a clear manner this new appreciation and pointed out the defeats imposed on working-class movements in the short space that separated the 2nd from the 3rd Congress and, mainly, the setbacks suffered in Poland by the Red Army in August 1920; by the movement of the Italian proletariat in September 1920; and by the insurrection of German workers in March 1921.[52] The conclusion reached by the *Theses on the World Situation* was of great impact and provoked protests from supporters of the offensive:

> The initial phase of the postwar revolutionary movement was marked by its elemental power, a lack of definition in its methods and goals, and the extraordinary panic it inspired among the ruling classes. This period now

---

50   The party's own data recorded that the KPD went from 359,613 members in early 1921 to 180,443 at the end of the same year (Broué 1997, p. 221).
51   Riddell 2015, p. 941.
52   Agosti 1974, p. 384.

seems to be essentially over ... The leaders of the bourgeoisie even boast of the power of state institutions, and everywhere they have launched both an economic and political offensive against the working masses.[53]

These *Theses* were in line with the *Report on the World Economic Crisis and the New Tasks of the Communist International*, presented by Trotsky in the same Congress.[54] In submitting the report, the Red Army commander surprised the delegates, and particularly the defenders of the offensive, when he said: 'Only now do we see and feel that we are not so extremely close to the final goal, the winning of power, the world revolution. At that time, in 1919, we thought it was a matter of months, and now we say it is perhaps a matter of years'.[55]

The judgement on the world situation and the development of the revolution separated the different wings of the Congress. The awareness of the new situation experienced by the workers' movement led Lenin and Trotsky to protest against the danger of untimely adventures, but this was not shared by Bukharin and Zinoviev, who formed an important minority in the Bolshevik representation in the Congress.[56] The speeches of Lenin and Trotsky on this occasion are a harsh criticism of extremism and Blanquism, probably the hardest made up to that moment by Bolshevik leaders to members of the International. The political consequences of this new characterisation can be seen in the *Theses on Tactics and Strategy*. Resuming that distinction between Russia and Western Europe present in the Report of the commander of the Red Army, the *Theses on the Tactics and Strategy* affirmed:

> *In Western Europe and the United States, where the working masses are organised in trade unions and political parties*, spontaneous movements are therefore for the time being quite infrequent. Given that fact, Communist parties are obliged to attempt, by mustering their strength in the trade unions and increasing their pressure on other parties based on

---

53   Riddell 2015, p. 902.
54   Riddell 2015, pp. 101–34.
55   Riddell 2015, p. 133.
56   Zinoviev and Bukharin inclined toward the 'offensive theory'. On the eve of the Congress, Lenin decided to impose the discipline of the political bureau of the Russian Communist Party (Bolsheviks) – PCR(b) – on the delegation, preventing Zinoviev and Bukharin from expressing their own position in the Congress of the International as well as voting against the proposal of the thesis advanced by the party. See Hajek 1984, p. 30. This measure deformed democratic centralism and thereby allowed the Russian delegation to present itself as united which made it possible to obtain a solid majority in the Congress, but it created a serious precedent later utilised by the Stalinist fraction.

the working masses, to enable the proletariat's struggle for its immediate interests to unfold on a unified basis.[57]

Unanimously approved, the theses *On Tactics and Strategy* represented an important inflexion in the politics of the International, but also the compromise between the different currents.[58] These theses, defended by Lenin and Trotsky, stated that the most important problem of the International was to 'win the majority of the working class to the principles of communism and how we organise the socially decisive layers of the proletariat for the struggle to achieve them'.[59] The anti-Blanquist content of the new tactic of the International was thus defined.

The policy of the united front was rooted in the deliberations of the 3rd Congress, but it had to wait for the meeting of the Executive Committee of the CI held in December 1921 to be finally announced. The delay expressed the difficult construction of a favourable political context in the International for such an important tactical change. In the *Theses* voted by the Executive Committee, this change was reflected in form and content: 'the general interests of the communist movement as a whole demand that the communist parties and the Communist International as a whole *support the slogan of the workers' united front*', announced the approved text.[60]

The directives adopted at the meeting of the Committee consistently presented for the first time the political formula of the united front proposing not only the unity of communist and social-democratic *unions*, but also the possibility of agreements between international organisations. In the *Theses* approved at that meeting, it was stated:

> Given that the Communist International is advancing the slogan of the workers' united front and of agreements of individual sections with the parties and associations of the Second and Two-and-a-Half Internationals, it cannot repudiate similar agreements on an international level.[61]

From then on, the policy of the united front was disseminated by the organisations of the International, but faced reservations in several of them and the open opposition of the French and Italian sections, the latter led by the Bordi-

---

57 Riddell 2015, pp. 939–40. Emphasis added.
58 See Hajek 1984, p. 33.
59 Riddell 2015, p. 924.
60 Riddell 2011, p. 1167.
61 Riddell 2011, pp. 1171–2.

gist extreme left. Although Gramsci manifested his adherence to the political formula of the united front, at first he remained close to the majority theses in the PCI. He claimed to be persuaded that 'not just the Popular Party, but also a part of the Socialist Party must be excluded from the proletarian united front, in accordance with the conception of the theses approved by the Enlarged Executive Committee, because to make an agreement with them would mean making an agreement with the bourgeoisie'.[62] And he considered that even a united front of the unions would be 'prejudicial for the political struggle in Italy'.[63]

Gramsci's position on this question underwent major changes over the years, without, however, abandoning the idea that the united front was a strategy 'that should begin with the centrality of the workers and the government of production',[64] the reason for which he considered it coherent to exclude fractions of the Socialist Party of Italy. This was a position close to the so-called left currents within the International. The evolution of Gramsci in this regard, however, developed in the opposite direction to that of the International itself.

The defeat of the German revolution in 1923 created within the CI the conditions for a new turn to the left that strengthened the sectarian traits of its political action. The formula of the united front was being questioned in an increasingly intense manner and at the 5th Congress held in 1924 after Lenin's death, it came to be considered a pure manoeuvre, only 'one mode of agitation in revolutionary mobilization'.[65] On the other hand, the application of the united front 'from below', that is, without the agreement of the leaders of the trade unions and other workers' parties, was considered 'always and in any part necessary', while the method of a united front 'from above', that is, with the agreement, was 'categorically and promptly rejected'.[66]

The Congress already reflected the theoretical and political decline of the International and the strengthening of the Stalinist faction within it. The excommunication of Trotsky, who until then had held a position of great importance in the congresses of the International, was announced from the tribune itself by delegates such as Ruth Fischer, who were as inexperienced as they were subordinate to the new Soviet leadership.[67] It was up to Radek then

---

62 SPW, p. 120.
63 SF, p. 520.
64 Del Roio 2005, p. 116.
65 Agosti 1976, p. 120. See Hajek 1984, p. 119.
66 Agosti 1976, p. 120.
67 Ruth Fischer herself was expelled from the German Communist Party in 1926 and sentenced to death in 1936 in the Moscow trials, accused of 'Trotskyism'. From the 1940s

to express a more acute defence of the united front formula in line with Trotsky, who did not even attend the Congress.⁶⁸

The sectarianism of the Congress resolutions resulted in the identification of fascism with social democracy, a thesis that would later be developed in the formula of 'social fascism', and the assertion that the united front as a coalition of communist parties and socialist democrats – the workers' government – was a distortion driven by right-wing tendencies. For the CI, the main goal of the united front tactic would be a struggle 'conducted mainly against the traitorous leaders of counterrevolutionary social democracy'.⁶⁹

A few months after the 5th Congress, in September 1924, Stalin wrote: 'Fascism is the bourgeoisie's fighting organisation that relies on the active support of Social-Democracy. Social-Democracy is objectively the moderate wing of fascism'.⁷⁰ From then on, the united front formula led a rugged life. Although it was maintained in the letter, successive resolutions withdrew its strength and ended up de-characterising it. The *Theses* adopted at the 6th International Congress defined a 'third period' in the world situation, marked by the accentuation of the 'contradiction between the growth of the productive forces and the contraction of markets' that 'will inevitably give rise to a fresh era of imperialist wars among the imperialist States themselves; wars of the imperialist States against the USSR; wars of national liberation against imperialism; wars of imperialist intervention and gigantic class battles'.⁷¹

The characterisation of the 'third period' resulted from a compromise between different positions within the International. In light of the crisis that began in 1929 and the Second World War it was not mistaken *a priori*, but the resolution was sufficiently ambiguous to allow for various interpretations, among them Stalin's, who, struggling against the influence of Bukharin in the International, bore the brunt of the catastrophic consequences of this characterisation.⁷²

Although the formula of the united front had not disappeared from the discourse of the leaders of the International, it assumed new connotations. Stalin, for example, in 1928, referred to a 'a united front among the workers of the

---

onwards, residing in the United States, she developed an intense anti-communist agitation and in 1947 participated as a prosecution witness in the McCarthyist tribunals.
68 Hajek, 1984, pp. 117–26.
69 Agosti 1976, p. 121.
70 Stalin 1954, Vol. 6, p. 294.
71 Degras 1959, p. 456.
72 See Hajek 1984, pp. 188–9. Trotsky was among the first to write that, despite formally leading the work of the 6th Congress, in the eyes of all, Bukharin's influence in the International was waning. See Trotsky 1989 and Broué 1997, pp. 483–5.

advanced countries and the working masses of the colonies'.[73] And in 1930 he used it as a synonym for the alliance of the workers with the small peasants.[74] But there is no mention in his writings from 1928 to 1934 of the united front as an alliance of trade unions and workers' parties. The idea of the united front 'from below' was fully consolidated, but contradictorily a new 'national united front' was advanced, that is, 'from above', but with the organisations of bourgeois nationalism, such as the Chinese Kuomintang.[75]

The prevailing sectarian interpretation of the resolutions of the 6th Congress had left the leadership of the PCI in a complicated situation. Gramsci and Terracini had been in prison since 1926, and the ruling nucleus of the party was composed of Palmiro Togliatti, Ruggero Grieco and Angelo Tasca. The dominant appraisal in the PCI on fascism was far from the simplistic and rudimentary view which came to prevail in the CI. The experience of the fight against the Mussolini government during the crisis that developed after the assassination of the Socialist deputy Giacomo Matteoti, had educated the leaders of the party in this respect and they were less prone to false identities between fascism and social democracy.[76]

In a report from June 1928, on the eve of the 6th Congress of the CI, Togliatti wrote that one of the peculiarities of the 'fascist reaction is precisely the fact that fascism, unlike most other European reactionary movements, excludes a compromise with social democracy'.[77] The distinction between fascism and social democracy was made even clearer in an article published for the first time in Russian in August 1928, in the journal of the CI:

> Fascism is clearly different from all reactionary regimes that have so far been affirmed in the modern capitalist world. It rejects all compromise with social democracy. Pursues it harshly; eliminates it from any possibility of legal life; forces it to emigrate.[78]

But although he disagreed on important points with the Soviet leaders, particularly those aligned with Stalin, Togliatti avoided a confrontation on 'Russian questions'. Nearest to Bukharin, Tasca did not adopt the same position

---

73 Stalin 1954, Vol. 11, p. 211. See also Stalin 1954, Vol. 13, p. 94.
74 See Stalin 1954, Vol. 12, p. 208.
75 See, for example, Agosti 1976, pp. 658–71 and Stalin 1954, Vol. 7, pp. 135–54 and Vol. 9, pp. 249–55.
76 See, for example, some of Gramsci's writings on the murder of Matteotti and the subsequent Italian situation. PPW, pp. 288–300, 301–5 and Spriano 1976, Vol. 1, pp. 381–404.
77 Togliatti 1973, Vol. II, p. 398. OT.
78 Togliatti 1973, Vol. II, p. 548. OT.

of conciliation and ended up committing the treasonous crime of expressing his opinion on such questions. They were severe criticisms. Tasca, in a letter to Togliatti dated 20 January 1929, called Stalin 'a regurgitator of the ideas of others, who steals unscrupulously and then presents it in a schematic way giving the illusion of a force of thought that does not exist'.[79] Even harder than the characterisation was the explanation: 'Stalin plagiarizes because he cannot do otherwise, because he is intellectually mediocre and infertile, and because he secretly hates the intellectual superiority of Trotsky and Bukharin'.[80] Obviously these criticisms would not go unanswered.

Togliatti's position was different. Having avoided defying Stalin's authority, he found himself in a situation that allowed him to deliver Tasca up to a campaign of defamation, thus reconstructing his position within the CI apparatus. Togliatti himself provided the arguments for the prosecution by execrating his former comrade in a speech to the Executive of the CI, calling him an 'ultra-opportunist' and 'opportunist to purism', affirming 'the anti-Marxist or simply stupid character' of his conception.[81]

As Stalin's struggle against Bukharin became acute in the International, the tensions inside the PCI increased.[82] The attack became more intense in December 1928, on the occasion of the meeting of the Executive Committee of the CI in which harsh criticism was directed at Jules Humbert-Droz, Angelo Tasca, and the German Communists Brandler and Thalheimer. On the occasion, Stalin stated that the presence in the CI of people like these leaders of the German Communist Party 'should no longer be tolerated'.[83]

The path to Bukahrin's conviction was thus cleared and in February 1929, Stalin himself stated: 'The majority of the comrades demand that this joint meeting of the Political Bureau of the CC and Presidium of the CCC should condemn the Right-opportunist, capitulatory platform of Bukharin, Tomsky and Rykov, that it should condemn the attempt of Bukharin and his group to form an anti-Party bloc with the Trotskyists'.[84] It was in this paranoid and persecutory context that the political bureau and the plenum of the central committee of the PCI, meeting between February and March 1929, decided

---

79 Cited in Fiori 1991, p. 33.
80 Ibid.
81 Ibid.
82 See Stalin's attack in his October 1928 full address to the Moscow Committee and Muscovite Control Commission of the Communist Party of the Soviet Union. Stalin 1954, Vol. 11, pp. 231–48.
83 Stalin 1954, Vol. 11, p. 324.
84 Stalin 1954, Vol. 11, p. 337.

to sacrifice Tasca, condemning his point of view and dismissing him from his position as the Italian representative on the Executive Committee of the CI.

A few days later in March 1929, the PCI journal *Lo Stato Operaio* announced that the discussion on international issues held at the Central Committee 'revealed the existence, also within its interior, of a differentiation that follows approximately the same lines of differentiation in regard to the acceptance or the "interpretation" of the decisions of the Sixth World Congress, in almost all other parties of the International'.[85]

The meeting of the 10th Plenum of the Executive Committee of the CI held in July 1929 in Moscow consolidated the sectarian turn of the CI. The Stalinist interpretation of the 'Third Period' was ratified and the inevitable character of new revolutionary situations announced.[86] The approved resolution also made official the formula of social fascism, stating that: 'In countries where there are strong social-democratic parties, fascism assumes the particular form of social-fascism ...'.[87] The united front was thus, finally buried, since even the left wing of social democracy could not be considered an ally in the struggle for the immediate demands of the working class:

> The plenum of the ECCI imposes on all the sections of the Communist International the obligation to intensify their fight against international social democracy, which is the chief support of capitalism. The plenum of the ECCI instructs all sections of the CI to pay special attention to an energetic struggle against the 'left' wing of social-democracy which retards the process of the disintegration of social-democracy by creating the illusion that it – the 'left' wing – represents an opposition to the policy of the leading social-democratic bodies, whereas as a matter of fact, it wholeheartedly supports the policy of social fascism.[88]

At the same meeting the Italian situation was debated intensely. The punishment for Tasca was considered insufficient and Dmitri Manuilski, representative of the CI, stated in his report on the Italian situation that Angelo Tasca's views were incompatible with militancy in the party. The Italian Party was severely censored and a cloud of suspicions about it arose, certainly thickened

---

85 Togliatti 1973, Vol. II, p. 703. See also Fiori 1979, pp. 319–21.
86 See Broué 1997, p. 493.
87 Degras 1964, p. 44.
88 Degras 1964, p. 47.

by the memory of Gramsci's letters opposing the modes employed in the struggle against the Trotsky-Zinoviev-Kamenev opposition.[89]

Although he expressed clear disagreement with the Opposition, the letter that Gramsci wrote in 1926, addressed to the Central Committee of the Russian Communist Party, stated that Zinoviev, Trotsky, and Kamenev had been the masters of the PCI and asked for assurances that the Communist Party of the Soviet Union did not intend to win 'a crushing victory in the struggle' and 'is disposed to avoid excessive measures'.[90] Togliatti, at the time in Moscow, replied to the letter reproducing the speech of the Stalinist fraction. Gramsci's reply, dated 26 October, manifested clear disagreement with Togliatti: 'This way of thinking gives me the most painful impression'.[91] It was, according to Fiori,[92] the consummation of the political and personal rupture between Gramsci and Togliatti.

In 1929, Gramsci's worst fears were realised. The removal of Bukharin and Humbert-Droz from the leadership of the International in July of that year was followed in Italy by the expulsion of Angelo Tasca in September 1929 and Amadeo Bordiga in January 1930.[93] At the same time that he led an internal purge, Togliatti publicly declared his acceptance of the theses of the Stalinist fraction and, in particular, the thesis of social fascism, thus abandoning his previous characterisations. Accordingly, in a speech delivered in February 1930 to the presidium of the Executive Committee of the CI, Togliatti defined the 'general line of development of the process' as 'an accentuation of the fascistization of social democracy'.[94] And he insisted on this question in his report to the same meeting: 'Italian social democracy became fascist with extreme ease … Behind every action that the elements of the democratic left seek to carry out, it can be demonstrated that this was accomplished under the inspiration of Mussolini'.[95]

---

89   Gramsci's letter was first published by Tasca in 1937 and Togliatti's letters had to wait for his death to come to light. The voluminous correspondence between Togliatti and the leaders of the PCI who were in Italy in 1926 was published by Daniele 1999.
90   PPW, p. 312.
91   Daniele 1999, p. 437. OT.
92   Fiori 1991, pp. 9 and 13.
93   Spriano 1976, Vol. II, pp. 227–9 and 254–5.
94   Togliatti 1973, Vol. III / 1, p. 154.
95   Togliatti 1973, Vol. III, p. 180. Commenting on this turn by Togliatti, the organiser of his *Works*, Ernesto Ragioneri states: 'It is a doubt in my opinion that is out of place or something that is impossible to resolve to ask oneself on this point to what extent the positions maintained by Togliatti in the course of these years corresponded to deep convictions or derived from tactical opportunity in the complex dialectic between the general line of the Comintern and the activity of the Italian party' (Togliatti 1973, pp. lxxi). Pro-

The turnaround led to the birth of a new internal opposition. The divergences exploded in January 1930 within the CPI's Political Bureau, giving rise to the so-called 'opposition of the three': Alfonso Leonetti, director of the illegal press; Pietro Tresso, head of the trade union movement; and Paolo Ravazzoli, from the bureau of organisation. The conflicts began with questions concerning the organisation of the party, but the struggle against fascism and criticism of the politics of the third period in the CI soon took centre stage, leading 'the three' to a rapid rapprochement with the International Left Opposition, led by Leon Trotsky, their expulsion on 9 June of the same year and the creation of the New Italian Opposition.[96]

Leonetti had been very close to Gramsci since the time of *L'Ordine Nuovo* and the positions held by the Italian opposition were not very different from the latter's defended before and during his arrest. Since 1926, the date of his correspondence to Togliatti expressing his disagreement on the course taken by the fight against the Unified Opposition, suspicion fell on the Sardinian Marxist in the CI as being pro-Trotskyist.[97] In this paroxysmal environment, characterised by the 'third period' turn in the CI and the 'svolta' (turning) in the Italian party, doubts about Gramsci's position on the expulsions must have come immediately.

---

found or not, such positions had negative practical effects on the PCI allowing hundreds of arrests to be effected. See Spriano 1976, Vol. II, pp. 287–97. The adventurous politics of the PCI in the early 1930s in resistance to fascism (Broué 1997, p. 513) reveals that in the 'dialectic between the general line of the Comintern and the activity of the Italian party' the first absolutely prevailed. Collating the different citations with respect to 'social fascism', Trotsky said in the heat of the moment: 'And the functionaries of the Comintern lost no time in re-aligning themselves. Ercoli [Togliatti] made haste to prove that precious as truth was to him, Molotov was more precious, and he ... wrote a report in defense of the theory of social Fascism. "The Italian social democracy", he announced in February 1930, "turns Fascist with the greatest readiness." Alas, the functionaries of official Communism turn flunkies even more readily' (Trotsky 1969a, p. 22).

96 One version of these episodes, hostile to the 'three' and sympathetic to Togliatti, is in Spriano 1976, Vol. II, chap. 13. The version of Togliatti (1973, see Vol. III, 1, pp. 248–80) can be read in his report to the Italian Commission of the Executive of the CI. The documents of the New Italian Opposition can be found in Massari 2004a. Massari 2004b and Marazzi 1990 highlight the similarity in this period between the positions of Gramsci and the New Italian Opposition as do Alfonso Leonetti 1974, p. 189 and Anderson 1976a, pp. 72–3.

97 Natoli 1990, p. 76. On Gramsci's critique of the Soviet bureaucracy and the opposition struggle in this letter, see Moscato 1999 and Vacca 1999, chap. VI. Moscato 1999, pp. 152–8 considers that the publication of this letter, blocked by Togliatti with the endorsement of the political bureau of the PCI, could have contributed positively to the struggle, mainly outside the Soviet Union.

At the request of Togliatti, Gennaro Gramsci, Antonio's brother, returned to Italy to visit him at the Turi prison, inform him of the expulsion of the 'three' and ask for his opinion. Back in Paris, Gennaro informed Togliatti: 'Nino [Gramsci] is totally in line with you'.[98] In testimony given to Fiori many years later, Gennaro told another version: 'The brother's line was that of Leonetti, Tresso and Ravazzoli. He did not justify their expulsion and rejected the new orientation of the International, shared by Togliatti, in his opinion, very hastily'.[99] According to Fiori, Gennaro considered that his attitude was the only one possible to save his brother: 'If I had given another answer ... not even Nino would have escaped expulsion'.[100] This version is considered 'credible' even by Spriano[101] although the existence of suspicions in the CI over Gramsci has been questioned or minimised by historians linked to the Togliattian tradition. But if Gramsci had been in Moscow, instead of the docile Togliatti, who could confirm that he would have survived the purges and executions?

Togliatti himself was responsible for building the legend of Gramsci as a partisan of Stalin by grossly disfiguring the positions of the Sardinian Marxist and claiming that in 1930 he said to Communists who were sympathetic to the ideas of the oppositionists that Trotsky was 'the whore of fascism'.[102] Gramsci was thus placed 'Under the invincible banner of Marx-Engels-Lenin-Stalin'.[103] Guido Liguori considers this statement 'unfounded and not justifiable today'.[104] In fact, the judgement that the Sardinian Marxist emitted in this respect in prison was very different, according to the testimony of Angelo Scucchia: 'On Trotsky, one day Gramsci said: "Great historian, great revolutionary, but he is self-centred, sees himself at the centre of all events and has no sense of the party"'.[105]

The psychological judgement expressed in this statement was not exclusive to Gramsci although it has been challenged by biographers such as Isaac Deustcher. Obviously, in this evaluation personal attitudes of antipathy or sympathy may be deduced, but not political positions. But the political judgement expressed in what 'Gramsci said one day' was radically different from that which Togliatti had sordidly imputed to him. The political differences that

---

98   Cited in Fori 1979, p. 312. OT.
99   Ibid. OT.
100 Ibid. OT.
101 Spriano 1976, Vol. II, p. 280.
102 Togliatti 2001, p. 88. OT.
103 Togliatti 2001, p. 89. OT.
104 Liguori 1996, p. 74. OT.
105 Quercioli 1977, p. 225. OT.

might have distanced Gramsci from Trotsky did not imply for the former an ignorance of the political position and historical significance that the latter occupied.

There is no doubt that Gramsci was at odds with the CI's position and with its application by Togliatti in the PCI and that an alternative policy that he advanced, the convening of a Constituent Assembly, was identical to that proposed by the New International Opposition. This identity was unknown by the oppositionists, but it seems to have at least been known to some extent by the author of the *Notebooks*, who was trying to find out about it. This is undoubtedly an uncomfortable position for Togliattian historiography. For if the 'war of position' was translated into the political formula of the united front, then, in 1930, the main representatives of the war of position were in the International Left Opposition, Trotsky among them.

Spriano attempted to resolve this embarrassing situation by reversing their roles in an implausible manner. For the historian of the PCI, it was Trotsky who came to share many of the positions of Gramsci and Terracini.[106] Without mentioning the criticism of the programme of the CI, written in 1928,[107] Spriano withdrew the critical anticipation of the 'third period' and the theory of 'social fascism' made by the Russian Marxist. Since in his narrative it was Trotsky who agreed with Gramsci rather than the contrary, this allowed him to rudimentarily highlight some passages from the *Notebooks* where Gramsci criticised Trotsky and stated that 'if calling Gramsci a Stalinist makes no exact sense, it makes even less sense to hypothesise his solidarity with Trotsky'.[108] And yet, there is Gennaro's 'credible' testimony and the coincidence of the antifascist politics shared between the Sardinian Marxist and the Russian ...

There is also no doubt that the news brought by Gennaro had a strong impact on his brother. In a letter dated 16 June, Gramsci himself confessed this impact to his sister-in-law: 'My brother came to visit me a short while ago; since then my thoughts have been zigzagging'.[109] According to Ercole Piacentini, one of the prisoners closest to Gramsci, after the visit of his brother, the communist leader began to speak of things to which he had not referred until then:

> he spoke of Stalin as a despot and claimed to know the testament of Lenin, in which it was maintained that Stalin was unfit to become secretary of the Bolshevik party ... He once spoke of the French Revolution. He said

---

106   Spriano 1976, Vol. II, p. 274.
107   Trotsky 1974.
108   Spriano 1976, Vol. II, p. 276.
109   LC, p. 350.

that at some point the revolutionaries had begun to cut the heads off of each other. They began by cutting that of Marat – which Gramsci sympathised with because he was of Sardinian origin – and ended up decapitating the revolution. And in this regard he also gestured toward a Soviet 'thermidor'.[110]

In July, according to the testimony of Giovanni Lai,[111] Gramsci began a series of conversations with his fellow prisoners in which the Constituent Assembly was one of the most important themes. Information about these conversations is not coincident. The period of the sectarian turn and agitation against social fascism and Gramsci's positions found strong resistance among some prisoners identified with the official line. Lisa, often quoted, did not narrate any misunderstanding between the prisoners. Umberto Clementi, for his part, said that Scucchia affirmed that Gramsci had adopted the 'position of a social-democrat'.[112] Sandro Pertini, who was imprisoned with Gramsci, describes that he was deeply isolated after exposing his positions.[113] And Scucchia described discussions, without Gramsci's presence, but with that of Lisa, in which the adjectives 'opportunism', 'antiparty positions', 'deviationism' and 'ideological betrayal' were often used.[114]

The outcome of such discussions provoked the breakup of the group of communist prisoners in Turi and the isolation of Gramsci in prison.[115] This isolation was aggravated by the fact that Gramsci fed suspicions that he had been abandoned or even betrayed by the Communist leadership and particularly by Togliatti. Such suspicions had existed since he received a letter from the communist leader Ruggero Grieco in 1928, which allegedly worsened his judicial situation. Gramsci considered this a 'strange letter',[116] a 'wicked act or an irresponsible prudence' and did not discard that who wrote it 'was irresponsibly stupid and someone else, a less stupid one, had induced him to write this letter'.[117] The other 'less stupid' one was, undoubtedly, Togliatti, with whom he had split on the occasion of the exchange of letters on the 'Russian question' in 1926.

All evidence suggests that the conclusions Gramsci reached about Grieco's letter and his situation in the prison were exaggerated. There was nothing in the

---

110 Cited in Fiori 1991, p. 40.
111 Quercioli 1977, p. 207.
112 Quercioli 1977, p. 199.
113 Quercioli 1977, p. 211.
114 Quercioli 1977, p. 222.
115 Fiori 1991, pp. 41–6.
116 LP2, Vol. 1, p. 201.
117 LP2, Vol. 2, pp. 236–9.

letter that the fascists did not know beforehand. At the present stage of documentary research, already aided by the opening of the archives of the former Soviet Union, it is also not possible to state that the communist leader had been abandoned by his party and convicted for that reason to perish prematurely. In this sense, fascism must be held responsible for the death of the communist leader, as Michele Pistillo demonstrates, based on extensive documentation.[118]

The conjunction of these episodes – the break with Togliatti in 1926, Grieco's letter, the sectarian turn of the PCI and the discussions in prison – made Gramsci cautious with the information he received. As late as December 1930, Gramsci continued to learn more about the expulsion of Leonetti, Tresso, and Ravazzoli. When Bruno Tosin, official of the PCI secretariat in Rome, arrived at the Turi prison, Gramsci insistently asked him about this subject.[119] After these initial conversations, Tosin said that his cellmates 'explained to him what had been the terms of the discussion with Gramsci and ... said that there had been virtually a rupture within our group of prisoners'.[120]

Apparently, after the visit of his brother Gennaro, Gramsci asked the prison authorities for permission to read some books by Trotsky with a view to forming a more solid opinion on the subject: 'his autobiography, translated also into Italian and published by Mondadori, and also these two: *La révolution défigurée* [*The Revolution Betrayed*] and *Vers le capitalism or vers le socialisme* [*Toward capitalism or toward socialism*]'.[121] A letter dated 1 December 1930 to Tatiana informs that his request was approved and that he asked her to send him the autobiography of Trotsky, but he makes no mention of the other two books.[122] Did Gramsci receive such books? Recalling his conversations with Gramsci in prison, Angelo Scucchia affirmed that 'in the prison Trotsky's *My Life* circulated and that it was common for the prisoners to talk about it "because almost everyone had read this book"'.[123] However, it is not possible to say with certainty that Gramsci was in fact among the readers or that he had read any of Trotsky's books he requested in prison. Indeed, none of these books were among those left in his library.

A careful analysis of the *Letters from Prison* and the *Notebooks* reveals a contradiction which should be taken into account in the analysis of the texts. As seen above, on 1 December of 1930 Gramsci still was not in possession of

---

118   Michele Pistillo 2003.
119   Quercioli 1977, p. 227.
120   Quercioli 1977, p. 228.
121   LP2, Vol. 1, pp. 348–9.
122   LP2, Vol. 1, p. 365.
123   Quercioli 1977, p. 225.

Trotsky's autobiography. The first mention of the Bolshevik leader's book in Gramsci's writings can be found in Notebook 3. In this passage, Gramsci considered it 'astonishing' that Trotsky had spoken of Labriola's 'dilettantism'.[124] Francioni[125] dates this paragraph, quite accurately, between June and July 1930, which clearly contradicts the letter. It is probable, then, that Gramsci was quoting the work without having it on hand, from third-party comments.

From the above-cited contradiction it is not possible to infer anything beyond the difficulties of the research and composition of the *Notebooks*. Access to the sources needed for research was precarious and Gramsci often sought to circumvent these difficulties by reviews and second-hand testimonials. He never ceased to be aware of these difficulties and several times he registered his discomfort about it. Unfortunately the reservations made were often ignored by interpreters and superficial readings with respect to the complex problems which substituted cautious research.[126] A careful reconstruction of the Gramsci-Trotsky relationship in the *Notebooks* therefore demands that the warnings of the author himself must be taken seriously.

Trotsky appeared for the first time in Notebook 1 in the important § 44 'Political class leadership before and after assuming governtment' ('Direzione politica di classe prima e dopo l'andata al governo'). This text is of fundamental importance for the structure of the *Notebooks* and advanced some of the most important themes that would be developed later. The concept of hegemony was outlined here based on 'politico-historical criterion on which our own inquires must be grounded':[127] the distinction between the functions of domination of the opposing classes and the leadership of the allied classes.

---

124   PN2, Q3, § 31, p. 30. For a non-Italian, it is not so astonishing that Trotsky referred to Labriola in this way. Manuel Sacristan, for example, in an essay that engaged the philosopher's reading, affirmed that his 'verbalism, sometimes pleased and other times shamed, could make it an uncomfortable read'. The same author mentioned the 'generic chirp of an academicism today considered anachronic' (Sacristan 1969, pp. 8 and 9).

125   Francioni 1984, p. 140.

126   Commentators who have been judicious about other issues have quickly passed over this theme. For example, Martelli 1996, pp. 91–5, Losurdo 1997, pp. 142, 204 and 242, and Coutinho 1999, pp. 150–2. With respect to the complex relations between Gramsci and Rosa Luxemburg and Leon Trotsky, Burgio, in a questionable manner, even states that in both cases 'the pages of the *Notebooks* can be deciphered without any particular effort' (2003, p. 148). Sena Jr. 2004 emphasised the inconsistencies and omissions of a Brazilian mythology with respect to Gramsci's anti-Trotskyism and the need for a more detailed analysis of the texts.

127   PN1, Q1, § 44, p. 136.

The distinction allowed its author to state that in order to reach power, a class should first lead and then, remaining a leader, also become dominant:

> There can and there must be a 'political hegemony' even before assuming government power, and in order to exercise political leadership or hegemony one must not count solely on the power and material force that is given by government.[128]

This declaration guided Gramsci's research on the concept of hegemony throughout the *Notebooks*. In its original context it provided a methodological criterion for the research on the formation of the governing Italian groups in the *Risorgimento*. Yet though its evolution, this question allowed him to address an important problem of the theory of revolution in the twentieth century:

> As regards the 'Jacobin' slogan which Marx directed at the Germany of 1848–49, its complex fortunes should be examined. Revived, systematized, elaborated, intellectualized by the Parvus-Bronstein group, it proved inert and ineffective in 1905 and afterward: it was an abstract thing that belonged to the scientific laboratory. The tendency which opposed it in this intellectualized form, however, without using it 'intentionally', in fact employed it in its historical, concrete, living form adapted to the time and place as something that sprang from all the pores of the society which had to be transformed, as the alliance of two classes with the hegemony of the urban class.[129]

The argument developed in this paragraph is rather subtle and complex. So Secco pronounces that in this passage Gramsci questioned Trotsky 'Once again as a theoretician opposed to the hegemony of the proletariat'.[130] The rough definition of Trotsky as an opponent of the 'hegemony of the proletariat', as documented by Secco,[131] was from Stalin's tillage.[132] Gramsci repeated this statement in an uncritical manner in the above-mentioned letter of 1926, in which he wrote:

---

128 PN1, Q1, §44, p. 137.
129 PN1, Q1, §44, p. 151.
130 Secco 2006, p. 75.
131 Secco 2006, p. 38.
132 Stalin 1954, Vol. 6, p. 107 ff.

It is the principle and practice of the hegemony of the proletariat that are put under discussion [by the opposition], they are the fundamental relations of the alliance between workers and peasants, that is, the pillars of the workers' state and the revolution.[133]

The rupture with Stalin and the Russian Communist Party was thus slow. Referring to the years 1924–25, Somai[134] states that Gramsci, as well as the majority of the PCI, was pressured on the one hand by the fascist reaction and by the CI, 'the main source of financial subsidies' and of hope. In this respect, too, there would also be 'confidence in the "old guard", the conviction that the main element was the continuity of the revolutionary tradition' of the Russian Communist Party.[135] The same commentator states that Gramsci, as well as much of the PCI, had 'little in-depth knowledge of the struggle within the RCP'.[136]

For these reasons, the said passage in the *Notebooks* should not be treated in a superficial way, making a more thorough treatment necessary. Although he did not have a deep knowledge of the matter, he showed that he was informed as much about the Marxian origins of the slogan 'Jacobin' as the 'permanent revolution', such as the role of Alexander Parvus (Israel Lazarevich Helphand) in its formulation prior to 1905.[137] The claim that the formula was 'intellectualist' in 1905 manifested Gramsci's discomfort with the question and was unfair, given Trotsky's role as a practical leader of the Petrograd Soviet during the events of that year. But the most important aspect of this passage, besides demonstrating certain knowledge of the theme, was that its author affirmed that the Bolsheviks applied 'in fact' the formula of the permanent revolution.

---

133   Daniele 1999, pp. 409–10.
134   Somai 1982, p. 91. OT.
135   Ibid. OT.
136   Somai 1982, p. 88. OT.
137   The sources of this may well have been the myriad of articles published in the International Communist movement seeking to affirm the Menshevik roots of the theory of permanent revolution. See, for example, Stalin's article 'The October Revolution and Russian Communist Tactics' of December 1924: 'It is not true that the theory of "permanent revolution", which Radek bashfully refrains from mentioning, was advanced in 1905 by Rosa Luxemburg and Trotsky. Actually, this theory was advanced by Parvus and Trotsky. Now, 10 months later, Radek corrects himself and deems it necessary to castigate Parvus for the theory of "permanent revolution"' (Stalin 1954, Vol. 6, p. 397). Maitan 1958 protested very mildly against the approximation that Gramsci made between Parvus and Trotsky. In an important work on the origins of the theory of the permanent revolution of Trotsky, Alain Brossat 1976, pp. 77–86 notes the latter's indebtedness to Parvus, while at the same time underscoring the differences.

This judgement, of great importance for the understanding of the Gramsci-Trotsky relationship, reproduced in a synthetic way the treatment given to this theme in a letter dated 9 February 1924. After mapping the different positions present in the Russian Communist Party, Gramsci stated in it:

> It is well known that as early as 1905 Trotsky stated that in Russia a socialist and workers' revolution could occur, while the Bolsheviks intended only to establish a political dictatorship of the proletariat allied with the peasantry, which would serve the development of capitalism, which should not be offended in its economic structure. It is also known that in November 1917, while Lenin and most of the party moved to Trotsky's position and intended to take in their hands not only the political government but also the industrial government, Zinoviev and Kamenev remained with the party's traditional view.[138]

The letter is clearly favourable to Trotsky and makes a crystal clear judgement on the events of 1917.[139] On the opposition programme, the author considered that it had the objective of increasing the weight of the working class in the internal life of the party, diminishing the bureaucracy and thus ensuring its socialist character.[140] It is not possible, however, to deduce from this letter complete solidarity with the platform of the oppositionists. On a theme of great importance, as was this balance of the defeat of the German revolution in 1923, the letter did not fully converge with Trotsky's position.[141]

However, the assessment made in this letter did not last long, and although Gramsci had, during 1925 and 1926, censured Trotsky several times and assumed positions favourable to the Stalinist fraction, the persistence of the position assumed by the Bolsheviks in 1917 was notable. There is no qualitative difference in this respect between the text of 1924 and § 44 of Notebook 1, probably written in February 1930.[142]

The peasant and labour alliance 'with the hegemony of the urban class' was the Bolshevik formula of the permanent revolution. It should be noted that this formula was very far from the 'democratic dictatorship of the proletariat and the peasantry', defended by Lenin in 1905. Gramsci had clearly perceived this

---

138   L, p. 224. OT.
139   On the positive judgement with regard to Trotsky issued in the letter, see Ortaggi 1974, Rosengarten 1984–85, p. 81, Massari 2004b, pp. 21–2 and Del Roio 2005, p. 115.
140   L, p. 224.
141   See Somai 1982, p. 85.
142   See Francioni 1984, p. 140.

in 1924. There were two fundamental differences between Lenin's original formula and that of Trotsky, which Lenin applied 'in fact'. The first difference was in the character of the revolution, which Trotsky claimed to be socialist and Lenin democratic, which implied that the revolution should serve 'the development of capitalism, which should not be offended in its economic structure'. The second difference was precisely in the 'hegemony of the urban class', since the Leninist formula did not define the leading role of the proletariat in the 'democratic dictatorship' and, for this reason the dictatorship was 'of the proletariat and of the peasantry' and not only 'of the proletariat'.

A new direct reference to Trotsky was made by Gramsci in the last months of 1930, after, therefore, the famous visit of his brother Gennaro. This new mention was of the discussion about the war of manoeuvre and the war of position. Once again the author of the *Notebooks* proceeded cautiously, feeling that he was advancing on unstable terrain:

> *War of position and war of maneuver, or frontal war.* One should determine whether Bronstein's famous theory about the *permanence* of maneuver is not a political reflection of the theory of maneuver (remember the observation by the Cossack general Krasnov); whether it is not, in the final analysis, a reflection of the general-economic-cultural-social conditions of a country in which the structures of national life are embryonic and unsettled and cannot become 'trench or fortress'. In that case, one might say that Bronstein, while appearing to be 'Western' was in fact a cosmopolitan, that is, superficially nationally and superficially Western or European. Ilyich, on the other hand, was profoundly national and profoundly European.[143]

In this passage, Gramsci seems to identify war of manoeuvre with permanent revolution, an identity that has been the object of a great number of often superficial comments.[144] It was not, however, the case of Frank Rosengarten, who highlighted 'the ambivalences, the contradictoriness, the shifts and changes in interpretation that one finds in Gramsci's whole interaction, on all levels, with Trotsky' and sought to compare the statements of the Italian Marxist with the Bolshevik leader's text itself.[145]

---

143 PN3, Q7, §16, p. 168.
144 Some commentators who sought to approach Trotsky-Gramsci (Harman 1983; Albamonte and Romano 2003) failed in their work due to a rudimentary knowledge of Gramsci's work, without the support of the critical editions. They therefore fell into extremely superficial analyses. Most of them did nothing but repeat Anderson's arguments (2002).
145 Rosengarten 1984–85, pp. 88–9.

The comparison does not fail to impress, for what one called 'permanent revolution' in the *Notebooks* is not the same as what the other wrote, yet, on the other hand, what the latter called permanent revolution was very close to the formula of political hegemony in some formulations of the former. The Marxist political lexicon reserved for the term Blanquism the designation of 'a political transformation carried out by a minority without the support of the masses'. The Gramscian conception of politics was clearly anti-Blanquist and its development was inserted into that theoretical current whose nodal question was 'that of the hegemony of the proletariat in the revolutionary process'.[146] This was precisely the question the former president of the Petrograd Soviet raised in a text published in 1906, *Results and Prospects*. Trotsky wrote:

> But the participation of the proletariat in a government is also objectively most probable, and permissible in principle only as a *dominating and leading participation*. One may, of course, describe such a government as the dictatorship of the proletariat and peasantry, a dictatorship of the proletariat, peasantry and intelligentsia, or even a coalition government of the working class and the petty-bourgeoisie, but the question nevertheless remains: who is to wield the hegemony in the government itself, and through it in the country? And when we speak of a workers' government, by this we reply that the hegemony should belong to the working class.[147]

In the distinction between leader and dominant, as well as in the avowal of the hegemony of the working class, the similarity between the lexicon of the two authors is impressive. This similarity was not always so strong, but even so it is not possible to identify the interpretation of Gramsci with the text of Trotsky. The difference is obvious in a text that every commentator should know, *The Permanent Revolution*, of 1929. Trotsky defined in it that in its first aspect the 'theory of permanent revolution ... demonstrates that the democratic tasks of the backward bourgeois nations lead directly, in our epoch, to the dictatorship of the proletariat ...'.[148] The other two aspects of the theory of permanent revolution concerned the permanent transformation of all social relations in the context of the process of building socialism[149] and the 'inter-

---

146   Del Roio 2005, p. 90. In terms of the so-called 'refoundation', Del Roio 2005 includes Lenin, Luxemburg and Gramsci. But there is no plausible reason for Trotsky not belonging in this strand.
147   Trotsky 1969b, p. 70. Emphasis in the original.
148   Trotsky 1969b, p. 132.
149   Ibid.

national character of the socialist revolution'.[150] In respect to this latter aspect, Trotsky clarified that the 'socialist revolution begins on national foundations', but it could only maintain itself in this restricted context under 'a provisional state of affairs, even though, as the experience of the Soviet Union shows, one of long duration'.[151]

The theory of permanent revolution is not, therefore, a definition of the situation, nor of the methods of struggle; it is not a description of an alleged 'permanent revolutionary situation' nor an apology for the 'frontal assault'. Thus, Rosengarten warns, if the statements of Gramsci in the paragraph quoted (Q7, §16) ceased to be expressed in the conditional mode, as a hypothesis of investigation, and were transformed into a definitive judgement, then it would be necessary to agree with Livio Maitan[152] who said that this interpretation of Trotsky's thought was a 'vulgar caricature'.[153]

At least in one passage, Gramsci was not so careful, leaving greater space for the interpretation denounced by Maitan. This is in Q6, §138 in which the path from the war of manoeuvre to the war of position was analysed. Gramsci considered this question 'the most important postwar problem of political theory' and declared that it was 'related to the issues raised by Bronstein, who, in one way or another, can be considered the political theorist of frontal assault, at a time when it could lead to defeat'.[154] What would be 'this one way or another' to consider Trotsky a theoretician of the 'frontal assault'? He 'may' or 'must' be regarded as such? The formulation was certainly less ambiguous than the previous ones, but it carried with it certain ambivalences. To ignore them is to ignore the complexity of the matter. If these ambivalences were suppressed, what would remain would be, once again, a 'vulgar caricature'.

The question was taken up in a B note in Part I of Notebook 10, written in April or May 1932. The terms of the note were still similar to those discussed above, assimilating Lenin to the theory of permanent revolution and identifying the theory of hegemony with the 'current form' of the theory of permanent revolution:

> in the same period as Croce, the greatest modern theorist of the philosophy of praxis [Lenin] has – on the terrain of political struggle and

---

150 Trotsky 1969b, p. 133.
151 To support his argument, Rosengarten 1984–85, p. 89 fully quotes this passage from the text of Trotsky. On the theory of permanent revolution, see Bianchi 2000.
152 Maitan 1958, p. 580.
153 Rosengarten 1984–85, p. 89.
154 PN3, Q6, §138, p. 109.

> organization, and with political terminology – in opposition to the various tendencies of 'economism', revalued the front of cultural struggle and constructed the doctrine of hegemony as a complement to the theory of the state-as-force and as a contemporary form of the 1848 doctrine of 'permanent revolution'.[155]

This passage reinforces the idea that the theory of hegemony was not in opposition to the theory of the 'state-as-force', but was its 'complement'. Coercion and consensus were not opposite terms in Gramscian thought, but they maintained a relation of unity-distinction, as we have seen. But besides being important for the precise appreciation of this relation, the cited text reinforces the idea that the author of the *Notebooks* aimed to construct his theory of hegemony as an updating of the theory of permanent revolution, revalorising it and transforming it, rather than simply cancelling it or substituting it.[156] Gramsci's theoretical operation was delicate. He sought to preserve what for him was the living content of the formula of permanent revolution and, for that reason, chose to preserve the expression instead of simply inventing a neologism.[157]

Its author advanced cautiously. He wrote that the doctrine of hegemony was a current form of the 'doctrine of 1848'. The explicit reference was therefore to Marx and not to Trotsky. Moreover, the formula of 'permanent revolution' appeared in quotation marks in the text, a resource that was used quite frequently when it came to a critical appropriation. Yet it was an appropriation of a formula whose development – and Gramsci knew this very well – was associated in an indissoluble way with the political thought of Trotsky. In a text probably contemporary with that quoted above, Gramsci meticulously elaborated this idea, and for that reason it is worth quoting more extensively and comparing the two versions:

Also, the question of so-called 'permanent revolution', a political concept that emerged around 1848 as the scientific expression of Jacobinism, at a time when the great political parties and large economic trade unions had not yet come into existence – a concept that would sub-	Political concept of the so-called 'permanent revolution', which emerged before 1848 as a scientifically evolved expression of the Jacobin experience from 1789 to Thermidor. The formula belongs to a historical period in which the great mass political parties and the great economic

---

155 GR, Q10 / I, §12, p. 195. See also LC, p. 661.
156 See Gerratana 1997, p. 113.
157 On the political lexicon of Gramsci and the process of theoretical production condensed there, see Burgio 2003, pp. 34–6.

sequently be absorbed and superseded by the concept of 'civil hegemony'.

The question of the war of position warfare and the war of manoeuvre, as well as the question of *arditism*, insofar as they pertain to political science; in politics the 1848 concept of the war of manoeuvre is precisely the concept of permanent revolution; in politics, the war of position is the concept of hegemony that can only come into existence after certain things are already in place, namely, the large popular organizations of the modern type that represent, as it were, the 'trenches' and the permanent fortification of the war of position.[158]

trade unions did not yet exist, and society was still, so to speak, in a state of fluidity from many points of view: greater backwardness of the countryside, and almost complete monopoly of political and state power by a few cities or even by a single one (Paris in the case of France); a relatively rudimentary state apparatus, and greater autonomy of civil society from state activity; a specific system of military forces and of national armed services; greater autonomy of the national economies from the economic relations of the world market, etc. In the period after 1870, with the colonial expansion of Europe, all these elements change: the internal and international organizational relations of the state become more complex and massive, and the 1848 formula of the 'permanent revolution' is expanded and transcended in political science by the formula of 'civil hegemony'. The same thing happens in the art of politics as happens in military art: war of movement increasingly becomes war of position and it can be said that a state will win a war in so far as it prepares for it minutely and technically in peacetime. The massive structures of the modern democracies, both as state organizations, and as complexes of associations in civil society, constitute for the art of politics as it were the 'trenches' and the permanent fortifications of the front in the war of position: they render merely 'partial' the element of manoeuvre which before used to be 'the whole' of war, etc.[159]

---

158 PN3, Q8, §52, p. 267.
159 GR, Q13, §7, pp. 232–3.

Francioni[160] cannot specify the date of Notebook 13 but states that all of it was written between May 1932 and early 1934. It is more likely, therefore, that §7 was written in the first months of that undertaking. The corresponding A text (Q8, §52), in turn, was written in February 1932.[161] The difference in form and content between the two versions is glaring. The text of the first version is surprisingly confusing and looks hurried or sloppy. Contrast this with the clear, meticulous, and elegant style of most of the paragraphs in the *Notebooks*, and particularly with this second version. Yet more important than issues of style are the contents of these paragraphs.

In the passage from the first to the second version, the mechanical identification between the war of manoeuvre and permanent revolution, as well as the war of position and hegemony, disappeared. Therefore, simplistic definitions gave rise to notions constructed through the description of the historical process of the state complex (in its strict sense) and civil society. Such a description emphasised the construction of the argument through the passage of the Marxian political formula of the 'permanent revolution' to the political formula of 'civil hegemony'. The political formula of hegemony was, thus, the 'contemporary form'[162] of the permanent revolution, 'expanded and transcended'.[163]

The text, in its second version, also helps to understand more clearly the war of manoeuvre itself in 'modern democracies', in which civil society constitutes a setback for the war of manoeuvre. The existence of private institutions requires the re-creation of forms of subaltern class struggle. In this context, the war of manoeuvre cannot sum up the whole struggle and must be only a 'partial' moment of this. But if it is a partial moment, it is because it exists in this new context. Gramsci protests against the transformation of the war of manoeuvre into an exclusive tactic, but he did not propose its suppression and therefore did not fall into the identical error in an inverted sense.

As of May 1932, Gramsci does not seem to insist on the identity of the war of manoeuvre with the permanent revolution, as can be seen in the suppression of this identity in the passage cited from Notebook 13. But the editors of the thematic edition of the *Notebooks* insisted on emphasising it. Thus, in 'Notes on Macchiavelli, on politics and on the Modern state' ('Note sul Macchiavelli, sulla politica e sullo Stato moderno'), in a paragraph in which the 'author' quoted the theory of permanent revolution, the editors announced in a footnote:

---

160   Francioni 1984, pp. 113–15 and 144.
161   Francioni 1984, p. 142.
162   GR, Q10 / I, §12, p. 195.
163   GR, Q13, §7, p. 233.

> The term permanent revolution is here used to indicate Trotsky's misinterpretation (*a political transformation carried out by a minority without the support of the masses*) of Karl Marx's formula. For this, the author put it within quotation marks.[164]

In this vulgar caricature, the theory of the permanent revolution would be the Blanquism against which Trotsky constantly fought.[165]

Less concerned with such caricatures and more with the proper placement of the problem through rigorous philological research, Valentino Gerratana addressed the question based on the Gramscian analysis of the 'Preface of 1859'. This text, the editor of the *Notebooks* said, can only be adequately understood if it is emphasised that Marx had in mind the definition of an 'age of social revolution'.[166] The Gramscian appropriation of the 'Preface' deconstructs the linear nexus between the objective and the subjective conditions, problematising those passages that had been read in such a mechanical and evolutionary manner. The relation between the two 'canons' of historical interpretation was not, thus, in Gramsci, a relation of immediate continuity, but a mediated relation. For a long historical period, to an 'age of social revolution', this mediation was encompassed by permanent revolution, Gramsci affirmed in the strategic § 17 of Notebook 13:

> It is precisely the study of these 'intervals' of varying frequency which enables one to reconstruct the relations on the one hand between structure and superstructure, and on the other between the development of the organic movement and that of the conjunctural movement in the structure. One might say that the dialectical mediation between the two methodological principles formulated at the beginning of this note is to be found in the historico-political formula of permanent revolution.[167]

The connotation that the expression permanent revolution (without quotes in the Gramscian text) assumes in this passage is frankly positive. The issue of permanent revolution – and, therefore, the Gramsci-Trotsky question – as it appeared in a note expressing the reflection of Gramsci's maturity was still not

---

164   Gramsci 1966a, p. 48. Emphasis added.
165   The accusation of Blanquism against Trotsky was, like so many other accusations, by Stalin who, with his characteristic prose, defined Lenin as a 'giant' and Trotsky as a Blanquist 'dwarf' (Stalin 1954, Vol. 6, p. 372).
166   Gerratana 1997, p. 111.
167   GR, Q13, § 17, p. 204. See Burgio 2003, pp. 68–9 in respect of this.

fully resolved by its author. But Gerratana indicated the path through which a solution could be found. For an 'age of social revolution' he says, it is necessary to understand 'whether it is the phase of the war of manoeuvre or that of the war of position, as a continuation of a revolutionary continuity, although in the discontinuity of the various forms and phases of the historical process'.[168] The reformulation of the concept of 'permanent revolution' in Gramsci was far from a simple cancellation of the formulas of Marx and Trotsky. As a current form of permanent revolution, the formula of civil hegemony presupposes the unity of the war of manoeuvre and the war of position.

It is not, therefore, a matter of understanding the complex Gramsci-Trotsky relation as one of antagonism or identity, as many have done; rather, the aim is to rediscover in these authors a common concern for the problems of their time and, in particular, of revolution in the capitalist West and an equally creative and anti-dogmatic commitment to the search for alternatives. The diversity of their approaches and the different solutions at which they arrived attest to the plurality of traditions that merged within the CI.[169] Their approaches, however, started from different points of view. While Gramsci assumed a perspective that emphasised the national particularities of political processes, Trotsky worked from an international point of view.

It is not possible here to deal in more detail with the methodological internationalism that characterises the thinking of the Russian communist.[170] However, it is worth registering that the characterisation of his point of view as 'cosmopolitan, that is, superficially national and superficially Western' is denied by his fine analysis of the particularities of the development of Russian society in his book *Results and Prospects*.[171] To the analysis of Russian society, it would be important to add his writings on England, France, and Germany in which he always tried to analyse the specificity of the development of capitalism in each of these countries and the distinctive characteristics of their labour movements.[172]

---

168 Gerratana 1997, p. 113.
169 On the diversity of these traditions, see Agosti 1988.
170 See Bianchi 2007a.
171 See, for example, Trotsky 1969b, pp. 37–46.
172 Anderson 1976a, p. 75. The accusation of cosmopolitanism was recurrent in the publicity of the Stalinist fraction and embodied a strong anti-Semitic content, since Lev Davidovich Bronstein was, as everybody knows, Jewish. Gramsci's reproduction of this unfounded accusation is one of the low points of his *Notebooks*, as well as the gross and astonishing comparison of the theory of permanent revolution with rape. See PN3, Q7, §16, p. 168. These moments are nonetheless rare in Gramsci's political life, in which he repeatedly rejected rudeness and brutality in political debate.

A judicious analysis of the texts will easily demonstrate that the various perspectives adopted by these different authors do not make the Italian a 'chauvinist' or the Russian a 'cosmopolitan'. In the interest of interpreting Gramsci's position here in a more detailed way, one may draw on his pre-prison writings. Several authors pointed out at different times and for different purposes the dissent that Gramsci expressed in relation to the leadership of the Russian Communist Party after Lenin's death and, particularly, his opposition to the premises and implications of the thesis of 'socialism in one country'[173] as well as the closeness between the positions of Gramsci and Bukharin from 1924 onwards, especially with regard to the workers' and peasants' alliance and the New Economic Policy.[174] But even his approach to Bukharin needs to be problematised in order to understand the harsh criticisms Gramsci directed towards him in the *Notebooks*.

Gramsci's character, his education and militant trajectory conditioned, however, a much more restrained style of opposition and a greater disposition to agreements with a view to preserving the unity of the Party and of the International.[175] A diverse position from this was, for example, that of Bordiga, always attentive to the international question and the struggle within the Russian Party. In February 1926, months before Gramsci sent the letter on behalf of the political bureau to Togliatti on the 'Russian question', Bordiga at the 6th Plenary meeting of the Enlarged Executive Committee of the CI had made a bold attempt to denounce Stalinism.[176] And it was Bordiga in the Italian delegation who asked Stalin, the main defender of the strategy of 'socialism in one country', if he believed that 'the development of the Russian situation and the internal problems of the Russian party were linked to the development of the international proletarian movement'. The incredible response he obtained summed up Stalin's interest in the discussion and his personality: 'This question ... has never been asked of me. I never believed that a Communist could do it. God forgive you for having done it'.[177]

If Gramsci was unlikely to act like Bordiga, he was not, contrary to Togliatti, predisposed to a capitulation to the Stalinist faction. As one may infer from the

---

173 Del Roio 2005, p. 165.
174 Paggi 1984, pp. 353–65 and Vacca 1999, chap. VI. It was up to Stalin to launch the slogan of 'socialism in one country' in a text dated 17 December 1924. His argument was based on a crude wordplay in which the construction of a dictatorship of the proletariat after the victory of the socialists in one country (Russia) would quickly be transformed into the 'victory of socialism in one country' (Stalin 1954, Vol. 6, p. 378).
175 See Rosengarten 1984–85, p. 91.
176 Rosengarten 1984–85, p. 92.
177 Cited in Vacca 1999, pp. 39–40.

correspondence with Togliatti in 1926 shortly before his arrest, Gramsci was moving, albeit slowly, toward more open dissent, a movement that until that moment was circumscribed within the scope of the PCI and not towards the Opposition. Inquiring about what would have happened if Gramsci had not been arrested is, however, a futile exercise.

In the *Notebooks*, only one reference was made to Stalin. In the constellation of the history of Bolshevism in the 1920s, Stalin's star did not shine brightly and there was nothing in his writing that would increase the brightness. Gramsci mentions in this passage the transcription of Stalin's interview with the 'First American Labour Delegation'.[178] In the interview there would be 'some essential points of the art and science of politics'. The reflection seems to have been motivated by the first question of the colloquium, in which a representative of the US delegation inquired about Lenin's contribution to Marx's theory: 'Would it be correct to say that Lenin believed in "creative revolution" whereas Marx was more inclined to wait for the culmination of the development of economic forces?'[179]

The question summarised themes dear to Gramsci, such as the relationship between economics and politics, structure and superstructure, questions that the *Notebooks* considered keys to the 'art and science of politics'. The question was interesting, but the answer belied the author's limits. Stalin asserted that Lenin was the 'most loyal and consistent pupil of Marx and Engels' and that he '"added" no "new principles" to Marxism'. And then he claimed that 'Leninism is the Marxism of the era of imperialism and proletarian revolutions'.[180] There are no references to these statements in Gramsci's text, which used the interview only as a pretext to address an issue that was crucial to him:

> The problem which seems to me to need further elaboration is the following: how, according to the philosophy of praxis (as it manifests itself politically) whether as formulated by its founder [Marx] or particularly as restated by its most recent great theoretician [Lenin] the international situation should be considered in its national aspect.[181]

Obviously, the 'founder' of the philosophy of praxis was Marx and his 'most recent great theoretician' was Lenin, not Stalin. The question that was posed concerned the national-international nexus in the revolution and the sub-

---

178 Stalin 1954, Vol. 10, pp. 97–153.
179 Stalin 1954, Vol. 10, p. 97.
180 Stalin 1954, Vol. 10, pp. 97–8.
181 GR, Q14, §68, p. 230.

sequent process of building socialism. It was a key problem for understanding the so-called 'Russian question' in its various manifestations as well as the evolution of the European communist movement.

Gramsci explained in his answer to this question a national-international point of view. The national relationship, he argued, is the

> result of a combination which is 'original' and (in a certain sense) unique: these relations must be understood and conceived in their originality and uniqueness if one wishes to dominate them and direct them.[182]

The development of this national unity was toward 'internationalism', or more precisely, toward its internationalisation in the double sense: formation that absorbs and expresses within it the trends of the international relations of forces, and formation that spills outwards, becoming a constituent part of this same relation of forces. The starting point, however, should be 'national' and in this regard it was necessary to focus attention on the development of an effective political action, but the line of evolution, 'the perspective', was necessarily international. Hence the need to study closely 'the combination of national forces that the international class should lead and develop according to the perspective and international directives'.[183]

The perspective presented by Gramsci was clearly distinguished from that which guided the Soviet state. The analysis of the particularities of a social formation implied the adoption of an originally national point of view, but not of a nationalist perspective. His point of view was not fixed on the national dimension, such as in the perspective of 'socialism in one country'. Initially focusing his gaze on this point, he then moved on to look at the process of the internationalisation of the revolution. The national-international nexus thus also indicated a desirable trajectory of the development of the political process.

If the initial point of view was national, this was due to the national character of political power. Only on the ground of the nation state could a class become a leader, resuming in its actions the solution to the problems that would afflict all the subaltern classes of a country. Thus,

> [a] class that is international in character has – in as much as it guides social strata which are narrowly national (intellectuals), and indeed fre-

---

182 GR, Q14, §68, pp. 230–1.
183 Ibid.

quently even less than national: particularistic and municipalistic (the peasants) – to 'nationalize' itself in a certain sense.[184]

It is in this process that the proletariat could become a state and absorb the whole of society in the 'scope' of its 'class'[185] thus unifying the subaltern classes.[186] The struggle for the construction of a new order, the process of the accomplishment of hegemony, could not, therefore, advance without any mediation to the international sphere.

It was from this perspective that Gramsci analysed in Notebook 14 the controversy over 'socialism in one country' involving Trotsky and Stalin. Although the criticism of Trotsky is clear and reproduces some of Stalin's own arguments, Gramsci did not affirm his solidarity with the thesis of 'socialism in one country', or with its author.[187] An original, though not always accurate, interpretation of the history of Bolshevism grounded the argument. What characterised Lenin's party and its history would be the insistence on 'purging internationalism of every vague and purely ideological (in a pejorative sense) element to give it a realistic political content'.[188]

The statement that attributed to Lenin the practical rather than the theoretical elaboration of a theory of hegemony as the current form of the theory of permanent revolution may now be better understood. The articulation of national demands in the concept of hegemony received a concrete response with the slogans of agrarian reform and peace that allowed the constitution of a workers' and peasants' alliance and gave a majority in the Soviets to the Bolsheviks. In this way, Lenin translated Marxism nationally, giving it a concrete content and making it historically effective.

Gramsci concluded his argument in that same paragraph by stating that 'non-national concepts (i.e. ones that cannot be referred to each individual country)' were wrong, because they could provoke passivity and inertia before and after the foundation of a new state. Before, because they could feed passivity and the expectation that all would begin the movement at the same time as the only way not to be defeated. After, because it would foment a form of 'anachronistic and unnatural form of "Napoleonism"'.[189] In these lines Gramsci did nothing but reproduce two arguments in the anti-Trotskyist campaign

---

184   GR, Q14, §68, p. 231.
185   PN3, Q8, §2, p. 234.
186   SPN, Q25, §5, p. 52.
187   Martelli 1996, pp. 91–2.
188   GR, Q14, §68, p. 231.
189   GR, Q14, §68, p. 232.

in the Soviet Union and the Communist International. The first of these concerned the alleged defeatism of the Trotskyist conception of revolution.[190] The second referred to a supposed 'Napoleonism', that is, Trotsky's desire to export the revolution through the Red Army, acting like Napoleon Bonaparte in the French Revolution.

Both arguments were extremely fragile. The first was evidently contrary to what Gramsci himself had written and created a schizophrenic image in which Trotsky was at the same time offensive and defeatist. The second did not correspond to what Trotsky himself repeatedly stated, rejecting the hypothesis of an intervention of the Red Army in the European scenario. Martelli[191] emphasised in a balanced way that 'Napoleonism' was put into practice by Stalin at the end of World War II and that, in this way, Gramscian anti-'Napoleonism' could paradoxically serve as a critique of Stalinist foreign policy, but not criticism of the opposition leader. Likewise, the criticism of defeatism would fall to Stalin in February 1917, when he considered impossible the advent of a workers' revolution and supported the government of Kerensky, but it is not possible to say that Gramsci was informed about such episodes.[192]

In order to properly discern the 'rational core' of this paragraph, it becomes necessary to criticise those written passages with an exclusively polemical bias and concentrate on what is at the heart of Gramsci's conception of the revolution. The national-international nexus that Gramsci sought to sustain led him to seek a third theoretical option, in which the rejection of Stalin's position did not imply an adherence to Trotsky. According to Martelli,[193] in this conception, the construction of socialism in the Soviet Union would be subordinated to two conditions: the development of the struggle for hegemony in the interior of the national state, and the development of the process of the European revolution.

---

190   The accusation of defeatism had been levelled against the Unified Opposition by Stalin in the written theses for the 15th Conference of the Communist Party of the Soviet Union in October 1926: 'in October 1917, the complicated situation and the difficulties of the transition from a bourgeois to a proletarian revolution engendered in one section of the Party vacillation, defeatism and disbelief in the possibility of the proletariat taking power and retaining it (Kamenev, Zinoviev), so now, in the present period of radical change, the difficulties of the transition to the new phase of socialist construction are engendering in certain circles of our Party vacillation, disbelief in the possibility of the socialist elements in our country being victorious over the capitalist elements, disbelief in the possibility of victoriously building socialism in the USSR. The opposition bloc is an expression of this spirit of pessimism and defeatism in the ranks of one section of our Party' (Stalin 1954, Vol. 8, p. 226).
191   Martelli 1996, pp. 94–6.
192   Somai 1982, p. 87.
193   Martelli 1996, p. 93.

The construction of socialism would have its beginning in a national dimension, but would only be completed on a world scale.

From the above conditions, it is not possible to establish an opposition between the positions of Gramsci and Trotsky, although the antagonism of both with the defence of 'socialism in one country' becomes evident. It has been said that Gramsci emphasised the national dimension of politics, while Trotsky emphasised the international dimension. For both of them, the national-international nexus did not express a relation of succession. In this regard, both agreed that the revolutionary process would have as its 'starting point' the nation state and, therefore, the international moment could only succeed the national moment. The question was, thus, which of those conditions occupied a determinant place in this relationship. It was the meaning of the translation of one term in the other that distinguished them. In this way it is possible to say that while Gramsci insisted on a *national*-international nexus, seeking to translate the international reality for a particular national situation, Trotsky held the position of a national-*international* nexus, which highlighted the uneven and combined development of contemporary capitalism.

It is not, therefore, a question of establishing a false identity between these authors, yet neither is there any sense in positing an inventive opposition of principles. The resumption of a dialogue between their works, interrupted by the simultaneous emergence of fascism and Stalinism, could have brought a positive influence on Marxism and stimulated critical research on the forms of social revolution. But for this, it would be necessary to leave prejudices aside, directly addressing the authors' own texts. For this purpose, research should be geared towards determining the really distinctive characteristics of each of these theories, seeking to particularise their contributions.

CHAPTER 7

Revolution/Restoration

A great historical sensitivity marked the Marxism of Antonio Gramsci to the point that one commentator stated that the *Notebooks* could be, for that reason, read as 'a great book of history: a history of the bourgeois West'.[1] Such a reading no doubt finds strong evidence in the Gramscian text itself, as well as in the various plans he wrote for them before and during their composition in which historical research occupied a central position. It should not be forgotten, though, that this sensitivity had a strong political orientation and sought both a more accurate understanding of the present and an alternative to the idealist and conservative historiography that prevailed in the Italian cultural environment.

'Absolute Historicism' was the polemical formula which summed up this sensitivity. The formula was strongly influenced by the thought of Benedetto Croce for whom history would not be possible without philosophical concepts and philosophy would have no life without history, since every philosophical proposition 'appears in the soul of a definite individual at a definite point of time and space and in definite conditions. It is therefore historically conditioned'.[2] History was philosophy in its concreteness and that would include the philosophy that would exist only in history and as history.[3]

From the idealistic identity established between history and philosophy, Croce concluded that the history of philosophy, as the history of a moment of the spirit, would condense all history in itself.[4] It was this idealism that Croce summed up in his mature work with the expression 'absolute historicism'.[5] It was this radical idealism that led the editor of *La Critica* to state that 'every true story is contemporary history' inasmuch as real history would be only that which would be presented as the object of thought, an act that could only occur in the present time. Contemporary cultural development, for example, would allow one to think of Hellenic culture or Platonic philosophy from the present incontrovertible problems, but outside of these problems they would not be

---

1 Burgio 2002, p. 3.
2 Croce 1917, p. 310.
3 Croce 1949, p. 19.
4 Croce 1917, p. 313.
5 Croce 1947b, p. 8.

history.[6] In this way, the present reflection on this culture and this philosophy would mark these in an unavoidable way, transforming them into part of our time.

One may perceive that although it explicitly rejected any attempt of identification between philosophy – and therefore history, its identical element – and politics, the Crocean historicist project contained a strong practical impulse. The philosopher recognised that the motivations of historical research could not fail to be practically oriented and in this he was clearly close to a Weberian theory of knowledge. But the results at which Croce arrived carried with them the political and cultural orientation implied in their origin. The affirmation of the contemporary character of history was marked so clearly by present politics that it made it enormously difficult to claim the principle of neutrality for the results of this research.

Croce's absolute historicism took shape in his ethico-political historiography. The research project of Crocean ethico-political history was not a mere exercise in erudition. He had the political-practical purpose of establishing a hegemonic programme for the reconstruction of the cultural and political life of the peninsula. Constructing a theoretical-political response to the crisis of liberalism, positivism and Catholicism, the philosopher from Pescasseroli developed a broad programme for the ideological and cultural renewal of Italian society.[7] And although this purpose could not be hidden, Croce remained faithful to the nexus of the distincts established by it and continued to debate the refusal of the identity between philosophy/history and *politics*.

A prisoner of the nexus of the distincts, the Crocean *oeuvre* was loaded with ambiguities and contradictions. His conception of true history as contemporary history rendered it imperative to confess that the indissoluble nexus between life and thought in history implied recognition of its usefulness.[8] At the same time, he affirmed that

> history never metes out justice, but always *justifies*; she could not carry out the former act without making herself unjust – that is to say, confounding thought with life, taking the attractions and repulsions of sentiment for the judgments of thought.[9]

---

6 Croce 1921, pp. 12–16.
7 See Kanoussi and Mena 1985, p. 46.
8 Croce 1921, p. 23.
9 Croce 1921, p. 89.

In his polemic with Bukharin, Gramsci, as is known, stated that the 'philosophy of praxis is absolute "historicism", the absolute bringing down to earth and worldliness of thought, an absolute humanism of history'.[10] And he stated this with the polemical purpose of marking the entire distance that separated philosophy from the praxis of the naturalistic scientism and positivism that thrived in Marxism in the early twentieth century. Gramscian historicism develops this affirmation by recognising the central importance of the historicity of social facts and disposing oneself to apply historical materialism to itself.[11]

If the distance between Gramscian historicism and naturalistic scientism is evident in Notebook 11, it was in Notebook 10 that it manifested itself with all its intensity in opposition to Crocean historicism. The appropriation of the notion of 'absolute historicism' by Gramsci was, like so many others, a radical reinterpretation and theoretical re-elaboration politically oriented with the purpose of eliminating all traces of political moderation. The incorporation of absolute historicism into the philosophy of praxis was preceded by the decantation of its original idealism. It thus ceased to be an expression of the movement of the spirit and became the expression of social struggles and conflicts.

It was in the analysis of European and Italian history that the radicalism of this enterprise and the notion of *passive revolution* occupied a central place.[12] It was through this notion that Gramsci engaged with Vincenzo Cuoco so that he could develop his historicist conception and so that his reflection in the *Notebooks* would reach its apex. The concept appears for the first time in Notebook 4, in a text probably written in November 1930:[13]

> *Vincenzo Cuoco and passive revolution.* Vincenzo Cuoco called the revolution that took place in Italy as a repercussion of the Napoleonic wars a passive revolution. The concept of passive revolution, it seems to me, applies not only to Italy but also to those other countries that modernize the state through a series of reforms or national wars without undergoing a political revolution of a radical-Jacobin type. Examine how Cuoco develops the concept with regards to Italy.[14]

---

10   SPN, Q11, § 27, p. 465. See also GR, Q15, § 62, pp. 263–4.
11   See Löwy 1988, pp. 122 and 128–32.
12   Kanoussi and Mena 1985, p. 13 even say that 'everything in the Notebooks has to do with the concept of passive revolution'.
13   See Francioni 1984, p. 141.
14   PN2, Q4, § 57, p. 232.

This passage seems to have preceded a note placed in the margins of the very important §44 of Notebook 1, shortly after Gramsci discussed the need for a political group to become a leader before coming to the government, exemplifying it with the political leadership that the Moderates exercised on the Action Party (Partito d'Azione), during the *Risorgimento*. The passage was already quoted more fully in Chapter 2.2 of this book, but it is worth repeating here:

> This truth is clearly demonstrated by the politics of the Moderates, and it is the solution of this problem that made the Risorgimento possible in the forms and within the limits in which it was accomplished as a revolution without revolution [or, in V. Cuoco's words, as a passive revolution].[15]

Strongly influenced by Machiavelli's realism and Vico's historicism, Vincenzo Cuoco had defined the Neapolitan revolution of 1799 as a passive revolution in which the masses were 'indifferent and inert'.[16] He distinguished therefore active revolutions in which 'the people on their own direct themselves immediately towards what effects them most'[17] from passive revolutions, in which 'the government's agent has to try to guess the mind of the people and present them with what they want but would not be able to procure on their own'.[18]

The references to Cuoco are, however, meagre in the *Notebooks* and his *Historical Essay on the Neapolitan Revolution* (*Saggio storico sulla rivoluzione di Napoli*) was not among the books that Gramsci had at his disposition. Gerratana states in the critical apparatus of the *Notebooks*[19] that it is likely that the appropriation of the concept of passive revolution had not come from a direct reading of this text, but rather an indirect source: *The Neapolitan Revolution of 1799* (*La rivoluzione napolitana del 1799*), by Benedetto Croce.[20]

The elitist liberalism of Cuoco, which manifested itself in the discourse of opposition to 'democratisation' certainly appealed to Croce. Although the absence of activity from a people conceived metaphysically as the embodiment of the ideals of the nation would leave the author of the *Historical Essay* dismayed, he disapproved of the direct participation of real people in politics and

---

15   PN1, Q1, §44, p. 137. The passage in parentheses at the end of the text was added to the margin by Gramsci at an uncertain date, but, evidently, after its first writing in February or March 1930.
16   Cuoco 2014, pp. 139–40.
17   Cuoco 2014, p. 108.
18   Ibid.
19   Q, pp. 2654–5.
20   Croce 1998.

restricted electoral participation to those who knew how to 'read and write' and 'own assets, or have a business, or exercise a trade that is not servile'[21] which excluded rural workers and many urban workers from political life. It is paradoxical, therefore, that Gramsci appropriated the formula of Cuoco and used it against Croce.

The appropriation of this formula had, however, a clear methodological inclination. Gramsci frequently resorted to an historical analogical method. Such a method cannot be confused, however, with vulgar empiricist comparison, that finding a few similarities between different historical events intends inductively, to formulate a 'historical law'. The Gramscian analogical method was intended not to affirm 'laws' but rather the construction of concepts capable of capturing the complexity of the historical movement. The historical process upon which Gramsci initially reflected by way of this concept was the formation of the Italian national state without a political revolution of the Jacobin type.

The formation of the modern state was for Gramsci the act of the very birth of modernity. Between the conquest of power by the bourgeoisie and the birth of the modern world, a strong correspondence was established.[22] As a canon of interpretation, passive revolution was a theoretical key to understanding the advent of capitalist modernity in most European countries. It was in contraposition to the idea of the political hegemony of the Jacobins that Gramsci theoretically elaborated the concept of passive revolution as a canon of historical interpretation. This contraposition was already evident in Notebook 1. In it, its author affirmed that the Jacobins had conquered

> their function of leading party by means of struggle: they imposed themselves on the French bourgeoisie, leading it to a much more advanced position than it would have 'spontaneously' wanted and even much more advanced than the historical premises would have allowed; hence, the acts of reaction and the function of Napoleon.[23]

To exercise this leading role, the Jacobins had to put aside their own corporative interests. The resistance of the old dominant classes and the determined activity of the followers of Robespierre removed the bourgeoisie from inertia and put it under the Jacobin leadership. The language and ideology of the Jacobins with their classicist phraseology were just apparently abstract, and in

---

21   Cuoco 2014, p. 235.
22   Burgio 2003, pp. 46–7.
23   PN1, Q1, § 44, p. 147.

fact, according to Gramsci, they reflected perfectly the needs of the time: 'to annihilate the enemy class or at least reduce it to impotence' and 'to enlarge the class interests of the bourgeoisie, discovering the common interests it shares with the other strata of the third estate'.[24]

Breaking with the economic-corporate narrowness that characterised the old feudal classes, the bourgeoisie created the conditions for the absorption of the whole of society into its productive economic universe through the assertion of an abstract equality obtained in the sphere of a market to which everyone would have access. At the same time, it extended political boundaries, incorporating the subaltern classes into the state sphere through the affirmation of a freedom that asserted itself in the sphere of abstractly equal civil rights for all. The maximum expression of this movement of economic and political expansion had been Jacobinism. For this reason, Robespierre's supporters were profoundly realistic:

> The Jacobins, therefore, forced their hand, but always in the direction of real historical development, because they not only founded the bourgeois state and made of the bourgeoisie the 'dominant' class, but they did more (in a certain sense), they made of the bourgeoisie the leading hegemonic class, that is, they provided the state with a permanent base.[25]

The nexus between the analysis of the French Revolution and the 'Preface of 1859' was not yet explicitly stated by Gramsci in Notebook 1. But in Notebook 4, in that first draft on the analysis of the relations of forces, he strongly established this link:

> These methodological criteria can acquire their full significance only if they are applied to the analysis of concrete historical studies. This might be usefully done for the events that took place in France between 1789 and 1870.[26]

In the light of the 'Preface of 1859' one can understand how Jacobinism may have become for Gramsci a fundamental interpretative historical category.[27] The Jacobins expressed on the political scene the 'necessary and sufficient conditions' already existent in France, politically resolving the contradictions that

---

24 PN1, Q1, §44, pp. 147–8.
25 PN1, Q1, §44, p. 148.
26 PN2, Q4, §38, p. 178.
27 See Medici 2004, p. 115.

manifested themselves in the structure of society. They did more than transform the bourgeoisie into a government, that is, into the ruling class. They made it a ruling and hegemonic national class, cohering around them the living forces of France, recreating their own nation and state, giving them a modern content and freeing the productive forces from the bonds of the old relations of production. In the analysis of the French Revolution and Jacobinism, the *Notebooks* thus established a close parallel between the 'process of the constitution of bourgeois hegemony and the logical-political theory of the relations of force that define hegemony in general'.[28]

The achievement of hegemony through revolution was what Gramsci called 'Jacobinism of content'. The content of Jacobinism was defined by the maximum development of national private forces, that is, by the constitution and strengthening of civil society and the creation of a wide network of institutions through which the moral and ethical consensus was permanently organised. Hence the Jacobins insisted on an identity between government and civil society, seeking to unify in the state, in a dictatorial way, the whole of national political life.[29]

The constitution of this modern state then had, as a presupposition, the extension of its own historical basis. To achieve its hegemony over the whole population, the bourgeoisie incorporated demands, fulfilled the aspirations of the nation, economically assimilated social groups, transformed their culture into the culture of the whole society. The enlargement of the historical basis of the state was thus accompanied by the economic and political expansion of the bourgeoisie. For Gramsci, the parliamentary legal regime was the result of this process of expansion, expressing civil society within political society itself:

> The development of Jacobinism (of content) found its formal perfection in the parliamentary regime which, in the period of the greatest abundance of 'private' energies in society, brought about the hegemony of the urban class over the whole population in the Hegelian form of government with permanently organized consent (with the organization being left to private initiative and thus having a moral or ethical character since it was, in one way or another, a 'voluntary' consent).[30]

Concerning the French Revolution, Gramsci consulted especially the first volume of the manual of Albert Mathiez, *La Révolution française* which he had at

---

28 Tosel 1994, p. 43. OT.
29 PN3, Q6, §87, p. 74.
30 PN1, Q1, §48, p. 155.

his disposal in prison. With a basis in this text, Gramsci attributed the disintegration of the 'urban block of Paris' to the Chapelier Law of 14 June 1791, which forbade workers' coalitions, and the Law of the 'Maximum' of September 1793, which froze prices and had as a consequence a crisis in the supply to Paris. Thus, the conditions for the execution of Robespierre and Thermidor were created. The limits encountered by the *Montagnards* in their action were thus the limits of bourgeois hegemony itself. To overcome these limits would be to go beyond what the 'necessary and sufficient conditions' allowed.

The Jacobins' trajectory was also that of the parable covered by bourgeois hegemony. While advancing the whole of society, freeing it from the chains of the past, the bourgeoisie, through the Jacobins, exercised its hegemony in a spontaneous manner, broadening the social bases of the state and constituting new spheres of economic activity. But reaching its limits, the limits of the bourgeois order itself, the 'ideological bloc' that sustained this hegemony presented its first fissures and promptly the spontaneous consensus was replaced by '"constraint" in forms which are less and less disguised and indirect, ending up in downright police measures and coups d'etat'.[31]

As a result, a situation arose in which the bourgeois universalism that had manifested itself in the revolutionary process revealed a particularist universalism.[32] In June 1848, on the streets of Paris, the limits of the social and political expansion of the bourgeoisie were evident. The sacrifices and concessions that it could make were restricted to an economic-corporate dimension. They could not encompass their fundamental interests or call into question 'the decisive function exercised by the leading group in the decisive nucleus of economic activity'.[33] The new dominant classes quickly reached a saturation point, closing off the access of the subaltern classes to politics and returning 'to the conception of the state as pure force'. After this point, the 'bourgeois class is "saturated": it has not only stopped growing, it is breaking down; not only has it stopped assimilating new elements, but it is losing a part of itself (or at least the losses are much more numerous than the assimilations)'.[34]

The limits, which in France appeared at the apex of the revolution in 1793, manifested themselves in Italy at the outset in 1848. There was no such party in Italy as that of Robespierre. The Action Party did not have the 'Jacobin spirit', that is, the will to become a 'leading party'.[35] Its leaders, like Mazzini

---

31 PN1, Q1, §44, p. 138.
32 Burgio 2003, p. 70.
33 GR, Q13, §18, p. 212.
34 PN3, Q8, §2, p. 234.
35 PN1, Q1, §44, p. 148.

and Garibaldi, were not large landowners, commercial or industrial entrepreneurs, did not belong to the dominant classes, and therefore could not exert a spontaneous attraction on them, such as that exercised by the Moderates of Piedmont. Although Mazzini considered that only the 'people' could be the creator of a new national unity, he repeatedly displayed an aversion to what he called the 'war of the classes', the attacks on private property, and every project of 'agrarian law'.[36]

In his analysis of the Moderates and the Mazzinians, Gramsci's argument assumed the form of a historical sociology of politics, in which comparative analysis was superimposed on research into the social bases of the different political forces, thus complementing the investigation of these latter forces. It was in this investigation of the social bases of these parties that the author of the *Notebooks* encountered the foundations of a diverse hegemonic capacity on the part of each of the groups:

> the Moderates represented a relatively homogeneous class, and therefore their leadership underwent relatively limited oscillations, whereas the Action Party did not found itself specifically upon any historical class and the oscillations which its leading organs underwent resolved themselves, in the final analysis, according to the interests of the Moderates.[37]

In order to become a ruling party, the Action Party needed to assume a Jacobin function and to act in a planned way with a government programme that could unify the yearnings of the nation. To impress on the *Risorgimento* a popular and democratic leadership, it had to have 'an organic program of government that embraced the essential demands of the popular masses and of the peasants in the first place'.[38] The absence of this programme confirmed the historical limits of the Action Party. The solution of the agrarian question in Italy was thus relegated to the margins and, consequently, also the solution to the question of clericalism and of the Vatican's place in the political life of the peninsula.[39]

The absence of a popular and democratic programme made the Action Party a political force dependent on the Moderates. The personal ties of some of its exponents, like Garibaldi, with the leaders of Piedmont intensified this subordinate character, transforming it into a mere instrument of political agitation of the Moderates. The Piedmont leader, Vittorio Emanuele II, was therefore cor-

---

36 See Procacci 1978, Vol. 2, p. 348.
37 PN1, Q1, § 44, p. 136.
38 PN1, Q1, § 44, p. 138.
39 See PN1, Q1, § 43, p. 136.

rect when he claimed to have the Action Party 'in his pocket'.[40] The leading role spontaneously employed by the Moderates in the *Risorgimento* allowed them to exercise their hegemony on the intellectuals of the peninsula, maximising their function of leadership at the same time in which they were indissolubly united with the organisers of the new state apparatus. The absence of a Jacobinism of content in Italy was compensated by the expansion of the intellectual strata capable of ideologically welding the nation and the diffusion of mechanisms of coercion that ensured the predominance of the functions of domination over the subaltern classes.[41]

This process of the construction of a modern state on the Italian peninsula remained in this unfinished mode. The hegemony of the North presupposed the support of policies that in the South represented the old social relations. Not only was the agrarian question not resolved; nor was the question of the Vatican. Worse, the alliance between the industrialists of the North and the landowners of the South based on a protectionist customs policy condemned the Mezzogiorno to backwardness, blocked the expansion of industrialism and the accomplishment of an 'economic revolution of national character', which incorporated new economic zones.[42] The conditions were thus created for a vicious circle which, in the name of the new, the separation between the two regions was reproduced, threatening national unity itself due to the division between the industrial North and the agrarian South.

Lampedusa in the novel *Il Gattopardo* synthesised the fate of this revolution without revolution in the statement that the young Tancredi made before his Uncle Fabrizio, the prince of Salina: 'Unless we ourselves take a hand now, they'll foist a republic on us. If we want things to stay as they are, things will have to change'.[43] Fabrizio returned to this idea during his conversation with Chevalley, who on behalf of the new government had offered him a post as senator of the Kingdom. Having refused the offer, he explained to him the natural reasons for the delay of the Mezzogiorno in a speech strongly marked by positivism. Chevalley could not fail to accept the refusal, but intimately pondered: 'This state of things will not last; our lively new modern administration will change everything'. Fabrizio's response also came under the form of an interior dialogue that carried a bitterness proper to his aristocratic cynicism: 'All this

---

40   See PN1, Q1, §44, p. 136 and SPN, Q15, §25, p. 113.
41   Buci-Glucksmann 1978, p. 130. On the place of intellectuals in the Gramscian analysis of the *Risorgimento*, see Vianna 1997, pp. 48–57.
42   PN1, Q1, §149, p. 228.
43   Lampedusa 2013, p. 19.

shouldn't last; but it will, always; the human "always", of course, a century, two centuries ... and after that it will be different, but worse'.[44]

Already in the very process of the constitution of the national state there appeared this phenomenon characteristic of Italian political life: denominated transformism or *gattopardismo*. Such a phenomenon spread with the rise of the 'Historical Left' (*Sinistra storica*) of Agostino Depretis and the incorporation into the government of the active and progressive elements of the 'Historical Right' (*Destra storica*) in 1882. In this way a moderately reforming block was formed, blocking the political action of the most radical groups in Parliament, a practice that would be developed in the governments of Francesco Crespi and Giovanni Giolitti.

The question of transformism was dealt with by Gramsci in his youthful political writings. In these texts, he first dealt with transformism as the result of the moderation of the radicals of the *Risorgimento* who not only changed their position, but also renewed the leadership centres of conservative political movements. In an article published in the newspaper *The Cry of the People* (*Il Grido del Popolo*), in March 1917 about the opponents of socialism, he said:

> The mentality of our opponents is transformist. The first nucleus of the current conservative parties was formed by men who in the period between 1860 and 1880 were converted from the extreme ideas of the time (Mazzinianism, antimonarchical radicalism, etc.) to the idea of order.[45]

They were not only the most tenacious opponents of the socialists who possessed a transformist thinking. This was the content of bourgeois mentality as well as that of some members of the Socialist Party itself, Gramsci wrote in an article entitled 'The Bozzacchine' ('Il bozzacchine'), published in *Forward!* (*Avanti!*), on 4 June 1917. As a way of acting and thinking, transformism was an expression of empiricism and pragmatism. A servant to contingency, bourgeois mentality limited action to the scope of small politics, reproducing the conditions of existence of the present. According to him:

> The content of bourgeois mentality is transformism, that is, the most trivial political empiricism. Some pseudo-socialists of today were only the bourgeoisie of the transformist tradition that only changed the market of contingencies; their brain was filled with surpassed proletarian oleo-

---

44 Lampedusa 2013, p. 175.
45 CF, p. 71. OT.

graphs, and so they called themselves socialists. And they continue: they judge socialists with this transformist and empirical mentality. They have no other criterion of distinction and of judgment other than the singular, isolated fact.[46]

The synonymy that Gramsci established between transformism and political empiricism did not constitute an explanation for the phenomenon, although it did allow for an ampler vision of it. In the article 'The regimen of the pashas' ('Il regimen dei pascià'), published in the newspaper *Forward!*, in July 1918, an explanation was outlined, strongly anchored in Italian political history. According to Gramsci, 'Italy is a country where there is always this curious phenomenon: political men, coming to power, have immediately reneged on the ideas and programs of action that they advocated as simple citizens'.[47] Thus, the defenders of the political liberty of the opposition once in government prohibit the congress of socialists, and the advocates of the economic freedom of the opposition, when they become ministers, advocate state interventionism. 'Why this phenomenon?', Gramsci asked.

In his response, he considered the claim of the lack of character and moral energy of individuals insufficient. It was therefore necessary to go beyond the article quoted in May of the previous year in *The Cry of the People* entitled exactly 'Character' (*Carattere*). The reasons for this 'curious phenomenon' reminded Gramsci of the formation of the Italian bourgeoisie itself and its organisation in parties. The absence of true national parties of the bourgeoisie, of a programme summarising the general interest of that class, allowed for the proliferation of interests. The absence of national parties corresponded to the lack of a 'national bourgeoisie' with common interests, an absence that was already evident in the *Risorgimento*. In place of these national interests of a unified class, all that remained were 'speculative local interests of local clientele'.[48] This was the explanatory key portrayed in Notebook 1 and developed in Notebook 19:

The Moderates continued to lead the Action Party even after 1870, and 'transformism' is the political expression of this leadership action; all Italian politics from 1870 to the present is characterized by	The Moderates continued to lead the Action Party even after 1870 and 1876, and so-called 'transformism' was only the parliamentary expression of this action of intellectual, moral and political hege-

---

46   CF, pp. 187–9. OT.
47   NM, p. 217. OT.
48   NM, p. 218. OT.

'transformism,' that is, by the formation of a ruling class within the framework determined by the Moderates after 1848, with the absorption of the active elements that arose from the allied as well as from the enemy classes. Political leadership becomes an aspect of domination, in that the absorption of the elites of the enemy classes results in their decapitation and renders them impotent.[49]

mony. Indeed one might say that the entire state life of Italy from 1848 onwards has been characterized by transformism – in other words by the formation of an ever more extensive ruling class, within the framework established by the Moderates after 1848 and the collapse of the neo-Guelph and federalist utopias. The formation of this class involved the gradual but continuous absorption, achieved by methods which varied in their effectiveness, of the active elements produced by allied groups – and even of those which came from antagonistic groups and seemed irreconcilably hostile. In this sense political leadership became merely an aspect of the function of domination – in as much as the absorption of the enemies' elites means their decapitation, and annihilation often for a very long time.[50]

The phenomenon of transformism precisely characterised the 'limits' and 'forms' of the hegemony of the Moderates. The political leadership of the Moderates over the subaltern classes was restricted to the direction it exercised over the ruling groups of these classes by means of transformism, enabling a 'regulated radicalisation' in which the political energy of the subordinates was placed under control.[51] In this context, political leadership would be converted into an aspect of the function of domination. According to Voza,[52] Gramsci attributed to the Moderates the accomplishment of a 'full hegemonic function, "leader" and "dominant" at the same time'. There is no denying that the Moderates exercised an effective hegemonic function, but it is necessary to qualify this. The leadership role was exercised on a narrow social basis: the industrial bourgeoisie itself, the southern agrarian bourgeoisie and the leaders of

---

49   PN1, Q1, § 44, p. 137.
50   GR, Q19, § 24, p. 250.
51   Braga 1996, p. 172.
52   Voza 2004, p. 191.

the Action Party. The dominant function, in turn, spread throughout the entire nation and encompassed both the ruling classes and the subaltern classes. The *full hegemonic function* cannot therefore be confused with *full hegemony* such as that exercised by the Jacobins. But a question remains that can only be responded to later: did the Moderates, in fact, exercise a 'full hegemonic function'?[53]

The contrast between France and Italy, the Jacobins and the Moderates/ Mazzinians, constituted a historical model for the analysis of the process of construction of the national European states. *Activity* and *passivity*, 'greater or less energy and radicalism of the revolutionary process'[54] provided the criteria from which it was possible to understand different ways of arriving at modernity. But an adequate appraisal of such criteria should establish the link between these two forms, understanding in a dynamic manner the conformation of the diverse paths followed. The political line through which the Italian *Risorgimento* developed was punctuated by international factors, according to Gramsci.[55] This line, which allowed the link between the French Revolution and the *Risorgimento*, was drawn precisely in § 151 of Notebook 1, entitled 'The historical relation between the modern French state created by the Revolution and the other modern European states':

> The question is of the greatest interest, as long as it is not resolved through abstract sociological schemes. It is the historical outcome of these elements: 1) Revolutionary explosion in France; 2) European opposition to the French Revolution and to its dissemination through class 'meatuses'; 3) Revolutionary wars by France under both the Republic and Napoleon, and the formation of a French hegemony disposed toward a universal state; 4) National insurrections against French hegemony and the cre-

---

[53] Gramsci emphasised the limited character of bourgeois hegemony in Italy in a 1926 text entitled 'The Italian Situation and the Tasks of the PCI'. He attributed to the intrinsic fragility of Italian capitalism the industrialists' need to resort, in order to survive, to economic and political compromises with the owners of land based on the solidarity of some existing interests between some privileged groups, in detriment to the general interests of production and the majority of workers. Just as it was not able to organise the national economy in its image and likeness, so the industrial bourgeoisie did not organise society and the state on its own: 'Its reinforcement and defence necessitate a compromise with the classes upon which industry exercises a *limited hegemony*: in particular, the landowners and petty bourgeoisie' (SPW, p. 344. Emphasis added).
[54] Burgio 2003, p. 54.
[55] PN1, Q1, § 44, pp. 148–9.

ation of modern European states in successive waves, but not through revolutionary explosions like the original French one.[56]

From the analytical point of view, Gramsci considered that this last phase, equivalent to the 'Restoration', represented the richest of meanings and was the one that should centralise his research. It was at this stage that the class struggle would find national contexts sufficiently elastic that would allow the bourgeoisie to come to power without going through the ordeal of revolution, without using the 'French terrorist device'. The elasticity of these contexts permitted that the old classes would cease to be leaders and become a 'governing stratum', furnishing intellectual cadres to the bourgeoisie, as in the case of England.[57]

The expansion of the bourgeoisie in Italy was thus exercised in a different sense from that which occurred in France. The cultural and economic backwardness of the bourgeois class prevented a progressive solution to the problem of the expansion of the social base of the state through the incorporation of the subaltern classes into their social and political sphere. The people were thus conceived primarily as the enemy and repelled from the framework of the ruling forces.[58] It was this cultural and economic backwardness, which led this class to believe little in their own forces and to rely on the old aristocracy for the functions of political leadership. Speaking in the name of modernity, Chevalley invited the noble Fabrizio to occupy a post in the Senate, but rejected the indication of the rude bourgeois Calogero Sedàra.

Although this paragraph makes mention of the Restoration, it was only in Notebook 8 in a note written between January and February 1932, that the relation between the concept of passive revolution and Edgar Quinet's formula of Revolution-Restoration was established, although it was still very preliminary. Gramsci's relationship with Quinet's work was rather distant. The mention of this author in the Notebooks is very rare and there is no direct reference to his work. The source seems to have been exclusively an article by Daniele Mattalia published in magazine *Nuova Italia* in November 1931. It was on the basis of this article that Gramsci wrote:

> Look up in Quinet the meaning and justification of the formula according to which revolution and restoration are equivalent in Italian history.

---

56   PN1, Q1, §151, pp. 230–1.
57   See PN1, Q1, §44, p. 150. Gramsci had in mind here Engels's 1892 introduction to the book *Socialism: Utopian and Scientific*. See MECW, Vol. 27, p. 298.
58   Burgio 2003, p. 57.

... Is it possible to establish a similarity between this concept of Quinet's and Cuoco's concept of 'passive revolution'? One would say that both Quinet's 'revolution-restoration' and Cuoco's 'passive revolution' express the historical fact that popular initiative is missing from the development of Italian history, as well as the fact that 'progress' occurs as a reaction of the dominant classes to the sporadic and incoherent rebelliousness of the popular masses – a reaction consisting of 'restorations' that agree to some part of the popular demands and are therefore 'progressive restorations' or 'revolutions-restorations' or even 'passive revolutions'.[59]

'Passive revolution' and 'revolution-restoration' are concepts that Gramsci mobilises at this point to express the limits and forms of the *Risorgimento*, of the constitution of the national Italian state. Although the analysis of the premises from which this process of 'Restoration' was confirmed was the result of an already mature reflection, it is not possible to state the same in relation to the analysis of the results of the political processes that would occur in this context. Gramsci had not yet elaborated his own notion of passive revolution, which meant that it was still defined in an oscillating manner, as one can glean from the differences between the first and second versions of the continuation of this text:

The 'successive waves' are produced by a combination of social class struggles and national wars, mostly the latter.[60]	The 'successive waves' are produced by a combination of social struggles of class, *of interventions from above of the enlightened monarch type* and by national wars, with the two latter phenomena predominating.[61]

Although it did not exhaust the notion of passive revolution, the leading role assumed by the state in the second version of the text began to have an even greater predominance over the other forms in the more mature phase of the elaboration of the *Notebooks*. This question so far was only intuited but it would be proclaimed in that formulation of the concept of passive revolution, inscribed in Notebook 4, a moment when Gramsci highlighted the modernisa-

---

59 PN3, Q8, § 25, p. 252.
60 PN1, Q1, § 151, p. 231.
61 SPN, Q10/II, § 61, p. 115. Emphasis added.

tion of the state 'through a series of reforms or national wars without undergoing a political revolution of a radical-Jacobin type'.[62]

Thus, a link was developed between passive revolution and the centrality of politics that would later be developed in the *Notebooks*.[63] Studying the different factors that allowed for the *Risorgimento*, Gramsci identified the central place occupied by the state apparatus of Piedmont in the process of the transition and formation of the unitary national state in Italy. The fact that the Italian case had taken place in the form of a passive revolution and not otherwise was because 'behind this development were the state of Piedmont and the Savoy dynasty'.[64] With its army, its diplomatic corps and its modern bureaucracy, Piedmont provided not only the military forces necessary for unification, but also the intellectuals capable of organising consensus.

For Piedmont to occupy this position, it was necessary, however, for the ascension of the liberal Cavour to power. Liberal supremacy endowed the house of Savoy with a unitary programme, overcoming both the 'municipalism' and the 'exclusivist Piemontese nationalism' from the right of Solaro della Margarita and the neo-Guelphism from the centre personified by Vincenzo Gioberti.[65] But Cavour and his supporters, Gramsci warned, were not Italian Jacobins:

> They go beyond Solaro's Right (though not qualitatively) because they conceive of unification as an extension of the state of Piedmont and of the patrimony of the dynasty – not as national movement from below but as a royal conquest.[66]

The place of politics in the transition occupied a central position in the mature thought of Gramsci. This seems to be the point of convergence of patient reflection that finds its material witness in the text of the *Notebooks*. At the decisive moment of this reflection, in Notebook 15, the 'Preface of 1859' could not fail to appear again, whose interpretation was 'the touchstone of reflection in prison,

---

62 PN2, Q4, §57, p. 233.
63 De Felice 1978, p. 200.
64 PN3, Q6, §78, pp. 59–60.
65 The neo-Guelphs defended an Italian unity under the supremacy of the papacy. Their denomination recalls the political faction of the Guelphs, active in the northern and central regions of Italy from the thirteenth century. The conflict between the Guelfi and the Ghibellini was portrayed by Machiavelli in Book II of his *Florentine Histories* (*Istorie Fiorentine*). Machiavelli 1988, pp. 52–104.
66 PN3, Q6, §78, p. 60.

the theoretical form of the role of subjectivity in the very history of philosophy of Gramscian praxis'.[67] Here Gramsci avowed:

> The concept of 'passive revolution' must be rigorously derived from the two fundamental principles of political science; 1. that no social formation disappears as long as the productive forces which have developed within it still find room for further forward movement; 2. that a society does not set itself tasks for whose solution the necessary conditions have not already been incubated, etc. It goes without saying that these principles must first be developed critically in all their implications, and purged of every residue of mechanicism and fatalism. They must therefore be referred back to the description of the three fundamental moments into which a 'situation' or an equilibrium of forces can be distinguished, with the greatest possible stress on the second moment (equilibrium of political forces), and especially on the third moment (politico-military equilibrium).[68]

The theoretical guideline from which 'passive revolution' should be interpreted was thus defined by those principles of the 'Preface of 1859'. They revealed the particular articulation between politics and the objective conditions in which a passive modernisation of society was possible. A national context in which objective conditions not yet fully developed prevailed and subjective conditions in which the old dominant classes had not yet exhausted all their potentialities created the possibility for the persistence of the old social and political forms within a renewed casing. The 'old' social formation still had sufficient historical energies that would allow it to persist. Gramsci accordingly established a strong link between the concept of passive revolution and a 'theory of persistence' that was constructed from the text of Marx.[69]

The revolution was passive, but the passivity that characterised it was that of the subaltern classes and not of the ruling classes. A new social structure and a renewed political form emerged as a result of the conflicts that counterpoised the new to the old and to the very new, the bourgeoisie to the old feudal classes and to the proletariat. Passive revolution was thus born from social struggle and constituted itself dynamically, altering the social and economic frameworks which characterised the preceding period.[70] For that reason, the modernity that was its result was pregnant with conflict.

---

67 Kanoussi 2000, p. 144. OT.
68 GR, Q15, §17, p. 263.
69 Burgio 2003, p. 66.
70 Burgio 2003, pp. 51 and 57.

'Preface of 1859' – Analysis of the relations of forces – Passive revolution. The strong points of Gramsci's political analysis were articulated in a synthetic mode in this paragraph. The flow of his reflection encountered in this moment the point of confluence. But this, it is always good to repeat, was the result of a patient reflection that at that moment was still unfinished. The attempts to transform Gramsci into a 'systematic' thinker by placing side by side passages written at different times end up imposing an artificial order and lose sight of the multifaceted character of the notions being constructed. This decisive moment of the Gramscian argument cannot therefore be considered a final moment, given the provisional character of the *Notebooks*.

In this thematic confluence, research in relation to the complex relations between structure and superstructure emerged in a different way from that which until then marked the *Notebooks*.[71] That which had been considered the fundamental question of the philosophy of praxis – 'how does the historical movement arise out of the structures?'[72] – was not mentioned which seems to reflect a certain distancing from the architectural metaphor and the difficulties, from it and from the sense that had been imposed by vulgar Marxism, in thinking of a process of transition in which politics occupied the central position.

Gramsci did not travel on this path without illustrious company. Lenin himself, in his analysis of the development of capitalism in Russia, had pointed to a non-revolutionary path, the Prussian way, as a possibility of the resolution of the agrarian-peasant question.[73] On the other hand, Trotsky had emphasised the role played by financial capital and by the Tsarist state in the process of the constitution of the capitalism in Russia, bypassing the bourgeois revolution.[74] On this point, what differentiated the Sardinian Marxist from his contemporaries was the attempt to construct a notion that would account for the analysis of the processes of the transition to capitalism, as they had done, but at the same time, one that had a broader methodological, historiographical, and political reach.

The notion of passive revolution was thus to occupy a strategic place in the Gramscian attempt to reconstruct the philosophy of the praxis, purifying it of all mechanicism, economicism, and fatalism. In this regard, it is important to

---

71 On Gramsci's different formulations in this regard, see Cospito 2004a, especially pp. 239–40 for the analysis of the Notebook 15.
72 PN3, Q7, §20, p. 171.
73 See LCW, Vol. 13, pp. 238–42. The Prussian way would be later developed by Lukács 1980. See Rego 1996.
74 Trotsky 1969b, pp. 37–45 and pp. 100–6.

pay attention to the subtle methodological construction announced by Gramsci in § 56 of Notebook 15:

> *Italian Risorgimento*. On passive revolution. The protagonists are the 'facts' as it were and not 'individual men'. How a certain political enclosure necessarily changes the fundamental social relations and new effective political forces arise and develop, which indirectly influence, with a slow but uncontrollable pressure, official forces that change themselves without realizing or almost.[75]

In his interesting essay on the concept of passive revolution, Weneck Vianna attributed a completeness and strategic character to this small paragraph quoted above. But in doing so he reduced the 'facts' to the structure.[76] But this is not the question in the passage cited. Assuming that the 'necessary and sufficient conditions', that is, the objective conditions, were already at least potentially defined, Gramsci affirmed the centrality of politics. Even if such conditions emerge, that is, the contradictory relation between the development of the productive forces and the relations of production have reached a saturation point, this is no guarantee that an active or passive revolution will occur. For such a revolution to take place, the concurrence of the effective determinations manifested within the superstructures and social conflicts are necessary. Historical 'protagonism' cannot, therefore, arise from an inert fact.

The 'facts' to which reference was made did not therefore comprise the structure; they were the movements and political parties that congregating an uncountable number of 'individual men' in a collective project assumed the dimension of a 'material force', as Marx declared.[77] It was for this reason that the author of the *Notebooks* opposed the 'facts' to 'individual men' and not to the 'collective man', to the political party.

Certainly Gramsci's goal was not to establish one of those separations between politics and economics that Croce mechanically established between the different 'spheres of the spirit', nor institute politics as a 'hidden god'. It is not, therefore, about affirming 'the primacy of the superstructure, but that of its unity with the productive forces, whose condition is in the conscious domain of the movement of these on the part of their bearers'.[78] The movement related by Gramsci in § 56 was, precisely, the movement of this unity. It was the pro-

---

75 Q15, § 56, pp. 1818–19. OT.
76 See Vianna 1997, p. 44.
77 MECW, Vol. 3, p. 182. See also Chapter 4 of this book.
78 Vianna 1997, p. 47.

cess of the slow maturation of (social) structural relations, which occur under a given *political* form, the emergence of new *political* forces, the explicit and implicit conflict between the new and old *political* forms and the slow *political* transformation of the latter. The passage lacked closure, indicating the political impact of this conflict on (social) structural relations, but Gramsci would provide this in other passages.

The relationship between structure and superstructure, which had been considered the fundamental question of the philosophy of praxis, received a political translation into the problem 'of the relations between the objective and subjective conditions of an historical event'.[79] Starting from the concepts of passive revolution and revolution-restoration, Gramsci clearly puts emphasis on the so-called subjective conditions defining its centrality. But the definition of this central position did not make them independent of objective conditions, as he explained:

> It seems obvious that the so-called subjective conditions can never be missing when the objective conditions exist, in as much as the distinction involved is simply one of a didactic character. Consequently it is on the size and concentration of subjective forces that discussion can bear, and hence on the dialectical relation between contrasting subjective forces.[80]

By adopting the principles deduced from the 'Preface of 1859' as methodological criteria with which the notion of passive revolution could be elaborated, the research would receive a new imposition. The fundamental theme ceased to be the formation of the Italian national state and the notion of passive revolution acquired deeper meanings. The starting point of the study was still, for Gramsci, 'the expression of Cuoco with respect to the Neapolitan revolution of 1799', but this was only one of the sources, since the concept is 'completely modified and enriched'.[81]

Central to this process was the identification of the function of the Piedmont in the Italian *Risorgimento*. This was, according to Gramsci, the function of a 'ruling class'.[82] Subject to their economic-corporate interests, the different fractions of the Italian dominant classes did not want to become leaders, that is, they were not willing to coordinate their interests with the interests and aspirations of the other fractions. They wanted to 'dominate' and not 'lead', Gramsci

---

79   SPN, Q15, § 25, p. 113.
80   Ibid.
81   Q15, § 17, p. 1775. OT.
82   SPN, Q15, § 59, p. 104.

argued.[83] It was then up to the state of Piedmont to perform this function, assuming a role equivalent to that of a 'party', that is, organising, centralising, and providing a programme to a social group.

The study of the role played by Piedmont in the process of the constitution of the state was essential for the elaboration of the Gramscian notion of hegemony. It revealed the possibility that the function of leadership was not occupied by a social group, but by a state that would lead for those that should have been leading. The investigation of this function was vital to widening the notion of passive revolution and Gramsci immediately recalled the functions similar to Piedmont carried out by Serbia in the Balkans and even by France after the revolution of 1789 in the European context. The author of *Notebooks* concluded his reflection in this respect with an observation of great importance:

> The important thing is to analyse more profoundly the significance of a 'Piedmont'-type function in passive revolutions – i.e. the fact that a State replaces the local social groups in leading a struggle of renewal. It is one of the cases in which these groups have the function of 'domination' without that of 'leadership': dictatorship without hegemony. The hegemony will be exercised by a part of the social group over the entire group, and not by the latter over other forces in order to give power to the movement, radicalise it, etc. on the 'Jacobin' model.[84]

The passage is, as was said, of great importance for two reasons: first, because the 'Piedmont' function was specified and became part of the concept of passive revolution, that is, passive revolution was understood in a more definite way as a process of modernisation in which the state occupied a 'leading' function; second, because Gramsci seems in this paragraph to modify, or at least to make more precise, his judgement on the Moderates. Only in a very restricted sense had they exercised a leadership function. The restricted character of this exercise of the supremacy of the Moderates was characterised by the absence of hegemony over the subaltern classes. Using strong words, Gramsci stated that it was a 'dictatorship without hegemony'.

It is now possible to return to the question raised with respect to the interpretation of Pasquale Voza: did the Moderates, in fact, exercise a 'full hegemonic function'? Only in the light of Notebook 15, the answer might be no.

---

83 SPN, Q15, §59, p. 105.
84 SPN, Q15, §59, p. 106.

Through the course of research, the slow process of the construction of a 'general theory of hegemony: a theory that could be applied both to proletarian hegemony and bourgeois hegemony'[85] was revealed. But in the construction of this general theory, the difference between proletarian hegemony and bourgeois hegemony became sharper.[86] Only the first, as an expression of the subaltern classes, can reveal all the antagonism that exists in society and, in this way, overcome the distance that separates leaders and led, denying the condition of their own subalternity. Bourgeois hegemony always remains as a restricted hegemony that hides the antagonism and thus reproduces the separation between leaders and led and the conditions of social subalternity.

1   Gioberti

In the historical analysis of the processes of transition and construction of modern national states in Europe, Gramsci showed that the revolution which met all the criteria of classicism – the French Revolution – was not the most universal.[87] The processes that became universal and conditioned the forms of social modernisation and politics on the European continent were those in which a nationalisation of transition occurred.[88]

To reach this conclusion it was necessary to overcome the narrow milestones in which the concept of passive revolution was confined in its first condition as a canon of interpretation of the Italian *Risorgimento*. From the first statement of this concept, this possibility was open. In that first reference to Vincenzo Cuoco in Notebook 4, Gramsci already pointed out the possibility that the concept could be applied to 'other countries that modernize the state through a series of reforms or national wars'.[89]

Initially, this extension of the concept covered only those countries that, at the beginning of the nineteenth century, had constituted modern states by successive waves of reform, thus avoiding an explosive revolutionary process, such as that in France. The passive revolution thus expressed not only a typically

---

85   Gerratana 1997, p. 122.
86   Obviously, Anderson 1976a does not realise that in the *Notebooks* different forms of hegemony are differentiated. For this reason, he accused Gramsci of simply extending the use of the notion of hegemony in the context of the bourgeois revolution for the context of the workers' revolution.
87   Bianchi 2006, p. 45.
88   See Buci-Glucksmann 1978, p. 130 and Braga 1996, p. 168.
89   PN2, Q4, § 57, p. 232.

Italian phenomenon and came to designate a form of transition to capitalism and of the social and political modernisation which became the general form of the nineteenth century. Gramsci was not free of doubts with respect to the scope of the concept and the possibility of generalising it, but in a patient and meticulous form he extended it gradually to encompass new social and political situations. §151 of Notebook 1 and the second edition thereof, written in Notebook 10, attest to this slow process of conceptual elaboration. After pointing out the different elements that historically characterised the 'Restoration', Gramsci asked himself:

> Can this 'model' for the formation of modern states repeat itself? This can be excluded, at least as far as its magnitude and large states are concerned. But the question is of the greatest importance because the French-European model has created a particular mentality.[90]

> Can this 'model' for the creation of the modern states be repeated in other conditions? Can this be excluded absolutely, *or could we say that at least partially there can be similar developments in the form of the appearance of planned economies*? Can it be excluded for all states, or only for the large ones? The question is of the highest importance, because the France-Europe model has created a mentality which is no less significant for being 'ashamed of itself' or for being an 'instrument of government'.[91]

It was in the second version that the analysis of the advent of fascism and the possibility of its modernising promise was treated, contained in the formula of a programmed economy, that is, economic planning. This could promote a development similar to that described by the concept of passive revolution when applied to the formation of national states in the nineteenth century. The criticism of Croce and fascism came together at this point and it was in the midst of the criticism of the philosophy and historiography of this philosopher that Gramsci developed an important part of his reflection on the regime of Mussolini.[92]

---

90 PN1, Q1, §151, p. 231.
91 SPN, Q10 / II, §61, p. 115. Emphasis added.
92 In his exposition of the development of the Gramscian interpretation of fascism, Adamson 1980 does not even mention this connection, although he has the merit of showing the successive elaborations of the interpretation and the substantial differences between the wording of the pre-prison writings and that which is contained in the *Notebooks*.

The high point of the reflection of the Abruzzian philosopher and his campaign against Marxism was identified by the author of the *Notebooks* in the historical works, mainly *History of Italy from 1871 to 1915* (*Storia d'Italia dal 1871 al 1915*) published in 1928, and *History of Europe in the Nineteenth Century* (*Storia d'Europa nel seculo decimonono*) originally published in 1932. In these works, the false antagonism created by Croce between ethico-political history and economic-political history led him to underestimate or even erase the moment of force of the class struggle and reduce all history to a part of it up until the moment of the consolidation of hegemony and cultural expansion.

The author's political moderation was transparent in these historical essays. In them, their narratives begin as early as 1815 and 1871, that is, from the very moment of the restoration. It was not by chance that his *History of Europe in the Nineteenth Century* began with the defeat of Napoleon Bonaparte:

> When the Napoleonic adventure was at an end and that extraordinary despot had disappeared from the stage where he had reigned supreme; while his conquerors were agreeing or trying to agree among themselves so that they could united in giving to Europe, by the restoration of old regimes and the timely manipulation of frontiers, a stable organization to replace the strongly held yet always precarious empire of the French nation – then among all the peoples hopes were flaming up and demands were being made for independence and liberty.[93]

At the end of the 'Napoleonic adventure', what remained was the restoration, whose history was written by Croce without the historical precedent of the revolution. The moment of the struggle was in this way suppressed from history. Gramsci protested that Croce excluded from history

> the moment in which the conflicting forces are formed, are assembled and take up their positions; the moment in which one ethico-political system dissolves and another is formed by fire and steel; the moment in which one system of social relations disintegrates and falls and another arises and asserts itself?[94]

In Croce's history, only the moment of cultural, or ethico-political, expansion occurred in which ruling groups had already consolidated their domination.

---

93 Croce 1933, p. 3.
94 GR, Q10 / I, § 9, pp. 265–6.

The cleansing that Croce produced in history aimed to create an ideological movement corresponding to that of the era of restoration, that is, a movement that allowed for the rise of the bourgeoisie without using the Jacobin-Napoleonic form, satisfying popular demands in small doses, through strict compliance of the law, thus keeping the old feudal classes safe, avoiding agrarian reform and an uprising of the popular masses.

The uprising of the masses. This continued to be the spectre that haunted Europe. An updated fear. It was no longer the fear of the *sans-culottes* hordes, inaugurated by the French revolution, but rather the dread provoked by the modern proletariat, which, if it was not created, was undoubtedly raised to the umpteenth power by the Russian Revolution. This fear was evident in the 'Epilogue' of the *History of Europe* in which Croce, demonstrating aristocratic fear of the barbarians, claimed that communism was 'sterile, and it suffocates all thought, religion, art, all these and other things that it would like to enslave and can only destroy'.[95]

Gramsci considered this Crocean historiography the continuity of the historiography of 'the Restoration reborn and adapted to the needs and interests of the present period'.[96] Such a current – namely that which, after 1848, was renewed by the moderate Hegelianism of the Spaventa brothers – was, in a certain way, a continuation of neo-Guelphism. Croce's affinities with this were strong and, for this reason, he even published, as part of the collection *Writers of Italy* (*Scrittori d'Italia*) by the publisher Laterza, the book *Del rinnovamento civile d'Italia* (*Of the Civil Renewal of Italy*) by Vincenzo Gioberti (1911–12) and *Della storia d'Italia dalle origini fino ai nostri giorni* (*The History of Italy from its Origins to Our Days*) by Cesare Balbo (1912–13), both political leaders of the Moderate Party. But the same space was not granted to Mazzini, who was left out of the collection.

The author of the *Notebooks* insists on the Gioberti-Croce link, which leaves one surprised. Gioberti's book, *On the Moral and Civil Primacy of the Italian Race* (*Del primato morale e civili degli Italiani*), published in 1843, had a great impact on public opinion at the time[97] and still impresses the modern reader, sometimes negatively, with his style full of 'glittering rhetorical and nationalistic tinsel'.[98] But this was the style that the era demanded. Abandoning the republican fancies of youth and distancing himself from Mazzini, with whom he became very close, Gioberti sought to demonstrate that Italy possessed in itself

---

95 Croce 1933, p. 353.
96 FSPN, Q10 / I, § 6, p. 488.
97 Haddock 1998, pp. 705–6.
98 FSPN, Q10 / I, § 6, p. 489. See also Woolf 1973, p. 351.

all the necessary conditions for a 'National and political *Risorgimento* and that for this to effectively occur *there is no need for internal revolutions nor invasions or foreign imitations*'.[99] The Piedmontese philosopher found these conditions in a reading of the history of the peninsula that emphasised the papacy as the main Italian institution, the leading force behind the great achievements of the past and the possibility for Italy to aspire to a prominent position in the concert of nations.[100]

Gioberti's proposal was supported by an assumed conservative realism. The principle of Italian unity, he argued, should be vivid, concrete, and real.[101] He was thus far from those like Mazzini, who professed to seek a unity based on the different peoples of the peninsula, who would understand each other between themselves and conspire to destroy their respective governments, making Italy a unified state.[102] Such unity would not be probable and therefore was impossible. But it also should be undesirable. The union would not occur if it were not 'quiet and stable' as opposed to 'agitated and hesitant'.[103]

The Jacobins, always them, were what should be avoided in Italy, according to Gioberti. The French Revolution showed how risky it would be to overthrow a legitimate power. Like most – if not all – liberals of the early nineteenth century, Gioberti demonstrated his fear of democracy and the dread that it would be converted into a 'demagogy'.[104] After 1789, the French state had been 'imprisoned by the fury of the plebs, by the tyranny of the demagogues and by the will of the soldier'. Gioberti did not fail to praise the restoration: 'good order was only reborn when the lineage of the old princes was solicited and restituted that part of the sovereignty which they completed directly'.[105] This return of the old rulers would indeed be unavoidable, since when disorder brought about by a revolution reaches its apex, 'the old order little by little is reborn; but, as its components were destroyed and the souls were ill-accustomed, it pitied itself a long time until it was restored'.[106]

Only the papacy could, according to Gioberti, correspond to an Italian specificity and be a national base for the union. The author of *On the Moral and Civil Primacy* proposed the constitution of an Italian confederation under the

---

99   Gioberti 1932, Vol. I, p. 92. OT. Emphasis added.
100   See Haddock 1998, p. 711.
101   Gioberti 1932, Vol. I, p. 92.
102   Gioberti 1932, Vol. I, p. 93.
103   Gioberti 1932, Vol. I, p. 95.
104   See Gioberti 1912, Vol. 3, chap. VI.
105   Gioberti 1932, Vol. I, p. 95.
106   Gioberti 1932, Vol. I, p. 96.

presidency of the Pope. This would be the 'true Italian unity' 'concrete, living and real'.[107] Gioberti's defence thus broke from a long tradition in Italian political thought, which, like Machiavelli in the *Discourses*, pointed to the Vatican's responsibility for the ruin and scourge of Italy.[108] Instead of the cause of riots, destruction, and violence, Gioberti saw in the papacy a power that was 'peaceful in essence and civil', 'perfectly ordered in itself and in its way of proceeding, because it is a power organised by God himself and constitutes the center of the most admirable society one can find or imagine among men'.[109]

Gioberti thought of the advent of an Italian national state more as a *union* rather than a *unity*. Unlike the Mazzinian project, he rejected the idea of one indivisible republic and proposed the constitution of a confederation in which Rome would be the seat of faith and Piedmont that of arms. The union of the 'holy city' with the 'warrior province' would create the conditions for the imagined union of the Italians and their chiefs. Weapons and religion, considered by Guicciardini the principal foundations of every kingdom, were incarnated in Gioberti's proposal in the King Carlo Alberto of Piedmont and in Pope Gregory XVI.

On the Moral and Civil Primacy had been carefully designed so as not to arouse the opposition of Rome or Turin. Gioberti omitted the discussion on the reform of the papal states and he also avoided references to the tendencies for political insulation of the Piedmontese.[110] He consciously relegated to a secondary level every programme of social reconstruction of Italy and assumed as his main objective the union of the provinces in the only way he thought was realistic, possible, and even desirable. The failure of the revolutions of 1848 and the reactionary role played at that time by Pope Pius IX led Gioberti to revise many of his views in *Of the Civil Renewal of Italy* (1911–12) and to affirm the centrality of Piedmont in the Italian union. In this way, he arrived at his neo-Guelph counter utopia.

What led Gramsci to approximate Croce to Gioberti was not, of course, the neo-Guelphism of the author of *On the Moral and Civil Primacy*, but this obsession with moderation and gradualism, the thinly veiled sympathy for the restoration shared by both. Hence Croce published in the collection he was coordinating for Laterza *Of the Civil Renewal of Italy* and not *On the Moral*

---

107 Gioberti 1932, Vol. I, p. 99.
108 Machiavelli 1996, pp. 36–9.
109 Gioberti 1932, Vol. I, p. 99. OT.
110 Haddock 1998, pp. 712–13.

and Civil Primacy of the Italian Race. The book published no longer defended the supremacy of papacy, but rather the 'leadership of the House of Savoy, its Italian mission'.[111]

The desired hegemony was that of the bourgeois class, as Gioberti made clear in *Of the Civil Renewal of Italy*. It was in the bourgeoisie that the Piedmontese philosopher hoped to find the successors of the pope. For him the unity of the people expressed itself in the unity of the plebe with the bourgeoisie. A 'material and affective force' would be demanded of the plebes while the bourgeoisie was solicited to provide the 'industrious and intellective' force.[112] On the one hand, the 'liberal conservatives' and 'muncipalists', and, on the other, the 'puritans' who wanted to give everything to the plebes, were a threat to this unity. Only the principle of self-moderation and the hegemony of class that had the intellectual conditions to run society could preserve it.[113]

It was in the Piedmont of the Savoy that Croce found his hero in the *History of Europe* and of bourgeois hegemony. But it was not Vittorio Emanuele, the successor of Carlo Alberto, but Camilo Benso, the Count of Cavour, the architect of the Italian passive revolution. Croce's serene prose, a subject of praise from so many, including Gramsci himself, was lost and became a ridiculous mystification when he met his hero and described him as:

> the man of genius whom Italy had produced from her midst, and who, after a long preparation of political studies and practical life, and after having participated in the events of 1848–49 as a publicist and journalist, now felt that his hour had arrived and came forward to assume the post of command, not, to tell the truth, 'pensif et palissant' like the man called by God to be the leader of peoples of whom the poet speaks, but active and gay like one who knows what he is called upon to do and knows that he is able to do it, and flings himself without reserve into the task and the fray.[114]

For Croce, Cavour was a lover of freedom who had among his great accomplishments the formation of an 'orderly parliamentary activity, with parties that represented needs and collected their forces, and were able if necessary to unite for certain common ends'.[115] The debates in the House and the subalpine

---

111 Croce 1933, p. 175.
112 Gioberti 1911, Vol. 2, p. 220.
113 See Badaloni 1973, pp. 972–3.
114 Croce 1933, pp. 210–11.
115 Ibid.

Senate, the legislative and political activity, the accords and the solution of the crises in the parliamentary ambit exemplified for this author what Cavour and Piedmont had given to Italy and to Europe.

The laudatory prose concealed those social and political problems that in the years after unification took their toll. No word was said about the restrictions that prevented the vast majority of the population from participating in the elections[116] or about growing poverty in rural areas. But even in what he revealed, Croce did not fail to show the limits of this bourgeois hegemony conducted by Cavour. The parliamentary accords and the '*connubio*' (union) that in 1852 had gathered together the liberals of Cavour with the democratic moderates led by Umberto Rattazzi were nothing more than the first step in transformism and implied the neutralisation of the democratic-revolutionary currents.[117] Croce's compliment to the '*connubio*' thus contained a positive revaluation of transformism itself.

The philosophical foundation of this Crocean valorisation of passive revolution and transformism was a mutilated dialectic, the dialectic of reaction. This dialectic of reaction, according to Grasmci, was based on an error of practical origin: the mechanical presupposition that in the dialectical process 'the thesis should be "preserved" by the antithesis so as not to destroy the process itself which is therefore "foreseen" as a mechanical, arbitrarily preordained repetition *ad infinitum*'.[118] This way of looking at the dialectical process is proper to the intellectuals, affirmed the author of the *Notebooks*. They conceive of themselves as arbitrators of any real political struggle, as personifications of the passage from the economic-corporative element to the ethico-political moment, in short, as the very synthesis of the dialectical process: 'what is practice for the fundamental class becomes "rationality" and speculation for the intellectuals', Gramsci affirmed.[119]

This shift in perspective was not without consequences for how intellectuals saw politics and the state itself. If 'for the fundamental productive classes (capitalist bourgeoisie and the modern proletariat) the state is only conceivable as the concrete form of a specific economic world, of a specific system of production',[120] the same does not occur with intellectuals. The latter see the state 'as

---

116 In the first general elections in the history of Italy, in 1861, the prevailing electoral law of Piedmont was adopted. Only 167,000 people had the right to vote in northern Italy, 55,000 in central Italy, 129,000 in Southern Italy and 66,000 in the islands. See Procacci 1978, Vol. 2, p. 390.
117 Woolf 1973, pp. 472–3.
118 FSPN, Q10 / I, § 6, p. 490.
119 SPN, Q10 / II, § 61, pp. 115–16.
120 SPN, Q10 / II, § 61, p. 116.

something in itself, a rational absolute', an artifact of thought and, therefore, of the intellectuals themselves:

> the state is the concrete form of a productive world and since the intellectuals are the social element from which the governing personnel is drawn, the intellectual who is not firmly anchored to a strong economic group will tend to present the State as an absolute; in this way the function of the intellectuals is itself conceived of as absolute and pre-eminent, and their historical existence and dignity are abstractly rationalized.[121]

This process of rationalisation that transforms the state into an absolute becomes rational for that which already exists. The problem was already posed in Hegel's *Elements of the Philosophy of Right* and the development given by the Hegelian right to this question converted classical German philosophy into a philosophy of restoration. It was with the intention of the formation of a philosophy of restoration that the southern intellectuals of the *Risorgimento*, among which the Spaventa brothers stood out, studied the 'pure' state. The political problem of the restoration thus manifested itself in the form of a philosophical problem. But when these intellectuals left their offices and entered into political life, Gramsci declared, then alongside the conception of the state itself marched 'the whole reactionary cortege which is their just company'.[122]

Gramsci was aware of the unity between philosophy and politics and, for this reason, strongly denounced Crocean neo-idealism. Like Gioberti, Croce was struggling with all his might against the very idea of revolution, trying to establish a course in the development of history in which the unwanted rupture with the past would not be necessary. For the dialectic of reaction it was necessary to preserve at all costs what was fundamental in the present. Now, Gramsci says,

> in history as it really is the antithesis tends to destroy the thesis, the synthesis that emerges being a supersession, without one being able to tell in advance what of the thesis will be 'preserved' in the synthesis ... That this may then happen in practice is a question of immediate 'politics', since in real history the dialectical process is separated out into innumerable partial moments.[123]

---

121 SPN, Q10 / II, § 61, p. 117.
122 Q10 / II, § 61, p. 1362. OT.
123 FSPN, Q10 / I, § 6, p. 490.

Crocean dialectics was a mutilated dialectic similar to that of Proudhon, who sought to reduce the contradictions of the real to a game of good/bad oppositions, to be eliminated by the suppression of one of its poles.[124] The suppression (rather than the dialectical overcoming) of contradiction through political cancellation on the bad side would make it possible to recreate reality on new bases. The result of this operation would be a constant reproduction of the previously existing through the process of improvement and harmonisation of the real.

Such a conception not only restricted the breadth of social transformation by putting harnesses on history, as it defined, in advance, what should be preserved from the old society and politics. Croce was criticised by Gramsci for his political moderation, 'whose only method of political action is posited to be that in which progress, historical development, stems from the dialectic of conservation and innovation'.[125] Crocean historicism was focused on the search in the past for what should constitute the present. Gioberti had found in Catholicism the moral foundation and in the papacy the political-spiritual matrix of Italian 'national classicism' that the union and the constitution of a new state should develop and preserve. In his *History of Europe*, Croce, in turn, judged that he found it in the realisation of the idea of freedom as the guiding thread that would give intelligibility to the course of the history, while at the same time it would fix the inheritance that could not be renounced.

But the Crocean idea of freedom was nothing more than the ideology of liberalism. His objective was not the elaboration of a 'history of the future', as in the philosophies of Hegelian inspiration, but a history of the 'past which is epitomized in the present'.[126] Freedom as the idea of our age and liberalism as its political horizon summarised the enterprise of the editor of *La Critica*. In modern language, Gramsci said, such a form of historicism is called reformism.[127] Croce's liberalism and reformism were not, however, radical and popular, like those of the collaborators of *L'Ordine Nuovo*, Piero Gobetti or Carlo Rosselli, founder of the anti-fascist movement *Giustizia and Libertà* (Justice and Freedom).[128] Croce's liberalism was deeply anti-egalitarian and was disposed 'to produce and promote not democracy, but the aristocracy, which is

---

124   See Marx's Critique in MECW, Vol. 6, p. 167.
125   FSPN, Q10 / II § 4lxiv, p. 524. For the relation between Benedetto Croce and the revisionist currents of his time, see Gramsci FSPN, Q10 / I, § 2, pp. 481–2. The theme is treated by Dias 2000, pp. 23–32.
126   Croce 1933, p. 354.
127   FSPN, Q10 / II § 4lxiv, p. 524.
128   Croce's relationship with liberal-socialism represented by the characters above did not cease to be ambiguous, since they had been deeply influenced by his philosophical think-

truly vigorous and serious when it is not a closed aristocracy, but open, ready, however, to repel the vulgar, but always ready to welcome those who rise from it'.[129]

In the olympic Crocean serenity there is no denying the delicate gesture of a decadent enlightened aristocracy that, to save its position, flirts with the liberal bourgeoisie and shows itself willing to accept its hegemony. This is similar to Fabrizio, the character in *The Leopard*. Longing for the old world he accepts the new in order to avoid what he considers to be worse. But this image is also a portrait of his painful impotence.

2   Fascism

The conservative character of the historiography of Benedetto Croce and its political consequences were promptly denounced by Gramsci. The book *History of Europe* was merely the history of a fragment of the historical period, 'the "passive" aspect of the great revolution which started in France in 1789'.[130] The revolution had been eliminated from the narrative, but it did not fail to guide the work of its author. The apology for restoration could have, according to Gramsci, the purpose of creating a cultural and political environment adverse to revolution and favourable to the restoration itself:

> The problem arises of whether this Crocean construction, in its tendentious nature, does not have a contemporary and immediate reference. Whether it does not aim to create an ideological movement corresponding to that of the period with which Croce is dealing, i.e. the period of restoration-revolution, in which the demands which in France found a Jacobin-Napoleonic expression were satisfied by small doses, legally, in a reformist manner in such a way that it was possible to preserve the political and economic position of the old feudal classes, to avoid agrarian reform, and, especially, to avoid the popular masses going through a period of political experience such as occurred in France in the years of Jacobinism, in 1831, and in 1848.[131]

---

ing. Concerning Italian liberal-socialism and Croce's relationship with it, see the book by Walquíria Leão Rego 2001, principally chapters 2 and 3.
129   Croce 1999, p. 336.
130   GR, Q10 / I, § 9, p. 266.
131   Ibid.

Crocean historiography sought to create a cultural and political environment conducive to a political programme that might resemble, in its function, that which the Renaissance had had in relation to the Bourbon Reform and Restoration in relation to the Revolution of 1789. Croce thus intended 'restoration as a reaction and response to the events of the revolution of [19]17, to the revolutionary movements in the West; a movement of building a reformed hegemony, a *passive revolution*'.[132]

The same question could be asked about the *History of Italy, 1871–1915*. Originally published in 1928, Croce's study[133] seems to have been conceived as a response to the book by the fascist historian Gioacchino Volpe, *Italy on the Way* (*L'Italia in cammino*), published in 1927. Like many historians of the early twentieth century, Volpe harshly criticised the existing political system and liberalism, both personified by the figure of Giovanni Giolitti, a leading figure in Italian politics, and stressed the distance separating the new social forces and a political class that was inert and refractory to a repositioning of Italy in the international context.[134]

If Cavour was the hero of Croce's *History of Europe*, Giolitti was that of the *History of Italy*. Tracing the history of Italy as a path along which the idea of freedom was realised, Croce emphasised the ethico-political elements of the narrative and pointed to the achievements of thought and culture that had been possible in the years of peace. Liberalism was thus a factor of progress responsible for the affirmation of the Italian national state and for economic expansion. The praise of Italian political life led the author of the *History of Italy* to naturalise transformism, considered as a phenomenon peculiar to parliamentary life, as well as positively valuing the conversion of the Socialist Party to parliamentarism.

The praise of Giolitti's Italian liberalism motivated a strong opposition from Fascist historiography. But Croce's work had, Gramsci asserted, a paradoxical result. For besides a profession of liberal faith, the *History of Italy* and the *History of Europe* were political manifestos favourable to the renewal of the economic, political, and cultural life of Italy by means of gradual reforms, a revolution without revolution. However, could liberalism play the role that Croce attributed to it? If Croce pursued his historical narrative beyond 1915 it was evident that Italian liberalism was historically impossible as a political movement capable of directing this new renewal. In the crisis highlighted by the First World War, there was another historical actor in a position to accomplish or aim

---

132   Kanoussi and Mena 1985, p. 45.
133   Croce 1963.
134   See Galasso 1990, pp. 379–80.

to accomplish the Crocean programme: fascism. Questioning Croce, Gramsci asked: 'But, in present conditions, is it not precisely the fascist movement which in fact corresponds to the movement of moderate and conservative liberalism in the last century?'[135]

The result of ethico-political history was thus surprising. Having developed his two major historical works in order to counteract the influence of Fascism and Marxism, Croce contributed to the 'reinforcement of Fascism furnishing it indirectly with an intellectual justification'.[136] Decanting its romantic irrationalism, fascist discourse actually revealed a political programme aligned with the aspirations of the philosopher. It was not without meaning, wrote Gramsci, that both Croce and Fascism in its early years claimed the legacy and tradition of the Historical Right of Cavour. And to this affinity, the admiration of both for the work of Georges Sorel, introduced in Italy by Croce, should also be added.

The links between Croce and Mussolini had been strong from 1922 to 1924, years in which the philosopher came to believe that fascism could re-establish authority and correct the defects of the parliamentary system. Like most liberals of his time, Senator Croce gave his vote in favour of the fascist electoral law, which modified the constitution and allowed Mussolini to obtain a large parliamentary majority.[137] At the first anniversary of the march on Rome, Croce publicly stated that fascism was not opposed to liberalism and that liberals had a duty to support the new regime.[138] Although Croce later sought to minimise the impact of his articles and interviews in which he expressed his support for the fascist movement, such support is well documented.[139] Just as well documented from 1925 onwards was his break from this movement and the opposition he came to exert against it,[140] although the shift was not accompanied by any self-criticism.

Gramsci seems not to have paid much attention to Croce's explicit support for fascism. Even at the time of this support, he never mentioned it in his writings.[141] In the *Notebooks* there is also no reference to these episodes. However, this did not stop him from identifying a deep affinity between Croce's his-

---

135 GR, Q10 / I, § 9, p. 266.
136 Ibid.
137 Smith 1974, p. 49.
138 Smith 1974, p. 48.
139 See also Destler 1952.
140 Galasso 1990, p. 342 ff.
141 It is not possible here to affirm this with complete certainty since the critical edition of Gramsci's writings of the period only covers material until 1920. In the texts gathered in *Socialism and fascismo: L'Ordine Nuovo (1921–1922)* and *La costruzione del Partito Comunista (1923–1926)* there are, however, no references to these episodes.

toriographical efforts and the fascist movement. The fundamental affinity that Gramsci asserted was of a programmatic character. The passive revolution that political-ethical historiography had converted into the desirable political form of the modernisation of state and society could be, for Gramsci, also a political form of fascism:

> One could think of it thus: a passive revolution takes place when through a 'reform' process, the economic structure is transformed from an individualistic one to an economy according to a plan (administered economy) and when the emergence of an 'intermediate' economy – i.e. an economy in the space between the purely individualistic one and the one that is comprehensively planned – enables the transition to more advanced political and cultural forms without the kind of radical and destructive cataclysms that are utterly devastating.[142]

> The ideological hypothesis could be presented in the following terms: that there is a passive revolution involved in the fact that – through the legislative intervention of the State and by means of the corporative organisation – relatively far-reaching modifications are being introduced in the country's economic structure in order to accentuate the 'plan of production' element; in other words, that socialisation and co-operation in the sphere of production are being increased, without however touching (or at least not going beyond the regulation and control of) individual and group appropriation of profit.[143]

In this passage, the elaboration and generalisation through which the concept of passive revolution had developed is evident. Originally conceived by Gramsci as a conceptual analogy that would allow an understanding of the process of the constitution of European nation states in the nineteenth century on the historiographical level, the notion came to acquire new meanings and assume a new function on a political level. In this new configuration, the notion of passive revolution was used for the analysis of phenomena whose dominant focus was the class shock between the bourgeoisie and the proletariat combined with a reflection on hegemony and its forms.[144] What Pasquale Voza[145] accurately demonstrates in his study of passive revolution is the complex dynamic through which the notion was successively broadened in the *Notebooks* to the extent that it encompasses social and political forms that took place in the

---

142 PN3, Q8, §236, p. 378.
143 SPN, Q10 / II, §9, pp. 119–20.
144 De Felice 1978, p. 194.
145 Voza 2004.

twentieth century. It is from the perception of the rhythm of construction of the notion of passive revolution that one can understand the evident differences between the first and the second version of the above-mentioned notes. The differences in these notes cannot be put in a logical order of succession, but they can be read in a complementary and non-antagonistic way, although the second version obviously expresses a more mature and careful elaboration.

Gramsci viewed state action in the economy as a possibility of the modernisation of capitalism and the development of the productive forces in a politically reactionary context. As such, the Gramscian interpretation was inserted in a reflection that had as a constant element an anti-catastrophic conception of the contemporary crisis.[146] The emphases presented in Notebook 8 allow one to understand that Gramsci conceived of passive revolution as a possibility for overcoming the crisis of the liberal economy ('pure individualist') different from the socialist economy ('planned in the full sense'). The note in Notebook 10 emphasises the 'intermediate' character of this economic alternative and demarcates that it was still capitalist.

The study of the different forms of the manifestation of politics in contexts of passive revolution allows one to approach through this notion the complex reality of 'modern, post-liberal, masses-state relations, hegemony-production'.[147] The passive revolution was thus to be developed on a theoretical-political plane as a way of overcoming or attenuating the postwar capitalist crisis and the achievement of a 'static equilibrium' between social classes. The material feasibility of this programme in the Italian context was, however, rather weak. The fascist plan of renovation was faced with a situation in which the colonial carve up had already occurred and competition with England, France or even Germany took place under conditions which were disadvantageous for the peninsula. But the practical unviability of this plan mattered in the first moment. Its political and ideological importance resided in its capacity of

> creating – and indeed [it] does create – a period of expectation and hope, especially in certain Italian social groups such as the great mass of urban and rural petit bourgeois. It thus reinforces the hegemonic system and the forces of military and civil coercion at the disposal of the traditional ruling classes.[148]

---

146 Di Bendetto 2000, p. 92.
147 Voza 2004, p. 204. OT. See also Baratta 2004, p. 177.
148 SPN, Q10 / II, §9, p. 120.

In the Gramscian analysis of fascism, the political forms of restoration proper to the government of the masses were closely linked to the ways in which production was or could be organised through a government of the economy.[149] This programme of the government of the economy would allow fascism to achieve its hegemonic function over the Italian dominant classes insofar as it represented a capitalist response to the crisis of Italian capitalism.

The United States provided the counterpoint from which Gramsci reflected on the possibility of fascism being, effectively, this response. As has already been seen, since the first plans of the *Notebooks*, as well as in correspondence with Tatiana, the desire to address the question of 'Americanism and Fordism' was manifested. The approach developed in Notebook 1 and then taken up again in Notebook 22 already indicated the two axes upon which the issue would be addressed. First, Americanism and Fordism as forms that could represent 'an intermediate phase of the current historical crisis'.[150] Second, a comparative approach between the United States and Europe/Italy that would allow one to recognise the particular forms of this phenomenon.

Gramsci's approach allowed him to construct a complex analysis of the relations between Europe and the United States, and to base this analysis on his investigation into the contemporary crisis. Methodologically, Gramsci proceeded from the first moment demarcating the differences existing between the continents in order to avoid the subsumption of historical specificities in the global movement of capital and a false generalisation. He highlighted, therefore, in Notebook 1 that, unlike Europe, the United States did not possess cultural and demographic residues of past historical forms that removed the dynamism of the Old Continent. There were no parasitic classes in the New World, '"producers of savings"; that is, a large class of "usurers" which not only extracts its own sustenance from the primitive labor of a specific number of peasants, but also manages to save'.[151]

The 'demographic rationality' of the United States made possible a 'formidable accumulation of capital, even though wages are relatively higher than in Europe'.[152] The historical conditions in which the development of capitalism occurred in the United States allowed industry to develop into a central position in the economy, organising all social life around it. 'Government of the masses' and 'government of the economy' converged in a spontaneous arrange-

---

149 De Felice 1978, p. 232.
150 PN1, Q1, §61, p. 167.
151 PN1, Q1, §61, p. 168.
152 PN1, Q1, §61, p. 169.

ment in which the structure dominated the superstructure, costs were minimised and results maximised. In the United States, Gramsci argued,

> This preliminary 'rationalization' of the general conditions of production which was already in place or was facilitated by history, permitted the rationalization of production, combining force (– destruction of trade-unionism –) with persuasion (– wages and other benefits –), so as to base the whole life of the nation on industry. Hegemony is born in the factory and does not need so many political and ideological intermediaries.[153]

However, this preliminary 'rationalisation' did not exist in Italy and much of Europe. The social strata without a direct function in the world of production consumed the national energies and the wealth produced, creating a short circuit in the process of the amplified reproduction of capital. The relationship between the potentially active population and that which effectively produced wealth was the most unfavourable, and Gramsci cited some of the reasons for this: emigration, the low level of employment of women in industry, endemic diseases, chronic malnutrition, unemployment and the existence of a huge parasitic population. These were problems that were present in a more intense way in the *Mezzogiorno* than in the North.

The convergence between 'government of the masses' and 'government of the economy' could not therefore be spontaneous in Italy. In the peninsula, only proletarian hegemony could be born of the factory. Bourgeois hegemony would have its genesis exclusively in politics. The superstructure should dominate the structure.[154] Kanoussi and Mena aptly stress that it is not a simple reversal of the Marxian determination of the superstructure by the structure, defined in the 'Preface of 1859'. It deals with a 'much more complex relationship in which the structural tendency of development is weak, but not non-existent, and where the role of superstructures is more visible, more decisive, since the beginning of the formation of the State'.[155]

Gramsci investigated these political forms through which the predominance of the superstructure could be seen in Italy in an important note in Notebook 1 in which he took as his object concepts developed by Massimo Fovel. From the writings of this theorist of corporatism, he considered relevant the concept of the corporation as an 'industrial-productive bloc destined to resolve in a modem way the problem of the economic apparatus in an emphatically

---

[153] Ibid.
[154] See Vianna 1997, pp. 64–5.
[155] Kanoussi and Mena 1985, p. 90. OT.

capitalistic manner'.[156] The conformation of such a block could represent the overcoming of the traditional forces of Italian society, the predominance of parasitic elements and the producers of savings present in it. The corporation could be a path towards a substantial increase in the production of surplus value that would allow for increases in wages and 'workers' savings', the expansion of the internal market, the elevation of profits and a capitalisation within the capitalist enterprise itself. The advantages of corporatism would lie in its ability to unlock the process of the broader reproduction of capital, bringing national economic life within the environment of industrial dominance.

In the *Notebooks* the analysis proceeded cautiously and the author's doubts appear to increase rather than decrease, redoubling the necessary care. In Notebook 1 he wondered whether this scheme of Fovel could come to fruition. The question did not depend on a unilateral act of will, but on the relation of forces. Once corporations were instituted with a view to economic renewal, workers could oppose and fight for the appropriation of these forms of the organisation of production, which had already occurred in the experience of *L'Ordine Nuovo*. The viability of this project depended, therefore, on its ability to articulate a consensus capable of supporting it. Was this, however, possible? 'One is necessarily declined to deny it', the author replied to this question, refusing in a categorical way its historical viability.[157] 'For the moment one is more inclined to be dubious',[158] he wrote more reticently in Notebook 22, answering the same question.

The legal form of the corporation, that is, the political will of the fascist state materialised in a statute was only a matter of immediate necessity, but not a sufficient condition. For the political power to be able to adjust to the economy, politics had to be previously adapted to the meaning of the transformation to be imposed. According to Gramsci,

> Americanization requires a particular environment, a particular social structure (or at least a determined intention to create it) and a certain type of state. This state is the liberal state, not in the sense of free-trade liberalism or of effective political liberty, but in the more fundamental sense of free initiative and of economic individualism which, with its own means, on the level of 'civil society', through historical development, itself arrives at a regime of industrial concentration and monopoly.[159]

---

156 PN1, Q1, §135, p. 221.
157 PN1, Q1, §135, p. 222.
158 GR, Q22, §6, p. 284.
159 GR, Q22, §6, p. 285.

In order to shape this environment in Italy, the disappearance of the parasitic strata of society was of great importance, and especially of the semi-feudal type of rentier that characterised the peninsula and, mainly, the *Mezzogiorno*. The state with its economic-financial policy was, for Gramsci, the instrument of this process under the condition that instead of stimulating new forms of parasitic accumulation, it would rationalise savings by amortising the public debt, instituting bonds and privileging direct taxes.[160]

The crisis of 1929, insofar as it put investments in shares under suspicion, would allow private savings to be channelled into state bonds which would become the institutional seat of the unification of income and profit.[161] In this way, the state 'thus finds itself invested with a primordial function in the capitalist system, both as a company (state holdings) which concentrates the savings to be put at the disposal of private industry and activity, and as a medium and long-term investor'.[162] Corporatism could be interpreted as an effect of this transformation of the functions of the state. Its increasing intervention in the productive universe would have the purpose of controlling its own investments. In this way, the state would be converted into 'an instrument of authoritarian control over production at the moment of universal diffusion of the autonomy of the productive forces'.[163]

But a 'vast design of integral rationalisation' that would allow the complete social and economic renewal seemed to be beyond the reach of fascist corporatism. This project would require an agrarian reform that would socialise the income from the land, incorporating it into a productive organism as a form of collective savings, and an industrial reform that reorganised the economy in the form of a 'medium economy' in which the orientation and the rhythm of production was not determined solely by a legal title of ownership.[164] Gramsci was quite pessimistic in this regard and, consequently, did not positively assess the effective capacity of corporatism to modernise Italian society.

Research on fascism and corporatism led its author to a very cautious approach between the concepts of war of position and passive revolution. The theme was addressed in a barely elaborated manner in Notebook 8, from April 1932 and resumed only one month later in the second version of this text in Notebook 10. In his first version, he pondered the theoretical possibility of approximating the 'passive' character of corporatism to that conception

---

160 Ibid.
161 De Felice 1978, p. 235.
162 SPN, Q22, §14, p. 314.
163 Di Benedetto 2000, p. 91.
164 SPN, Q22, §14, p. 315.

that 'one might call "war of position" as opposed to war of movement'.[165] In the second version, he seems to give way to an assertive formula and corporatism and the promise of conservative modernisation that were held by the ruling classes would serve 'as an element of a "war of position" in the international economic field ... just as "passive revolution" does in the political field'.[166]

The gradualism that characterised both the war of position and passive revolution allowed Gramsci to establish this identity. The war of position would be the preponderant form of conflict in a passive revolution, that is, throughout 'an entire historical period'.[167] From the affirmation of this identity Gramsci wrote that in the war of position that took place after the defeat of the German revolution in 1921, fascism was its representative 'both practical (for Italy) and ideological (for Europe)'.[168]

As a form of social conflict, the war of position enabled the Fascist passive revolution, blocking the war of manoeuvre of the subaltern classes and disarticulating the opponent. A reactionary reformism that expressed the restricted dynamics of the dominant classes thus occurred. The spaces of politics were reconfigured, the limits of conflict conditioned and the intensity of these was modulated, affirming a new relationship of forces in which the passivity of the subaltern classes was assured. The passive revolution thus became 'the war of position brought to the West by the ruling classes to prevent the advance of the hegemony of the subalterns'.[169]

Gramsci certainly could not define fascism and its systematic violence against the organisations of the labour movement as a war of position if he believed that this was a peaceful means of obtaining a normative consensus. As the name says, the war of position is a form of war, and is therefore marked by conflict and not by the tranquil communicative interaction of agents. The identity established between this war of position and the passive revolution stresses that this form of conflict is imposed by the dominant classes, blocking the subaltern classes' 'concentrated and instantaneous form of an insurrection'. The form of the conflict thus becomes inescapable, leading the subaltern classes to a form of 'diffused' and 'capillary' form of struggle, which is the premise for a resumption of the war of manoeuvre.[170]

---

165 PN3, Q8, §236, p. 378.
166 GR, Q10 / I, §9, p. 267.
167 SPN, Q15, §11, p. 108.
168 GR, Q10 / I, §9, p. 267.
169 Tosel 1994, p. 44.
170 SPN, Q15, §11, p. 110.

The war of position and the passive revolution are the setbacks that made it difficult for the subaltern classes to affirm their societal project. A programme of passive anti-revolution can only be achieved by means of a struggle that disarticulates the war of position of the dominant classes and accelerating historical time. The political action of the subaltern classes assumes the dimension of a struggle for the reappropriation of their own time that has been denied to them. To conquer this time is to change the relation of forces and define the conditions under which the struggle must take place.

CHAPTER 8

Conclusion

The *Prison Notebooks* has had a troubled life. Saved from the prisons of Mussolini, they were taken to a second prison. The operation of editing the Gramscian writings in the immediate postwar period and the political and theoretical canonisation of its author by the PCI leadership had a lasting effect. The Gramsci of Togliatti, the one who was under the 'invincible banner of Marx-Engels-Lenin-Stalin', gave way to that of Eurocommunism which was then supplanted by post-communism which, in turn, seems to have been succeeded by post-modernism. The prisoner was the same; only his jailers changed.

There is no denying it: the complexity of Gramsci's thinking and the fragmentary character of his work facilitate this imprisonment. As a provisory effort, it can be rebuilt, rearranged, and re-presented in various forms. With regard to a work of difficult understanding it becomes easy to replace the written by the said. A vulgarly 'sociological' 'common sense' thus prevails that proceeds through the construction of rudimentary ideal-types and the affirmation of binary conceptual oppositions: state *versus* civil society, Orient *versus* West, war of manoeuvre *versus* war of position. The morphological notions constructed by Gramsci to account for the complexity of the real thus give way to narrow concepts. And this with a Gramsci who protested so much against 'sociology' ...

Gramsci's thinking is not characterised by the construction of dichotomies, but by research on the radical unity that exists in radical diversity. It would have been easier if Gramsci had written a philosophical and political system. But he was not like Croce, who planned and classified all his work, even before he wrote it. Maybe this is one of the reasons why today Gramsci is more widely read than Croce. Any attempt to systematise, manipulate, catalogue, thematise, and order the *Notebooks* will produce a work that is different from that written by its author. But the open character of this work cannot be an alibi for a hasty interpretation.

'Gramscian' common sense finds its habitat in the apparatuses of hegemony: research centres, universities, non-governmental organisations and political parties. 'Common sense' becomes politics and a reading increasingly marked by slogans of agitation: 'civil society against the state', 'occupy spaces', 'democratise democracy', 'revolutionary reformism'. For many, Gramsci provided the exit door that allowed for many to bid farewell to the proletariat and to the forms of struggle and organisation identified with it.

CONCLUSION

What is the relation between this common sense and the work that supposedly inspired it? A considerable part of it rests on superficial readings. Kate Crehan[1] denounced that Gramsci's omnipresence in cultural studies hides the fact that he is not quoted from his own texts but by commentators. Buttigieg[2] came to a similar conclusion for the social sciences. Instead of the texts of the author, commentators; in place of the critical edition, thematic editions or anthologies. Gradually, common sense moved away from the work that inspired it. The sources that support these versions are therefore remote from the text written by Gramsci in prison. The result is an instrumentalised commentary on a work that would not even be recognised by its own author.

A critical resumption of the text of the *Prison Notebooks*, valuing the rhythm of its theoretical elaboration, considering the sources of research mobilised by its author and effectively contextualising the production of the text, can contribute to a better clarification about Gramsci's thinking and criticism of this common sense. Yet a rigorous reading and an effective contextualisation will not resolve all issues. The *Notebooks* is an incomplete work, and, therefore, is more open to interpretation than other texts. Research that is conscious of the demands of the philological-historical method will not result in the discovery of what Gramsci 'really said'. Rigorous research cannot nourish the naïve and mainly misguided hope of finding the 'true Gramsci'.

In that tangle of notes, he said many things and some clearly in contradiction with others. He cancelled texts using oblique strokes, with a schoolish whim, so that they could still be read. He inserted the same notion into conceptual constellations distant from one another. He attributed to a single text more than one meaning, shifting it from one thematic to another. He experimented with a new writing of history, anticipating the diffusion of hypertext. How do we get out of this mess with a single interpretation? Impossible!

Philological-historical analysis – or genetic-diachronic, as Giorgio Baratta prefers to call it – is not the only legitimate one. Nor is it the only one that can be said beforehand that it will produce the best results. Neither is it the safe-conduct for an axiological neutrality that frees one from all political-ideological contamination, leaving the text of Gramsci to 'speak for itself'. Rigour is a requirement of theoretical practice; it is the guarantee of objectivity. But it should always be treated, as Gramsci warned, as that which is 'humanly objective'. After all, in the selection of the theme, in the sequence of the arguments, in the literary style itself, is it Gramsci 'who speaks' or his interpreters hidden

---

1 Crehan 2002.
2 Buttigieg 1994, p. 100.

behind feigned scruples and love for the 'truth'? Rather than 'psychographing' the text, then, it would be better to reproduce the text line by line, paragraph by paragraph, page by page. But we already have this text. Gerratana gave us this work. These are the *Notebooks*!

A rigorous philological-historical analysis that seeks to patiently reconstruct the intricate conceptual and thematic network that its author wove in detail in prison, responding to the challenges of his time, can never result in a new 'truth', but it can arrive at a more solid interpretation, more consistent in its internal logic and less fragile in the face of empirical evidence. One can follow paths that are epistemologically blocked to other approaches. One may, finally, reach *another* Gramsci.

What sense does it make, however, to travel this difficult path at the beginning of the twenty-first century? Why do we need to read Gramsci one more time? The dissemination of his ideas in Latin America provides a clue in trying to answer this question. If it makes sense to return to Gramsci it is because he still has something to say. The diffusion in this continent of his books and comments on them speaks to the vitality of this thought. It is true that one may question the quality or appropriateness of these readings. Their results and conclusions can be questioned. But Gramscian common sense only prospered because it was anchored in reality. It cannot be denied that these readings reflect – not always in a precise way, but a reflection nonetheless – the force of thought that has become part of theoretical and political debate. It is necessary to read Gramsci because he has become unavoidable.

First, Gramsci has become unavoidable in order to think about this continent. In cultural studies, relevant research was stimulated by the notion of the national-popular forming the basis for a renewed investigation of subaltern cultures. And the notion of a passive revolution, which was first developed with a view to interpreting the processes of the formation of European nation states in the nineteenth century, has been fruitful in important approaches to the past and present in Latin America. The incomplete modernity of the continent facilitated the identification of a past that is recognised, sometimes in an exaggerated way, in that analysis of the *Risorgimento*.

Second, from the late 1960s, Gramsci became an unavoidable reference in political debate and the subject of this debate itself. Political parties and social movements from a broad political spectrum organised their discourses and guided their practices around notions such as hegemony, historical bloc, and civil society. In the context of the end of the dictatorships of the Southern Cone, references to Gramsci became more frequent and marked the intense discussions that took place at that time.

In the troubled process of the theoretical and political diffusion of Gramsci's ideas in Latin America, the readings made in Italy and France about them exerted significant influence. But that did not stop original studies from being carried out. One can find important reasons for the importance of passive revolution to understand the particularities of capitalist development in this continent demonstrated in studies by Kanoussi and Mena[3] and Vianna,[4] while in Europe interest in the subject has come quite late. And perhaps because the active revolutions and political and social upheavals were still so close in time to the writings of the young Gramsci, these have aroused unexpected attention as shown in the research of Dias, Schlesener, and Del Roio.[5]

Just as in Italy, a 'struggle of hegemonies' has had and continues to have a place in the theoretical and political legacy of the countries south of the equator. The conditions under which this 'struggle' occurs are, however, different. The weight of the Stalinist tradition and the communist parties in most Latin American countries was much smaller than in Western Europe. The debate did not suffer, therefore, the same blockages imposed by the leaden Soviet bureaucracy and its representatives. Here the Sardinian could dialogue more freely with Rosa Luxemburg, Leon Trotsky, and Georg Lukács, with José Carlos Mariategui, Che Guevara, and Paulo Freire. It has thus become possible to re-establish clashes and confluences that had been barred by the concomitance of fascism and Stalinism.

Several prison mates reported that Gramsci had a habit of taking them by the arm to walk while they talked. This was a walk he never gave up. For some time these conversations in prison were anxiously awaited by several of them who saw them as an opportunity to learn from the 'head of the Italian Communists'. They were not, however, monotonous monologues. Gramsci asked, inquired and stimulated his interlocutors to say what they thought in order to later, in a patient and calm manner, advance his own arguments and illustrate them with imaginative metaphors so that they could be better understood.

How many of these conversations would later be found, in a literary and theoretically elaborated form, in the *Notebooks*? And how many new dialogues could be stimulated from his paragraphs? Taking an author by the arm for a roving dialogue with other authors, in other times and other geographies is something that the text itself seems to require. Gramsci gave a piece of advice that can still stimulate these confrontations and confluences, and serve to orient a renewed political-theoretical practice: pessimism of the intellect, optim-

---

[3] Kanoussi and Mena 1985.
[4] Vianna 1997.
[5] Dias 2000, Schlesener 2002 and Del Roio 2005.

ism of the will. A programmatically oriented will flourishes on the ground of research on the tendencies of contemporary reality with caution, serenity, and parsimony as methodological presuppositions. The investigation does not cease to be passionate or politically oriented, but it must not submit to the contingencies of the will.

A slow and careful reading that manifests its impatience may contribute to an understanding of the present and help to unlock the theoretical debate and political practice of the Latin American left. Such a reading is still a challenge which, of course, was not transposed here. This book does not present anything but provisional results of a research project that seems to have no end. It is, therefore, the portrait of an incomplete reflection. But how could an interpretation of a work that was not concluded by its author be any different? And is it not in the incompleteness and provisional nature of knowledge, in the absence of a definitive 'truth', that there is an ever-renewed possibility for new, critical, and surprising results?

References

Adamson, Walter L. 1980, 'Gramsci's Interpretation of Fascism', *Journal of the History of Ideas*, 41, no. 4: 615–33.
Agosti, Aldo 1974, *La Terza Internazionale: Storia documentaria, 1919–1923*, t.I, Roma: Riuniti.
Agosti, Aldo 1976, *La Terza Internazionale: Storia documentaria, 1924–1928*, t.II, Roma: Riuniti.
Agosti, Aldo 1979, *La Terza Internazionale: Storia documentaria, 1928–1943*, t.III, Roma: Riuniti.
Agosti, Aldo 1988, 'As correntes constitutivas do movimento comunista internacional', in *Historia do marxismo*, Vol. 6, edited by Eric Hobsbawm, Rio de Janeiro: Paz e Terra.
Albamonte, Emilio and Manolo Romano 2003, 'Trotsky y Gramsci: convergencias y divergências', *Estrategia Internacional*, 19.
Althusser, Louis 1980, 'O objeto de O Capital', in Louis Althusser et al., *Ler o Capital*, Rio de Janeiro: Zahar.
Anderson, Perry 1976a, 'The Antinomies of Antonio Gramsci', *New Left Review*, I/100: 5–78.
Anderson, Perry 1976b, *Considerations on Western Marxism*, London: New Left Books.
Anderson, Perry 2002, 'As antinomias de Gramsci', in *Afinidades seletivas*, São Paulo: Boitempo.
Anderson, Perry 2004, *Considerações sobre o marxismo ocidental. Nas trilhas do materialismo histórico*, São Paulo: Boitempo.
Aricó, José 2005, *La cola del diablo: itinerário de Grasmci en América Latina*, Buenos Aires: Siglo XXI.
Badaloni, Nicola 1973, 'La cultura', in VVAA, *Storia d'italia: dal primo Settecento all'Unità*, Turim: Eiunaudi.
Badaloni, Nicola 1978, 'Liberdade individual e homem coletivo em Gramsci', in Instituto Gramsci, *Política e história em Gramsci*, Rio de Janeiro: Civilização Brasileira.
Badaloni, Nicola 1991, 'Gramsci: a filosofia da práxis como previsão', in Eric Hobsbawm (ed.), *História do marxismo*, Vol. X, Rio de Janeiro: Paz e Terra.
Badaloni, Nicola and Carlo Muscetta 1990, *Labriola, Croce, Gentile*, 2 ed., Bari: Laterza.
Baker, Gideon 1998, 'Civil Society and Democracy: The Gap between Theory and Possibility', *Politics*, 18, no. 2: 81–7.
Balbo, Cesare 1913–14, *Della storia d'Italia dalle origini fino ai nostri giorni: sommario. A cura di Fausto Nicolini*, 2 vols, Bari: Laterza.
Balibar, Étienne 1995, *A filosofia de Marx*, Rio de Janeiro: Jorge Zahar.
Baratta, Giorgio 2004, *As rosas e os Cadernos: o pensamento dialógico de Antonio Gramsci*. Rio de Janeiro: DP&A.

Bellamy, Richard 1987, *Modern Italian Social Theory*, Stanford: Stanford University Press.
Bellamy, Richard 1990, 'Gramsci and the Italian Political Tradition', *History of Political Thought*, 11, no. 2: 313–37.
Bensaïd, Daniel 1995, *La discordance des temps: essai sur les crises, les classes, l'histoire*, Paris: Passion.
Bensaïd, Daniel 1996, *Marx l'intempestif: grandeurs et misères d'une aventure critique (XIXe–XXe siècles)*, Paris: Fayard.
Bianchi, Alvaro 2000, 'O primado da política: revolução permanente e transição', *Outubro*, 5: 101–15.
Bianchi, Alvaro 2002, 'Crise, política e economia no pensamento gramsciano', *Novos Rumos*, 36: 28–37.
Bianchi, Alvaro 2004, 'Resenha de Antonio Gramsci, Cadernos do cárcere, Rio de Janeiro: Civilização Brasileira, 1999–2002, 6v', *Outubro*, 10: 134–42.
Bianchi, Alvaro 2006, 'Revolução passiva: o futuro do pretérito', *Crítica Marxista*, 23: 34–57.
Bianchi, Alvaro 2007a, 'O marxismo de Leon Trotsky: notas para uma reconstrução teórica', *ideias*, 14: 57–99.
Bianchi, Alvaro 2007b, 'Democracia e revolução no pensamento de Marx e Engels (1847–1850)', *Outubro*, 16: 109–43.
Bobbio, Norberto 1955, *Politica e cultura*, Turim: Einaudi.
Bobbio, Norberto 1975, 'Gramsci e la concezione della società civile', in Pietro Rossi (ed.), *Gramsci e la cultura concemporanea: Atti del Convegno internazionale di studi gramsciani tenuto a Cagliari il 23–27 aprile 1967*, Vol. 1, Roma: Riuniti/Istituto Gramsci.
Bobbio, Norberto 1979, 'Gramsci and the Conception of Civil Society', in Chantal Mouffe (ed.), *Gramsci and Marxist Theory*, London: Routledge, Kegan and Paul.
Bonetti, Paolo 2000, *Introduzione a Croce*, Roma: Laterza.
Borghese, Lucia 1981, 'Tia Alene in bibicletta, Gramsci traduttore dal tedesco e teorico della traduzione', *Belfagor*, 36, no. 6: 635–65.
Braga, Ruy 1996, 'Risorgimento, fascismo e americanismo: a dialética da passivização', in Edmundo Fernandes Dias et al. (eds), *O outro Gramsci*, São Paulo: Xamã.
Brewster, Ben 1974, 'Introducción al trabajo de Luckacs sobre el "Manual" de Bujarin', in Nicolai Bukharin, *Teoría del materialismo histórico*, Madrid: Siglo XXI.
Brossat, Alain 1976, *El pensamiento político del joven Trotsky: en los orígenes de la revolución permanente*, México: Siglo XXI.
Broué, Pierre 1997, *Histoire de l'Internationale Communiste: 1919–1943*, Paris: Fayard.
Buci-Glucksmann, Christine 1978, 'Sobre os problemas políticos da transição: classe operária e revolução passiva', in Instituto Gramsci, *Política e história em Gramsci*, Rio de Janeiro: Civilização Brasileira.

REFERENCES

Buci-Glucksmann, Christine 1980a, 'Entrevista com Christine Buci-Glucksmann', *Revista Mexicana de Sociologia*, 42, no. 1: 289–301.

Buci-Glucksmann, Christine 1980b, *Gramsci e o Estado: por uma teoria materialista da filosofia*, Rio de Janeiro: Paz e Terra.

Buci-Glucksmann, Christine 1987, *Gramsci and the State*, London: Lawrence and Wishart.

Bukharin, Nicolai 1925, *Historical Materialism: A System of Sociology*, New York: International Publishers, available at: https://www.marxists.org/archive/bukharin/works/1921/histmat/intro.htm

Bukharin, Nicolai 1971, 'Theory and Practice from the Standpoint of Dialectical Materialism', in *Science at the Crossroads: Papers Presented to the International Congress of the History of Science and Technology held in London from June 29th to July 3rd, 1931 by the delegates of the USSR*, London: Frank Cass.

Bukharin, Nicolai 1974, *Teoria del materialismo historico: ensayo popular de sociologia marxista*. Madrid: Siglo XXI.

Burgio, Alberto 2003, *Gramsci storico: una lettura dei 'Quaderni del carcere'*, Bari: Laterza.

Burgos, Raúl 2004, *Los gramscianos argentinos: cultura y política en la experiencia de Pasado y Presente*, Buenos Aires: Siglo XXI.

Buttigieg, Joseph A. 1990, 'Gramsci's Method', *boundary 2*, 17, no. 2: 60–81.

Buttigieg, Joseph A. 1994, 'Philology and Politics: Returning to the Text of Antonio Gramsci's Prison Notebooks', *boundary 2*, 21, no. 2: 98–138.

Chambers, Simone and Jeffrey Kopstein 2001, 'Bad Civil Society', *Political Theory*, 29, no. 6: 837–65.

Cochrane, Eric 1961, 'Machiavelli: 1940–1960', *The Journal of Modern History*, 33: 113–36.

Codato, Adriano Nervo 2005, 'O Dezoito Brumário, política e pós-modernismo', *Lua Nova*, 64: 85–115.

Codato, Adriano Nervo and Renato Monseff Perissinotto 2001, 'O Estado como instituição: uma leitura das obras históricas de Marx', *Critica Marxista*, 13: 9–28.

Cohen, Jean and Andrew Arato 2000, *Sociedad civil y teoría política*, México D.F.: Fondo de Cultura Económica.

Cospito, Giuseppe 2000, 'Struttura e sovrastruttura nei "Quaderni" di Gramsci', *Critica Marxista (nuova serie)*, 3–4: 98–107.

Cospito, Giuseppe 2004, 'Struttura-superstruttura', in Fabio Frosini and Guido Liguori (eds), *Le parole di Gramsci: per un lessico dei Quaderni del carcere*, Roma: Carocci.

Costa, Sérgio 1997, 'Categoria analítica ou passe-partout político-normativo: notas bibliográficas sobre o conceito de sociedade civil', *BIB – Revista Brasileira de Informação Bibliográfica em Ciências Sociais*, 43: 3–25.

Coutinho, Carlos Nelson 1976, 'Um certo senhor Gramsci', *Jornal do Brasil*, Caderno Especial, Rio de Janeiro, 29 fev: 3.

Coutinho, Carlos Nelson 1980, *A democracia como valor universal: notas sobre a questão democrática no Brasil*, São Paulo: Ciências Humanas.

Coutinho, Carlos Nelson 1981, *Gramsci*, Porto Alegre: L&PM Editores.

Coutinho, Carlos Nelson 1999, *Gramsci: um estudo sobre seu pensamento político*, Rio de Janeiro: Civilização Brasileira.

Coutinho, Carlos Nelson 1999a, 'Introdução', in Antonio Gramsci, *Cadernos do cárcere*, Rio de Janeiro: Civilização Brasileira.

Coutinho, Carlos Nelson 2003, 'O conceito de política nos Cadernos do cárcere', in Carlos Nelson Coutinho and Andréa de Paula Teixeira (eds), *Ler Gramsci, entender a realidade*, Rio de Janeiro: Civilização Brasileira.

Coutinho, Carlos Nelson 2006, *Intervenções: o marxismo na batalha das ideias*, São Paulo: Cortez.

Coutinho, Carlos Nelson and Andréa de Paula Teixeira 2003, 'Apresentação', in Carlos Nelson Coutinho and Andréa de Paula Teixeira (eds), *Ler Gramsci, entender a realidade*, Rio de Janeiro: Civilização Brasileira.

Crehan, Kate 2002, *Gramsci: Culture and Anthropology*, London: Pluto.

Croce, Benedetto 1909, *Aesthetics as a Science of Expression and General Linguistics*, translated by Douglas Ainslie, London: Macmillan.

Croce, Benedetto 1913, *Philosophy of the Practical: Economic and Ethic*, translated by Douglas Ainslie, London: Macmillan.

Croce, Benedetto 1915, *Historical Materialism and the Economics of Karl Marx*, translated by C.M. Meredith, London: George Allen & Unwin Ltd.

Croce, Benedetto 1917, *Logic as the Science of the Pure Concept*, translated by Douglas Ainslie, London: Macmillan.

Croce, Benedetto 1921, *Theory and History of Historiography*, translated by Douglas Ainslie, London: George G. Harrap & Co. Ltd.

Croce, Benedetto 1923, *Filosofia della pratica: economia ed ética*, 3 ed., Bari: Laterza.

Croce, Benedetto 1927, *Materialismo storico ed economia marxistica*, 5 ed., Bari: Laterza.

Croce, Benedetto 1933, *History of Europe in the Nineteenth Century*, translated by Henry Furst, New York: Harcourt, Brace and Company.

Croce, Benedetto 1934, *Contro le sopravvivenze del materialismo storico: nota letta all'Academia di Scienze Morali e Politiche della Società Reale di Napoli*, Napoli: Torella.

Croce, Benedetto 1945a, 'La "mia" filosofia', *Quaderni della 'Critica'*, 2: 1–9.

Croce, Benedetto 1945b, *Politics and Morals*, translated by Salvatore J. Castiglione, New York: Philosophical Library.

Croce, Benedetto 1946a, *Estetica come scienza dell'espressione e linguistica generale: teoria e storia*, 8 ed., Bari: Laterza.

Croce, Benedetto 1946b, *Storia della Etá Barocca in Italia: pensiero – poesia e letteratura – vita morale*, Bari: Laterza.

Croce, Benedetto 1947a, 'Rivista bibliografica: Antonio Gramsci – Lettere dal carcere. – Torino, Einaudi, 1947', *Quaderni della 'Critica'*, 8: 86–8.

Croce, Benedetto 1947b, *Logica come scienza del concetto puro*, 7 ed., Bari: Laterza.

Croce, Benedetto 1948, 'Rivista bibliografica: Antonio Gramsci – Il materialismo storico e la filosofia di Benedetto Croce. – Torino, Einaudi', *Quaderni della 'Crítica'*, 10: 78–9.

Croce, Benedetto 1949a, 'Rivista bibliografica: Antonio Gramsci – Gli intellettuali e l'organizzazione dela cultura. – Torino, Einaudi, 1949', *Quaderni della 'Crítica'*, 13: 95–6.

Croce, Benedetto 1949b, *My Philosophy*, translated by E.F. Carritt, London: George Allen and Unwin.

Croce, Benedetto 1949c, 'Rivista bibliografica: Antonio Gramsci, Il Risorgimento. Torino, Einaudi, 1949', *Quaderni della 'Crítica'*, 14: 112.

Croce, Benedetto 1950, 'Un giuoco che ormai dura troppo', *Quaderni della 'Crítica'*, 17–18: 231–2.

Croce, Benedetto 1962, *Storia d'Italia dal 1871 al 1915*, 12 ed., Bari: Laterza.

Croce, Benedetto 1963, *A History of Italy, 1871–1915*, translated by Cecilia M. Ady, New York: Russell and Russell.

Croce, Benedetto 1993, *Cultura e vita morale: intermezzi polemici*, Napoli: Bibliopolis.

Croce, Benedetto 1994, *Etica e política: a cura di Giuseppe Galasso*, Milano: Adelphi.

Croce, Benedetto 1998, *La Rivoluzione napoletana del 1799*, Napoli: Bibliopolis.

Croce, Benedetto 1999, *Storia d'Europa nel secolo decimonono: a cura di Giuseppe Galasso*, Milano: Adelphi.

Croce, Benedetto 2001, *Teoria e storia della storiografia: a cura di Giuseppe Galasso*, Milano: Adelphi.

Cuoco, Vincenzo 1999, *Saggio storico sulla rivoluzione di Napoli*, Milano: Rizzoli.

Cuoco, Vincenzo 2014, *Historical Essay on the Neapolitan Revolution of 1799*, edited and introduced by Bruce Haddock and Filippo Sabetti, translated by David Gibbons, Toronto: University of Toronto Press.

Damen, Onorato 1988, *Gramsci tra marxismo e idealismo*, Milano: Prometeo.

Daniele, Chiara (ed.) 1999, *Gramsci a Roma, Togliatti a Mosca: il carteggio del 1926*, Turim: Einaudi.

Daniele, Chiara (ed.) 2005, *Togliatti editore di Gramsci*, Roma: Carocci.

De Felice, Franco 1978, 'Revolução passiva, fascismo, americanismo em Gramsci', in Instituto Gramsci, *Política e história em Gramsci*, Rio de Janeiro: Civilização Brasileira.

De Sanctis, Francesco 1968, *Storia della letteratura italiana*, Turim: Utet.

Degras, Jane (ed.) 1959, *The Communist International, Documents, 1923–1928*, Vol. 2, London: Royal Institute of International Affairs.

Degras, Jane (ed.) 1964, *The Communist International, Documents, 1929–1943*, Vol. 3, London: Royal Institute of International Affairs.

Del Noce, Augusto 1978, *Il suicidio della rivoluzione*, Milano: Rusconi.

Del Roio, Marcos 1998, 'Gramsci contra o Ocidente', in Alberto Aggio (ed.), *Gramsci: a vitalidade de um pensamento*, São Paulo: Unesp.

Del Roio, Marcos 2005, *Os prismas de Gramsci: a fórmula política da frente única (1919–1926)*, São Paulo.

Destler, Chester McArthur 1952, 'Benedetto Croce and Italian Fascism: A Note on Historical Reliability', *The Journal of Modern History*, 24, no. 4: 382–90.

Di Benedetto, Donatella 2000, 'Americanismo e corporativismo in Gramsci', *Critica Marxista*, 3–4: 88–97.

Di Lampdeusa, Guiseppe 2013 [1958], *The Leopard*, New York: Knopf.

Dias, Edmundo Fernandes 1996a, 'Hegemonia: racionalidade que se faz história', in Edmundo Dias et al., *O outro Gramsci*, São Paulo: Xama.

Dias, Edmundo Fernandes 1996b, 'Sobre a leitura dos textos gramscianos: usos e abusos', in Edmundo Dias et al., *O outro Gramsci*, São Paulo: Xama.

Dias, Edmundo Fernandes 1996c, 'Gramsci no Brasil: o rabo do diabo', in Edmundo Dias et al., *O outro Gramsci*, São Paulo: Xama.

Dias, Edmundo Fernandes 2000, *Gramsci em Turim. A construção do conceito de hegemonia*, São Paulo: Xamã.

Durante, Lea 1999, 'Il libro del convegno di Napoli', *International Gramsci Society Newsletter*, 9: 3–13.

Finocchiaro, Maurice A. 2002, *Gramsci and the History of Dialectical Thought*, Cambridge: Cambridge University Press.

Fiori, Giuseppe 1979, *A vida de Antonio Gramsci*, Rio de Janeiro: Paz e Terra.

Fiori, Giuseppe 1991, *Gramsci, Togliatti, Stalin*, Bari: Laterza.

Foley, Michael W. and Bob Edwards 1996, 'The Paradox of Civil Society', *Journal of Democracy*, 7, no. 3: 38–52.

Fontana, Benedetto 1993, *Hegemony and Power: On the Relation between Gramsci and Machiavelli*, Minneapolis: University of Minnesota.

Francioni, Gianni 1984, *L'Officina gramsciana: ipottesi sulla struttura dei 'Quaderni del carcere'*, Napoli: Bibliopolis.

Francioni, Gianni 1987, 'Gramsci tra Croce e Bucharin: sulla struttura dei Quaderni 10 e 11', *Critica Marxista*, 25, no. 6: 19–45.

Francioni, Gianni 1992, 'Problemi di filologia gramsciana: le traduzioni nei "Quaderni del carcere"', *Studi Storici*, 23, no. 1: 7–32.

Frosini, Fabio 2003, *Gramsci e la filosofia: saggio sui Quaderni del cárcere*, Roma: Carocci.

Frosini, Fabio 2004a, 'Filosofia della praxis', in Fabio Frosini and Guido Liguori (eds), *Le parole di Gramsci: per un lessico dei Quaderni del cárcere*, Roma: Carocci.

Frosini, Fabio 2004b, 'Reforma e Rinascimento', in Fabio Frosini and Guido Liguori (eds), *Le parole di Gramsci: per un lessico dei Quaderni del cárcere*, Roma: Carocci.

Galasso, Giuseppe 1990, *Croce e lo spirito del suo tempo*, Milano: Il saggiatore.

Galastri, Leandro de Oliveira 2007, 'Gramsci leitor de Georges Sorel: um "diálogo" sobre história e revolução', *Temáticas*, 26: 121–49.

Garaudy, Roger 1970, *Le grand tournant du socialism*, Paris: Gallimard.
Garaudy, Roger 1971, 'Rèvolution et bloc historique', *L'Homme er la Societé*, 21: 169–77.
Garin, Eugenio 1996, *Intellettuali italiani del XX secolo*, 3 ed., Roma: Riuniti.
Gentile, Giovanni 2003, *La filosofia di Marx*, Firenze: Le Lettere.
Germino, Dante 2003, 'Interpretando Gramsci', in Carlos Nelson Coutinho and Andréa de Paula Teixdeira (eds), *Ler Gramsci, entender a realidade*, Rio de Janeiro: Civilização Brasileira.
Gerratana, Valentino 1997, *Gramsci: problemi di método*, Roma: Riuniti.
Gill, Stephen 2007, *Gramsci, materialismo histórico e relações internacionais*, Rio de Janeiro: UFRJ.
Gioberti, Vincenzo 1911–12, *Del rinnovamento civile d'Italia: a cura di Fausto Nicolini*, 3 vols, Bari: Laterza.
Gioberti, Vincenzo 1932, *Del primato moral e civile degli italiani: introduzione e note de Gustavo Balsamo-Crivelli*, 3 vols, Turim: Utet.
Gramsci, Antonio 1949, *Il materialismo storico e la filosofia di Benedetto Croce*, Turim: Einaudi.
Gramsci, Antonio 1966a, *Note sul Machiavelli sulla politica e sullo stato moderno*, Torino: Einaudi.
Gramsci, Antonio 1966b, *Socialismo e fascismo: L'Ordine Nuovo (1921–1922)*, Turim: Einaudi.
Gramsci, Antonio 1973, *Lettere dal carcere: a cura di Segio Caprioglio e Elsa Fubini*, Turim: Einaudi.
Gramsci, Antonio 1977, *Quaderni del carcere: edizione critica dell'Istituto Gramsci a cura di Valentino Gerratana*, Turim: Einaudi.
Gramsci, Antonio 1978, *La costruzione del Partito Comunista 1923–1926*, Turim: Einaudi.
Gramsci, Antonio 1980, *Cronache Torinesi. 1913–1917: a cura di Sergio Caprioglio*, Turim: Einaudi.
Gramsci, Antonio 1982, *La città futura. 1917–1918: a cura di Sergio Caprioglio*, Turim: Einaudi.
Gramsci, Antonio 1984, *Il nostro Marx. 1918–1919: a cura di Sergio Caprioglio*, Turim: Einaudi.
Gramsci, Antonio 1991, *Maquiavel, a política e o Estado moderno*, 8 ed., Rio de Janeiro: Civilização Brasileira.
Gramsci, Antonio 1992, *Lettere 1908–1926: a cura de Antonio A. Santucci*, Turim: Einaudi.
Gramsci, Antonio 1999ss, *Cadernos do cárcere*, 6 vols, Rio de Janeiro: Civilização Brasileira.
Gramsci, Antonio 2005, *Cartas do cárcere*, 2 vols, Rio de Janeiro: Civilização Brasileira.
Gruppi, Luciano 1987, *'Tudo começou com Maquiavel: as concepções de Estado em Marx, Engels, Lênin e Gramsci'*, 8 ed., Porto Alegre: L&PM.
Gruppi, Luciano 2000, *O conceito de hegemonia em Gramsci*, 4 ed., Rio de Janeiro: Graal.

Guicciardini, Francesco 1933, *Scritti politici e ricordi: a cura di Roberto Palmarocchi*, Bari: Laterza.

Haddock, Bruce 1998, 'Political Union without Social Revolution: Vincenzo Gioberti's Primato', *The Historical Journal*, 41, no. 3: 705–23.

Haddock, Bruce 2006, 'Between Revolution and Reaction: Vincenzo Cuoco's Saggio storico', *European Journal of Political Theory*, 5, no. 1: 22–33.

Hajek, Milos 1984, *História de la Tercera Internacional: la política de frente único (1921–1935)*, Barcelona: Critica.

Harman, Chris 1983, *Gramsci versus Reformism*, London: Socialist Workers' Party.

Hegel, G.W.F. 2003, 'Linhas fundamentais da Filosofia do Direito ou Direito natural e ciência do Estado em compêndio. Terceira parte – A Eticidade. Segunda seção – A sociedade civil', translated by Marcos Lutz Muller, *Cadernos de Tradução*, 6.

Hegel, G.W.F. 2008, *Outlines of the Philosophy of Right*, Oxford: Oxford University Press.

Hughes, H. Stuart 1979, *Consciousness and Society: The Reorientation of European Social Thought 1890–1930*, Brighton: Harvester.

Hunt, Geoffrey 1987, 'The Development of the Concept of Civil Society in Marx', *History of Political Thought*, 8, no. 2: 263–76.

Jacobitti, Edmund E. 1975, 'Labriola, Croce and Italian Marxism (1895–1910)', *Journal of the History of Ideas*, 36: 297–318.

Jacobitti, Edmund E. 1980, 'Hegemony before Gramsci: The Case of Benedetto Croce', *The Journal of Modern History*, 52: 66–84.

Jesus, Antônio Tavares de 1998, *O pensamento e a prática escolar de Gramsci*, Campinas: Autores Associados.

Kanoussi, Dora 2000, *Una introducción a los Cudernos de la Cárcel de Antonio Gramsci*, México D.F.: Benemerita Universidad Autonoma de Puebla/International Gramsci Society/Plaza y Valdez.

Kanoussi, Dora and Javier Mena 1985, *La revolución pasiva: una lectura a los Cuadernos de la Cárcel*, México D.F.: Universidad Autónoma de Puebla.

Kautsky, Karl 1909, *The Road to Power*, Chicago: S.A. Bloch, available at: https://www.marxists.org/archive/kautsky/1909/power/index.htm

Kautsky, Karl 1978, *A revolução social. O caminho do poder*, México: Siglo XXI.

Kohan, Nestor 2005, 'Gramsci y los gramscianos argentinos', *Clarín – Revista Ñ*, 71: 10–11.

Krieger, Leonard 1953, 'Marx and Engels as Historians', *Journal of the History of Ideas*, 14, no. 3: 381–403.

Labica, Georges 1990, *As 'Teses sobre Feuerbach' de Karl Marx*, Rio de Janeiro: Jorge Zahar.

Labriola, Antonio 1912, *Socialism and Philosophy*, translated by Ernest Untermann, Chicago: Charles H. Kerr & Company.

Labriola, Antonio 2000, *Saggi sul materialismo storico: introduzioni e cura di Antonio A. Santucci*, Roma: Riuniti.

Lampedusa, Giuseppe Tomasi di 1958, *Il gattopardo*, Milão: Feltrinelli.

Le Goff, Jacques 1993, *Intellectuals in the Middles Ages*, London: Wiley-Blackwell.

Le Goff, Jacques 2003, *Os intelectuais na Idade Média*, Rio de Janeiro: José Olympio.

Lefort, Claude 1986, *Le travail de l'oeuvre: Machiavel*, Paris: Gallimard.

Lefort, Claude 1990, *As formas da história: ensaios de antropologia política*, 2 ed., São Paulo: Brasiliense.

Lenin, V.I. 1960ss, *Collected Works*, 4 ed., Moscow: Progress Publishers.

Leonetti, Alfonso 1974, *Notes sur Gramsci*, Paris: Edi.

Lepre, Aurelio 2001, *O prisioneiro: a vida de Antonio Gramsci*, São Paulo: Record.

Liguori, Guido 1996, *Gramsci contesso: storia di un dibattito, 1922–1996*, Roma: Riuniti.

Liguori, Guido 2006, *Sentieri gramsciani*, Roma: Carocci.

Liguori, Guido and Chiara Meta 2005, *Gramsci: guida allá letura*, Milão: Unicolpi.

Lisa, Athos 1981, 'Discusión política con Gramsci, en la cárcel', in Antonio Gramsci, *Escritos políticos (1917–1933)*, México D.F.: Siglo XXI.

Losurdo, Domenico 1997, *Antonio Gramsci dal liberalismo al 'comunismo critico'*, Roma: Gamberetti.

Löwy, Michael 1962, 'Consciência de classe e partido revolucionário', *Revista Brasiliense*, 41: 138–60.

Löwy, Michael 1988, *As aventuras de Karl Marx contra o Barão de Münchhausen: marxismo e positivismo na sociologia do conhecimento*, 2 ed., São Paulo: Busca Vida.

Lukács, Georg 1966, 'Technology and Social Relations', *New Left Review*, I/39: 27–34.

Lukács, Georg 1980, *The Destruction of Reason*, Atlantic Highlands, NJ: Humanities Press.

Lukács, Georg 1999, *History and Class Consciousness: Studies in Marxist Dialectics*, translated by Rodney Livingston, Cambridge, MA: The MIT Press.

Lukács, Georg 1974, 'Tecnologia y relaciones sociales', in Nicolai Bukharin, *Teoria del materialismo histórico*, Madrid: Siglo XXI.

Lukács, Georg 1989, *História e consciência de classe: estudos de dialética marxista*, Porto: Escorpião.

Lukács, Gyorgy 1968, *El asalto a la razon: la trayerctoria del irracionalismo desde Schelling hasta Hilter*, 2 ed., Barcelona: Grijalbo.

Machiavelli, Niccólo 1971, *Tutte le opere*, Florença: Sansoni.

Machiavelli, Niccólo 1988, *Florentine Histories*, translated by Harvey C. Mansfield and Laura Banfield, Princeton: Princeton University Press.

Machiavelli, Niccólo 1996, *Discourses on Livy*, translated by Harvey Mansfield and Nathan Tarcov, Chicago: University of Chicago Press.

Machiavelli, Niccólo 2005, *The Prince*, translated by Peter Bondanella, Oxford: Oxford University Press.

Maitan, Livio 1958, 'Intervento', in Studi Gramsciani, *Atti del convegno tenuto a Roma nei giorni 11–13 gennaio 1958*, Roma: Riuniti/Istituto Gramsci.

Marazzi, Antonella 1990, 'Prefazione', in Leon Trotsky, *Scritti sull'Italia: introduzione e cura di Antonella Marazzi*, Roma: Erre Emme.

Martelli, Michele 1996, *Gramsci filosofo della politica*, Milano: Unicolpi.

Martelli, Michele 2001, *Etica e storia: Croce e Gramsci a confronto*, Napoli: La Città del Sole.

Marx, Karl and Friedrich Engels 1976ss, *Collected Works*, New York: International Publishers.

Massardo, Jaime 1999, 'Gramsci in America latina. Questioni di ordine teorico e político', in Alberto Burgio and Antonio A. Santucci, *Gramsci e la rivoluzione in Occidente*, Roma: Riuniti.

Massari, Roberto (ed.) 2004a, *All'opposizione nel Pci con Trotsky e Gramsci: Bollettino dell'Opposizione Comunista Italiana (1931–1933)*, Bolsena: Massari.

Massari, Roberto 2004b, 'Introduzione', in Roberto Massari (ed.), *All'opposizione nel Pci com Trotsky e Gramsci: Bollettino dell'Opposizione Comunista Italiana (1931–1933)*, Bolsena: Massari Editore.

McLellan, David 1990, *Karl Marx: vida e pensamento*, Petrópolis: Vozes.

Medici, Rita 1990, *La metafora Machiavelli: Mosca, Pareto, Michels, Gramsci*, Modena: Mucchi.

Medici, Rita 2000, *Giobbe e Prometeo: filosofia e politica nel pensiero di Grasmci*, Firenze: Alinea.

Medici, Rita 2004, 'Giacobinismo', in Fabio Frosini and Guido Liguori (eds), *Le parole di Gramsci: per un lessico dei Quaderni del cárcere*, Roma: Carocci.

Mirsky, D.S. 1931, 'The Philosophical Discussion in the CPSU in 1930–31', *The Labour Monthly*, October: 649–59.

Monasta, Attilio 1985, *L'educazione tradita: criteri per una diversa valutazione complessiva dei Quaderni del Carcere di Antonio Gramsci*, Pisa: Giardini.

Moscato, Antonio 1999, 'Gramsci e lo stalinismo', in Marco Proto (ed.), *Gramsci e l'internazionalismo: nazione, Europa, America Latina*, Bari: Piero Lacaita.

Napolitano, Giorgio 1970, 'Roger Garaudy et le "nouvelle bloc historique"', *La Nouvelle Critique*, 34, no. 215: 7–10.

Natoli, Aldo 1990, *Antigone e il prigioniero: Tania Schucht lotta per la vita di Gramsci*, Roma: Riuniti.

Ortaggi, Simonetta 1974, 'Gramsci e Trockij. La lettera del 9 febbraio 1924', *Rivista di Storia Contemporanea*, 4: 478–503.

Paggi, Leonardo 1973, 'La teoria generale del marxismo', *Annali Istituto Giangiacomo Feltrinelli*, 15: 1318–70.

Paggi, Leonardo 1984, *La strategia del potere in Gramsci*, Roma: Riuniti.

Pistillo, Michele 2003, *Gramsci in carcere: il lento assasinio del capo del PCI*, Roma: la R.

Portantiero, Juan Carlos 1979, 'Gramsci y el análisis de conyntura (algunas notas)', *Revista Mexicana de Sociologia*, 4, no. 1: 59–73.

Portelli, Hugues 1977, *Gramsci e o bloco histórico*, Rio de Janeiro: Paz e Terra.
Poulantzas, Nicos 1977, *Poder político e classes sociais*, São Paulo: Martins Fontes.
Poulantzas, Nicos 1978. *Political Power and Social Classes*, London: Verso.
Prestipino, Giuseppe 2004, 'Dialettica', in Fabio Frosini and Guido Liguori (eds), *Le parole di Gramsci: per un lessico dei Quaderni del carcere*, Roma: Carocci.
Procacci, Giuliano 1977, *Storia degli italiani*, 12 ed., 2 vols, Roma: Laterza.
Quercioli, Mimma Paulesu 1977, *Gramsci vivo nelle testimonianze del suoi contemporanei*, Milão: Feltrinelli.
Ragazzini, Dario 2002, *Leonardo nella societá di massa: teoria della personalità in Gramsci*, Bergamo: Moretti Honegger.
Rego, Walquíria Leão 1996, 'Questões Sobre a Noção de Via Prussiana', in Walquíria Leão Rego and Ricardo Antunes (eds), *Lukács: um Galileu no seculo xx*, São Paulo: Boitempo.
Rego, Walquíria Leão 2001, *Em busca do socialismo democrático*, Campinas: Unicamp.
Riddell, John (ed.) 2015, *To the Masses! Proceedings of the Third Congress of the Communist International, 1921*, Leiden: Brill.
Riddell, John (ed.) 2011, *Toward the United Front: Proceedings of the Fourth Congress of the Communist International, 1922*, Leiden: Brill.
Righi, Maria Luisa (ed.) 1995, *Gramsci nel mondo: Atti del Convegno Internazionale di Studi Gramsciani*, Roma: Fondazione Istituto Gramsci.
Rosengarten, Frank 1984–85, 'The Gramsci-Trotsky question (1922–1932)', *Social Text*, 11: 65–95.
Sacristán, Manuel 1969, 'Por qué leer a Labriola', in Antonio Labriola, *Socialismo y filosofía*, Madrid: Alianza.
Saes, Décio 1994, *Estado e democracia: ensaios teóricos*, Campinas: IFCH/Unicamp.
Sassoon, Anne Showstack 1997, *Gramsci's Politics*, Minneapolis: University of Minnesota.
Schlesener, Anita Helena 2002, *Revolução e cultura em Gramsci*, Curitiba: UFPR.
Secco, Lincoln 2002, *Gramsci e o Brasil: recepção e difusão de suas ideias*, São Paulo: Cortez.
Secco, Lincoln 2006, *Gramsci e a revolução*, São Paulo: Alameda.
Semeraro, Giovanni 2001, *Gramsci e a sociedade civil: cultura e educação para a democracia*, 2 ed., Petrópolis: Vozes.
Semeraro, Giovanni 2006, *Gramsci nos embates da filosofia da práxis*, Aparecida: ideias & Letras.
Sena, Jr., Carlos Zacarias F. de 2004, 'Gramsci: mais um antitrotskista?', *Outubro*, 10: 49–68.
Simionatto, Ivete 2004, *Gramsci: sua teoria, incidência no Brasil, influência no Serviço Social*, 3 ed., São Paulo/Florianópolis: Cortez/UFSC.
Smith, Denis Mack 1973, 'Benedetto Croce: History and Politics', *Journal of Contemporary History*, 8, no. 1: 41–61.

Somai, Giovanni 1982, 'Sul rapporto tra Trockij, Gramsci e Bordiga (1922–1926)', *Storia contemporanea*, 13, no. 1: 73–98.
Sorel, Georges 1930, *Réflexions sur la violence*, Paris: Marcel Rivière.
Sorel, Georges 1999, *Reflections on Violence*, Cambridge: Cambridge University Press.
Spriano, Paolo 1976, *Storia del Partido comunista italiano*, 5 vols, Turim: Einaudi.
Sraffa, Piero 1991, *Lettere a Tania per Gramsci: introduzione e cura di Valentino Gerratana*, Roma: Riuniti.
Stalin, J.V. 1954, *Works*, 14 vols, Moscow: Foreign Languages Press.
Studi Storici, 'L'Edizione Nazionale e gli studi gramsciani', 52, no. 4: 787–9.
Texier, Jacques 1975, 'Intervento: Prima seduta di lavoro', in Pietro Rossi, *Gramsci e la cultura concemporanea: Atti del Convegno internazionale di studi grasmciani tenuto a Cagliari il 23–27 aprile 1967*, Roma: Riuniti/Istituto Gramsci.
Texier, Jacques 1988, 'Significati di società civile in Gramsci', *Critica Marxista*, 26, no. 5: 5–35.
Togliatti, Palmiro 1973ss, *Opere: a cura de Ernesto Ragionieri*, Roma: Riuniti.
Togliatti, Palmiro 2001, *Scritti sur Gramsci: a cura di Guido Liguori*, Roma: Riuniti.
Tosel, Andre 1994, 'Gramsci e a revolução francesa', *Novos Rumos*, 9, no. 22: 41–5.
Trotsky, Leon 1969b, *Permanent Revolution and Results and Prospects*, New York: Pathfinder.
Trotsky, Leon 1970, *La révolution permanente*, Paris: Gallimard.
Trotsky, Leon 1972, *The First Five Years of the Communist International*, 2 vols, London: New Park.
Trotsky, Leon 1973, *Writings of Leon Trotsky (1932)*, New York: Pathfinder Press.
Trotsky, Leon 1974, *The First Five Years of the Communist International, Vol. 2*, London: New Park, available at: https://www.marxists.org/archive/trotsky/1924/ffyci-2/index.htm
Trotsky, Leon 1979, *Revolução e contra-revolução na Alemanha*. São Paulo: Ciências Humanas.
Trotsky, Leon 1980, *Literatura e revolução*, 2 ed., Rio de Janeiro: Zahar.
Trotsky, Leon 1989, 'Qui dirige aujourd'hui l'IC?', in *Oeuvres*, Aout 1928/Fev. 1929. 2e série, Grenoble: Institut Léon Trotsky.
Trotsky, Leon 1990, *Scritti sull'Italia: introduzione e cura di Antonella Marazzi*, Roma: Erre Emme.
Trotsky, Leon 2005, *Literature and Revolution*, edited by William Keach, Chicago: Haymarket Books.
Vacca, Giuseppe 1983, 'Il marxismo e gli intellettuali: da Kautsky a Lukács, da Labriola a Gramsci: duelinee a confronto', *Critica Marxista*, 21, no. 5: 45–128.
Vacca, Giuseppe 1999, 'Gramsci a Roma, Togliatti a Mosca', in Chiara Daniele (ed.), *Gramsci a Roma, Togliatti a Mosca: il carteggio del 1926*, Turim: Einaudi.
Vianna, Luiz Werneck 1997, *A revolução passiva: iberismo e americanismo no Brasil*, Rio de Janeiro: Iuperj/Revan.

Voza, Pasquale 2004, 'Rivoluzione Passiva', in Fabio Frosini and Guido Liguori (eds), *Le parole di Gramsci: per un lessico dei Quaderni del carcere*, Roma: Carocci.

Wolf, Stuart J. 1973, 'La storia politica e sociale', in VVAA, *Storia d'italia: dal primo Settecento all'Unità*, Vol. 3, Turim: Eiunaudi.

Zanardo, Aldo 1974, 'El "Manual" de Bujarin visto por los comunistas alemanes y por Gramsci', in Nicolai Bukharin, *Teoria del materialismo histórico*, Madrid: Siglo XXI.

Zarone, Giuseppe 1990, *Classe politica e ragione scientifica. Mosca, Croce, Gramsci: problemi dela scienza politica in Italia tra Otto e Novecento*, Napoli: Edizioni Scientifiche Italiane.

Name Index

Agosti, Aldo 193, 196–198, 218
Agosti, Hector 25–26
Althusser, Louis 24–25, 277, 279–280
Anderson, Perry 186, 188–189, 202, 211, 218, 247
Arato, Andrew 161, 163
Aricó, José 2, 25–26

Badaloni, Nicola 74, 78, 89, 97, 110, 120–121, 161, 253
Baratta, Giorgio 18, 20, 23, 31–33, 261, 269
Bellamy, Richard xv, 33, 78
Bensaïd, Daniel 33–34
Bobbio, Norberto vii, x, 25, 83, 86, 114, 145, 152, 157–161, 279
Bonetti, Paolo 83–86
Bordiga, Amadeo x–xi, 201, 219
Braga, Ruy 5, 237, 247
Buci-Glucksmann, Christine 4, 10, 49, 50, 156, 165, 234, 247
Brouè, Pierra 192–193, 197, 200, 202
Bukharin, Nikolay xi, 18, 25, 39, 40–41, 49–54, 65–68, 71, 76–77, 108–113, 194, 197–201, 219, 227
Burgio, Alberto 148, 207, 214, 217, 225, 229, 232, 238–239, 242
Buttigieg, Joseph 13–14, 17, 20, 34, 111, 269

Cohen, Jean 161, 163
Cospito, Giuseppe 120, 138, 153, 243
Coutinho, Carlos Nelson x, 2, 26–31, 34, 68, 70, 150, 160, 163–164, 190–191, 207, 274, 275, 278, 280–281
Croce, Benedetto ix, 5, 8, 11–12, 15, 21–25, 29, 38–46, 49, 50, 53–54, 68, 76–104, 111–117, 125–130, 135–139, 146, 156, 159–162, 166, 171–172, 213, 225, 226–229, 244, 248–259, 268, 274
Cuoco, Vincenzo 5, 10, 36, 227–229, 240, 245, 247

Daniele, Chiara 201, 209
De Felice, Franco 121, 241, 260, 262, 265
De Sanctis, Francesco ix, 128
Del Roio, Marcos 5, 137, 191, 191–192, 196, 210, 212, 219, 271

Dias, Edmundo Fernandes x, 2, 6, 28, 97, 122, 139, 159, 256, 271

Engels, Friederich 22–23, 42–44, 50, 70–73, 79, 91, 95, 103, 106, 203, 220, 239, 268

Finocchiaro, Maurice 78, 89, 124, 128, 130
Fiori, Giuseppe 7, 10, 199–203, 205
Fontana, Benedetto 84, 87, 96, 129
Francioni, Gianni 6, 10–14, 22–25, 30–33, 39, 59, 74, 108, 120, 124–125, 129, 155, 161, 165, 169, 176, 179, 183, 207, 210, 216, 227
Frosini, Fabio 16–18, 32, 39, 40–41, 44–45, 65, 101, 129–130, 169–170

Galasso, Giuseppe 86, 258–259
Galastri, Leandro 118, 181
Garaudy, Roger 118–119
Gentile, Giovanni 5, 38, 44, 68, 72–78, 87–91, 118, 137
Gerratana, Valentino 12–15, 23–25, 28–33, 95, 108, 122–123, 166, 214, 217, 218, 247, 270, 281
Gruppi, Luciano 33, 68, 70, 190
Guicciardini, Francesco 5, 38, 132, 133, 166–167, 252

Haddock, Bruce 66, 250–252
Hajek, Milos 177, 192–197
Hegel, Georg 40, 46–47, 50, 68, 84, 90, 115, 122, 157, 159, 160–161, 231, 250, 255–256

Kanoussi, Dora 6, 56–57, 94–96, 116, 226–227, 242, 258, 263, 271
Kautsky, Karl 107–108, 123

Labriola, Antonio 38, 42–43, 44–47, 56, 72, 79, 95, 125, 207
Lampedusa, Giuseppe Tomasi di 234–235
Lefort, Claude 125, 131, 133, 134
Leonetti, Alfonso xi, 202–203, 206
Lenin, Vladimir Ilich 22–23, 38, 41, 72, 101, 187–196, 203–204, 210–213, 217–222, 243
Liguori, Guido 2–3, 22–23, 28, 32, 156–158, 160–163, 203
Lisa, Athos 4, 11, 57, 124, 150, 205

NAME INDEX

Losurdo, Domenico   47, 75, 88, 91, 137, 189, 207
Löwy, Michael   26, 227
Lukács, Georg   48, 71, 243, 271
Luxemburg, Rosa   180, 207, 209, 212, 271, 274

Machiavelli, Noccolò   5, 11–15, 21, 24–29, 38, 86, 96, 124–136, 137, 165–174, 179, 228, 241, 252, 274–275
Maitan, Livio   209, 213
Martelli, Michele   4, 43, 46, 51, 68, 70, 73–75, 82, 90–91, 129, 162, 207, 222–223
Marx, Karl   ix–xii, 2–8, 13, 20–25, 32–34, 37–83, 86–116, 119–137, 143–145, 152–153, 157–162, 165–168, 170–171, 174, 177–178, 185–189, 199, 202–214, 216–227, 242–244, 249, 256, 259–260, 263, 268, 273–281
Massari, Roberto   202, 210
Medici, Rita   5, 32, 44, 96, 122, 125, 128–134, 137, 161, 230
Mirski, D.S.   40–41
Mussolini, Benito   22, 198, 201, 248, 259, 273

Paggi, Leonardo   42–43, 49, 51–53, 122–124, 138, 149, 219
Portantiero, Juan Carlos   144, 150
Poulantzas, Nicos   24–25
Prestipino, Giuseppe   150, 162, 163
Procacci, Giuliano   233, 254

Quercioli, Mimma Paulesu   57, 148–149, 203–206

Rego, Walquíria Leão   30, 243, 257
Rosengarten, Frank   xv, 186, 210–213, 219

Sassoon, Anne Showstack   57–58
Schucht, Tatiana (Tania)   6–8, 11–13, 16–21, 30, 39, 80, 92, 97, 206, 262, 274
Secco, Lincoln   2, 26, 208
Semeraro, Giovanni   119, 159–160
Somai, Giovanni   209–210, 223
Sorel, Georges   ix, 38, 42–43, 79, 93, 117–118, 135–137, 259
Spaventa, Bertrando and Silvio   250, 255
Spriano, Paolo   198, 201–204
Sraffa, Piero   xi, 9, 17, 66
Stalin, Josef   xi, 10, 22–23, 40, 42, 197–204, 208–209, 217–223, 268

Terracini, Umberto   198, 204
Texier, Jacques   25, 160, 163
Togliatti, Palmiro   xi, 21–23, 27, 30, 118, 191, 198–206, 219–220, 268, 274, 279
Tosel, André   108–110, 231, 266
Trotsky, Leon   x–xi, 24, 38, 41, 149, 181, 185–189, 192–194, 196–214, 217–218, 222–224, 243, 271–273

Vacca, Giuseppe   42, 202, 219
Vianna, Luiz Werneck   234, 244, 263, 271
Voza, Pasquale   237, 246, 260–261

Subject Index

Americanism   xii, 9–12, 15, 16, 29, 39, 59, 262
Autonomy of the political   84, 86, 127–130

Civil society   2, 61–62, 99–101, 136, 150–166, 169–175, 182–186, 189–191, 215–216, 231, 264, 268–270
Coercion   61, 100–101, 155–156, 164–171, 174–175, 214, 234, 261
Conception of the world   32, 44, 48, 51–55, 60, 64–67, 87, 126, 130–131, 147
Consent   61–62, 99, 156, 165–168, 171–172, 175, 231
Contradiction   17, 44, 47, 69, 77, 106, 110–111, 117, 143–145, 151, 197, 206–207, 226, 230, 256, 269
Contribution to the Critique of Political Economy [Preface of 1859]   50, 74, 103, 106–122, 137–138, 142–143, 151, 155, 217, 230, 242–245, 263
Culture   5, 8–9, 11, 15–16, 21–26, 37, 42–47, 52, 67, 77, 87–89, 92–97, 99, 106, 123, 225–226, 231, 258, 274–277

Dialectics   46, 76, 99, 118, 129, 162, 165, 201–202, 254–256
Dictatorship of the proletariat   210, 212, 219

East and West   vii, 176, 180–181, 185–192
Economism   23, 83, 90, 98–101, 108, 111–112, 122, 141, 160, 163, 180, 214
Empiricism   235–236
Ethico-political   85, 97–101, 117, 136, 148, 160, 166, 226, 249, 258–259
Eurocommunism   268, 278, 279

Fascism   10, 75, 158, 169, 176, 189–192, 197–206, 224, 248, 257–262, 265–266, 271–273
Fordism   xii, 9–12, 15–16, 29, 39, 262

German Revolution   196, 210, 266

Hegelianism   46, 250
Hegemonic apparatus   158
Hegemony, bourgeois   231, 232, 238, 247, 253–254, 263

Hegemony, civil   215–218
Hegemony, political   36–37, 136, 208, 212, 229
Hegemony, proletarian   186, 247, 263
Hegemony   2–3, 24, 29, 35–37, 46, 57–65, 78, 97–102, 116, 136, 139, 146–148, 152, 155–160, 163–170, 174–176, 183–188, 207–218, 222–223, 229–234, 237–238, 246–249, 253–254, 257–263, 266–270
Historical bloc   2, 99, 117–119, 139, 270
Historical epoch   47, 53, 128
Historicism, absolute   225–227
Historicism   24–25, 45, 72, 96, 101, 225–228, 256
Historiography   4, 9–10, 16, 34, 39, 80, 86, 93, 97, 100–101, 127, 143, 180, 204, 225, 248–250, 257–260
Humanism   72, 131, 227

Idealism   39–47, 54, 66–68, 71–72, 75–77, 87–91, 94–96, 117, 122, 131, 136, 160, 225, 227, 255
Ideology   42, 53, 60, 70, 96, 99, 107, 114–115, 134, 229, 256, 277
Ideology/philosophy   4, 5, 8, 12–15, 18, 21–25, 29, 37–56, 60, 64–87, 91–103, 109, 112–117, 125–133, 170, 220, 225–227, 242–245, 248, 255, 274, 277, 279, 280
Integral state   146, 155, 163, 172, 173, 185
Intellectuals   4, 7–26, 29, 39, 54–55, 63, 67, 88, 91–93, 96–99, 105, 124, 153–157, 164, 170, 221, 234, 241, 254–255

Jacobinism   11, 137, 214, 230–231, 234, 257

Liberalism   27, 30, 41, 45, 90, 136, 139, 226–228, 256–259, 264, 276–277
Linguistics   7–8, 80
Lorianism   11, 14–15, 46, 111

Materialism, historical, 18, 21–25, 39–46 50–51, 68, 72, 79, 82, 89–90, 94–100, 108, 111, 114, 119, 153, 180, 185, 227, 274
Metaphor   58, 66, 67, 130, 180–181, 184, 188–189, 243, 271
Metaphysics   46, 77, 89

SUBJECT INDEX

Modern Prince   130, 147

National/international   xi, 2–5, 10–11, 15, 21–22, 25, 29, 32–33, 42, 57, 66, 107, 111, 121, 124, 127, 136–137, 141, 146, 149, 152–156, 175, 185–189, 192–204, 209–215, 218–224, 227–229, 231–242, 245–252, 256–258, 263–266, 270, 274–275, 278, 281
Neo-Idealism   46, 68, 75, 87, 88, 94, 117, 122, 255

Objectivity   68–73, 126, 131, 134, 269
Orthodoxy   47–49

Passive revolution   xii, 10, 29, 36–37, 227–229, 239–248, 253, 258, 260–261, 265–267, 270–271, 277
Permanent revolution   24, 105, 209, 210–218, 222
Philosophy of praxis   23–24, 37, 43–49, 52, 55–56, 64–65, 71–72, 76–77, 92–95, 100–101, 109, 112–117, 125–126, 129–133, 170, 220, 227, 243, 245
Political power   24, 167–169, 183, 185, 221, 264
Political society   61–62, 101, 152–163, 166, 169, 174–176, 183–185, 231
Positivism   68, 78, 87, 111, 226, 227
Practice   63–65, 73–74, 80, 83–87, 119, 126–131, 134–136, 147, 173, 209, 223, 235, 254–255, 269–272

Reformation   11, 45–47, 95, 128, 147–148
Relations of force   119, 133, 138, 144–145, 149–151, 189, 221, 230–231, 243
Religion   52–53, 60, 67–88, 89, 126, 129, 166–167, 175, 250–252
Renaissance   11–12, 45–47, 78, 88, 95, 127–128, 258
Risorgimento   11, 14–15, 21, 25, 28–29, 35, 66, 88, 124, 128, 149, 176, 208, 228, 233–241, 244–247, 251, 255, 270
Russian Revolution   89–91, 121, 188–189, 250

Science   5–6, 8, 22, 41–42, 46–48, 51, 54–55, 60, 66–70, 74, 77, 80, 84–86, 90, 93, 98, 100, 108, 113–116, 124–134, 145, 182–184, 215, 220, 242, 269
Social Democracy   93, 107–108, 121, 146, 1970–202

Social forces   50, 102, 105, 113, 153, 174, 258
Socialism in one country   219, 221, 222, 224
Sociology   14–15, 42, 50, 51, 77, 171, 233, 268, 277–278
State, integral   146, 155, 163, 172, 173, 185
State   xii, 5, 7, 11–13, 16–29, 32, 36, 42–44, 48, 53–58, 61–63, 68, 71–76, 79–80, 83–87, 91–93, 96–107, 110–117, 125–131, 135–139, 143, 146–177, 182–191, 194–216, 220–248, 251–265, 268, 270, 274–277, 279
Structure   3–4, 9, 16, 23, 34, 39, 49, 58, 60–61, 64, 72, 75, 83, 90, 103, 109–122, 129–131, 136–147, 151–154, 157–163, 166, 179–182, 186, 192, 207, 210–211, 215–217, 220, 231, 242–245, 260, 263–264, 280
Subaltern classes (or groups)   15–16, 65, 117, 146147, 159, 182–183, 191, 221–222, 230–234, 237–239   242, 246–247, 266–267
Subjectivity   121, 242
Superstructure   4, 23, 60–61, 64, 75, 83, 90, 103, 110–121, 129–131, 138, 141–147, 151–154, 157–162, 179–182, 217, 220, 243–245, 263, 280
Syndicalism   136, 146
Stalinism   xi, 10, 22–23, 192–196, 200–201, 204, 210, 218, 219, 223–224, 271

Temporality   35, 104, 142, 188
Theory   1, 4, 9, 10, 16, 22, 24, 3–44, 47, 50–51, 55–57, 63–65, 70–71, 74, 77–81, 86, 93, 97, 100–103, 108, 111–112, 115–117, 121, 125–127, 129, 134, 136, 144, 148, 160, 172–173, 176, 179–180, 185–188, 194, 202–204, 208–222, 226, 231, 242, 247
Theses on Feuerbach   43, 47, 72, 74, 75
Third period   192, 197, 200–204
Transformism   36, 235–237, 254, 278
Translation   13–14, 17, 25–30, 73–75, 95, 98, 101, 110, 120, 124, 166, 224, 245
Truth   36, 85, 87, 92, 108, 131–132, 162, 174, 180, 202, 228, 253, 270, 272

United front   192, 195–198, 200, 204

War of movement (manoeuvre)   x, 176–178, 180–186, 189–192, 196, 211–218, 266–268
War of position   176–185, 189–192, 204, 211–218, 265–268

www.ingramcontent.com/pod-product-compliance
Lightning Source LLC
Chambersburg PA
CBHW070911030426
42336CB00014BA/2371